HANDICRAFTS AND HOBBIES
for
PLEASURE AND PROFIT

HANDICRAFTS
AND
HOBBIES
FOR PLEASURE AND PROFIT

Edited by
MARGUERITE ICKIS

Author of Arts and Crafts, Working in Plastics, Working in Leather, Pastimes for the Patient, Nature in Recreation, The Square Weaver and Pattern Weaving, The Christmas Book, Knotted and Braided Belts

THE GREYSTONE PRESS ∾ NEW YORK

ACKNOWLEDGMENTS

Grateful acknowledgment is due to the following organizations and persons for illustrations of original articles and other material:

American Crayon Company (Prang Textile Colors) and N. E. Zistel; American Textile Company; Extension Service, College of Agriculture, University of Arkansas; Victoria Bedford Mitchell, Studio of Binney and Smith Company, for finger paintings; C. Howard Hunt Pen Company and Henry Frankenfield, author of "Block Printing with Linoleum," and Charles J. Stoner; Children's Bureau, U. S. Department of Labor; U. S. Department of Commerce; Extension Service, Cornell University; Delta Manufacturing Division, Rockwell Manufacturing Company and Walter E. Schutz; Eastman Kodak for photographs from "How to Make Good Pictures"; Felt Crafters and Dick Keezer; Fisher Body Craftsman's Guild and Bernard W. Crandell; Fun with Felt Company; H. E. Harris Company and S. F. Harris, for stamp illustrations; Higgins Ink Company and B. Cholet; Lionel Corporation; National Recreation Association; National Soap Sculpture Committee and Henry Bern; New York Association for the Blind; Rohm and Haas Company and G. F. Finnie; Scott Publications; Spool Cotton Company; Universal School of Handicrafts and Edward T. Hall; X-Acto Crescent Products Company and Karl G. Kolish for their copyrighted material on pages 19-38 and 71-90; and to these model railroaders who graciously permitted the use of pictures of their roads: Bradford Van Ness, Frank C. Ellison, John Mushacke, Warren F. Morgan and E. M. Robbins.

This book owes much to Mrs. J. V. Miller, who wrote and illustrated the chapter on drawing, and drew many of the other illustrations; James Stevens, Jr., author of the chapter on stamp collecting; Gordon K. Zern, editor of *Model Builder Magazine,* who wrote the chapter on model railroads; Mrs. Isabelle Stevenson and Frederick Drimmer, my Publishers' editors, who made many helpful suggestions in the planning stages of the book and when it was being written; Chester Lawrence and Lester Leventhal, of the Publishers' art department, who did the layout; and Richard Robbins, well-known hobby consultant, who advised on the original outline.

ABOUT THIS BOOK . . .

This book holds rich store for you. Whether you are young or old—an experienced hobbyist or a beginner looking for a creative outlet—you will find in these pages much to please you. For here are dozens of engrossing occupations you can engage in for pleasure or for profit, any one of them worthy of being a major interest, and having, besides, the virtue of entertaining and relaxing you when practiced from time to time, as the desire moves you.

Not that I am suggesting aimless dabbling or taking-and-leaving. What I do advocate is real recreation—doing things in the spirit of play and because they are fun. If you've never had time for hobbies before, you may have to try out several until you find one that really appeals to you. A hobby is in the nature of an adventure and, when you are adventuring, if you don't like one trail it is perfectly good practice to back-track and try another.

Yet this volume is not presented merely in a spirit of fun, with suggestions for pleasant ways to while away your time. Many of the crafts to which it introduces you are solid and substantial, and a door may hereby be opened to a serious and remunerative activity which you can practice either for pin money or as a full-time occupation. The attractive and useful articles you are shown how to make in the plastic, woodworking, felt, weaving, pottery, netting, metal, leather craft and many other chapters are all natural money-makers. Your state department of commerce will be glad to advise you about markets and packaging, if you will write to it.

This book takes nothing for granted. The instructions and illustrations are clear and thorough, and can be readily followed by the beginner without other help. The expert hobbyist will find in it countless novel projects he will enjoy making. Each chapter is complete in itself and there is such diversity in the various crafts and hobbies that every taste and temperament will be satisfied.

I am confident that among these exceedingly varied recreations there will be more than a few you will like. There may be one that will really take root and enrich your life to a degree you cannot imagine. Some great things have developed from hobbies.

MARGUERITE ICKIS

CONTENTS

Page

About This Book v

How to Enlarge or Reduce Patterns and Designs x

PLASTIC CRAFT AS A HOBBY.. 1
Care of plastic—how to use a pattern—cutting plastic—how to saw
plastic—punching and drilling—turning—how to file—scraping—how
to sand plastic—buffing—forming—heating the plastic—joining plastic
—design—dyeing—how to paint plastic—a novel method—carving plastic—diagrams and directions for plastic projects: drawer compartments; broom holders; shelf bracket; corner shelf; towel rack; pen and
pencil tray; paper knife; photograph frame; pad holder; salad or sugar
tongs; book ends; cocktail tray; bud vases; cigarette box.

ADVENTURES IN WHITTLING.. 19
Tools—woods to use—whittling in plastics—cutting techniques—steps
in work—finishing and painting—diagrams and directions for whit-
tling projects: Pig; What-zit; Tommy; Hanzel; Colt; Fawn; Molly;
Fido; Jumbo; Katchina Indian dolls, large and small—Rain Maker—
Clown—Storyteller—Water Maiden; Scottie and turtle made of cedar.

IT'S FUN TO MAKE MODEL BOATS... 33
How to carve concave areas—templates—sawing—how to carve difficult
convex surfaces—how to cut notches and corners—attaching the keel—
how to make undercuts—Eskimo kayak—diagrams and directions for
making sailing model—rigging for two other models (ketch and yawl).

MAKE YOUR OWN MODEL CARS.. 41
Your designing tools—the French curve—making your design—dia-
grams for model cars—the plaster-cast method of making a model car
with complete directions and step-by-step photographs—wheels for
your car—steps in making wheels—how to mount wheels—wooden
wheels—plaster wheels.

EVERYBODY'S GUIDE TO MODEL RAILROADING................................... 59
Where to begin—scale and tinplate trains—railroad gauges—planning
your purchases—locating the railroad—three railroad systems—the
point-to-point road—turning trains at terminals—laying out the road
—cars that build interest—building an open-work table—how to add
ballast—how to create scenery—making rock from plaster—how to
paint the terrain—the scenic backdrop—buildings—your railroad in
operation—how to run way freights—naming your railroad.

BUILDING MODEL PLANES THAT FLY... 71
Words for model builders—the propeller is important—carving the
prop—sanding and drilling—construction hints—covering and doping
—wire fittings—flying your model—diagrams and instructions for making airplanes: outdoor glider; all-balsa R.O.G.; outdoor cabin flyer.

HOW TO ENJOY STAMP COLLECTING... 91
What you can learn from stamps—the different types of collectors—
what you should know about the stamp itself—perforations—outer
edge of the sheet—face of the stamp—errors that add value to stamps—
cancellations—types of watermarks—building a special collection—care
of stamps—materials and tools needed—kinds of albums—using the
catalogue—how to use hinges—how to handle stamps—tools for stamp
identification—how to develop and enlarge a collection—buying
stamps in quantity—auctions and traders—stamp clubs and their value
—displaying your collection.

THE ART OF SOAP SCULPTURE... 101
  Subjects for soap sculpture—holidays offer interesting possibilities—historical and art subjects—other ideas—making a woman—working hints—preparing the soap—tracing the pattern—roughing out design—joining a sculpture to a base—joining two cakes—polishing—progressive steps in soap carving—diagrams and instructions for carving: eagle; cat and mouse; squaw and papoose; polar bear; pelican; fish.

BOOK BINDING MADE EASY... 107
  Equipment—tools—materials—preparation—book make-up—end sheets—how to sew—knocking down—how to glue—trimming—shaping—headbands—the super—the case—full binding—how to recase—titling.

PAPER DECORATING AND PORTFOLIO MAKING... 115
  Paper decorating—butterfly method—crackle—color—water-printing—crackle and drip—splash tone—mounting—things to decorate—how to make a portfolio—materials needed—size—backing—assembling—covering—corners—tapes for tying—lining—finishing.

FINGER PAINTING FOR THE FAMILY... 121
  Paints and paper—steps in finger painting—painting a picture—how to design your pictures—rhythm—proportion—balance—forms—practical uses for finger paintings—baskets and scrapbook—decorated book ends.

PAPER PULP MODELING AND CRAYON CRAFT... 127
  Paper pulp modeling—how to make models—decorating the figures—steps in crayon craft—paint hints—for the party—poster-making—a magic trick.

SQUARE KNOTTING—A USEFUL CRAFT... 129
  Equipment and material—making a square knot in one operation—the half-knot—the half-hitch—the picot—making a belt—patterns—diagonal knotting—finishing with a loop or "keeper"—buckles—a braided lanyard—the braiding process—whipping the ends—diagrams and directions for making belts: twelve-strand belts; eight-strand belts; six-strand belts.

NETTING FOR FUN AND PROFIT... 137
  Equipment needed—glossary—how to make netting—diagrams and directions for netting projects: hammock of seine cord; doll hammock; tassel trim; landing net; landing net frame and handle; circular net; lawn tennis net; basket ball net; badminton net; saddle bags; shopping bag; shawl with ruffle.

LOVELY DOLLS ANYONE CAN MAKE... 149
  Faces for character dolls—changing faces—how to make wigs—doll proportions—how to make a body armature—diagrams and directions for making dolls: apple dolls; dolls carved from wood; storytelling dolls; dancing dolls; costumes for character dolls.

HOW TO MAKE DOLL HOUSES AND MINIATURE FURNITURE.......... 156
  Materials and dimensions for doll house—making the doll house—how to decorate it—lights for the doll house—diagrams and directions for making doll house accessories: doll-house rugs; oilcloth mats. How to make miniature furniture—miniature furniture patterns—decorating and finishing the furniture.

DECORATING TEXTILES AS A HOBBY.. 160
Plain dyeing—batik-dyeing with designs—tie-dyeing—crackle batik—
batik with wax—batik without wax—decorating cloth with textile
colors—things to decorate—how to decorate—helpful suggestions—adding color with stencils.

BLOCK PRINTING WITH LINOLEUM................................ 167
Uses of block printing—tools—facts about linoleum—mounting linoleum—cutting linoleum to size—brayer, ink and slab—the press—other
necessary materials—making a linoleum block print—proper way of
cutting—single-line cutting—background technique—lettering: single
stroke and single stroke shaded—how to cut blocked letters—how to
hand-block textiles.

WORKING WITH LEATHER.................................... 179
Minimum tools for leather work—material and sources—making a key
case—tooling—setting eyelets—stitching or lacing—diagrams and directions for leather projects: braided leather belts; book ends; buttons;
lapel ornaments; link belts; leather belts; billfold; cigarette case;
knife sheath; leather covers.

METAL CRAFT FOR FUN AND PROFIT......................... 189
Tools and equipment—metals and their uses—how to work in metal—
cutting—sawing—transferring design—annealing—pickling—shaping—
how to solder—raising—decorating metal—finishing—repoussé—diagrams and directions for metal projects: repoussé plaque and pin;
antelope plaque; giraffe book ends; bracelets; paper knives; attractive
projects from scrap metal; ashtrays and plates; a link bracelet; cuff
links; coin necklace; flower necklace; telephone memo pad.

ANYONE CAN DRAW................................ 201
Artist's equipment—drawing with your eyes shut—develop your ability
to observe—an easy drawing lesson—form, light, and shade—how to
develop a still-life drawing—the first sketch—movement—shading and
color—hints for original composition—distance and proportion—
drawing techniques—drawing with circles and triangles—how to draw
figures—face drawing made easy—planes of the face—different features
for different expressions.

• **THE USEFUL ART OF LETTERING**.............................. 212
Story of the alphabet—Old English text—Roman letters—the letter
and its parts—principles of good lettering—height of letters—correct
letter spacing—developing your skill—how to ink in letters—lettering
for designs—alphabets to study and copy.

ADVENTURES IN INDOOR GARDENING....................... 223
Collecting seeds—how to start a window garden—nationalities of
flowers—diagrams and directions for garden projects the herb garden;
dish gardens; a garden in a bottle; potted plants; eggshell gardens;
terrarium; hanging gardens; scenic gardens.

PHOTOGRAPHY FOR EVERYONE
and **How to Make Your Own Apparatus**.................... 231
How the camera works—shutter speed—how the image is formed—the
film—these common picture-making errors are easy to avoid—developing—the darkroom—diagrams and instructions for making your own
apparatus: enlarger; printing box; developing bench; safelight box;
print dryer; copying stand; retouching easel; negative dryer; trays;
tripod; pinhole camera; printing frame. How to mount your prints—
things to remember.

FUN WITH FELT.. 241
How to sew felt—twelve common stitches—moulding of felt—how to
make patterns—diagrams and directions for felt projects: flowers and
flower clusters; crushed felt flowers; roses; water lily; felt pot-holders;
appliqué belts; bridge table cover; curtain tie-backs; stuffed rabbit;
stuffed horse; woman's envelope bag.

POTTER'S CLAY—HOW TO USE IT............................... 253
Clay to use—wedging the clay—how to work with clay—slip method—
ball method—slab method—slip casting—how to make pottery—decorating pottery—how to glaze pottery—bisque firing—how to make pins
and belt links—how to make busts and figures—how to make a plaster
cast.

CARD TRICKS, MENTAL FEATS, AND MAGIC................ 259
Tricks with cards and dominoes: the queens dig for diamonds; a card
trick with a mathematical basis; the domino oracle; guessing the ends
of a domino line; like with like, or how to keep a hotel; the four
knaves; the magic courts of Zoroaster. Mental feats: the figure he
struck out; the certain game; the dice guessed unseen; to find a number thought of; another way to find a number thought of; to discover
two or more numbers thought of. Magic tricks: the balanced coin; the
balanced Turk; the erratic egg; to light a candle without touching the
wick; the Spanish dancer; the bridge of knaves.

WEAVE YOUR OWN BASKETS.. 268
Materials and equipment—general directions for making baskets—
cutting the ribs—different type weaves—bases for baskets—how to make
borders—how to shape the basket—how to make a handle—diagrams
and directions for making baskets: nut basket made with double over-
and-under weave; a small basket in pairing weave; tall flower basket
using pairing and triple weave; basket made with knot weave; tall
flower basket of splints and honeysuckle; sandwich basket made of
splint oak.

HOW TO MAKE FLIES AND FISHING RODS................... 281
Fly-making tools—varieties of fishing flies—how to make a hackle fly—
dry flies—feather streamers—bass flies—parts of a fly—how to make a
mallard quill—how to make other flies—how to make a fly book—how
to make fishing rods.

BUILD IT YOURSELF—Woodworking and Toys Anyone Can Make............ 287
How to select wood—woodworking terms—tools—glues and how to use
them—how to paint—helpful woodworking shop suggestions—diagrams and directions for woodworking projects: folding bench ladder;
adjustable book ends; linen closet; tool chest; salt box; waste-paper
basket; dog house; sled; plank train; pull toys; wooden wagon; three
boats; kitchen string holder; child's desk; modern night table; pin-up
lamps.

EASY WEAVING ON SMALL LOOMS............................... 302
Materials to use—weaving words—pattern weaving—the purse loom—
directions for stringing loom—how to weave purses—the square weaver
—how to use patterns—directions for making square weaver—directions for stringing loom—diagrams and instructions for making popular patterns: diagonal weave; Irish chain; log cabin; double diamond.
Diagrams and directions for things to make: afghan and robe for car;
attractive scarfs; knitting bags; woven belts; berets for children; zipper
purses and handbags.

HOW TO ENLARGE OR REDUCE PATTERNS AND DESIGNS

In many cases it will probably be necessary to enlarge or reduce the size of the drawings in this book. There are several ways of doing this, but for our purpose the method illustrated is easiest. This is done by ruling squares of equal dimension on the original drawing or picture, and then preparing a paper for the enlargement by ruling squares of larger proportions. Assuming that the squares on the original are ¼ inch or (2/8 inch) and you wish to enlarge it to 1½ times the original size, the squares for the enlargement must measure ⅜ inch. For enlarging to twice the original size, make the squares measure ½ inch. This is illustrated by the accompanying drawings of a key case. To reduce the size, simply scale downward.

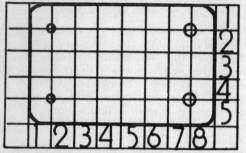

To make the enlargements, point off on the larger squares, using the same comparative proportions, wherever the original crosses the lines of the smaller squares. Next connect these points, taking care to follow the original drawing.

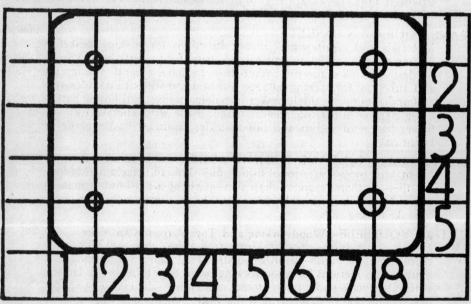

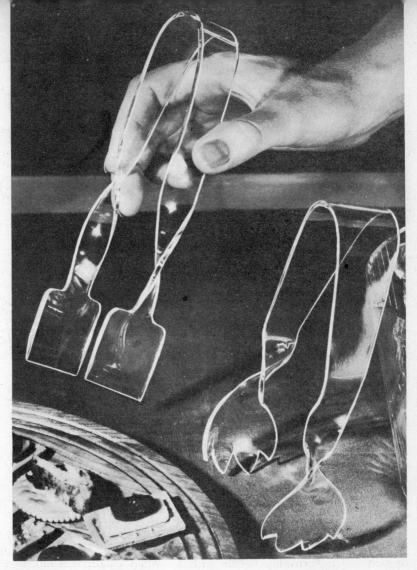

PLASTIC CRAFT AS A HOBBY

The hobby of working with plastic has an enthusiastic following of people from many walks of life. As a means of recreation it is enjoyed as much by the beginner with a few simple hand tools as by the skilled mechanic with an elaborately equipped shop, for many useful and attractive articles may be made entirely by hand.

The widespread use of plastics in home shops started during World War II. Over two million members of the air forces and tens of thousands of civilian workers

in aircraft plants became acquainted with plastic bomber noses, gun turrets, canopies and other parts of the plane. Many of these people saw in this plastic an intriguing and highly valuable material for home crafts.

Recommended projects for the beginner are those requiring no machine processes, no cementing and no intricate forming operations. Rings, pendants, brooches, bracelets and earrings are favorite items. Photograph frames, lamps, and trinket boxes are also popular.

[1]

CARE OF PLASTIC

Plastic should be stored vertically on edge or kept flat, and fully supported. If it stands at an angle or hangs over an edge, it will warp, and must be laid flat for a time to bring it back to its normal shape.

Masking Paper. The gummed masking paper covering the plastic sheet should be left in place as long as possible during the fabrication process, since it is easier to avoid scratches than to remove them. It is good practice, however, to peel the paper off sufficiently to examine a sheet before using it. A slow, steady pull removes the paper. It is readily replaced, following inspection, by simply pressing back in place. Warming in an oven a minute softens the adhesive and facilitates removal of the paper.

Cleaning Plastic. Ordinary dirt can be removed from plastic with soap and water. Use pure soaps—not pumice or scouring types—and do the cleaning with a very soft cloth or preferably just the bare hand. Oil or grease smears that do not wash off can be removed with a little kerosene or white gasoline followed by the soapy water. After rinsing, the plastic can be dried by patting with a damp chamois, soft damp cloth or crumpled soft tissue.

Dust particles, held to the plastic surface by static charge, may be blown off or removed by brushing lightly with a damp cloth.

As a final step in cleaning, or as the last operation in fabricating, the plastic should be given a thin coat of some recommended wax of the Simonize type. Apply the wax with a damp cloth and polish with clean cotton flannel or jersey.

HOW TO USE A PATTERN

In most cases a pattern or a folded-up model is recommended when starting to make an article of plastic. The pattern can be transferred to the paper masking the plastic by marking around the pattern or by tracing over it through carbon paper laid on the masking paper (Fig.

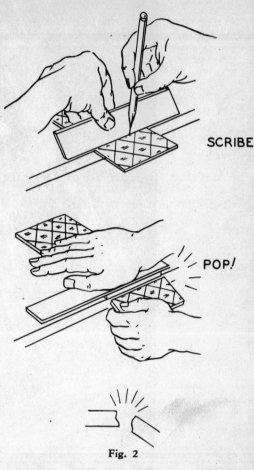

SCRIBE

POP!

Fig. 2

1). Free-hand sketching or drawing with drafting tools directly on the masking paper is, of course, entirely practical when a pattern is not used.

CUTTING PLASTIC

Thin plastic, up to $\frac{1}{8}$ inch thick, can be cut by a method similar to that used in cutting window glass. A scribe mark is run across the sheet along a straight edge, making a deep scratch. Then, by holding the plastic rigidly under the straight edge on one side of the mark and pressing the other side down over the edge of a table, the plastic will break along the scratch. The method is not recommended for long breaks or thick material (see Fig. 2).

Hot plastic is rubbery and can be cut like heavy rubber. Hence, for cutting hot

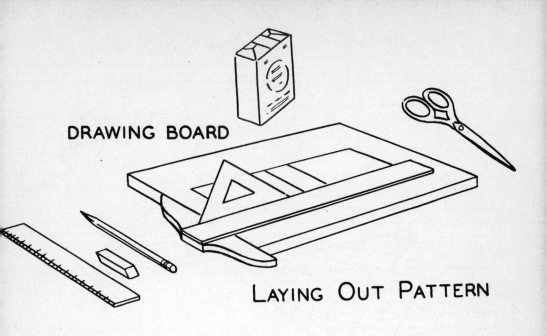

DRAWING BOARD

LAYING OUT PATTERN

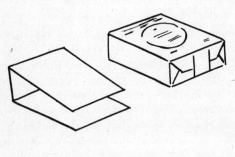

FOLDING PATTERN
FOR SIZE

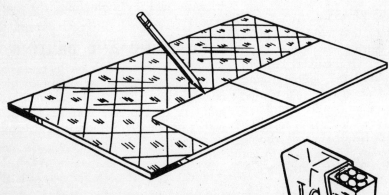

TRANSFERRING PATTERN
TO MASKING PAPER

Fig. 1

[3]

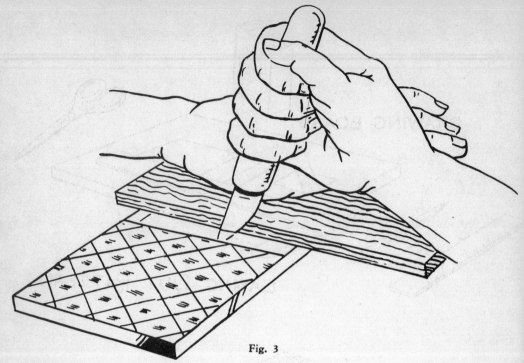

Fig. 3

plastics, tin snips, the guillotine-type of paper cutter, or even a heavy knife can be used (Fig. 3).

Curved cuts can be made by shears along a scribed line or wax crayon mark, but a margin must be provided for finishing the edge, since the edge from scissors cuts is often rough and warped.

HOW TO SAW PLASTIC

Plastic may be sawed with any type of wood or metal-cutting saw, either hand or power operated. Of the many kinds of hand saws available, the hollow-ground straight saw and the deep-throat coping saw are usually found most useful, although compass saws, hack saws and various other types of hand saws may also be used. A straight saw having eight to ten teeth per inch with very little set is recommended.

The saw should be used with little pressure and it should be kept straight, since if the saw binds, the plastic may be cracked.

Straight hand saws should be held at an angle of about 45° from the vertical, to engage two or more saw teeth in the material at one time. In the case of the

coping or scroll saw, very narrow blades usually give best results.

Clamps, jigs and miter boxes are very helpful—almost essential—accessories in hand-sawing plastic. A simple but very useful clamp is made by bolting a straight wooden bar on the table top, arranged so that the plastic can be slipped under it and held by tightening the bolts (Fig. 4).

PUNCHING AND DRILLING

Holes in plastic are made by punching or drilling. In the home shop punching does not have wide application. Small holes in cold plastic may be punched with a hot needle, withdrawing it before it cools.

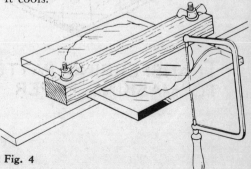

Fig. 4

[4]

An adaptation of this "hot-wire punching" is used in inserting small screws or fasteners in plastic. The metal fastener is merely heated and pushed into place in the plastic. As it cools it "freezes" in place quite firmly.

Finishing a Hole. For the best possible finish in a hole, the drill should have polished, slow, spiral flutes. These enable the drill to clear the hole of shavings and leave a good finish on the walls of the hole. The flutes should be wide enough to clear the widest chip the cutting edge can produce. Fuzzy or irregular finish is caused by the shavings rubbing on the walls of the hole, melting and smearing or "burning" the walls.

TURNING

Plastic can be turned on either wood or metal turning lathes. The metal turning type, commonly known as the engine lathe, is preferred because of its rigidity and the wide range of operations which can be performed with it. Sizes of lathes vary from the tiny precision lathe used by jewelers to enormous floor models used for large machining operations. The home craftsman will find a 9- or 10-inch bench lathe satisfactory for ordinary requirements in turning plastic.

In general, the recommended procedure for turning plastic is about the same as that used in working with brass.

Lathe Work. The lathe is the only practical means of producing most turned

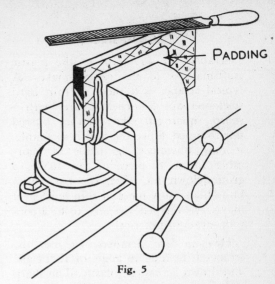

Fig. 5

parts. Knobs, furniture legs, vases, lenses —all such circular parts call for lathe work. In addition, the ingenious home craftsman will find many other operations for which the lathe can be used. The machine is not dangerous and it is not particularly noisy.

HOW TO FILE

Plastic files quite easily and can be brought to a surface ready for the final polishing by filing alone if the job is correctly done. For filing edges to remove tool marks, a 10- to 12-inch smooth-cut flat file is recommended.

Filing should be done in one direction, keeping the file flat on the surface of the material, but at an angle with the direction of motion that will prevent grooving of the plastic by the file teeth (Fig. 5).

To keep the file in good condition, it should be cleaned frequently, using a wire or fiber file brush. Files used in working plastic should not be used for filing metal or other materials that would dull or gum the teeth.

Special Files. Half-round or rat-tail files are useful for smoothing the inner surface of holes. A triangular file is useful for notches or grooves. A set of very small files is excellent for finishing fine scroll work. Files that can be inserted in a jig saw will prove very useful for shaping, cutting or finishing a profile.

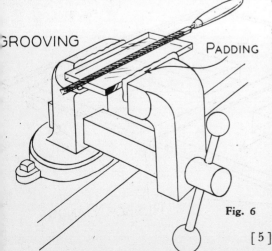

Fig. 6

SCRAPING

Scrapers are as useful to the plastic craftsman as to the cabinet-maker. A typical scraper is a piece of thin hard steel, perhaps 3 inches square, with a sharp, square-cut edge, neither burred nor rounded. Since the tool is so simple, it may, obviously, be made in many other forms. A piece of saw blade, a ground-down file edge, the back of a knife blade—any piece of thin hard steel may serve. Shaped scrapers, to fit a contour, are also practical.

How to Use Scrapers. In use, the scraper is held at an angle of about 45° and drawn across the plastic. The sharp right-angled edge removes a thin shaving, leaving a smooth surface ready for polishing. Repeated strokes of the scraper will, of course, continue to remove material, so that it is possible, although tedious, to shape a plastic part, as well as to prepare it for polishing, with the scraper. Figure 7 illustrates a few typical applications for scrapers.

HOW TO SAND PLASTIC

Sanding is commonly the last step in finishing before the buffing operation. There are a number of power sanding devices, but the home craftsman will probably find that for his purposes sanding is still largely a hand operation—tedious but very essential for a well-finished article.

For most work "wet-or-dry" sandpaper, used wet, is recommended for work on plastic. Beginning with a relatively coarse paper (about 240 to 300 grit) the work is sanded until all scratches except those caused by the sandpaper itself are removed. Keep the plastic wet during all the sanding operations, but wipe it dry to inspect the progress of the work.

After the work with the first paper, shift to a finer grit—perhaps 320 or 400—and, if the nature of the piece will permit it, sand across the scratches left by the first sanding. When all of the marks left by the first paper are removed, change to a still finer grade of paper, change direction again, and repeat the operation. Observation and experience will help determine just how many different grades of paper to use for the most efficient work. The final paper (600 grit) should leave the work satin smooth and ready for easy buffing to a high polish.

Sanding Small Parts. In hand sanding of small parts it is often easier to fix the sandpaper and rub the plastic across it. The craftsman may find various ways to do this. One practical method is to fasten the sandpaper to a sheet of plate glass with rubber bands. (Glass is recommended because it is flat and is not affected by water.) A piece of glass about 12 by 19 inches is recommended since this size permits four sheets of paper (giving four different grits) to be fastened to it. Two sheets are placed on each side of

WET SANDING BY HAND

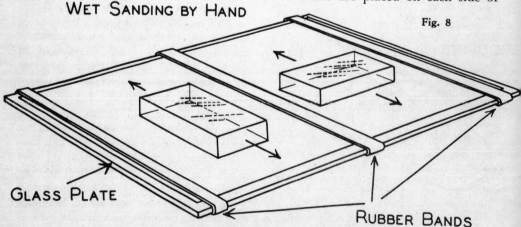

Fig. 8

GLASS PLATE

RUBBER BANDS

[6]

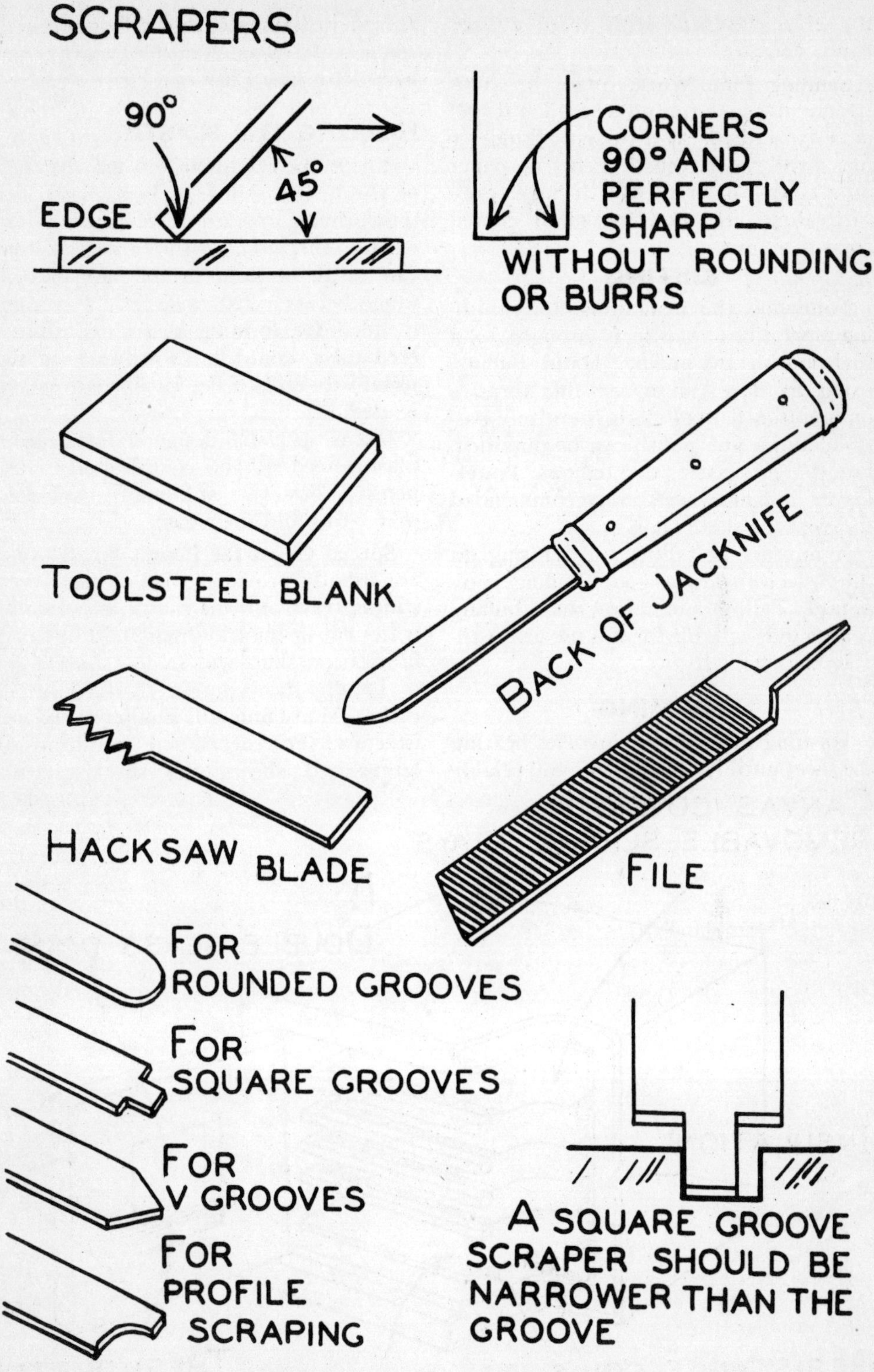

SCRAPERS

90°

45°

EDGE

CORNERS 90° AND PERFECTLY SHARP — WITHOUT ROUNDING OR BURRS

TOOLSTEEL BLANK

BACK OF JACKNIFE

HACKSAW BLADE

FILE

FOR ROUNDED GROOVES

FOR SQUARE GROOVES

FOR V GROOVES

FOR PROFILE SCRAPING

A SQUARE GROOVE SCRAPER SHOULD BE NARROWER THAN THE GROOVE

Fig. 7

the glass, fastened with three rubber bands (Fig. 8).

Sanding Fine Work. Strips of sandpaper, wrapped around a wooden dowel or a twist drill, serve to sand holes or fine scroll work. Small pieces of paper on a cloth pad or used with finger pressure alone are used for small curved areas.

BUFFING

Following the machining and finishing operations, plastic is brought to a high polish by buffing. Hand buffing, using dry Bon Ami or *very* fine abrasive on a cotton flannel cloth is entirely possible, and a fine polish can be obtained, but the process is very tedious. Power-driven buffing wheels are recommended for even the small shop.

A mixture of tallow and whiting on the wheel makes a good buffing compound. Tallow and tallow base buffing compounds suitable for this use are available commercially.

FORMING

Forming sheet plastic involves heating the sheet until it becomes soft and pliable and then shaping it to the form desired, using hand or mechanical means as the particular case requires.

HEATING THE PLASTIC

The home craftsman can use the oven of the kitchen stove to heat plastic for the forming operations. Such ovens are usually thermostatically controlled and can easily be kept in the temperature range between 220° and 300° F. recommended for forming plastic. Cloth-covered trays should be substituted for the usual wire racks if the kitchen stove oven is used.

Ovens specially designed for heating plastic need not be complicated or expensive, however, and many craftsmen prefer to build their own.

Special Ovens for Plastic. Small ovens are usually provided with cloth-covered sliding trays, and the plastic is heated as it lies flat in the tray (Fig. 9). The small fabrication shop will seldom have need to handle sheets larger than 36 by 48 inches. Many find still smaller ovens satisfactory. For occasional handling of larger-sized sheets, the sheet can be

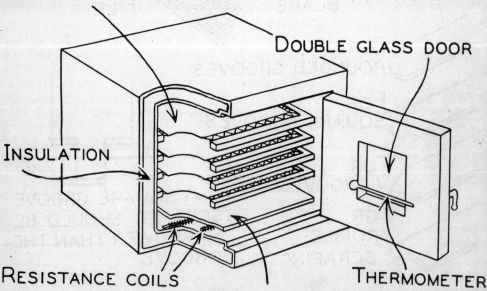

CANVAS COVERED
REMOVABLE SLIDING TRAYS

Fig. 9

DOUBLE GLASS DOOR

INSULATION

RESISTANCE COILS

METAL BAFFLE

THERMOMETER

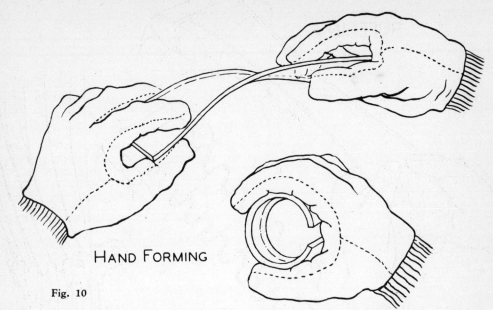

HAND FORMING

Fig. 10

folded over a strip heater before being placed in the oven. In this case, cotton flannel should be inserted in the fold to prevent the surfaces of plastic from touching.

Heating the Oven. Any of several methods may be used to heat the ovens—steam, gas, electric coil and infra-red all have their place. For ovens in the small shop, the electric coil is probably the most convenient source of heat.

Heat Carefully. Regardless of the method used to heat the plastic, care must be taken to avoid heating the material too long or at too high a temperature, since excessive heating tends to produce a slight yellow color.

FORMING TECHNIQUES

Only a few of the more fundamental methods of forming heated plastic are described here. There are, of course, many possible variations of the methods and the fabricator will work out processes suitable to his particular problems.

Soft cotton flannel gloves should be worn when working with hot plastic. With most gloves, a softer surface is obtained if the gloves are turned inside out. Double thickness gloves are helpful for holding hot plastic while it cools.

Many forming processes are done entirely by hand (Fig. 10) or with the aid of only a vise or clamp. In others, simple jigs may be provided, but an elaborate set-up of jigs and equipment is rarely needed in the home shop. The production fabricator will, of course, need more equipment in order to secure the necessary efficiency of operation.

Twisting. Twisting a strip of plastic by clamping one end of the material and twisting the other by hand is a simple means of producing pleasing articles (Fig. 11).

To keep the twist regular, the strip should be rubbed as it is twisted, or twisted part at a time. After twisting, the piece may be held straight or quickly turned to form a circle, spiral, or other shape as desired.

TWISTING

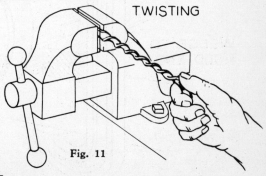

Fig. 11

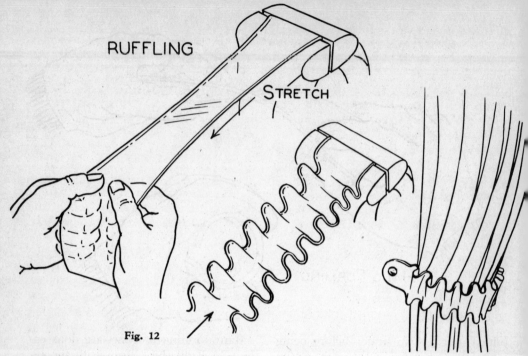

RUFFLING

STRETCH

Fig. 12

Ruffling. Ruffling is produced by stretching a strip of plastic as shown in Fig. 12. The edges of the material cool before the center, and, if a half-cooled, stretched piece is released, the attempt of the plastic to return to its former length will cause a ruffling effect along the edges. Curved into loops, ruffled pieces of this sort make decorative tiebacks for curtains.

Jigs and Clamps. Simple jig and clamp arrangements permit forming of a variety of shapes. A spiral, such as might be formed for a bracelet, is easily made with the clamp device shown in Fig. 13.

Curves. Draping plastic over a form, either convex or concave, is a useful means for shaping shallow three-dimensional curves. The method is illustrated in Fig. 14. A wood or plaster form covered with stretched cotton flannel or flocked rubber, is generally used. The hot

Fig. 13

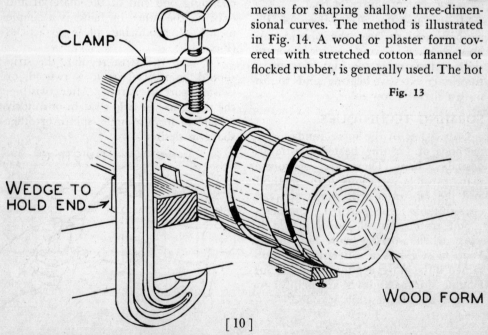

CLAMP

WEDGE TO HOLD END→

WOOD FORM

[10]

plastic is placed on the form and rubbed gently with cotton gloves or a ball of flannel to bring the material to the contour of the form.

With some types of molds, rubber bands can be used to hold the edges of the plastic to the form until the plastic cools. In other cases, it will be easier for the craftsman to hold the plastic in place by simply continuing to press it against the form with the flannel or gloves until it cools and hardens.

JOINING PLASTIC

The usual types of adhesive cements or glues, such as are commonly used in woodworking, have little use in working with plastic. They may be employed to join flat opaque or translucent sheets where the joint is not seen or to fasten cloth, wood, metal or other material to the plastic. When glues and cements of this type are used, the plastic should be sanded to provide a surface with a little "tooth" to increase the strength of the bond, and flexible adhesives such as are commonly sold as "household cements" should be used.

For regular fabricating operations, however, adhesive glues and cements are not recommended. A cohesive cement is needed; that is, one that softens the surfaces of the plastic so that the two parts actually become a single unit. Find out the type of plastic used and ask your local dealer for cement for that particular plastic.

Just before the cement is applied, the area around the joint should be masked with a pressure adhesive tape that will not be affected by the cement. The tape should be carefully rubbed down to prevent seepage of cement under it, and removed when the joint has set up, before it is quite hard. With proper care and a steady hand, masking may be omitted in many types of joints, but is a worthwhile precaution.

How to Apply Cement. The cement may be applied in several ways. The most usual method is to soak one of the edges

DRAPING

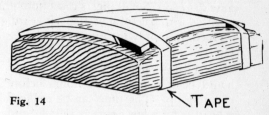

Fig. 14

TAPE

to be joined until it is swollen into a "cushion" by the solvent action of the cement. The time required to produce the necessary cushion will vary according to the cement used and the joint to be made, but 30 seconds to 3 minutes are the usual periods. Soaking time should be long enough to form an adequate cushion, but if too deep a cushion is formed too much material will be extruded at the joint and a long hardening period must be allowed.

Bringing Edges Together. When sufficient cushion has been obtained, the two edges are brought together without delay, while the cushion is still wet with solvent. The solvent causes the opposite dry surface to swell into the cushion, forming the joint. The cushion serves to hold the cement needed in the joint and helps to close a joint that is not perfectly fitted.

Use of Jig. As soon as the edges are joined, the assembly is placed in the clamp or jig and left to harden. Just

Fig. 15   SHOT SACK OR WEIGHT

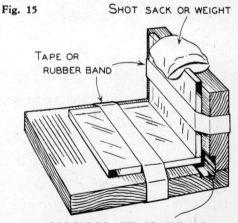

TAPE OR RUBBER BAND

GROOVE TO KEEP CEMENT FROM SEEPING BETWEEN WOOD AND PLASTIC

enough jig pressure to squeeze out the air bubbles is recommended. Greater pressure will squeeze out the cement and cause dry spots. Small pieces can often be weighted with bags of shot, tied with cord, or taped, to supply the required pressure (Fig. 15).

For Firmer Joints. Cemented joints should be left at least 24 hours before "cleaning up." The time can be reduced by heating for a few hours at 150° F., and the resulting joint will be stronger. Heat should not be applied, however, until the joint has set up—usually fifteen to twenty minutes.

Caution. Solvent cements are toxic and most of them are inflammable. Inhaling the concentrated vapors for extended periods may cause illness, so the worker should provide adequate ventilation, away from fire, for the operation.

DESIGN

The craftsman will find the proper design of a plastic part is often of greater importance than its decoration. An object of poor design cannot be corrected by any amount of decoration; on the other hand, an article that is pleasing in proportions and designed to fulfill its functions often needs no decoration.

Good design involves more than these considerations of proportion and function. It includes, also, choice of proper materials and the correct use of the materials chosen. The designer must know the characteristics of the material he works with—its limitations as well as its advantages.

The worker in plastic will be especially interested in the following about the material:

Heat Sensitiveness. The fact that plastic softens when heated and, in this condition, can be shaped as desired has been discussed previously as one of the valuable properties of the material. Obviously, however, this characteristic makes the acrylic plastics unsuitable for use near fire or excessive heat. The acrylics will burn slowly (about like wood) when placed in an open flame, although red-hot metals will not ignite them (Fig. 16).

DYEING

Clear plastic carries light practically undiminished and therefore produces great brilliance. Coloring or tinting the material naturally decreases the brilliance since some light must be absorbed by the coloring material. If the plastic is surface-dyed, rather than colored all the way through, there is, of course, less diminishing of the brilliance.

A plastic dye is simply a color dissolved in a liquid that will penetrate the surface but not seriously injure it. Great care should be taken to be certain the solvent of the dye does not harm the plastic.

Annealing the object before dyeing is a good policy since it removes surface strains which, if present, would be apt to develop a pattern of tiny fissures. This effect, called crazing, can best be seen by looking along the surface of the sheet.

BURNING AND DEFORMING

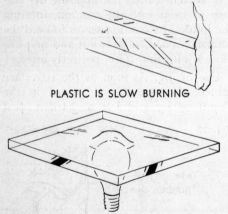

PLASTIC IS SLOW BURNING

IT SOFTENS AGAINST AN INCANDESCENT BULB

BUT NOT AGAINST A FLUORESCENT TUBE

Fig. 16

After dyeing it is well to anneal again to remove the tendency to craze caused by the dye.

Dip Dyes. "Dip" dyes are popular with craftsmen. These are dyes that can be used, as the name implies, by simply dipping the object in the dye. The intensity of color is regulated by varying the time the plastic is in the dye. The surface should be quite clean to produce a uniform color. Unpolished surfaces become more intensely colored than highly polished ones.

When the desired color is obtained, the object is removed from the dye, rinsed, dried and waxed.

It is best to do all the dyeing required in one operation. Crazing is more likely to occur if the plastic dries between two or more separate dye dips.

A Good Dyeing Mixture. A satisfactory mixture may be made with 60 per cent acetone and 40 per cent water. A dye is dissolved in the acetone, the water added, and the mixture filtered. A disadvantage of this type of mixture is that the dye precipitates due to evaporation of the acetone, weakening the color. For this reason, it is best to make up a stock solution in a large bottle and work from a small bottle which is refilled as needed from the stock solution.

Rub Dyeing. This is a simple method of coloring plastic in selected spots. A cloth dipped in the dye is rubbed on the area where color is wanted (Fig. 17). A surface thus tinted appears vividly colored when viewed in such a way as to get internal reflection. For example, a rear surface bevel tinted in this way appears brilliantly colored when viewed through the front surface. The effect of iridescence is obtained when colors are mixed by rub dyeing.

After tinting, the object is rinsed, dried and waxed. The dyes will stay on the surface unless they are buffed off.

With either dip or rub dyes, a design can be colored, leaving the rest of the sheet clear, by carefully masking the sheet to outline the design.

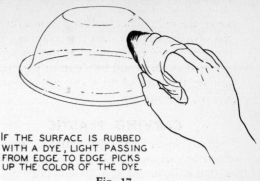

IF THE SURFACE IS RUBBED WITH A DYE, LIGHT PASSING FROM EDGE TO EDGE PICKS UP THE COLOR OF THE DYE.

Fig. 17

HOW TO PAINT PLASTIC

For many applications remarkably decorative effects are produced by using opaque paints. Many processes are used, but almost without exception the paint is applied to the reverse side of the plastic to be viewed through the transparent sheet. Seen in this way, the color appears brighter or richer—just as a painting takes on richer tones when it has been varnished.

Since the paint is to be viewed through the surface on which it is applied, the technique of application must, of course, be different. The "top coat" must be applied first, followed by such undercoats as may be desired. Naturally, there can be no correction of color or appearance after the paint is applied, since the "top coat" is inaccessible.

A NOVEL METHOD

An interesting variation in the process of decorating with paint consists of reversing the order of application. The background color is applied to the plastic first and allowed to dry. Then with orange stick or plastic point, the color is scraped off where a design of different color is desired. This area is painted with the new color, allowed to dry, and space for another color scraped away. The process can, of course, go on indefinitely to make whatever design is wanted.

A sketch of the completed picture, placed under the plastic, while the decorating is in progress can be used as a guide, since it becomes visible in the section being worked as the paint is scraped away, the only difficulty being in locating the proper point to start the scraping. A more accurate but somewhat more complicated guide would be a cutout pattern laid on the back of the sheet, directly on the painted surface.

CARVING PLASTIC

Many home craftsmen will be interested in carving plastic. It is not carved with a knife or chisel, as in wood carving, but is scraped away, being worked in much the same manner as brass. Small, pointed tools and variously shaped scrapers are used for the purpose. With such tools, plastic may be carved as desired, but the operation is exceedingly tedious and has only limited use.

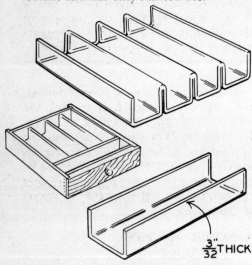

DRAWER COMPARTMENTS

First, measure the drawer in which the compartments are to be fitted and measure width and height of each compartment. It is better to make each compartment in one separate piece as plastics generally come in small sheets and it would be almost impossible for the home craftsman to heat and form all of them at one time. The sides may be cemented together after they are shaped if necessary.

Use plastic 3/32 inch in thickness. Cut out each compartment. Heat in an oven and bend over a wooden block. File and polish edges.

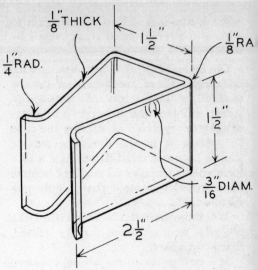

BROOM HOLDER

Cut a strip of 3/16-inch plastic 6½ by 1½ inches. Drill a 3/16-inch hole in the center. This project should be heated twice—first, heat and bend at the center leaving 1½ inches at the center bend. Next, place the two ends in boiling water —it will become soft in two or three minutes. Bear down with the hand until ends begin to bend back. Then remove from the water, cover with a cloth and complete curve with fingers.

Smooth the edges with fine sandpaper and file the corners. Polish with a little jeweler's rouge.

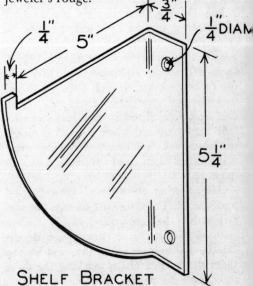

SHELF BRACKET

SHELF BRACKET

This bracket is cut from a piece of 3/16-inch plastic 6¼ by 6 inches. Mark out the pattern on paper covering plastic and cut around edges with a coping saw. Drill two ¼-inch holes on the straight side about ½ inch in from the edge.

Remove paper and smooth edges with sandpaper and a file. Place in oven to heat and bend over a block ¾ inch in thickness.

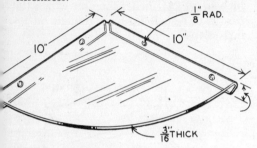

CORNER SHELF

Cut a piece of 3/16-inch plastic 12 by 14 inches. Round off one corner as shown in the illustration. At the opposite corner, cut out a small piece 1 by ¼ inch to allow for the bending.

Next, drill two ⅛-inch holes in each straight side about ½ inch from the edge.

After edges are filed and sanded, heat in an oven for bending. Shelf can be shaped over the corner of a table.

TOWEL RACK

Cut a piece of 3/16-inch plastic into a strip 19½ by 1¼ inches. Drill two 3/16-inch holes in either end about ¾ inch in from the edge as indicated in the illustration.

The bending of this particular project can be made simpler by bending one side at a time, and heating it in boiling water instead of an oven. Have enough water in the pan to cover the part you want heated and hold the end of the rack in the boiling water until it becomes soft (about 3 minutes). When quite flimsy, remove and shape it over a block 1¼ inches high. The end with the holes can be spread out on the table. Finish by filing and polishing edges.

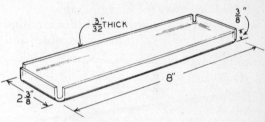

PEN AND PENCIL TRAY

This tray is cut from a piece of 3/32-inch plastic 8½ by 3¼ inches. At each corner cut out a small piece ⅛ by ⅜ inch to allow for bending the corners. Finish off edges by sanding and polish with jeweler's rouge. Heat in the oven and bend over a piece of three ply wood cut to the same dimensions as the bottom of the tray.

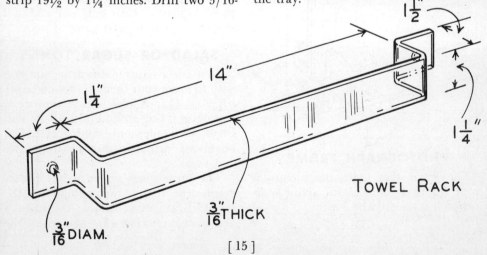

TOWEL RACK

[15]

PAPER KNIFE

Trace pattern on paper covering 3/16-inch plastic and saw around the outline. Trace your monogram on the handle and drill a small hole in the corner of each letter. To cut out the letters, insert the saw blade in the hole and fasten each end in a coping or jeweler's saw. Cut around the outer edge until the letter has been removed.

The frame around the letters is made by filing away the background.

File edges of knife until they are thin, smooth off with fine sandpaper and polish.

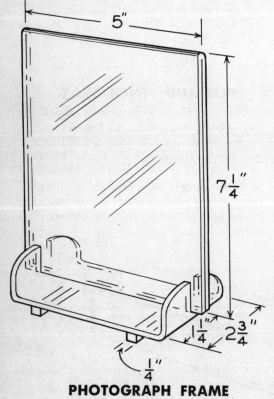

PHOTOGRAPH FRAME

The frame that holds the picture is made from very thin plastic about 3/32-inch in thickness; 14 by 5 inches is a good size.

Heat a line through the center and bend, leaving just enough room for a picture. The base is made from 1/4-inch plastic. Draft a pattern as shown in the illustration, making the slits in sides to fit the frame after it is bent. Cut two 1/4-inch strips 2¾ inches long on which the base is to rest. Bend base, cement on 1/4-inch strips and finish all edges.

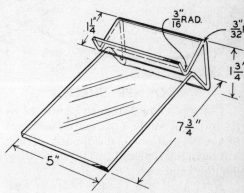

PAD HOLDER

This is a problem in cutting and bending. The measurements given in the accompanying illustration are for an ordinary pad; if you use a different size, change the dimensions.

It is not necessary to heat the entire piece of plastic. Heat only one end and shape over a triangular piece of wood.

SALAD OR SUGAR TONGS

First cut a paper pattern the size you wish to make your tongs. Trace on paper covering 1/8-inch plastic (use thinner if you desire). Cut around outline, smooth edges with file and sandpaper. Heat about a 1-inch strip through the center and bend.

The sugar tongs shown in the photograph are cut the same, except that the two ends are shaped. Heat the handles and twist them (Fig. 11), then reheat the

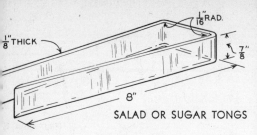

1/16" RAD.

1/8" THICK

7/8"

8"

SALAD OR SUGAR TONGS

bowls and round them by forcing the plastic in shallow depression such as a spoon.

BOOK ENDS

These beautiful book ends are made from 3/4-inch plastic. The center piece not only aids in holding the side and bottom together but also lends interest to the design. The problem involved is simply cutting the plastic to shape, finishing and polishing the edges and finally cementing together.

COCKTAIL TRAY

This tray is cut in one piece of plastic 16 by 13½ by 3/16 inches. Cut small pieces from each corner 3/4 by 1/4 inch for bending. Note detail of bending corners. Bend the two ends with handles first and then the sides.

See suggestions given earlier in this chapter for decoration, if you wish to add color to the tray.

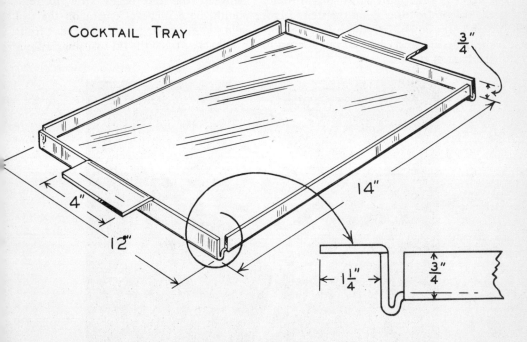

COCKTAIL TRAY

3/4

14"

4"

12"

3/4

1 1/4"

3/4

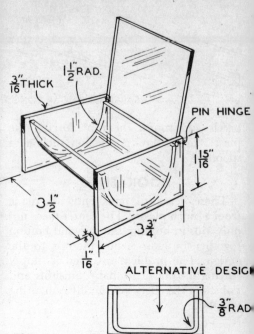

PIN HINGE

ALTERNATIVE DESIGN

BUD VASES

First draft a pattern the size of vases you wish and cut out the different parts to see if they fit together.

The flower holder is a hollow plastic tube easily obtained at any craft store. Cut the tube to the desired height, then cut the plastic strips and drill two holes the size of the tube. Bend the strips in an S and slip down over the tubes. Cement the tube and lower part of the S strips to the base of the vase.

CIGARETTE BOX

First cut the four pieces of plastic needed for the box to dimensions given in the diagram. Heat the bottom piece and shape it over a mold. The distance between the top edges after forming should be 3 inches. Cement on the two side pieces, leaving a 1/8-inch space front and back. Attach the lid by using two pin hinges.

ADVENTURES IN WHITTLING

Anyone can learn to whittle expertly. It depends primarily on the proper use of the knife and may consist of simply cutting shavings, or the carving of objects of art. The most necessary qualification for the beginner is the desire and urge to carve—with this and some perseverance, carving will soon be an accomplishment.

Carving began almost as far back as man himself. Since knives were not available, he was forced to use the sharpened edge of a stone and to chisel away bits of wood or cut it out in chips. Today we have knives made from the finest steel, with blades sharp enough to cut away shavings too fine for the eye to see.

[19]

TOOLS

You can buy knife blades in almost any size or shape. The large strong blades are used for rounding out the block of wood and rough work, and the smaller blades for fine detailed work. In selecting a knife, take the one that feels comfortable and well balanced in the hand.

WOODS TO USE

The best wood to use for most whittling projects is a clear grained, soft wood such as sugar pine or white pine. Bass, cottonwood and poplar are also good whittling woods. Other good woods are cedar, which gives a beautiful grained effect, and willow, which has a gray finish. It is best to avoid the hard woods such as maple, walnut and mahogany, until you have made several projects and have become fairly expert.

The harder grades of balsa wood are also good for beginners as even the hardest grade is soft and works easily.

Make sure that the block you use is free from cracks and knots. Try to get wood that has been kiln dried as it is less likely to have internal cracks which are known as checks. Make sure that the grain runs in the direction shown in the instructions, otherwise you will find pieces split off if the grain runs across instead of along the thin parts.

WHITTLING IN PLASTICS

The new materials of the modern age are the plastics, created chemically by man from raw material such as coal, water and air. Plastics have many uses in handicrafts. The softer plastics are good for whittling. Cellulose acetate, from which cellophane and celluloid are made, is available in blocks suitable for carving. It is best to begin on wood to learn the methods of whittling before beginning on plastics.

Some of the advantages which plastics have are the absence of grain, the beautiful colors in which it is available, the high polish and not least the low expense. Try your hand at a project in plastic.

CUTTING TECHNIQUES

There are two basic ways of handling the knife for whittling. They are the push and the pull methods illustrated below.

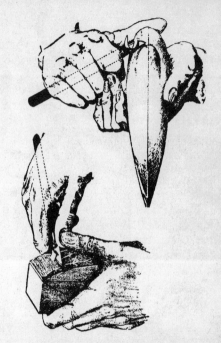

As you work on various projects you will probably develop your own variations on these techniques to suit your own individual needs. Remember that a knife is a sharp instrument and it is not advisable to try to stop a cut with your thumb against the blade.

Remember also that a sharp knife is less dangerous to use than a dull knife as you can control it more easily. Certain types can be kept sharp with replaceable blades.

STEPS IN WORK

The first step after you have picked the project and have a suitable piece of wood is to cut out the blank. Lay the pattern of the project over the block of wood, making sure that the grain of the wood runs in the correct direction as shown in the illustration. Place a piece of carbon paper between the pattern and the block of wood. Using a hard pencil trace the pattern onto the wood through the carbon paper. Following the outline on the wood cut the shape out with a band saw or a coping saw.

After you have cut out the blank, start whittling with your knife. First rough out the general shape of the object. At this stage you can make large cuts taking off fairly large chips. As the block comes closer and closer to the final shape, make your cuts smaller and smaller and take more and more care that you don't cut off something that you may have to glue back on as part of the finished project.

All dimensions shown on instructions and drawings refer to the full-sized finished projects.

Start with an easy job to learn how to handle your knife and the wood. The best project to start with in this chapter is the pig on this page. As you become more skilled you can tackle the harder projects. If you start with something difficult you may become discouraged and then drop whittling and never know the possibilities of the art.

FINISHING AND PAINTING

The whittled object can be finished off with paint, wood stain or in natural wood finish using varnish or shellac. To get a high gloss finish, sandpaper the figure to a smooth surface before painting and give the figure several coats of paint, sanding lightly after the first coat has dried. After the paint has thoroughly dried, rub in floor wax, using felt or similar cloth. If you use wood stain, finish with several coats of shellac or varnish and wax.

That's all there is to it except to stick to it and try to make each piece better than the one before. And above all have a good time—the more fun you get out of whittling, the better will be your work. And the better your work the more fun it will be.

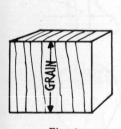

Fig. 1

Fig. 2

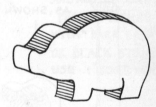

Fig. 3

PIG

This fellow is easy to make because he is so round and fat.

Start with block size 3 inches wide, 2 inches high and 1½ inches thick.

Trace Fig. 2 to side of block, Fig. 1.

Outline with coping saw, also cut between legs as shown in Fig. 4 (note arrows).

Figs. 5 and 6 show front and back views that will help get the picture.

Fig. 7 shows Mr. Pig, round and fat, standing without base on a shelf.

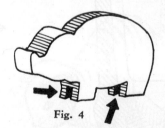

Fig. 4

Fig. 5

Fig. 6

Fig. 7

"Hansel"

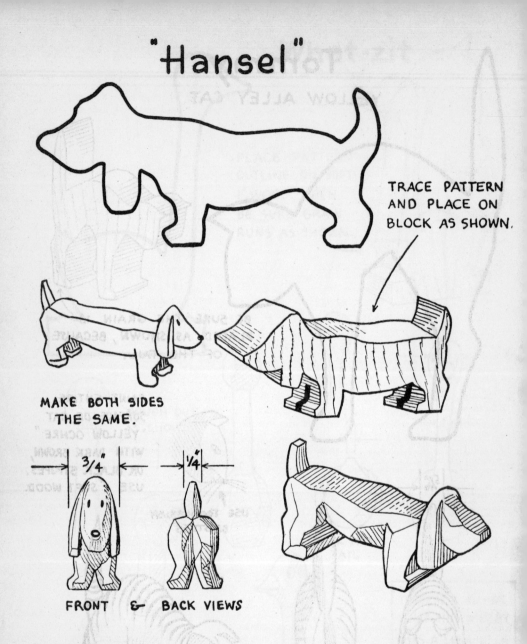

TRACE PATTERN AND PLACE ON BLOCK AS SHOWN.

MAKE BOTH SIDES THE SAME.

3/4"   1/4"

FRONT & BACK VIEWS

FINISH - DARK BROWN STAIN, WITH WHITE SPOTS FOR EYES. KEEP "HANSEL" LONG AND LOW FOR BEST EFFECT.

Colt

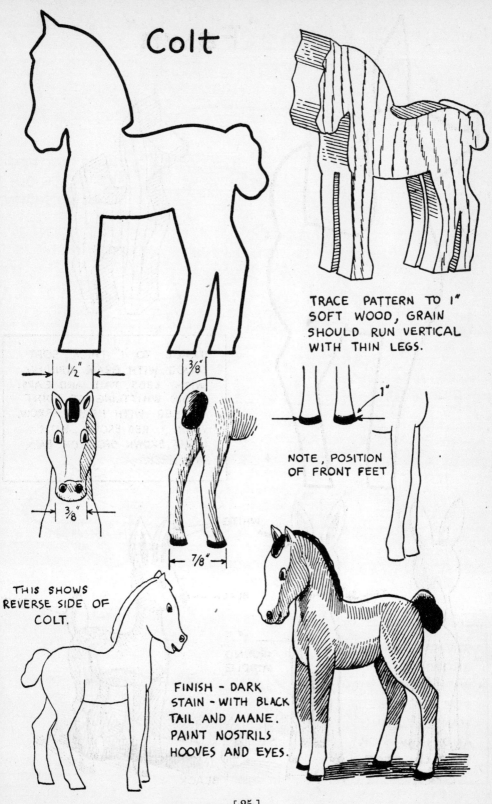

TRACE PATTERN TO 1"
SOFT WOOD, GRAIN
SHOULD RUN VERTICAL
WITH THIN LEGS.

1/2"

3/8"

3/8"

7/8"

1"

NOTE, POSITION
OF FRONT FEET

THIS SHOWS
REVERSE SIDE OF
COLT.

FINISH - DARK
STAIN - WITH BLACK
TAIL AND MANE.
PAINT NOSTRILS
HOOVES AND EYES.

"Fawn"

TRACE TO 1" THICK SOFT WOOD, WITH GRAIN RUNNING WITH LEGS, TAIL AND EARS. BEGIN WHITTLING AT POINT MARKED WITH HEAVY ARROW. FINISH • RED·BROWN, WITH LIGHT BROWN SPOTS ON BACK AND NECK.

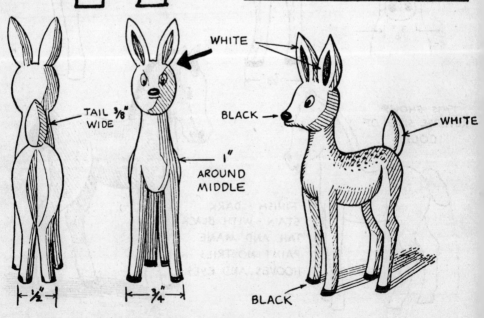

TAIL 3/8" WIDE

WHITE

BLACK

WHITE

1" AROUND MIDDLE

½"

¾"

BLACK

Molly

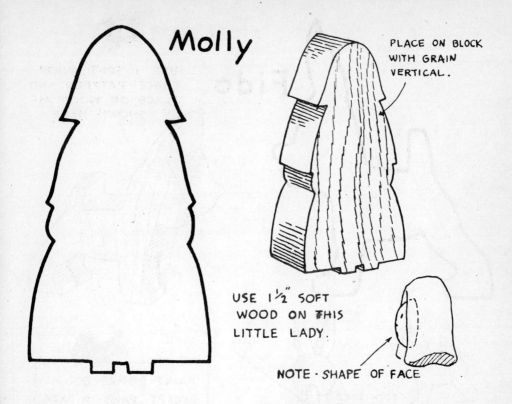

PLACE ON BLOCK WITH GRAIN VERTICAL.

USE 1½" SOFT WOOD ON THIS LITTLE LADY.

NOTE · SHAPE OF FACE

NOTE - WRINKLES

FINISH - BY PAINTING WITH BRIGHT COLORS. FACE SHOULD ALSO BE PAINTED TO ROUND SURFACE

Fido

USE 1" SOFT WOOD
TRACE PATTERN AND
PLACE ON WOOD AS
SHOWN HERE.

BOTH SIDES
ARE THE
SAME.

TAIL ¼" WIDE.

PAINT ENTIRE DOG,
EXCEPT PAWS, A DARK
BROWN THEN FINISH
BY VARNISHING TO A
HIGH GLOSS.

INSIDE EARS
V-CUTS.

DO NOT
PAINT PAWS

PAWS ARE
ABOUT ⅜"
WIDE

1"

MAKE V-CUTS
FOR TOES.

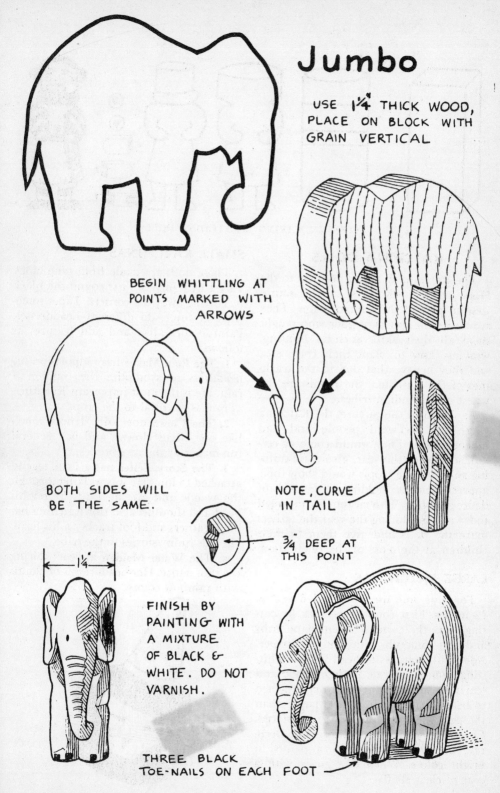

Jumbo

USE 1¼" THICK WOOD, PLACE ON BLOCK WITH GRAIN VERTICAL

BEGIN WHITTLING AT POINTS MARKED WITH ARROWS

BOTH SIDES WILL BE THE SAME.

NOTE, CURVE IN TAIL

¾" DEEP AT THIS POINT

1¼"

FINISH BY PAINTING WITH A MIXTURE OF BLACK & WHITE. DO NOT VARNISH.

THREE BLACK TOE-NAILS ON EACH FOOT

[29]

STEPS IN MAKING A KATCHINA DOLL

KATCHINA DOLLS

The Katchina dolls are peculiar to the Hopi Indians who live in the south-western part of the United States. They symbolize the spirits or gods who taught them all their skills such as hunting, weaving, how to plant their corn, etc., and they believe that due to the teachings of the Katchina, the Hopis are the wisest of the Indian tribes.

As shown in the picture, the Katchina were very awkward people and had hideous faces. They would come at certain seasons of the year, give their training and then the Hopis would show their appreciation by holding a festival of dance and song. This custom is continued today and all during the year the fathers make the dolls and give them to their children at the close of the celebration.

LARGE KATCHINAS

For large dolls use pine block 6 by 6 by 12 inches. First round the block by cutting away the corners. Then shape arms and feet. Smooth with fine sandpaper. Add small features to head by first whittling from a separate piece of wood and leaving a small peg at end to be attached to head. Drill a hole a little larger than the peg where the piece is to be placed. Cover peg with glue and insert it. Decorate the dolls with tempera paints in bright colors. When dry, cover with a coat of clear shellac.

SMALL KATCHINAS

These dolls are made from pine block 4 by 4 by 6 inches. First round the block by cutting away the corners. Taper somewhat at top. Add different headdresses. Paint bodies alike and add features as follows:

1. The Rain Maker has tadpoles on his headdress to symbolize the coming of rain. He is the most important Katchina, as rain is essential to the crops.

2. The Clown does silly dances, much like our circus clowns, and is a general fun-maker at the ceremonies.

3. The Story Teller has a little legend attached to him. He was walking through the woods and all the birds lit on his head and shoulders. So this Katchina has bird feathers and foot tracks on his head. He tells funny stories to the tribe.

4. The Water Maiden appears during the rain dance. Her headdress is of clouds with rainbow colors.

[30]

RAIN MAKER WISE MAN CLOWN OLD WOMAN CORN GROWER

2

3

4

[31]

SCOTTIE AND TURTLE MADE OF CEDAR

Obtain two blocks of cedar of the desired size, one for the Scottie and one for the Turtle. Trace the-pattern of each animal, or enlarge, and transfer to the respective blocks. Whittle according to directions given in this chapter and smooth with fine sandpaper. Polish wood with floor wax.

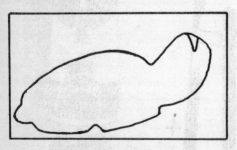

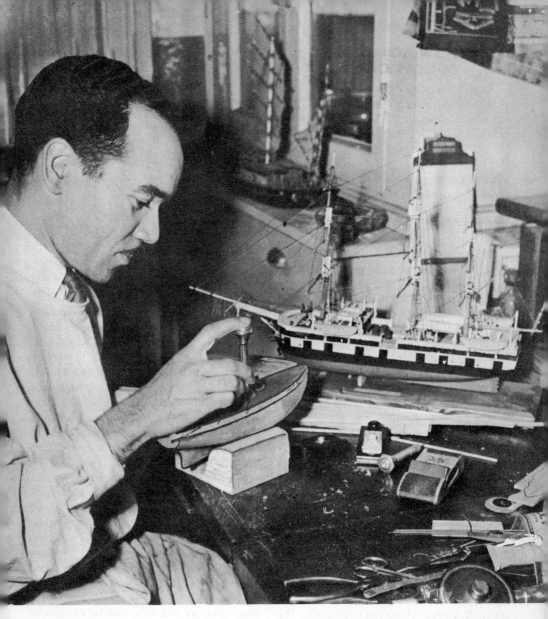

IT'S FUN TO MAKE MODEL BOATS

One of the most satisfying forms of whittling is the making of boat models. Not only will you enjoy making them— you'll find they add a nautical touch to your favorite room, where they may be anchored on a mantelpiece, shelf, or table. And some models, like the sailboat described in the following pages, are actually "seaworthy," and may be launched in a lake or pond, to the delight of the shipbuilder and the younger members of his family.

The preceding chapter took you through basic techniques of whittling wood. The making of boat models involves certain special procedures which are fully discussed in this chapter. Once you have mastered them, you will be equipped to make many different types of vessels.

HOW TO CARVE
CONCAVE AREAS

Among the most difficult whittling jobs is that of fashioning concave areas. Typical of these are the forms plotted by the bowlines and buttock lines of a ship's hull.

These curves are very beautiful, very intricate and *very important*. Incorrect rendering of these curves affects very seriously the performance of a ship—particularly its speed and its behavior in the water.

The *kinds* of curves we mean are those in which there is no fixed center; no fixed focus—for the many radii that determine the curvature. And to bring this out clearly a front plan and bottom views, showing a ship's bowlines, are given.

On the top side of the piece of wood you will use, draw the longitudinal center line. It scarcely matters which way the grain runs, since difficult compound curves must be cut at the stern as well as bow. One end will always be easier. Take your choice. At right angles to the center-line, draw cross lines, completely around the block. Mark these A, B, C, etc., so that the *plane* of each line represents actual cross-sections of the hull at A, B, C, etc.

Now make templates for each of these cross-sections—as many as needed to give a complete contour picture of the bow-line curve. Make these templates of cardboard, about a sixteenth of an inch thick. In depth, these cardboards should exceed the depth of the projected hull by at least an inch, to give them strength under the keel. On *each* of these cardboards, lay out the bowline curve as it should be at that point, both starboard and port. You will

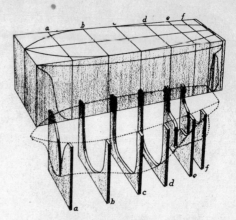

Fig. 2. Method of laying out block for ship hull and templates for gauging contour accuracy.

see how a succession of these points, joined into an unbroken, smooth surface, will be the curve you seek. The purpose of the cardboards is two-fold, (1) to show the shape of the cross-section at a known point; (2) to act as a checking template, into which you will fit the actual curve as you whittle it. So, when your hull-curve fits all the templates, each held at its correct cross-sectional position, your hull-curve is correct—and you will be very proud of a job well done.

Proceed as follows: (1) lay out the deck plan from bow to stern, using celluloid curves. Be sure that starboard and port are *exact* reciprocals of each other. (2) On both *sides* of the block, lay out the bow profile, from deck to keel. Saw out roughly the chunks that can be eliminated in this way. Saw as close to your plan lines as you can, but be careful to leave yourself plenty of stock for whit-tling. If you are adept with a small coping saw, you can remove much more

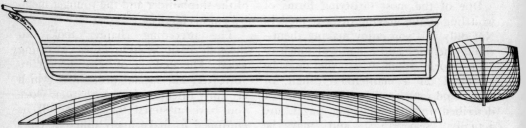

Fig. 1. Contour lines of typical clipper hull.

[34]

Fig. 3. Make first rough cuts with saw and follow with knife as explained in text.

wood than in any other way, leaving you less to carve.

If the model be small, hold it in your left hand, *keel up,* to carve the port bow, bow pointing toward you. If the grain runs toward the bow, cut by the "draw" method. If it runs toward the stern, cut by the "thumb-push" method. To do the starboard bow, the steps are exactly the same, but with the stern toward you. Use either cutting method depending on grain direction. Don't try to remove too much wood per cut. Your eye is generally a close-enough check till you get to where real accuracy begins to count. We advise

Fig. 4. Begin finishing with knife, using either thumb push or draw method, depending on grain. *Always* cut with the grain.

you to do one side up to about that point —then do the other—so that finishing may be done on both sides as you go along. More will be said of this a little later. After every few cuts, try the hull in the

bowline templates to check where more wood must be removed. Of course this can be done only if you have shaped both port and starboard to about the same degree.

In making these cuts, remember that the right fingers, curved around the knife handle, control the angle and direction of the blade. Without taking the knife out of your hand, or changing your hold on the block, see that the edge and flat of the blade come closer and closer to producing

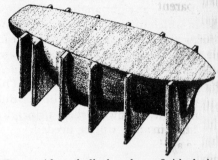

Fig. 5. After hull has been finished it should fit snugly into templates.

the curve you want. Remember—small cuts.

Gradually you will find the templates beginning to fit; still there are the areas between the templates. Test both starboard and port bows by drawing the

Fig. 6. Dependable test for accuracy is feeling between fingers. Any slight irregularities can thus be easily discovered.

[35]

thumb and index finger together slowly, starting back almost amidships and ending at the water break. Any irregularity or roughness of surface on either side will be apparent immediately—and the correction can be made. When you have whittled as closely as you think you can, test again with the fingers for minute bumps —some small enough to be almost invisible. Still holding the knife with the fingers curved around the handle turn the latter in your hand so that the flat will be at right angles to the bow surface, and the edge at right angles to the direction in which you had been cutting. Now, moving the knife toward you, but steadied by the thumb on the wood ("draw" method) *scrape* the high spot *very delicately,* till it has been removed. This scraping, if done properly, will not dull the blade. By following these principles, very little sanding will be needed.

Fig. 7. Irregularities can be scraped easily with knife.

If the piece you wish to form be too large to hold in the hand, hold it in a vise, high enough above the bench or table, to give you plenty of elbow room. However, on large hulls, the first cuts to remove stock quickly, may be made with a draw-knife or spoke-shave. The former cuts faster; the latter is easier to control.

These methods, of course, are equally efficacious on work of all sorts, including many of the depressed areas encountered in sculpture, for example.

HOW TO CARVE DIFFICULT CONVEX SURFACES

The procedure is exactly the same as described under concave surfaces, care being taken not to remove *any* wood till you are sure it *should* come off. But the cutting methods should be the same; and you should endeavor to cut *with* the grain, if at all possible.

HOW TO CUT NOTCHES AND CORNERS

Lay out the limits of the notch or corner in pencil. Hold the work on a hardwood board or bench, steadying with the left hand. With the knife held in the right hand, like a pencil, set the point exactly at the angle apex. The flat of the knife should be held at whatever angle the sides are to have, except that they should never be undercut at this stage. Pierce repeatedly, as deeply as moderate pressure will accomplish. Then cut along the edges.

Take out excess wood by making cross cuts. The wood will then be easy to lift out with the point of the knife, and there will be no danger of splitting.

Repeat these operations till the notch or angle has reached the desired depth. Smooth sides and apex.

Fig. 8. In cutting convex surfaces, *always* cut with the grain. Solid black in above illustration indicates wood to be removed.

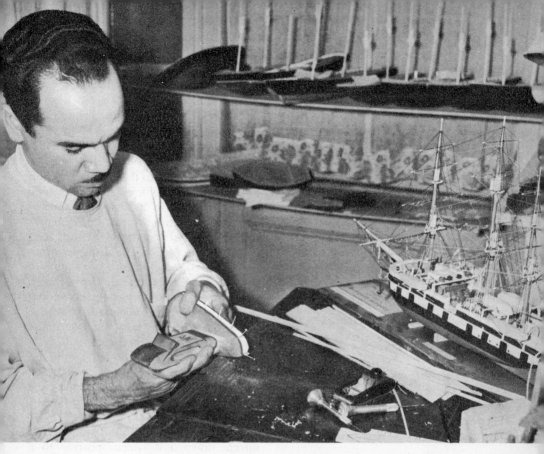

HOW TO MAKE UNDERCUTS

Undercuts are difficult or easy depending on the depth and angle of the undercut, and its position in relation to other parts of the work. Any undercut can be made readily with a sharp blade, so long as the angle of the cut, together with the height of the overhang, above the rest of the work, permits free manipulation of the knife.

Assuming that there is room for manipulation, make a long cut along what is to be the upper edge of the overhang. Hold your knife against a straight edge or curve (or free-hand, if the line be irregular) and cut the full length. The blade should lie with its flat canted to the approximate angle of the undercut and the cut should be carried deeply in successive stages. Now make piercing cuts, like in fashioning a corner at the extremes of the undercut. If it be a long one, make a series of such cuts along its reach. These cuts should be at right angles to the long axis of the undercut, and extend from what is to be its outer, top edge to where its base is to be. In other words, as you

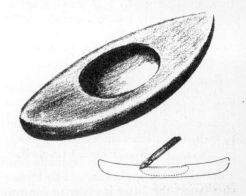

Fig. 9. Eskimo kayak is good example of undercutting. Diagram shows how knife accomplishes this.

cut downward from the desired edge of the overhang, you cut *inward*, too, at the angle of the proposed undercut, or as close to it as possible.

By making these small cuts from 1/16 to 1/8 inch apart, the wood in between lifts out easily with the blade point and —this is important—practically all danger of splitting the wood or chipping the overhang is eliminated. This method suffices for usual straight or curved under-cuts of more or less uniform depth. In cases where such regularity does not exist, your ingenuity will devise, readily enough, such modifications of the fore-going as may be necessary.

SAILING MODEL

Once you have mastered the use of a knife and understand the techniques in-volved in making the hull, you will want to make a complete boat. Why not start with a simple sailing model? The one described here is a serviceable boat, fun to make and easy to handle.

MATERIALS

Hull. Pine 18 by 4⅞ by 2⅞ inches (normally 5 by 8 inches).

Deck. Pine 18 by 4⅞ by 3/32 inches.

Mast. Pine, 24 inches long—⅜ inch maximum diameter.

Booms. Pine, 1 piece 12 by ¼ inch diameter, 1 piece 6 by 3/16 inch diameter.

Lead for Keel. 1 piece approximately 6 by 3 by ⅛ inch full.

Screw Eyes. 1 dozen brass ⅜ inch, buy No. 000.

Rigging Cord. 1 hank fine.

Sail Cloth. 1 yard.

Eyeballs. 6 small brass.

Sundries. 1 packet brass fretwork pins ⅜ inch, 1 small can undercoating paint, 1 small can cellulose enamel, 1 tin shellac.

DIRECTIONS

1. Plane block of wood until it is per-fectly smooth and draw a pencil line along center of block. Then draw fine lines square across the top of the block and down the sides to divide off the sec-tions, Fig. 1.

2. Draw a curved line through the marks on each side of the station lines, making it as much like the deck lines shown in Fig. 3 as possible.

3. Saw the block to the shape of the top outline, and when finished it will look something like Fig. 2. Now draw vertical lines on each side of the sawed block, squaring them down from the top; then on these lines set off the distances from the top of the block to the lowest line of the profile at each section. Draw curved lines through these points corresponding to the profile of the hull; then saw off the unwanted pieces at bow and stern, the block then looking like Fig. 3.

4. You are now ready to hollow out the inside of the hull. Do not remove too much wood at a time; work from each end toward the center, using good sharp chisels or gauges.

5. To shape the outside, turn the hull upside down and fasten securely to a heavy board or table. Remove a little wood at a time and use templates corre-sponding to each section so each side of the boat is exactly the same. Your boat is now ready for the Fin Keel and should have the appearance of Fig. 4.

6. The Fin should be marked out full size on a piece of mahogany 3/16 inch thick and cut to shape with a fret saw. The grain should run vertical with the boat—not lengthwise.

Chisel a groove along the exact center line of the hull about ½ inch deep (Fig. 5), and 3/16 inch wide so that the fin will fit closely into the groove. Take great care that the fin stands perfectly upright and hold in place by filling in gaps with plastic wood. Smooth out to interior and give the whole hull a coat of shellac for protection.

7. Cut a piece of very thin pine to the shape of the deck and fasten it in place temporarily with two small screws. Mark exact position of the hole for the mast

[38]

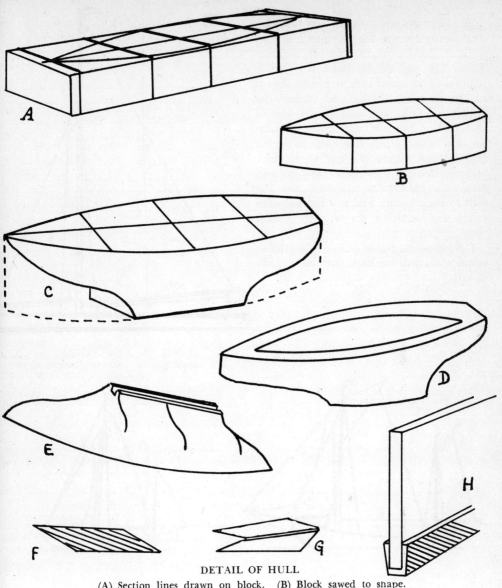

DETAIL OF HULL

(A) Section lines drawn on block. (B) Block sawed to shape.
(C) Second stage of shaping. (D) Hull partly hollowed.
(E) Groove for fin. (F, G, H) Shaping and fixing lead keel.

which measures ⅜ inch in diameter. Drill a hole through the deck and let the drill go on through it and make a shallow hole in the bottom of the hull.

Remove the deck and finish both the top and bottom by giving it several coats of shellac and smoothing it down each time.

8. The next step is to attach lead to the keel; otherwise your boat will float well above the water level of the hull. It usually takes about ¾ of a pound, depending on how much you have hollowed out the inside of your boat.

Bend over the sheet of lead along the middle of its length, fit it tightly to the bottom of the fin as shown in Fig. 6 and secure it with rivets or screws. Again test the boat and if it sinks below water level, scrape off some of the lead.

[39]

9. The masts and sails are easy to make. The size and shape are given in Fig. 9, as well as details of the simple rigging. Taper the end of the mast with sandpaper and fix screw eyes at points shown in the drawing. Make and fit up the booms the same way and give a coat of shellac. You can use fine cambric muslin for sails or sail cloth. Use stout twine for rigging cord. Fasten one end to the deck and put free end through a screw eye and fasten the cord to an eye bolt. Sew the sails to their booms and sew the halyards to the top corners of the sails; then hoist them in place.

Give the hull a coat or two of cellulose enamel, varnish the deck and she is ready to sail.

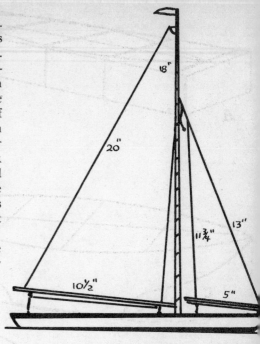

SAIL PLAN OF MODEL
The measurements indicate dimensions of the sails.

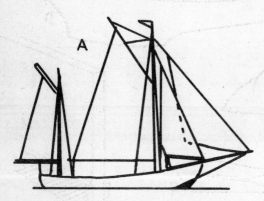
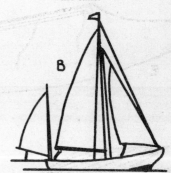

Detail for rigging two other sailing models.
(A) Ketch, (B) Yawl.

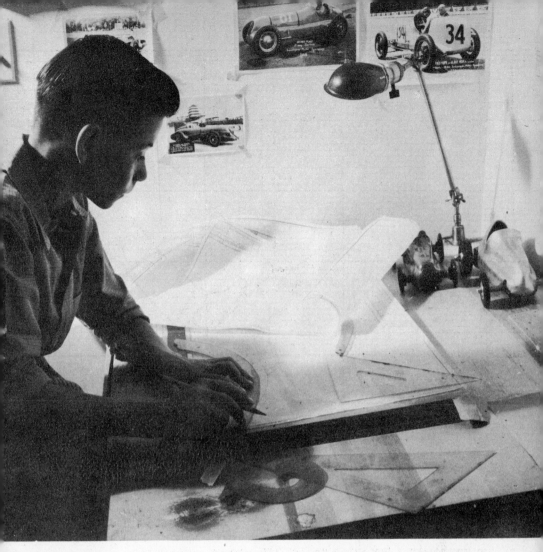

MAKE YOUR OWN MODEL CARS

Almost everyone has, at one time or another, said to himself: "Now if I were going to make an automobile I'd do it like this. . . ."

This chapter is planned to help you realize that ambition. It explains the basic steps in designing and then how to proceed to make a rubber mold and a finished plaster model of your car which you can produce in quantity.

The only limitations placed upon a model car builder who wants to try out his theories and ideas in car designing, are requirements of safety and practi-

cality. Like professional car designers, a model builder must think about leg and head-room, ground clearance in the center of the car and on the front and rear overhang as well. The first step is to study plans of model cars and design one with the features you prefer.

For the first drawings you need only a pencil, a soft eraser and blank paper of any kind. You have decided, after some research and thought, about what kind of an automobile you want to build. Now you begin to translate those ideas to rough drawings.

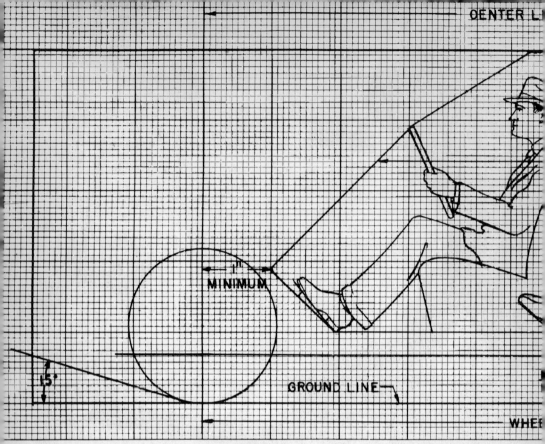

MINIMUM

GROUND LINE

15°

WHE

Overall Length of Model 15 13/16 inches
Overall Height of Model 5 inches
Overall Width of Model
6¼ inches—6 inches
Wheelbase Is Flexible

A GUIDE FOR DESIGNING A MODEL

Do not attempt to make a finished sketch at first. Instead, just make a rough outline. Make a few side views, experiment with the front appearance, the general sweep of the car, and the outline from the rear. These rough sketches may change your mind as to whether you do or do not want running boards or fenders, whether you should have more window space, and whether your car will have "lines" and proportion. It may also bring to light some conflicts in basic design which will have to be corrected.

The rough drawings need not be according to size or scale. They are merely to begin charting what general shape your car is going to take. Make as many rough sketches as you need until you have satisfied yourself completely that you are ready to start the final design.

The next step is to begin your design according to scale and exactness on ruled paper.

YOUR DESIGNING TOOLS

Before beginning a discussion of the final design, it might be well to look at a few of the tools you should have. Actually, the complete design can be made with nothing more than a sharp pencil, an eraser, a drawing compass and a ruler. It will help, however, if you have such drawing equipment as a French curve, a T-square, a triangle, and similar drafting accessories. For pencils, it is recommended that you use an H pencil for your drawings, and a 3 or 4-H for tracing. Keep your pencils sharpened to the finest possible point, and to do this you can use

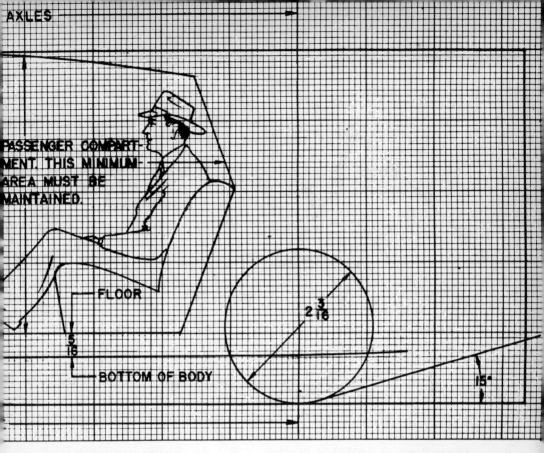

PASSENGER COMPART-
MENT. THIS MINIMUM
AREA MUST BE
MAINTAINED.

FLOOR

BOTTOM OF BODY

$2\frac{3}{16}$

$\frac{5}{16}$

15°

CAR WITH ENGINE IN FRONT

sandpaper, an emery board, or an ordinary nail file.

Use the compass to make circular lines, such as headlights or the wheels. Nearly any line describing an arc should be made with the compass, like the sharper portion of the fender curves. If your compass is quite large, you can, as mentioned earlier, make your entire design with it and a ruler.

THE FRENCH CURVE

The French curve is composed of various types of curves, from gentle swerves to sharp contours. It will make lines which vary from a straight line but which cannot be done so easily with a compass. For example, the sloping sweep of the car roof. To use it, you sketch in lightly the general line you want to follow. Then take the portion of the French curve which most nearly simulates your curve, and trace your line in more heavily. Keep moving the French curve as often as necessary, always using just that portion of it which gives you the curve you want.

MAKING YOUR DESIGN

Instead of starting your design on the ruled paper itself, it might be better to place some thin drawing paper over the lined paper. Tack or tape it down firmly over the lined paper, and you will be able to see the lined paper clearly through the drawing paper. Now start making your design to scale. By using the thin paper, instead of the ruled paper itself, you can draw and erase as much as you wish without erasing the ruled lines.

Perhaps the first view you will want to

[43]

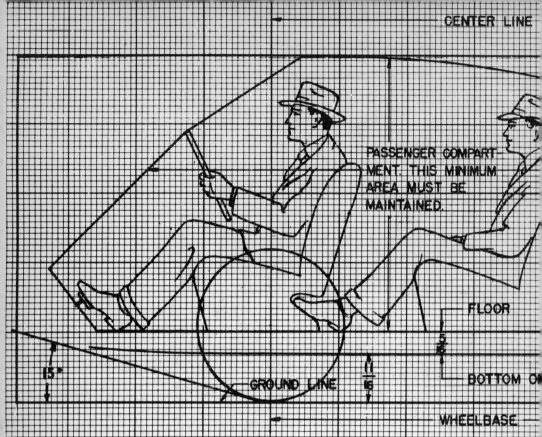

PASSENGER COMPART-
MENT. THIS MINIMUM
AREA MUST BE
MAINTAINED.

FLOOR

GROUND LINE

BOTTOM O

WHEELBASE

15°

Overall Length of Model 15 13/16 inches
Overall Height of Model 5 inches
Overall Width of Model
6¼ inches—6 inches
Wheelbase Is Flexible

A GUIDE FOR DESIGNING A MODEL

draw will be the side view. You can use a sheet of carbon paper to transfer your drawing onto the ruled paper itself. Or, if you have no carbon paper, just blacken with a thick lead pencil the back of your thin sheet and, placing it over the lined paper, trace your drawing. Whichever method you use, be sure the paper is held tightly in place, and use a good sharp pencil to make an accurate, true line.

Once you have the side view in a clean, neat drawing on the ruled paper, follow the same procedure with the top view, or front or rear views—whichever you prefer to do next. All the views must be kept in the same proportion.

Next do the same with the rear view and the top view, and always keep checking them for proper positioning so that the doors, fenders, wheels, all are in the

same relative position in each drawing. Your design should now be complete.

THE PLASTER CAST METHOD OF MAKING A MODEL CAR

Modeling clay can be used advantageously in several different ways by model car builders. You may want to make your finished models by molding instead of using wood or other material.

Regardless of what material you choose for the finished product, it is wise to make a clay model of your car for the purpose of checking your drawing and design. This, incidentally, is how the professional car designers do it.

Suppose you intend to make a wood model. You have completed your design and are ready to start. No one can visualize exactly, from the drawing, what the

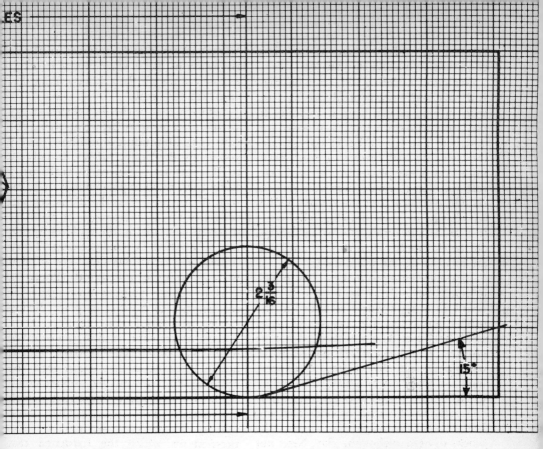

AR WITH ENGINE IN REAR

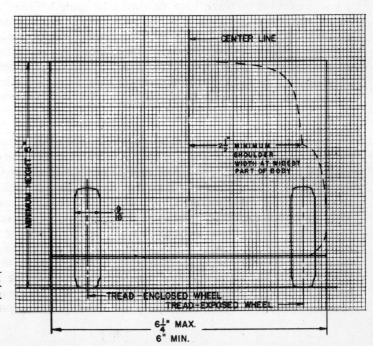

GUIDE FOR DEVELOP- G FRONT AND REAR EWS OF MODEL CAR DESIGN

finished car will look like, so now is a good time to make a clay model.

Ordinary modeling clay can be used and your model can be made any size you wish so long as you keep it to scale. In clay, you will see a replica of what you designed. You have a better opportunity for checking and correcting your drawing in case some phases of the car do not suit your taste. Every time you make a change, of course, be sure to make a similar change in your drawing. Obviously it is easier and quicker to make changes on the clay model than to wait until you are at work on the wood model.

If you are going to make a clay model, it should be built up on a ¾-inch baseboard with mock wheels attached at the proper points to give the correct tread and wheelbase. The wheels need not be finished. Rough-cut wheels nailed to the baseboard will do. Then, if desired, blocks of wood can be glued or nailed on to build up a rough wooden core. These will make the bulk of the body and will save clay. Holes may be drilled in the blocks to help anchor the clay. Next put on the clay, pressing it in firmly against the wood as you fill out the form of your car according to your design (Photo 1).

You may wish to make your finished models with plaster of paris or dental plaster or stone and rubber molds. This is an interesting method of making the model and some suggestions on it are presented on the following pages.

First make your model from regular modeling clay to full size (Photo 2). Dust the clay model with talcum powder for ease in removing the rubber mold when finished (Photo 3). Next paint onto the model 8 or 10 coats of rubber molding liquid, such as latex, making sure that all coats are free from bubbles (Photo 4). This can be accomplished by blowing on the surface where the bubbles have formed. Apply the rubber by dipping, spraying or painting with a soft brush. If you use a brush, an inexpensive camel-hair type about 1 inch wide is best. After each coat rinse your brush thoroughly in water and let it soak in water until you are ready to use it again, for if it is left exposed to the air the rubber will harden and ruin the brush.

Let each coat of the liquid rubber *dry at room temperature* before applying the next coat. Depending upon how thickly you apply the liquid rubber, usually 10 to 12 coats are sufficient to build up a fairly thick mold approximately ⅛ of an inch. If you wish to make it thicker and stiffer, layers of cheesecloth or bandage material saturated in the molding liquid can be applied as reinforcement. Three or four layers of rubber should be applied first, before using cheesecloth (Photo 5).

Your rubber mold is now ready for casting, but to hold it in place during casting you need some reinforcement. This reinforcement, or shell, can be made of marbletop or plaster of paris. And it has to be made so that it can easily be removed from around the rubber mold.

Check your model for undercuts, which are places where your rubber mold sharply changes contour, making a depression in which the hardened cast would catch when you attempt to remove it. For each section involving a problem of this nature, an additional piece must be made for your shell so that the model may be easily removed and replaced. In our particular model shown in the accompanying picture story, it was found best to make the plaster shell in three pieces—building up first one side and half of the rear, then the front, and then the other side and remaining half of the rear (Photos 6, 8 and 9). The shell should be at least ½-inch thick and notches should be cut around the edges so that the edges of the 3 sections will interlock (Photo 10).

To avoid trouble in making the sections interlock, it is necessary, before pouring the second shell section, to coat the splice edge of your finished first section of shell with two coats of ordinary rubber cement to prevent the sections from sticking together (Photo 11).

Temporary dams to prevent the plaster from spreading may be made of wax or

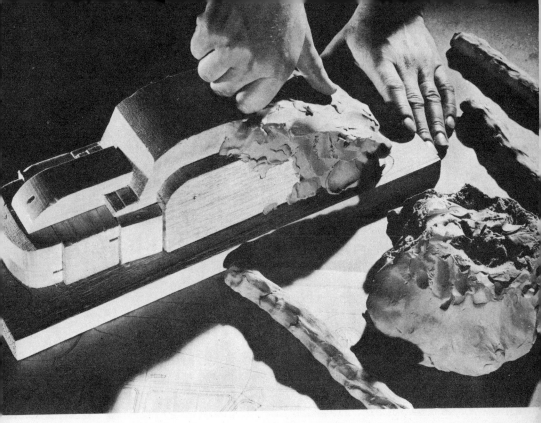

1. (*Top*) Applying modeling clay to rough block

2. (*Bottom*) Finishing clay model

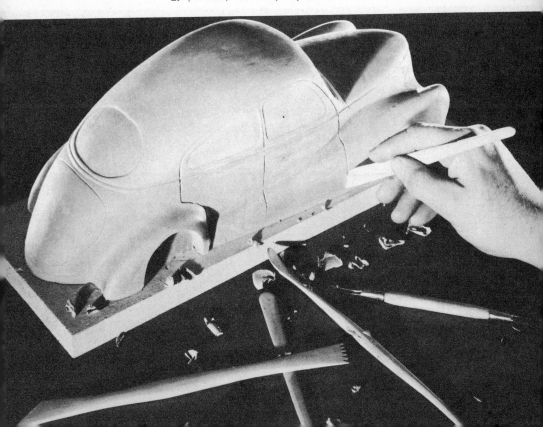

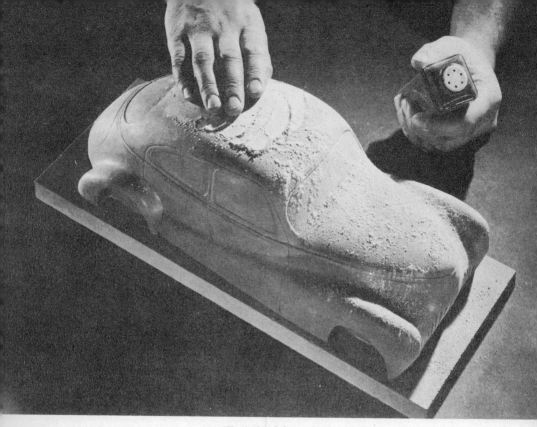

3. (*Top*) Applying talcum powder

4. (*Bottom*) First coat liquid rubber

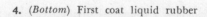

5. (*Top*) Reinforcing with gauze after 5th coat

6. (*Bottom*) Forming first section of plaster shell

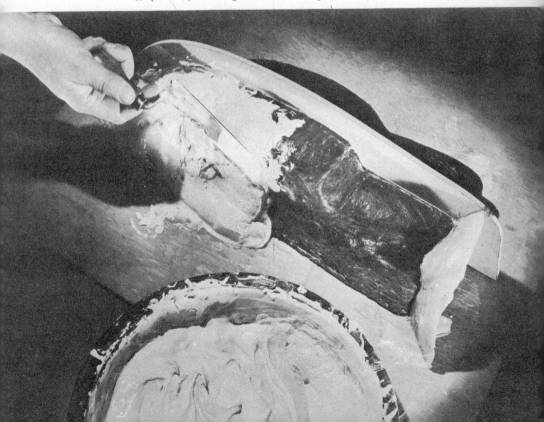

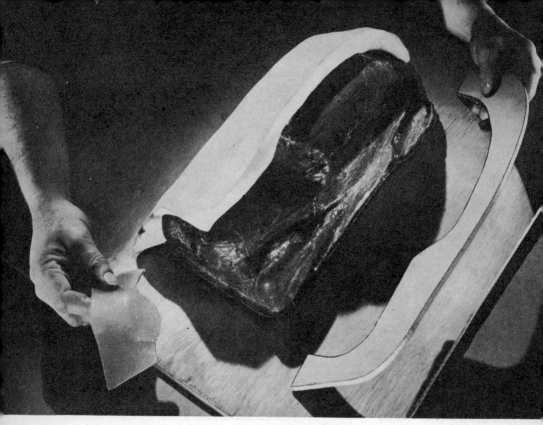

7. (*Top*) Removing wax (*left*) and wood dams

8. (*Bottom*) Forming front end plaster shell

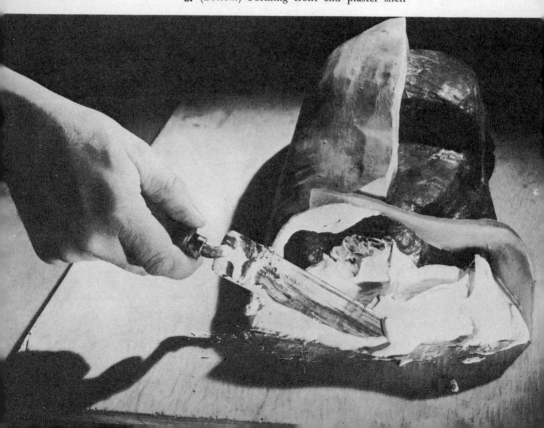

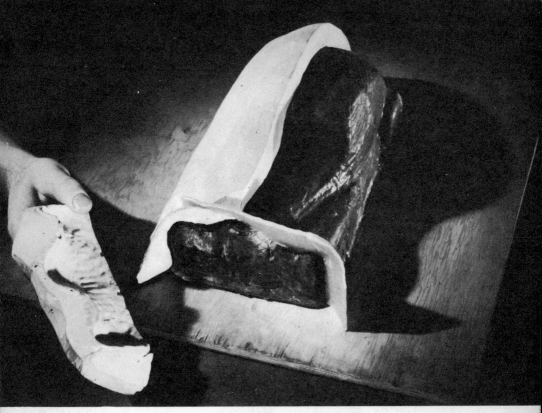

9. *(Top)* Removing finished front section of shell

10. *(Bottom)* Sawing locking notches

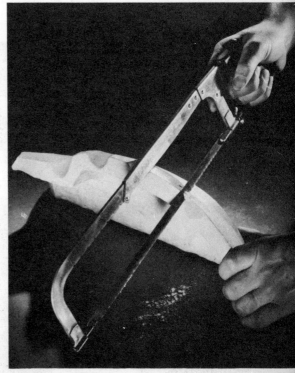

wood. Any gaps between the wood dam and the rubber mold may be plugged with candle wax which also serves to hold the wood in position (Photo 7).

When the shell is finished (Photo 12), remove it from the rubber mold (Photo 13), remove the clay from the inside of the mold, turn the mold upside down, and you are ready to begin casting the final product.

Casts made of plaster of paris can be hardened by soaking them in a solution made by dissolving one part of alum in six parts of hot water. Large casts should be permitted to stay in the water two or three days. Carpenter's glue diluted with twice its usual amount of water forms an efficient hardener for use with plaster of paris.

To lighten your completed casting, you should make a wooden core which can be roughed from a piece of soft wood. The core should be about $\frac{3}{8}$ to $\frac{1}{2}$ an

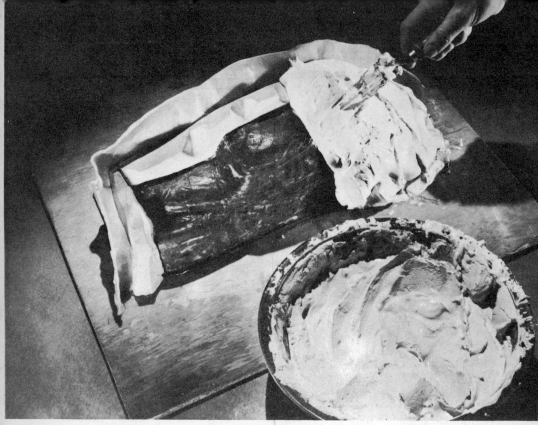

11. *(Top)* Making third section interlock; wax dam *(front to rear)* prevents overflow

12. *(Bottom)* Completed plaster shell

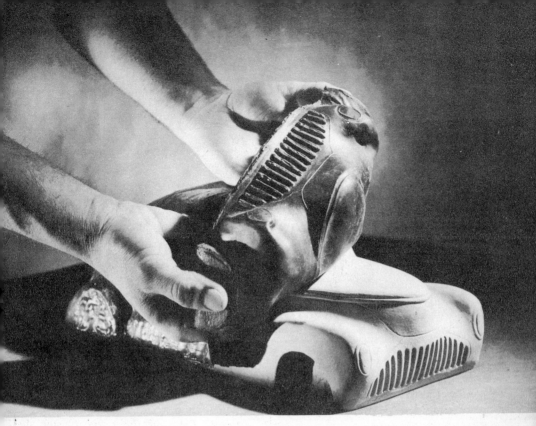

13. (*Top*) Removing rubber mold from clay model

14. (*Bottom*) Starting final casting of car

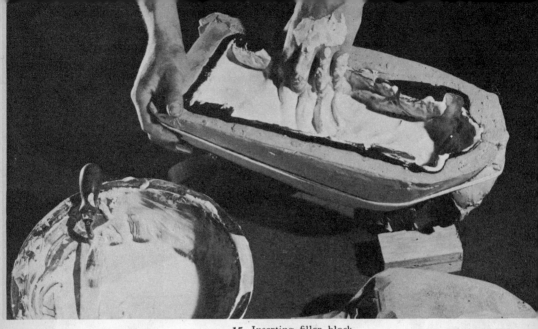

15. Inserting filler block

inch smaller than the mold all the way around the mold. A few holes should be bored into the core to strengthen the bond with the plaster, and shellac or paint should be applied to prevent absorption of moisture.

If you wish to make your final casting of plaster of paris or dental plaster or stone, your local dentist can tell you where it can be obtained. It should be mixed with a little water to a molding consistency, about 100 parts plaster to 33 parts water. It sets hard in about 30 minutes and produces a strong finished surface.

The model may be further lightened by mixing the plaster with a filler such as ground cork—five parts plaster to three parts cork by volume. Now you are ready to start casting. Work rapidly to complete the molding before the plaster sets. Mix enough plaster to half fill the mold. Take some of the soft plaster and wet the inside of the mold with it. This is to help the air escape and thus prevent air bubbles in the casting. Pour the plaster into the rubber mold (Photo 14), then insert the wooden core by pressing it down into the plaster (Photo 15). Slight shaking of the core will aid in getting the core into position and in eliminating air bubbles.

Fill in any empty spaces with more plaster.

The casting will set hard enough to work on in half an hour (Photo 16), at which time it can be removed from the mold. Take off the outer plaster shell first, then work the rubber mold off the casting carefully (Photo 17). It may be that some small defects will show up in the casting. These can be repaired with a filler substance, with a rubber eraser acting as a squeegee. After that, prepare the surface of your casting for a coat of sealer. Rub the sealer down after it is dry with finishing sandpaper. Apply a coat of primer, let it dry, and rub it down again. Now look at the model in an oblique light to see if there are any slight depressions or irregularities in the surface. If there are, these should be built up with filler. Then apply a final coat of primer, sand down, recheck, and if it is now satisfactory, the car is ready for its first coat of paint. Three or four coats should be sufficient, and each coat except the last should be rubbed down with finishing sandpaper that has been dipped in water to prevent scratching the painted surface. After the last coat is dry, rub it to a glossy surface with a combination of rottenstone and oil, and wax if you prefer.

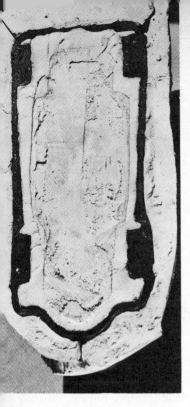
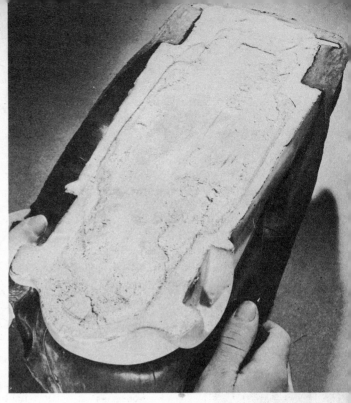

. (*Top Left*) Drying casting in mold

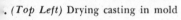

17. (*Top Right*) Removing casting from mold

18. (*Bottom*) Finished casting and mold

WHEELS FOR YOUR CAR

Wheels can be made either of wood or plaster. Wood wheels can be turned out by hand, or on a lathe if one is available. To make wheels of plaster, a clay mold can be used.

The accompanying Figs. 1, 2, 3 and 4 illustrate a simple fixture, designed for making a clay wheel-mold, and a fixture for scribing tire threads on the wheels.

MATERIALS REQUIRED

Mold Forming Fixture—Block of wood 1 by 6 by 6 inches, for base of fixture (Fig. 1). Spike or rod 3/16 inch in diameter,

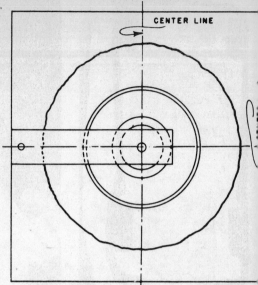

Fig. 2. Mold-forming fixture (*top view*) with wheel mold

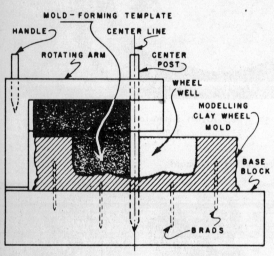

Fig. 1. Wheel Mold-forming fixture (*side view*); cross-section of wheel mold

4 inches long, for center post. Two dozen brads to anchor clay to base block. Piece of hard wood ½ by 2 by 3½ inches for rotating arm. Piece of heavy tin or metal 1/32 by 2 by 2 inches for mold-forming template.

Mold—One-half pound of modeling clay.

Tire-treading fixture—Extra spike or rod 3/16 inch in diameter, 4 inches long, for scriber post (Fig 4). Piece of metal 1/32 inch thick, for tire-tread scriber.

Wheels—One-and-a-half pounds dental-type plaster.

STEPS IN MAKING WHEELS

Use the following procedure in making the wheel mold-forming fixture, forming the clay wheel-mold, casting the wheels, and scribing tire treads:

1. Draw center lines on the base block (Fig. 2) and drill a hole at their intersection into which the center post will fit tightly.

2. Make the rotating arm, using Figs. 1 and 3 as guides. Drill a hole in the rotating arm for the center post. This hole must be a snug fit for the center post or irregularities in the finished wheel will result. It is suggested that you use a drill press to drill the holes in the base block and in the rotating arm because the center post must be absolutely vertical to the base block to make a perfect mold.

3. Now cut out and file the mold-forming template (Fig. 1). The design of the wheel you have developed for your car will determine the shape of your template. Since the cutting edge of the template will form the wheel mold in the modeling clay, it must have the same contour as the wheel, measuring from the hub, around the tread to the rear edge of the tire. In transposing your wheel dimensions to the template you must subtract

[56]

one-half the diameter of the center post from the hub end of the wheel template. This will compensate for the amount of space taken up at the center of the wheel mold by the center post.

4. Bend the wheel template to fit the rotating arm as seen in the perspective illustration of these two parts (Fig. 3),

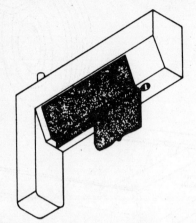

Fig. 3. Perspective of rotating arm and mold-forming template

making sure when placing the template that it forms a radius from the center post. The template may be attached to the rotating arm with a few short brads.

5. Drive approximately 12 brads into the base block (Fig. 1), letting them project the maximum length possible without touching the rotating arm or template as they are rotated around the center post. Make a biscuit of your modeling clay and press it on the base block around the center post so that the brads will anchor it firmly.

6. Place the rotating arm in position over the clay and rotate it carefully, making the template cut the wheel mold into the clay. It is necessary to remove excess clay frequently from the template as it cuts into the clay. If the clay develops ragged edges, try warming it slightly. Should this fail, a few drops of oil may be used to moisten the ragged area to soften the clay.

7. After the mold has been cut to the proper wheel depth, remove the rotating arm, leaving the center post in position.

If oil has been used, remove any remaining on the surface of the mold to eliminate the possibility of pitting the finished wheel.

8. Now you are ready to pour plaster into the mold; use a hard dental plaster. While pouring plaster, agitate it in the mold to eliminate any trapped air bubbles.

9. It is necessary to make a new mold for each wheel because you distort the mold when you remove the finished plaster wheel. If you use a dental-type plaster, it will harden and be ready for removal in about 30 minutes.

10. When all wheels are finished, remove the clay and the small brads from the block. Leave the center pole in place.

11. Drill a hole in one corner of the base block (Fig. 4) and insert the scriber post.

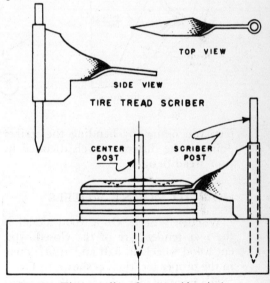

TOP VIEW

SIDE VIEW

TIRE TREAD SCRIBER

CENTER POST

SCRIBER POST

Fig. 4. Tire treading fixture (side view); tread scriber in cutting position

12. Mount the scribing tool, which you have made as illustrated in Fig. 4, on the scriber post.

13. To make the tire treads, place the plaster wheel on the center post (Fig. 4); press the scriber into the plaster; and rotate the wheel until a groove of desired depth is formed. These grooves can be spaced as in Fig. 4, or in any tread pat-

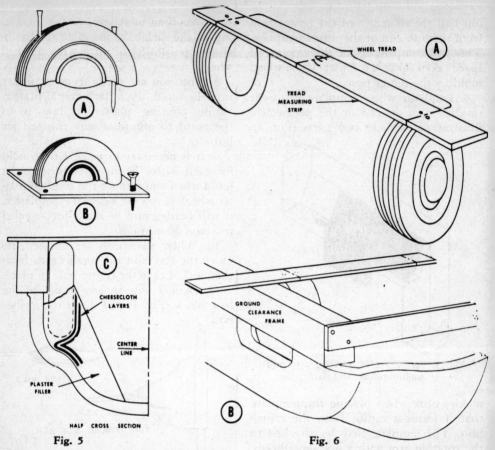

Fig. 5

Fig. 6

tern you desire, by bending the scriber point to the different levels dictated by your tread design.

HOW TO MOUNT WHEELS

Wooden Wheels. On a wood model, if the rear fenders are of the closed type, cut wood wheels in half and attach them in the proper location, as shown in Fig. 5.

For front or rear wheels of the exposed type (on wood models), the fenders need only be cut out and the wheels glued in place. If your model has closed front fenders, allow clearance for the wheels to turn in steering. Proper clearance is indicated in Figs. 5B and 5C.

Plaster Wheels. Figure 6 shows details of a simple method for mounting plaster wheels securely to a plaster-cast model.

Attach wheels lightly to strips of wood, positioning them according to your tread measurement (Fig. 6A). Make a frame of wood which will fit over the edges of your over-turned model (Fig. 6B); the side strips of this frame should be cut to the same depth as the ground clearance of your model. Lower the wheels (attached to your tread-measuring strip) into the ground-clearance frame (set in place on your model). This will position each wheel as shown in Fig. 5C.

First, fill in between the wheel and the side of your model with wet plaster mix. Then soak strips of cheesecloth in wet plaster and lay them over the top half of the wheel and along the side of your model (Fig. 5C). (Allow each cheesecloth layer to set before applying next.) Finally, build up a solid filler of plaster over the wheel and side of your model as shown (Fig. 5C). When the plaster filler has set and dried, the wheels will be an integral part of the plaster casting.

EVERYBODY'S GUIDE TO MODEL RAILROADING

There is no universal, all-embracing hobby, but if an open race were held, we might find miniature railroading well up among the leaders.

Perhaps we can explain just how model railroading can be all things to all men. In the first place, model railroading depends only in the very slightest degree upon income, so it can be the hobby of the wealthy or the avocation of those of very modest means. However, the bigger point is that there is a place in the hobby for every sort of skill. Carpentry, painting, decorating, electricity, machine shop work, building, management, or operations, all play a part in making a model railroad come to life as a living, throbbing empire.

Are you an architect? There are plenty of buildings to be erected in order to give your trains a reason for running, yet many model railroaders never put buildings on their roads for they prefer to manipulate the trains and merely imagine the accessories. On the other hand, you may want the buildings but have no skills that will enable you to design and erect them. In that case, there are kits of every imaginable sort available at modest cost, and from them you can build an industrial center, a terminal, or a residential section. And so it goes.

WHERE TO BEGIN

Suppose we follow the progress of a model railroader from the very start, explaining as we go along.

You, the mythical hobbyist (with several hundred thousand parallels in real life), first are made aware of the hobby by meeting a neighbor, seeing a newspaper or magazine article, reading one of the several magazines in the field, or even by a visit to one of the model railroad clubs that are in evidence over most of the country. First you decide to make the hobby your own, and secondly you make several decisions.

Possibly the first decision will be whether or not to do your model railroading at home. This depends on the space available, of course, but a little ingenuity can often solve a space problem by putting a layout under a bed or on a table which folds against the wall or which is sectionalized so that it can be hidden away in a closet. If there is a club available, it may be that you will want to join it, though many fans prefer to work alone. Numbers of club members have their club activities *and* a railroad at home, often of a different gauge or variety.

SCALE AND TINPLATE TRAINS

So far as variety goes, there are scale trains and tinplate trains, and the difference is rather simple. Tinplate trains, so-called from the style of the track, are those which are purchased complete and ready to run. Scale model railroading in the fullest sense of the term is that wherein every part of the model railroad and its trains is hand built. There are railroaders who can build a locomotive given nothing but an electric motor and some pieces of metal, and these men also turn out cars and any needed accessories. The scale fan also tacks down his own track spike by spike, builds his own switches and crossings and generally conducts his road as close to a real or prototype road as possible.

Naturally, scale railroading takes a certain amount of experience plus a knowledge of machine work, soldering, electricity and other skills. Actually, there are relatively few hobbyists who do not draw a middle line by combining to a greater or lesser degree the merits of each division. Thus you may find a hobbyist who buys his engines but builds all his other materials, or you may find a hobbyist who builds only engines but purchases the remainder, and that variety of choice is one reason for the wide appeal of miniature trains.

RAILROAD GAUGES

Then, too, you must make a decision about the gauge of your road. Gauge actually refers to the distance between rail heads, but it has a direct relationship to the scale of the buildings and trains. In the tinplate field, O gauge is far and away the most widely used and it is the size generally seen in purchased sets. Its accompanying scale is quarter inch, which means that each quarter inch represents one foot of the real item and therefore a six-foot man is reduced to one and a half inches, a twenty-four-foot tower to six inches, or a fifty-foot-long box car to twelve and a half inches.

Next smallest of the gauges is OO, for which the scale is 4 millimeters equals one foot, and after that comes HO (half O gauge), in which 3.5 millimeters equals one foot. Naturally, the smaller gauges mean that more railroading can be done in the same amount of space, but in turn other problems arise in building and powering the set.

A good case can be made by the advocates of any gauge or scale, including the relatively new S gauge at 3/16 inches to the foot and the very tiny TT gauge, in which a locomotive is about the size of a penny matchbox. The beginning hobbyist would be wise to look around for some time weighing space, skills, and other advantages against the disadvantages of each gauge.

The larger scales have the advantage of being generally easier to handle and maintain, since the smaller gauges become more and more delicate as the size of the train decreases. The biggest advantage of the small gauges is the fact that more railroading can be done in a given amount of space.

With the immediate decisions made, you can start to work. You will find that model railroading, in common with many other hobbies, requires just about the amount of money you have available for it. You can buy a car kit for as low as a dollar, or you can even drop under that price if you want to follow plans in one or another of the magazines available.

PLANNING YOUR PURCHASES

Similarly, you can begin with a very modest selection of track that is lightly fastened down, and then expand as you desire. About the only mistake that is possible at this time is wildly spending too much money on poorly selected purchases. There is plenty of time available to all model railroad fans, and they can make good use of it, especially since a heavy investment in one particular gadget or device may turn out to be ill advised in the course of time. Therefore, even if large sums of money are available, it will pay to go slowly, absorbing each purchase into your entire assembly as time goes on.

Let's project an ideal situation for you, our mythical railroader, and endow you with a limited amount of ready cash, but with a middle-sized cellar, a plentiful accumulation of lumber, and a patient and sympathetic spouse. The last, of course, is not absolutely necessary, but the patience will be invaluable, the sympathy will help, and if the wife is handy with her fingers she can perform miracles on a model layout.

LOCATING THE RAILROAD

First you will determine what part of the cellar is not cluttered up with sinks, furnaces and other relatively immovable objects, and secondly you will figure out which part you wish to use now. Even-

A HOMEMADE GAS STORAGE PLANT
The oil drums are small sections of dowel, the tanks are cans covered with silver paper marked with a clock-work gear for rivets, the fence is wire screen.

tually, perhaps, you may find that you want your trains to disappear occasionally behind the furnace, and you may even want to run a high level line on a narrow shelf above the laundry tub, through some closets and under or over your workbench, but all that can and should come later.

Starting with a limited space we can probably figure out a yard area that can be built, a station area and a place for the trains to come and go. The last point raises a brand new question: What kind of system to have?

THREE RAILROAD SYSTEMS

Railroad systems in miniature or prototype can be of three sorts. First, there is the continuous loop which is nothing but a circle of track no matter how much it be varied with sidings and accessories. Second, there is the out-and-home-again, whereby the train starts out of a terminal and circles around and returns to the same terminal. Perhaps it should be explained that at a station the trains continue on through, while at a terminal they are stopped by the end of the line. Lastly, there is the point-to-point system.

A TERMINAL

A very compact terminal is shown before completion. It is built on the general idea of the Grand Central Terminal in New York, the loop enabling trains to be turned around and rerouted with a minimum loss of time, while the stub tracks can be used for longer halts.

THE POINT-TO-POINT ROAD

The point-to-point road goes, as its name implies, from one terminal to another. It may help you to lay out your ideal road in one fairly straight line, indicating spurs, sidings, buildings and terrain features. Several stations can be located between terminals. Then, when you have a road which you think would be interesting, start looping the track around and around like a piece of folded spaghetti until it fits into your space. By having grades you will be able to cross over tracks, and by the adroit use of tunnels and hills you can conceal the fact that the lines are actually running around in loops. It may be that your terminals will actually be located on the same end of the table, but at different levels.

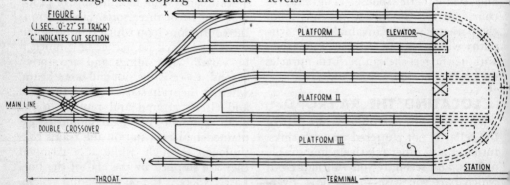

FIGURE I
(1 SEC. "O"-27" ST TRACK)
"C" INDICATES CUT SECTION

X

PLATFORM I ELEVATOR

MAIN LINE

PLATFORM II

DOUBLE CROSSOVER

PLATFORM III

Y

C

STATION

THROAT TERMINAL

TURNING TRAINS AT TERMINALS

Each of the terminals must have some provision for turning trains or engines, and there are three methods for achieving this. You may use a loop, a wye, or a turntable. The last is most impressive, it is true, but it is also hardest to build and is actually the least useful, so in the beginning it may be wisest to use the other two, one at each terminal.

All of these systems can be found in prototype railroading, but even so the vast majority of prototype roads go from one point to another point. Therefore, most model railroaders prefer a point-to-point road where it is at all practical. This will call for a longer and narrower layout than a single loop, but still has certain advantages in operation and in applying scenery and backgrounds.

With location selected, you should make some notes about available space and existing obstructions and then make a carefully scaled drawing of the chosen area. In that area you can project a number of ideas about your railroad and after some consideration choose the one that most meets your desires, abilities, pocketbook and existing or forthcoming equipment.

LAYING OUT THE ROAD

You should know or figure that freight **trains** are inherently more interesting than passenger trains, for there is much more switching and maneuvering to be done with them. You should calculate where you can put your switches and how you can arrange to turn your trains by a loop, a wye, or even a turntable. Calculate your grades, holding them wherever possible to 5 per cent or less.

CARS THAT BUILD INTEREST

In tinplate railroading especially, freights are most interesting, for the manufacturers provide an astonishing number of accessories which are tied in with specific cars. There are log loaders that work on one track or between two tracks. There are coal loaders that can be used with a single line or between two lines. Electro-magnetic cranes are a popular item, and so is one gadget that consists of a milk car and platform. When the car is stopped, a man pops out of the door and places cans on the platform. There are dozens of these items, many of which are used by model fans to liven their pikes.

PLAN FOR EXPANSION

Finally, in planning your road, you should look ahead to expansion. What if Cousin Ambrose should give you a lot of track that is just cluttering up the attic, or what if the Treasury Depart-

A WYE

This winter scene shows a wye combined with a crossing in a complicated track pattern near a station. The suburban backdrop gives the impression of space and a town while actually using up no train space whatsoever.

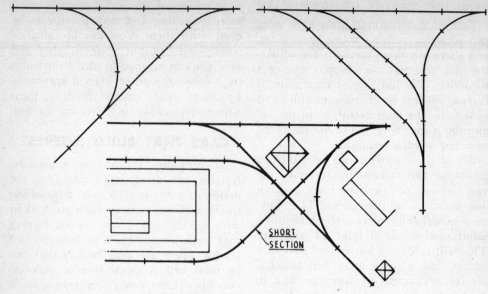

WYE VARIATIONS

In all of these, a train can be turned by backing up one leg and going down the other. The wye is a common feature of real railroads and is nearly always seen where a branch line meets a mainline.

ment finds they have received $280.67 too much for your last income tax return? In either case, or around holidays, it is wise to figure out just what to do if fate or kindly friends deposit an extra locomotive on your hands. And this, too, is the way the prototype road figures its problems.

RAILROADING ON A BUDGET

Let us be very specific about building an actual model road on a limited budget. If the case does not exactly fit your needs, at least it may show how problems are solved.

With a little over one hundred dollars available over a period of months, and with some track and old trains in the attic, and with some odd-sized lumber in the cellar, here is how the road might begin.

First let us assess the trains on hand. The track is slightly rusty, but some sandpaper and oil will fix that. The switches are hand operated, so they should go in the yards near the operator although they can be rigged with small wires for distant operation. The old engine still runs, but it is a short, stubby electric engine of the type called "tunnel engine." The cars are very old-fashioned and use very old couplers.

Let us build our table, of which more later, and perhaps purchase a piece of plywood for a few dollars. With nails and old lumber we can build the table, and perhaps with luck we can find some paint to give it two coats.

On it we can fasten the usable track which we will assume is O gauge. O gauge comes in several sizes and varieties, but all can be connected together with a bit of ingenuity and the result is often better than with O gauge of one type. With the old track fastened down we can now calculate what we need.

ADD A FREIGHT SET
AND SWITCHES

If we first buy a freight set, that will provide a small transformer which can be coupled with the old one we now have. There will be an engine, three cars, a caboose, and an assortment of

[64]

A TURNTABLE

The handy model maker can build a turntable and power it if he wishes, although many are turned by hand or by mechanical cranks.

track which we can readily use and it will cost from thirty to seventy-five dollars, depending upon the set chosen. Let us choose a middling figure of forty-five dollars and also buy a pair of remote control switches for about seventeen dollars. This brings our purchases up to sixty-five dollars all told.

MAKE YOUR OWN SCENERY

If there is another ten dollars around, some wire screen and some plaster will add scenery, while the paints normally found around a house will color the settings. This will use up three or four of the ten dollars, and the rest can be spent on some artist's board, model cement and the other odds and ends that you need to build a switch engine.

BUILD A SWITCH ENGINE

Build a switch engine! Why, certainly. With the motor from your beat-up old tunnel engine and two of the trucks from one of the old cars you can turn out a splendid little switcher and tender that will chug around your yards in-

A COAL ELEVATOR

A coal elevator is an excellent excuse for switching cars around your layout. A bucket elevator carries it to the bin at the top and the coal is dumped into the car below.

definitely. Most of the model magazines carry conversion plans at one time or another, and you can get a copy of one such article. Even if it is not about the same engine that you want to build, it should give you enough information to turn out a switcher.

VARIETY FOR YOUR RAILROAD

It is a good rule to absorb each new purchase into your layout before making the next one, so even if there is another twenty-five dollars left, don't rush out yet. Depending on your space and your wishes, you might want to spend your remaining funds on a working electromagnetic crane. On the other hand, you might like to work with kits and spend

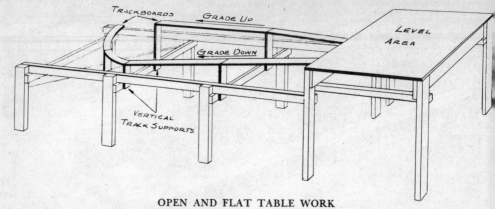

OPEN AND FLAT TABLE WORK

Open table work has many advantages, even where a flat table is also used. Here on the right is an area suitable for a yard or station or other flat area, while from it a grade rises and one descends. The track boards carry the rails, while the area between can be covered with screen that has been shaped to fit and then coated with plaster and painted. By this means, realistic tunnels, streams and bridges may be introduced into a layout that really combines railroad practice with miniature flexibility.

all of it on kits for passenger cars, freight cars and buildings of various sorts. A few of the dollars might go for background scenery, or a couple might be spent in the local radio shop buying some electrical switches so that you can cut sidings and spurs in and out of your circuits. You might do all of this eventually, but there's not much point to any of it until you build some tables, so here are some tips about them.

A TABLE FOR YOUR RAILROAD

Tables can be either open work, flat top, or a combination of both. The combination provides the best features of

each, and so is recommended. Generally the flat or closed top is used for yards, stations and terminals or other places where the trackwork is flat and there are a number of adjoining tracks. Open work makes scenery easier, uses less lumber, and actually makes trackwork more simple.

A flat area can be made from building board or plywood, and tracks are usually directly attached to it, since in yards and similar areas there is little or no track ballast to worry the builder.

BUILDING AN OPEN-WORK TABLE

Open work involves a frame with crosspieces at fairly regular intervals. The tops of the crosspieces should be below the flat level since you will want grades that go down from the median

BUILT-UP TABLE WORK

The merits of built-up table work are aptly shown in this use of bridges, for on a flat table there is no need for them. Here a girder bridge and a truss bridge were combined to form a standard railroad structure. Lichen moss, crushed rock, and crumpled heavy wrapping paper form the scenery. The wrapping paper makes excellent rockwork if carefully used, but it should be varnished after shaping and then tinted to give shadows and reflected colors.

point as well as those that go up. On the crosspieces are attached small sections of four-inch board fixed vertically to the desired height. Running from one to another of these verticals are the track boards, straight and curved, level and graded. Thus the trains run over an open network that can later be filled or covered with scenery of almost any desired sort.

HOW TO ADD BALLAST

Track is fixed and ballast is added. With any sort of rail, you will probably want ballast eventually. The spaces between ties can be built up with cardboard or almost any materials. A coating of glue or cement is spread and small, finely crushed rock is spread on. This can be repeated until ballast of sufficient depth is achieved.

HOW TO CREATE SCENERY

With the roadbed down, trains ready to roll and power applied, you can now run your road, and with a little vision you can see towns and cities, factories and farms, but it is an unquestioned fact that your friends may look at you with odd expressions if you attempt to tell them that you are spotting a box car at the local glue factory when it is as plain as the nose on your streamliner that there is nothing but a big hole beside the track.

So let's please them.

Your basic beginning for scenery is some rough mesh wire and some plaster. Fine mesh wire can be used, but it is more expensive than the rough mesh and it adds nothing to your road. The wire can be tacked to various members

EASY-TO-MAKE SCENERY
Scenery is very easy where it need not stand too close inspection from the onlookers. Here fine crushed rocks form the bed of the main line while the two passing sidings are ballasted with coffee grounds. Other materials can be used for roadways and ground surface, while small bits of sponge of various sorts make excellent shrubs if dyed green.

of the supporting unit including the underside of the track boards, and it can be roughly molded and punched into shape. Mountains and valleys, farms and lakes can all be roughed out with a little pressure and imagination. Then a coating of plaster is spread over the wire and, when it is dry, you'll be able to stand on it without damaging it.

MAKING ROCK FROM PLASTER

It is amazing how simple it is to sculpt rock forms from plaster. You can, if you

A MAN-MADE CLIFF
Here plaster has been molded with a kitchen knife and a fork to imitate a grassy slope and rocks. The rocky sections use wooden block bases, but the slope is plaster on wire screen. The soft texture of the slope is gained by painting the surface with glue or cement and, while wet, applying dyed and natural sawdust. Rocks are carefully colored with a variety of hues to indicate weathering.

USE A PAINTED BACKDROP
You can make yourself or purchase the city background painting, which adds perspective and justifies the heavy traffic of the two-level junction.

wish, gather some rocks and embed them, or for a cliff you can usually pick up some whole pieces of cork at a florist's, but lacking either of them, a kitchen knife and some wet plaster will turn out a remarkably realistically shaped terrain.

HOW TO PAINT THE TERRAIN

Painting the terrain is not very difficult. Small brushes are most useful, and an assortment of oil paints with browns, blues and greens predominating should be gathered. One worthwhile tip is that many hobbyists tint their plaster with either brown or green, depending upon whether the terrain is largely rock or grass. Do a little observing of some terrain and of some oil paintings in magazines before you start. Notice that there are never any flat colors in nature, but that even a field of wheat will vary in its shade of brown from corner to corner and spot to spot. As the distance from the eye increases, colors dim, greys appear and more blues and purples show through.

Basically you are after a color scheme that will fool the eye, and incidentally, this is easiest if you seat your guests so that their eyes are as close to table-top level as possible.

USE OF THE SCENIC BACKDROP

Eventually you will want to put in a background. This can be purchased, or you can paint one yourself, but in either case there is a trick that works wonders. Always, without exception, arrange your scenery so that there is no visible joint between the flat background and the relatively level table. Do this by always having a row of hills, a string of buildings, a factory, or a high-level route placed close to the wall. Drop the scenic backdrop below it with a two- or three-inch gap between. This three-inch gap will fool the eye completely, for so long as there is no visible junction, there will be nothing to establish distance other than that which imagination supplies.

BUILDINGS

Buildings give a strong touch of realism to any layout. You will want stations and all of the usual railroad buildings. In addition, if you have industrial buildings, many of them, you also have an excuse for switching your cars frequently. Lastly, you will want a few residences.

Many a fan spends a tremendous amount of time and effort and even a few dollars in order to build a fine-looking residential town with a string of stores and theatres. Unfortunately this is not effective for two reasons. Even a very small town is usually spread out for a mile or so, and it takes 110 feet to equal one O gauge mile—in short you don't have room to do a good job. Secondly,

AN OLDTIME WESTERN ROAD

Notice that on this ancient branch of his railroad, the model maker uses old-fashioned cars. A town such as this could be the basis for an entire layout.

if you do have room, the residences will give you no reason at all for switching cars or moving anything other than an occasional passenger train.

Thus, we recommend that you follow this scheme. Put plenty of industrial buildings along your right of way—that usually is the way it is in real life—and put two or even three buildings on each spur. It is true that industries presuppose a town, so get yourself a painted background that can be located just behind the industries. Thus you will have buildings in the foreground and behind them a town stretching off to the horizon, or even beyond it if you wish. You can't get 110 feet of town on your table, but you can get several hundred on a painted backdrop. It is a good rule never to add a building that doesn't give you some excuse to do more railroading, with the possible exception of a farm that fills up a space between towns. Even on the farm you can occasionally load livestock or milk to go to the nearby slaughterhouses or dairies.

So there you are. You've got rolling stock, trackage, scenery and buildings, all mounted on a table where people can admire them, and where you can manipulate the destinies to your heart's content.

But even so, you haven't begun to exhaust the hobby of all of its potentialities. There is plenty to be learned about various railroad tricks of track laying, about schedules and timing and a host of other things.

YOUR RAILROAD IN OPERATION

Once things are rolling, it is very wise to name all of your passenger trains—this gives them a greater semblance of reality. If you have only one train, you can easily start it on a run from one terminal to another under the name of the Hutsut Limited. When it reaches its destination and the passengers are unloaded, shift to a yards track, shunt the engine around for water and coal, drop the baggage car if you have one. In a very few minutes you can call out the Hotshot Express (ignoring the fact that it is the same train) and send it off, and by doing the same thing at the other end you can eventually return in time to get the original Hutsut Limited ready for its return run at night.

Trains should be numbered, freights as well as passenger, and these too can be maneuvered so that one train gives the impression of three or four.

HOW TO RUN WAY FREIGHTS

The most interesting of the freights are the way freights. These are usually short trains of six to eighteen cars (hence ideal for model railroading) and they are unscheduled and thus must clear the main lines for all scheduled trains. They run up or down the line, picking up a car here and dropping one there to do the local work that is necessary so that the major yards can be fed with traffic. A way freight may leave its train sitting on the mainline, back into a siding and pick up a full box car and couple it onto the front of the train. Leaving the caboose still sitting, it may drop an empty in the same place by backing it into the siding and cutting it loose. Then it picks up the caboose and rolls off the main while the Idaho Limited flashes by. Then at the next plant a full gondola is left to be unloaded and an empty one is taken away, and so the little freight works its way laboriously from one terminal to the next.

NAMING YOUR RAILROAD

You can pick your own name for your road or you can pattern it after one of the big roads. You can learn about the short lines and choose one of them as your prototype. There are old-fashioned roads, Western roads, logging railroads, coal roads and almost any combination of any sort that can be imagined.

There are plenty of aids available at your hobby store, and the only limitation lies in your own imagination and ability. You too can be an empire builder!

[70]

BUILDING MODEL PLANES THAT FLY

Anyone can build model airplanes—models that actually fly. All you have to do is follow the simple instructions presented in this chapter. It explains the basic vocabulary of plane building, how to carve propellers, how to cover and dope fuselage, and gives many helpful pointers on construction, as well as how to test and fly your models. Then there are complete plans and directions for three models that are fun to make and fly.

WORDS FOR MODEL BUILDERS

The following is a list of basic words the model builder will need in his work. You don't have to master them right now. Refer back to the list for the definitions of new words you encounter later on in this chapter.

Ailerons. Hinged surfaces at the trailing edge of the wings to bank the airplane.

Airfoil. The profile or cross-section shape of a wing or rib section.

Bank. Tipping of the wing in either direction preparatory to making a turn with the use of rudder.

Bearing. A piece of tube, washer, or flat metal surface used to reduce friction between moving parts of a wheel, propeller shaft, washer, etc.

Bulkhead. A frame or former of any shape designed to carry basic fuselage longerons or stringers.

Camber. The curve of an airfoil section or tail section extending from leading to trailing edge.

Cowling. A circular or similarly shaped piece of metal or wood used to enclose

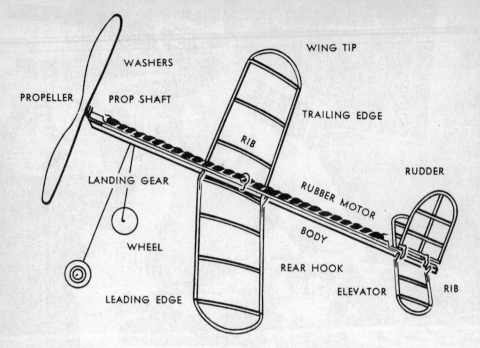

PARTS OF A MODEL AIRPLANE

a motor or cover a part of the nose section.

Crutch. Backbone for a frame-type fuselage consisting of the main longerons and cross pieces.

Diameter, Propeller, Wheel. The size of object measured from tip to tip or edge to edge.

Dihedral Angle. The angle at which the tips of the wings are raised above the center section portions of the wing. Its effect is to lower the center of gravity of the airplane and increase stability.

Elevators. Hinged surfaces attached to the horizontal stabilizer causing the plane to nose up or down by their movement.

Form. A jig-like device formed of pins or small nails set into a bench or working board and designed to hold parts of the fuselage or wing while they are being assembled or cemented.

Fuselage. The body of the airplane which carries engine and tail (on conventional models).

Incidence, Angle. Setting of the wing at a slight upward or downward angle against the fuselage. The angle is fixed.

Jig. See Form.

Landing Gear. The combination of wheel(s) and strut(s) attached to wing or fuselage, or both, which supports the model while taking off, landing or at rest.

Longerons. The main fore and aft members which combine to make the basic frame of a fuselage.

Lubricant. Paste, grease or liquid-grease preparations which, when rubbed into rubber strands, aid in increasing their elasticity and number of windings, and add to their life span.

Nose Plug. A conical or similar shape of wood into which the propeller thrust bearing is inserted for support.

Polyhedral Angle. A modified dihedral angle in which the outermost wing panels are tilted higher than the natural dihedral setting. This provides extra-lateral stability.

Rudder. A part of the tail surface hinged to the vertical fin and used to turn the plane in the direction of bank.

Side Thrust. Off-setting of the propeller or thrust bearing so that the model will fly slightly to one side for purpose of flying adjustments.

Spars. The span-wise structural member of a wing or stabilizer which carries false or full-length ribs.

Stabilizer. Fixed horizontal or vertical tail surface.

Stability. Tendency of aircraft to remain at, or return to, level flight after being disturbed from level flight.

Stall. Complete loss of lift due to an extreme angle of climb. Result is usually an abrupt dive or tailspin.

Sweepback. Angle of wing setting from the center toward the tips as viewed from above. Setting is designed to increase stability.

Tabs. Small adjustable sections located at trailing edges of ailerons, elevators, rudder, for delicate flight adjustments.

Tail Surfaces. The rearmost controlling surfaces of an aircraft composed of stabilizers, rudder, elevators and tabs.

Tail Skid. On model aircraft it may be made of wood, wire, and is used to elevate the tail section off the ground. Sometimes it is used in wheel form.

Template. Metal, wood or cardboard pattern used to trace its outlines onto another surface for purpose of making one or more duplicates.

Thrust Bearing. A washer, metal fitting, or tube attached to the nose block or plug, accommodating the propeller shaft. Also known as propeller hangar.

Torque. Reactive force created by the propeller which tends to turn the model in opposite direction of the propeller's rotation. This is remedied by effecting counter reaction through use of rudder, tabs, washin or washout as required.

Trailing Edge. Rearmost edge of a wing or tail surface.

Washin. A twist worked into a wing at its tip to raise the leading edge.

Washout. A twist worked into a wing at its tip to raise the trailing edge.

THE PROPELLER IS IMPORTANT

In a model plane, the propeller is a most important part. There are all types of propellers each designed for a special job, and in its finished form the propeller provides pulling or pushing power, speed or climb.

USE THE RIGHT TOOLS
A drawing board, a T-square, and a curve are useful equipment for the model builder.

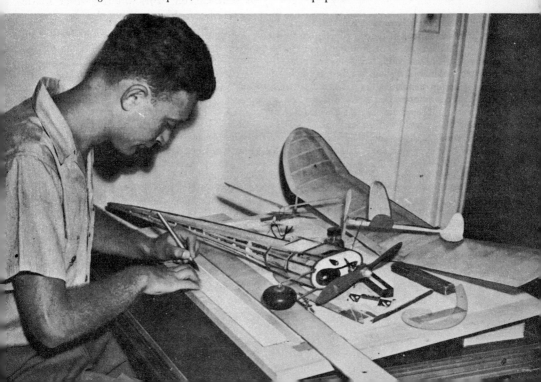

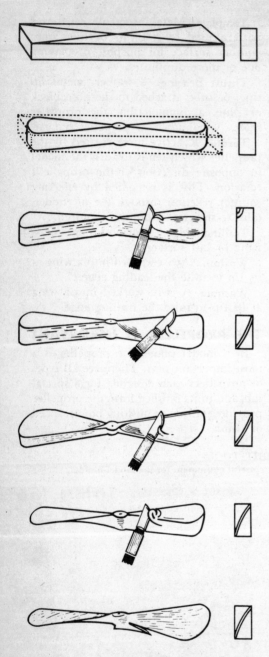

of the model you've just built, use your knife and go to work.

The beginner builder would do well to follow the propeller design given when building a model from plans. It is assumed that the designer of the model has tested his craft thoroughly to get the best results with the propeller in question. Indoor models as a general rule are flown with propellers whose dimensions are about ½ the span of the wing. On outdoor models (excluding gas jobs) propeller sizes are about ⅓ the span and are designed for higher speed.

CARVING THE PROP

The block of wood chosen for the prop is called a "blank." A properly dimensioned blank may be purchased at any model shop. First step is to draw diagonal lines across the face and back of the block. The "X" blank is then cut to shape with your knife or saw. Be sure the hub section is left fairly thick. The sketches illustrating the carving steps are simple to follow. Work easily and carefully across the face of the blade from hub outward in a gentle scooping out or concave motion. Do not attempt deep cuts and do not cut close to the outer edges. When one blade is semi-carved, work on the other blade in similar fashion.

Next turn the prop over and carve the CONVEX shape in the blades. Working out from the hub where it is thickest, remove the top surfaces in easy cuts until the blade has a tapered thickness at the edges of at least ⅛ of an inch. For the time being the hub should be the thickest part since strength is needed in the center portion because pressure is applied by the weight of carver's hand.

SANDING AND DRILLING

The next step is sanding the blades down smoothly. Using your fingers under the right hand blade (opposite if a "lefty") as a means of support, rub medium grade sandpaper over the surface to remove the rough spots. Finish with fine sandpapering. Round off the

For the type of models shown in this chapter, the most efficient prop here illustrated is known as the STANDARD type. It is one of the easiest to carve.

A study of the various stages of carving a prop will convince you that without further hesitation, you can select your propeller block as specified by the plans ends of the blades as shown in the sketches.

Now mark the center of the prop, drill a hole the same size of the wire prop shaft to be used and then balance horizontally. The heaviest side of the blade will naturally drop down. Sand lightly over the surface and balance again until the prop remains perfectly still in a horizontal position. (See sketch of prop balancer.)

Cutting away a part of the hub at the rear of the prop in a scalloping effect, as illustrated in Step 7, makes for lightness and efficiency. Insert the prop shaft, bend the front end to shape and push firmly back into the face of the hub. Apply lots of cement over the joinings. Next, slip a few washers on the shaft before bending the rear end of the shaft into a hook. It is a good idea to cement one washer flush to the rear of the hub.

CONSTRUCTION HINTS

A quick and simple method of making a fuselage of the type illustrated here is done by placing a sheet of wax paper directly over the plan layout. The wax paper being transparent allows the lines of the original drawing to show clearly.

Upper and lower longerons are set in position. Use pins as a jig and place them both along the inside and outside of the strips. They help in holding the bottom curve of the lower strip as well as in keeping the top strip steady while the upright members are cemented in position.

Modelers who are a bit impatient prefer to make both frames of the body at the same time without waiting for the first to set before removal from the plan. If you think you're expert enough to try it, all that has to be done is to place another set of upper and lower longerons on top of the first frame, then cement the upright members directly over the lower set. Just apply cement to the tip ends of the uprights, so that a cement contact is made only with the longerons. Do not allow any cement to get on the sides of the uprights or you'll find the sides difficult to separate later.

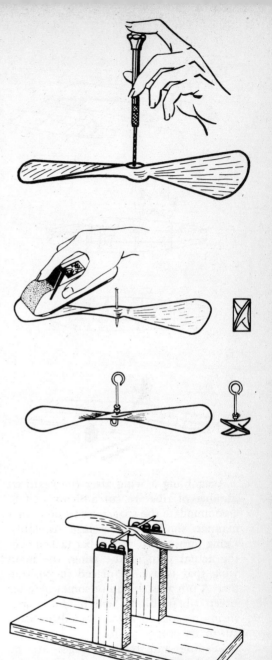

Be sure the jig pins are set snugly so that the frame does not get out of shape. When both frames are ready to be joined by top and bottom cross braces, remove the jig pins. Next, use a sharp knife to separate the two frames by carefully poking between them where they seem most likely to have gotten stuck together.

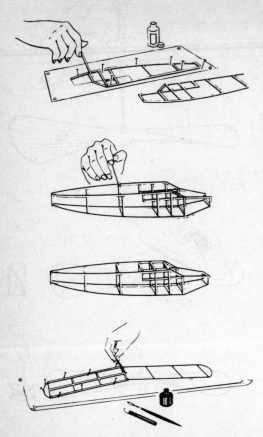

COVERING AND DOPING

The covering of wing, fuselage and tail surfaces often decides success or failure of a flying model. The tissue which covers the lifting surfaces must be as tight as possible. A good job requires time, experience and technique—but in this case they are fairly easy to achieve. By working unhurriedly and carefully, even your first covering job will turn out to be a good one.

Jap tissue, which is used for covering both indoor and outdoor models (even

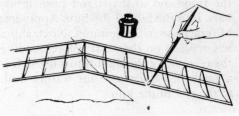

Fig. 1

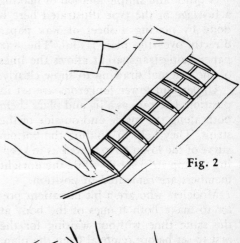

Fig. 2

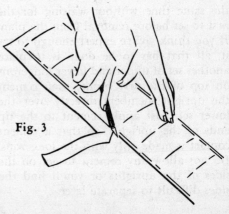

Fig. 3

Assembling a wing after the required number of ribs are cut and notched to accommodate the spar, may be done in a manner similar to fuselage assembly. Using transparent wax paper tacked over the actual plan of the wing, the main wing spar is usually placed in position first. A pin at each end or somewhere between rib positions, will hold the spar steady as you go about cementing each rib in its proper position.

Leading and trailing edges are cemented in place next. Apply the cement with a thin applicator so that the cement touches both the rib and edges.

If rudder and elevator are of the built up kind, that is of frame type construction, the use of pins to hold the various members in position is recommended. This jig-like device prevents the parts from getting out of position or warping while the cement is drying.

small gas models, too) costs only a few cents. It comes in a fairly large size and may be folded softly for carrying. If badly wrinkled, spread out flat on a table cloth and with a warmed iron, slide over the surface. The wrinkles will vanish.

In covering a wing, first place the wing under the tissue as illustrated in Fig. 1. Then using your knife, trim the paper leaving at least half an inch margin all around. If too large it may be trimmed even shorter depending upon the type of wing design and construction. Covering

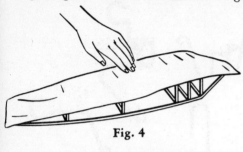

Fig. 4

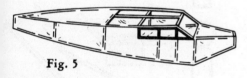

Fig. 5

Fig. 6

some types of wings, is done by attaching a single piece to the bottom first and then wrapping over the top after the ribs have been dabbed with banana oil, Figs. 2 and 3. Another method is to cover the bottom or top side first with separate sheets. A good job is secured by either method.

To attach the tissue to balsa surfaces, banana oil is used. Applied with a small brush and dabbing a portion at a time, the paper is then pressed to the surfaces gently and smoothed out in all directions to prevent wrinkling. This must be done immediately upon placing the tissue on the wood. Allow a minute or so for the glue to dry before applying more to the next section. When extending the covering, stretch out the tissue as you go along. The longest time devoted to building a model is the covering and the time spent doing it carefully is worth the results in both flying and over-all appearance.

The trailing edges of the wing and tips are finished off by trimming as close to the edge as possible, just allowing enough overhang to wet and tuck in flat, Fig. 4. See also Fig. 5 on fuselage covering.

Before applying a dope finish on the covered surfaces, shrink the covered parts with water which may be applied by dabbing a wad of absorbent cotton in a glass, wetting it, but not too thoroughly, and brushing it along the surfaces lightly until the paper is dampened evenly. The water-spray method illustrated in Fig. 6 is suggested for the beginner. Your first result will be a saggy looking frame which hardly seemed possible after the careful work you did to make a tight surface in the first place.

Set the dampened surfaces upright against a wall or table in a room of even temperature. Don't ever place it against a radiator or gas heater in order to make it dry faster. The results will be a wing twisted like a prop. Allow the covered surfaces to dry normally for as long as it takes to become taut throughout. If a wrinkle shows up here and there, moisten the area with another dab of damp cotton. Only by trial and error can you

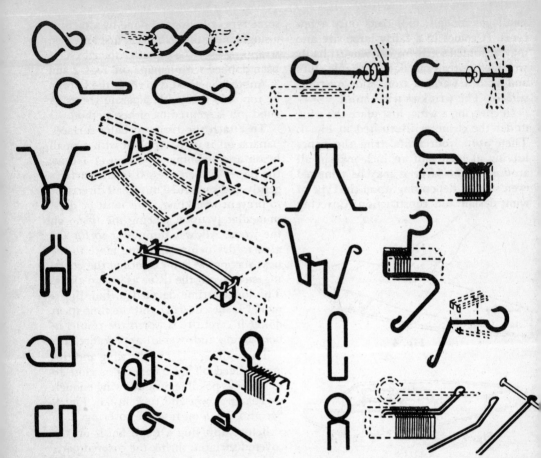

achieve good results. The experience of your first try is always educational anyway.

After the job of water-spraying is done, the entire surfaces are gone over with specially prepared dope or banana oil. This tightens the surfaces still better and makes them water proof. A poor covering is like a sloppily dressed man.

WIRE FITTINGS

In rubber powered models, where tension and stress is applied to certain parts, metal fittings necessarily have to be used. Light weight, easily shaped, piano wire is best suited for the purpose. Wire may be purchased by asking for it by Gauge number which identifies the diameter of the wire itself. For the most common purposes, at least for the type models presented in this chapter, Gauge Numbers 6, 8, 10, 12 and 14 are used for fittings.

Propeller shafts, cans, rear hooks, "S" hooks, tail skids, thrust bearings, and common type wing clips may be purchased ready-made in many model shops.

Look at accompanying illustration; it shows the most commonly used fittings. You will see some of them repeated directly on the model plans themselves. Practice shaping all types of metal fittings. The cost of a length of wire is less than having to buy ready-made sets of fittings.

FLYING YOUR MODEL

The finest flying model plane isn't worth the effort spent on building it if it won't fly properly. Getting the best possible performance depends upon the final adjustments of the model. Adjustments may include the setting of the wing for glide, greater climb, warping wings to offset torque or, to get a spiral climb, turning the rudder slightly or warping the elevators to make for better glide or climb. All have a special purpose. The manner of adjusting for one model may be different than required for another type.

What determines whether the model will fly at all is the glide test. Hold the model between the fingers of the right hand at the approximate balancing point —the point where the wing is attached according to the position shown on the plans. The nose of the model should be pointed slightly down. If testing outdoors, be sure you face the wind—that is with the wind blowing in your face. The wind should be not more than a light breeze for if the model is launched without power into anything stronger, your craft will stall and flop to the ground.

With the nose pointed down, give it a slight push forward. Fig. 1 shows the three possible results of the launching. If the model stalls it indicates that the wing is too far forward. In the rubber powered model, where the wing is held on by clips, the wing should be removed, from its present position and moved back a little. Attach it once more; go through the launching process again. Do this until you obtain as long a glide as possible. When satisfied that it is the best the model can do, mark the position of the wing with pencil so that if the wing becomes loose, you won't have to go through the gliding test all over again.

The second result of a glide test may be a steep dive before the model has a chance to pull out. This is caused by the wing being set too far back. Using the same method of resetting, move the wing up ahead a little at a time; the best gliding angle can thus be found.

On a glider, the addition or removal of modeling clay around the nose will help you find its best gliding angle. Where a piece of lead weight is used, the weight can be removed and filed or cut down bit by bit.

On a cabin model such as shown in this chapter, the wing location has been predetermined and does not require too much re-setting. By adding small pieces of lead weight in either the nose section or at the tail end, proper balance may be had. To make the model climb at a steeper angle and give it more lift without stalling, a small piece of balsa wood, measuring either 1/16 inch or 3/16 inch thick may be placed under the leading edge of the wing thus providing an angle of incidence.

Adjustments apply for the models shown in this chapter and are of the simple variety. It isn't necessary to warp the wings, or tail surfaces of all rubber powered models unless there is an excessive torque making the model fly in tight right or left circles. This can be remedied

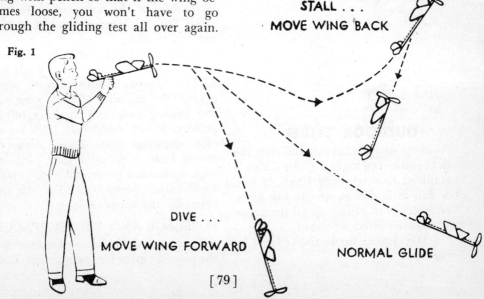

Fig. 1

STALL . . .
MOVE WING BACK

DIVE . . .
MOVE WING FORWARD

NORMAL GLIDE

by warping the trailing edge of the outer portion of the wing on the side to which it turns. The warping will lift up the banked side, thus keeping the wings on an even keel. Warping the rudder to off-set a tight turn may also be tried.

In flying a model with landing gear attached such as on the stick and cabin models shown in this chapter, turn up the propeller until a single or double row of knots is wound. Place the model on a smooth spot, with the left fingers holding

Fig. 2

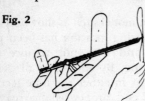

the top blade of the propeller in vertical position, and the right thumb and fore-finger holding the rear end of the body or at the top of the rudder. A slight push or just release of the propeller will send the model off.

Fig. 2 shows a stick model without the wire landing gear attached. Your stick models too can be flown in this manner if you decide to leave the landing gear off altogether. Apply the same method of glide testing. Sketch shows manner in which the model should be launched, when ready to fly.

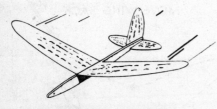

OUTDOOR GLIDER

From the simple plans shown, even the rank beginner can make a glider which is guaranteed to give many hours of out-door fun as it climbs, spirals and soars.

First step is to round up all the neces-sary materials listed as follows:

Fuselage. 1 piece hard balsa ¼ by ½ by 9 inches.

Wings. 2 sheets soft balsa 1/16 by 2⅛ by 5¼ inches.

Tail Surfaces. 1 sheet soft balsa 1/32 by 2 by 6½ inches.

Bottle of cement, sander, typewriter carbon paper, sharp knife, several small pins, lump of modeling clay.

In order to trace the outlines of the various surfaces of the plan onto balsa wood, simply place a sheet of typewriter carbon underneath it (dull side against back). Then place a sheet of manila paper against the shiny face of the carbon sheet. Use a sharp pencil over the outlines. It is not necessary to make a tracing of the cross section of the fuselage or elevator.

WINGS

Start with the wing first. Cut out the pattern exactly and check for accuracy by placing the cut-out over the original drawing. Next, place the pattern over one of the pieces of 1/16 inch balsa sheets and trace its outlines. Cut out the shape. Note the cambered shape of the wing section. Draw this shape against the straight edge and with a little shav-ing round off the leading edge. Work out the rest of the curve throughout the entire length of the wing with a sander.

The right half is made by turning your pattern over on its back and again trac-ing its outlines on a second piece of 1/16 inch sheet. Be sure the rounded part of the wing is on the right end of the balsa piece. Use the same method of camber-ing and sanding.

With both wing panels completed next step is to put the sweep-back angle into it. This is done by using a ruler placed against the top side of each wing near the joining ends and marking off the position shown by dotted lines on the plan drawing. Slice clean along the dotted lines. Now place each wing half edge against the other and note how the wing halves sweep back. For the time being lay the wings aside.

FUSELAGE AND TAIL SURFACES

Trace the shape of the fuselage onto the piece set aside for that purpose. Carve

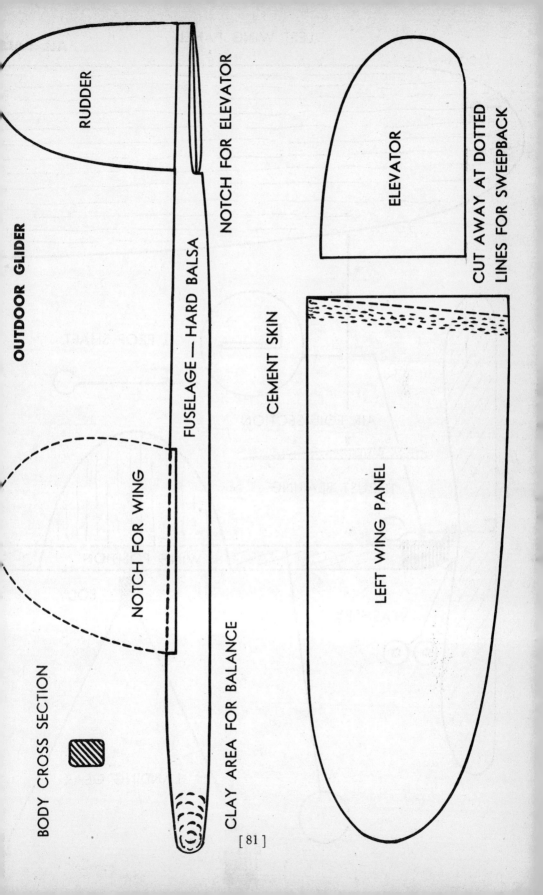

OUTDOOR GLIDER

RUDDER

NOTCH FOR ELEVATOR

FUSELAGE—HARD BALSA

NOTCH FOR WING

CLAY AREA FOR BALANCE

BODY CROSS SECTION

[81]

ELEVATOR

CUT AWAY AT DOTTED
LINES FOR SWEEPBACK

CEMENT SKIN

LEFT WING PANEL

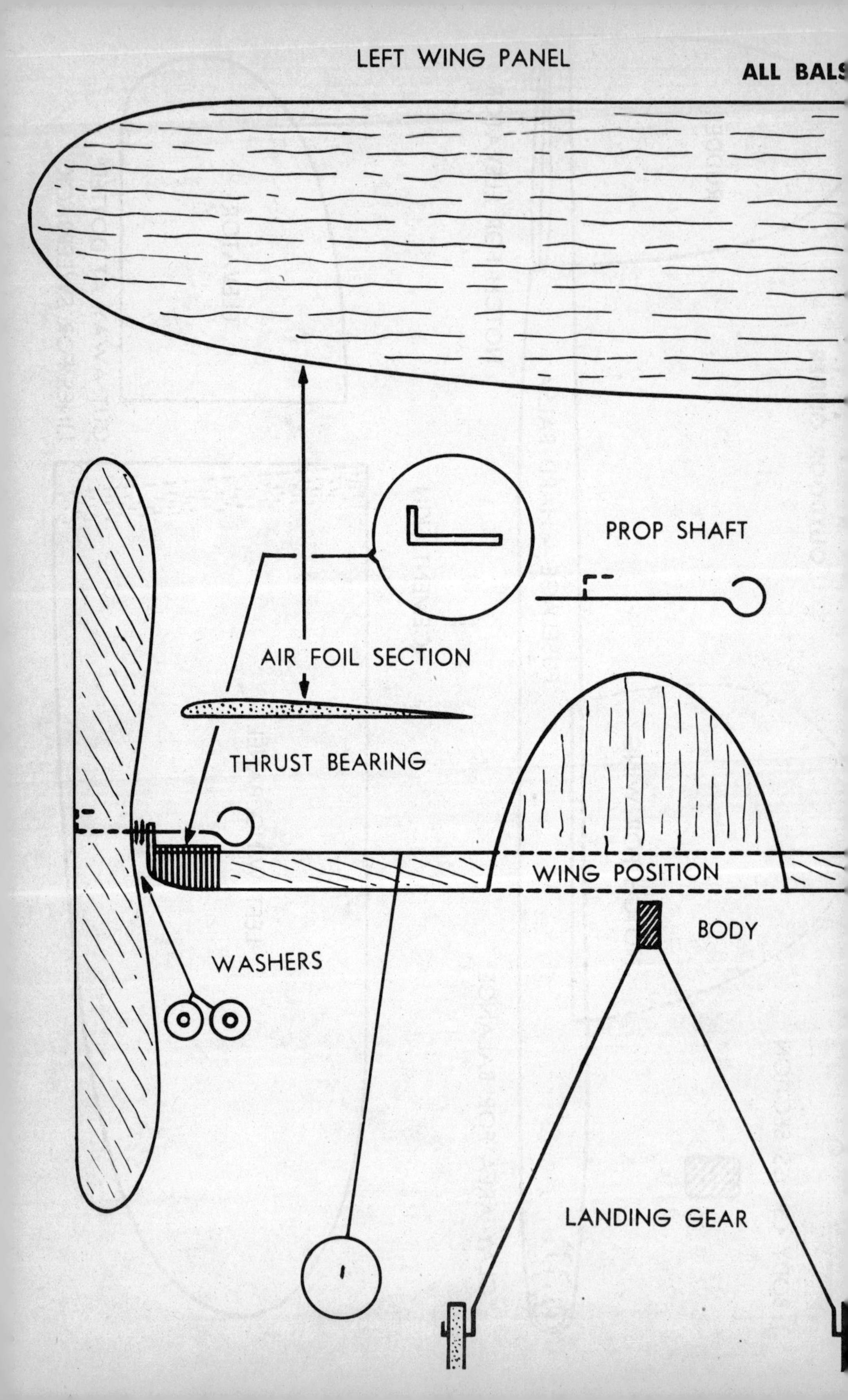
LEFT WING PANEL
ALL BALS
PROP SHAFT
AIR FOIL SECTION
THRUST BEARING
WING POSITION
BODY
WASHERS
LANDING GEAR

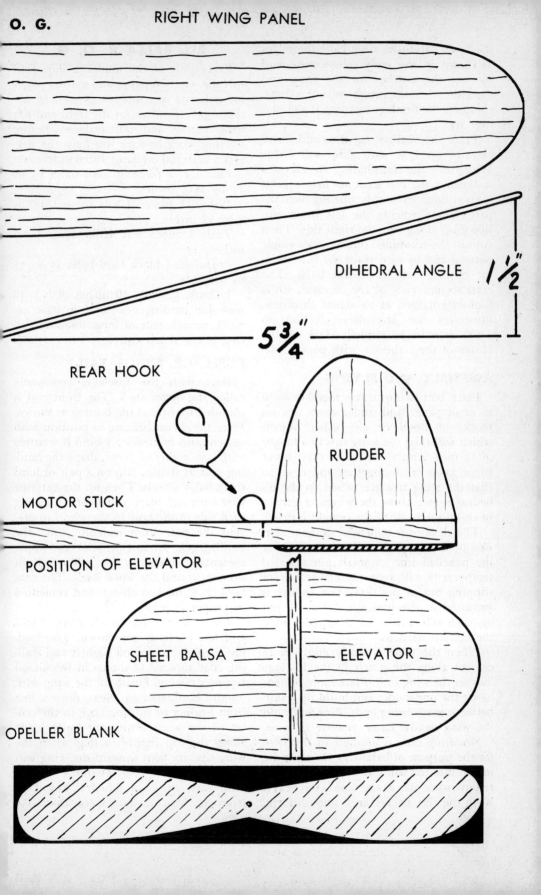

DIHEDRAL ANGLE

$1\frac{1}{2}''$

$5\frac{3}{4}''$

REAR HOOK

MOTOR STICK

RUDDER

POSITION OF ELEVATOR

SHEET BALSA   ELEVATOR

OPELLER BLANK

the body carefully, round off the edges as shown in the body cross-section and cut out the notches for the wing and elevator. After the rough cutting is done, complete the fuselage by using the sander over it.

Trace the outlines for the rudder and elevator on 1/32 inch sheet soft balsa. While only the right half of the elevator is shown, actually it is cut out in one piece. This is done by simply turning over the pattern and tracing the left hand outline flush along side the right side. Then cut out the combined outlines as a single pattern and in turn trace the full elevator outline onto the sheet balsa. The cross section view of the elevator, while slightly enlarged as to actual thickness, illustrates the streamline section to which it must be sanded. Mark off the center of the stabilizer with pencil line.

ASSEMBLY AND FLYING

Place both wing panels together on a sheet of paper and under their tips set blocks of wood or any other objects which will raise the wing tips to a height of 1/2 inch. Apply cement to their inner edges, press firmly together and re-set so that the wing tips are raised to the dihedral angle. Allow the wings to remain in this position until the cement is dried.

The elevator is cemented to the underside of the fuselage and centered along the penciled line. A small pin inserted temporarily will keep the elevator from slipping out of position. The rudder is mounted in the position shown. A pin on each side will hold it straight until the cement hardens.

When the wing is ready apply more cement along the notch in the fuselage and set the wing in it. Place more cement along the undersides and build up a skin between the joining ends. Pins will hold the wing steady. Later, remove all pins.

Modeling clay is applied to the nose for the purpose of balancing. Launch the model into the wind. If it dives abruptly, remove some clay as the nose is too heavy. Keep the clay packed in a smooth form.

ALL BALSA R. O. G.

Every part of the model is shown in full size. Carbon paper and manila paper for patterns or templates is used in obtaining the outlines for the right and left wing panels and tail surfaces. Before starting work be sure you have the necessary material on hand, listed as follows:

Fuselage. 1 piece of hard balsa 1/8 by 1/4 by 10 1/8 inches.

Wings. 1 piece of soft balsa 1/16 by 2 by 12 inches.

Tail. 1 piece soft balsa 1/16 by 6 inches.

Propeller. 1 block hard balsa 1/2 by 3/4 by 5 inches.

1 thrust bearing, 10 inches of No. 10 wire for landing gear and fittings, cement, sander, pair of long nose and cutting pliers, sharp knife.

FUSELAGE, WINGS, TAIL

Start with the fuselage, commonly called the motor stick. The front end is rounded slightly at the bottom as shown. Place the thrust bearing in position with cement and immediately bind it securely with strong thread. Next, shape the landing gear as shown. Slip on a pair of hard sheet balsa wheels. Turn up the extreme wire ends and place a drop of cement on each side of the hole in the wheel to prevent the hole from widening. Slip the landing gear around the stick and apply cement generously so that a skin is built up over it and the wood itself. The rear hook is shaped as shown and cemented in proper position.

The wing is made in one piece. Right and left portions are shown. The leading edge is rounded off slightly and trailing edge tapered as shown in the airfoil section drawing. Finish off the wing with smooth sandpapering. Next, draw a line from leading to trailing edge in the center of the wing. Run your knife blade along the top lightly so that when the wing tips are bent upward the wing will crack along the line, enabling you to raise each tip to a dihedral anywhere from 3/4 inch to not more than 1 1/2 inches. Once the dihedral angle is chosen, apply cement generously along the crack, place on a flat surface and set "blocks" under the wing tips to hold them at the raised angle until the cement has hardened.

Elevator and rudder parts are cut, sanded and streamlined to match with their outlines on the plans. The elevator is cemented to the underside of the motor stick at the very end. The rudder is cemented on top of the stick as shown. Use a few small pins to aid in holding the tail parts steady until the cement dries. Then remove pins.

Carve the propeller following the method illustrated earlier in the Propeller Carving section. Drill a hole in the hub and insert the wire shaft and shape accordingly.

ASSEMBLY AND FLYING

Before attaching the wing in a permanent position, place the prop shaft through the thrust bearing. Then attach a single loop of 1/8 inch flat rubber between shaft and rear hooks. Now take the wing, hold it against the bottom of the motor stick in the same position shown on the plans. Insert two or three small pins through the wing right into the stick for a temporary attachment.

Glide the model with a slight push forward. If the model dives steeply, remove the pins and move the wing forward. If the model noses up steeply and stalls, move the wing back. Keep shifting the wing forward or backward slightly until you get the best possible gliding angle so that when the model touches the ground the tail drops easily.

At the correct position of the wing, apply cement generously to the underside of the motor stick as well as the top part of the wing. Press the wing firmly to the stick, insert a few small pins and allow to dry for a couple of hours. Later remove the pins, and apply more cement between the stick and wing, filling in the open cracks so as to build up a solid joint.

Take the model outdoors and wind up the propeller until the rubber strand is well knotted. Face into the wind, place the model on the ground, and with a slight push it will rise off the ground.

OUTDOOR CABIN FLYER

Constructing a cabin model usually gives the builder the feeling that at last he is out of the "beginner's" class. For the cabin type model has all the appearances of a real airplane as it takes-off, flies and glides to a landing like a big ship.

Plans are full size on the accompanying illustrations. The wings are built up. The nose plug is removable. Tail surfaces are solid. An oversize propeller gives it a fast rate of climb.

All the required materials are listed below:

Fuselage. 8 strips of hard balsa 1/16 by 1/16 by 12 inches for framework.

Wings. 1 strip medium balsa 3/16 by 3/16 by 20 inches for leading edges.

Wings. 1 strip medium balsa 1/8 by 3/16 by 20 inches for trailing edges.

Wings. 1 strip medium balsa 1/8 by 3/16 by 20 inches for main spars.

Wings. 1 piece soft sheet balsa 1/16 by 3 by 24 inches for ribs and tail parts.

Propeller. 1 block of hard balsa 9/16 by 1 1/2 by 7 1/4 inches.

Nose Plug. 1 piece hard wood balsa 1 1/4 by 3/4 by 3/8 inch.

Nose Former. 1 piece hard balsa 3/16 by 1 by 1 1/4 inches.

Also No. 12 wire for landing gear, prop shaft, rear hook, tail skid, cement, Jap tissue, banana oil, dope, copper washers, 50 inches of 1/8 inch flat rubber.

FUSELAGE ASSEMBLY

First examine the sketch which shows the method of construction. Then study the plans. The frame work is made of 1/16 inch balsa. Make one side at a time. Use small pins to hold the longerons in position until the cement dries hard. In the meantime, cut out the nose former to the exact shape shown. Remove the

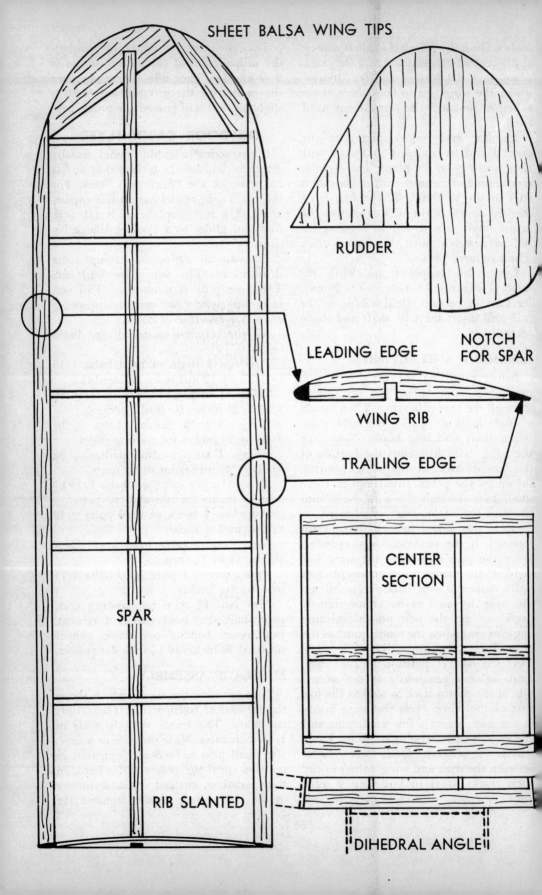

SHEET BALSA WING TIPS

RUDDER

LEADING EDGE

NOTCH FOR SPAR

WING RIB

TRAILING EDGE

SPAR

CENTER SECTION

RIB SLANTED

DIHEDRAL ANGLE

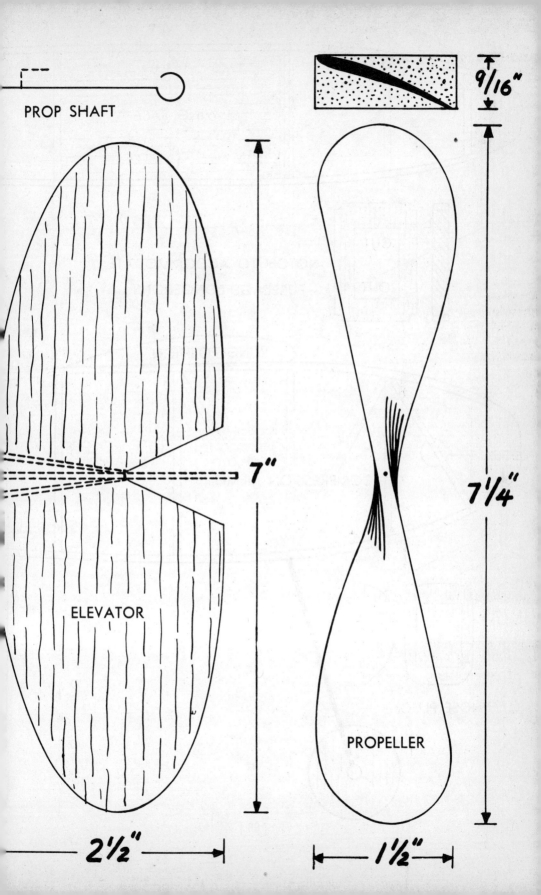

PROP SHAFT

ELEVATOR

7"

2½"

9/16"

7¼"

PROPELLER

1½"

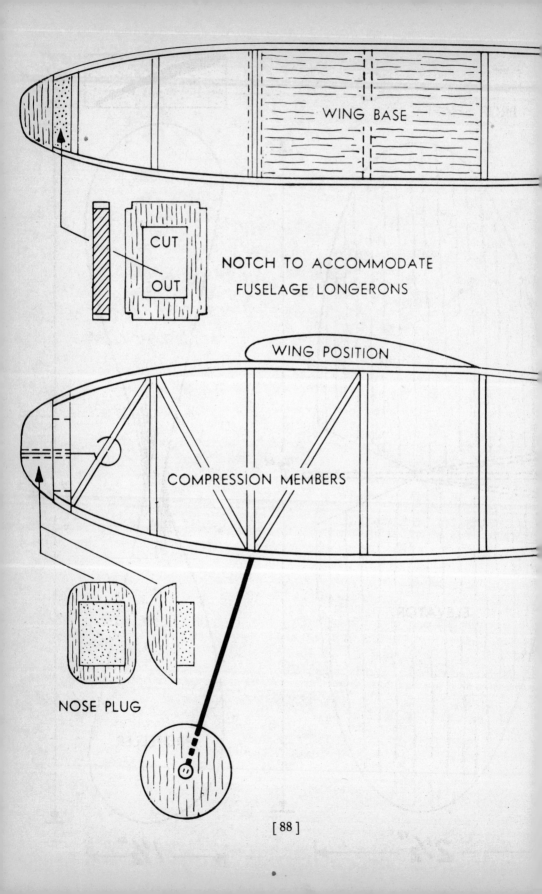

WING BASE

CUT OUT

NOTCH TO ACCOMMODATE
FUSELAGE LONGERONS

WING POSITION

COMPRESSION MEMBERS

NOSE PLUG

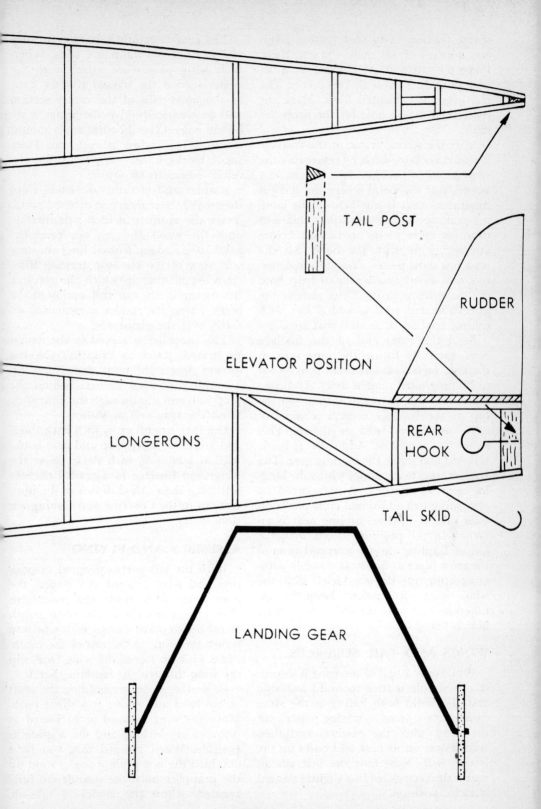

TAIL POST

RUDDER

ELEVATOR POSITION

LONGERONS

REAR
HOOK

TAIL SKID

LANDING GEAR

center portion. Top and bottom edges are notched 1/16 inch square. Next, shape the tail post. After that, carve the nose plug. It is made in two pieces. The rear piece is cemented flush. Mark the center and drill a hole for the propeller shaft.

After the second frame of the fuselage is ready, assemble both by cementing the cross pieces in position. It is best to start assembly at the point where the body is straightest—that is just behind the landing gear. See Side View. Allow sufficient time for cross pieces to harden before attempting to work the bend. Set the next few cross pieces along top and bottom and insert small pins to help hold the curve temporarily. Later remove the pins. The tail post is added last with cement applied all around that area.

Bend the front end of the fuselage next, carefully fitting the longerons in the nose former. Insert small pins to aid in holding until cement dries. Add cross pieces and side braces as shown. On the top of the fuselage cement a piece of 1/16 inch sheet balsa as shown. This serves as a wing base. Add the rear hook, tail skid and shape the landing gear. The bottom cross brace under which the landing gear is attached, is re-enforced by cementing two additional cross pieces on each side of it. The landing gear is attached in the position shown with the aid of binding thread wrapped around the cross piece as firmly as possible without cutting into the wood itself. Coat the whole joint with cement. Keep the tail raised in level position while the landing gear is being set.

WINGS AND TAIL SURFACES

While only a half of the wing is shown, it is a simple matter to build one side first. To build both halves at the same time, place a piece of tracing paper over the wing, trace the outlines and then turn it over on its back and build up the second half. Note how the first rib on each half is cemented in a slightly slanted outward position.

The center section is built separately and in itself is a miniature wing. When both wing panels are attached to the center section the slanted ribs set flush to the outer ribs of the center section will automatically give the wings a dihedral angle. The dihedral angle should measure $1\frac{1}{4}$ inches at each tip. Place small blocks under each tip while the cemented panels set firmly.

Rudder and elevator are made from sheet balsa. Note direction of wood grain. Trace the outlines of each part directly onto the wood and cut out carefully. Sand rough edges. Dotted lines showing side view of the elevator drawing illustrate the manner in which the elevator lies on top of the tail end section of the body. Later, the rudder is cemented directly over the elevator.

The propeller is carved to the design illustrated. Refer to Propeller Carving section. Insert the prop shaft, place on a couple of copper washers behind the prop hub and slip through the nose plug. Bend the rear end as shown.

Use four strands of $\frac{1}{8}$ inch flat rubber and attach to both prop and rear hooks with at least a $\frac{3}{4}$ inch slack. Cover the wings and fuselage in a careful manner following the method shown in the illustrations in the Covering and Doping section.

ASSEMBLY AND FLYING

With the tail parts cemented in position and wing covered and doped, the next phase is to ready the model for glide tests. Use some of the extra length of rubber to make a band with which to secure the wing to the top of the cabin. Place wing on top of the wing base, slip the wing through the fastening band.

Glide the model by holding the craft at eye level and giving it a slight push. Move the wing forward or backward in order to get as long and flat a glide as possible. When satisfied that you have obtained the best gliding angle, wind up the propeller until the strands are fully knotted. Allow the model to take-off.

AROUND THE WORLD WITH STAMPS

Stamps take us around the world and show us the geography, customs, interests, and events of foreign lands. *(Top row, left to right)* A Norwegian fjord; the Moscow subway; a Bulgarian woman plowing. *(Center row)* A native Fiji canoe; skiing in Austria. *(Bottom row)* A Canadian vessel named *The Bluenose;* capturing wild horses in Mongolia; and a desert family in French West Africa.

HOW TO ENJOY STAMP COLLECTING

Stamp collecting ranks high among the hobbies known and enjoyed by man today. A leisure-time activity that appeals to all age groups and all classes of people, it can be as interesting as you desire to make it. It is the aim of this chapter to help you make it as interesting and profitable as possible, by explaining the pleasures and benefits of collecting stamps, the types of collections and how to build them, the care of stamps, how to develop and enlarge a collection, and the advantages of joining an organized stamp club.

Stamps were first used by foreign countries as a means of receipt, showing the carrier that the transportation of the messages had been paid for. Many of the early stamps looked much like the postmarks found on our envelopes today. A

typical one consisted of a stamp made on the wrapper of the letter, bearing the name of the place from which the letter was sent. Another early form was the postmaster's signature with "Paid" written on the wrapper or envelope.

Later stamps were printed on paper. This required an engraved steel plate or block with the design carved on it so the stamp could be printed many times. These stamps were not separated by perforated holes so they could be torn apart easily. They had to be cut apart with shears or a knife.

As mechanical operations became more widely used, they were applied to the production of stamps. Today one would be amazed at the number of steps required to produce a new stamp.

HISTORY IN STAMPS

Stamps in top row portray a nation's birth. *(Left)* Emperor Franz Josef of Austria on Bosnian stamp issued before World War I. *(Center)* "Hatred Surcharge" used by Bosnia after Austrian Empire collapsed. *(Right)* First issue of Jugoslavia (a union of Bosnia, Serbia, Montenegro), symbolizing escape from Austrian tyranny. The stamp on left commemorates a spark that set the world afire. Pictured are the Austrian Archduke and Archduchess, who on June 28, 1914, visited Sarajevo, in the subject-province of Bosnia. Their assassination by a Serbian terrorist plunged the world into war.

WHAT YOU CAN LEARN FROM STAMPS

The field of stamps opens up many treasures of knowledge for the collector. Individuals often find stamps from new countries previously unknown to them. This is true even today, with international relations foremost in the news. A stamp collector should have a world map available and, as he gets stamps from each country, he might fill that country in on the map with colored crayon. It is fun to see how many countries there are from which stamps may be collected.

Foreign stamps are usually very colorful and possess fine detailed designs. The kind of money, stamps tell us, varies from country to country, and none of it is the same as our own currency. France uses the franc; China, the yen; Spain, the centavo; and Italy, the lira. Adults as well as children learn about foreign money through stamp collecting.

Then, too, stamps reflect the countries' history and growth. There are heads of their rulers or famous persons, such as Queen Wilhelmina on the Dutch stamp, Lenin on the Russian stamp, and King George on the British stamp. Stamps also reflect important historical events. The coronation of the King and Queen of England was honored by a series of British stamps. The death of King Alexander of Yugoslavia was memorialized by the regular stamp being printed with a black border. The Olympics are graphically displayed, usually by every country participating, by a series of stamps picturing various athletes in action. United States stamps record many memorable events in the history of this country.

Through stamps, one may also learn what animals inhabit different countries. Good illustrations of this are the Canadian stamps with the beaver, while the Newfoundland stamps have the codfish, caribou and the famous Newfoundland dog. Then too, many countries have stamps showing how the people live and till their soil.

A stamp is not, therefore, just a piece of paper which laws require one to purchase in order to mail a letter or send a package. Every stamp issued carries its own little story. Every one is of interest and value if it is properly understood and taken care of. So stamp collecting is not only fun, it is educational as well.

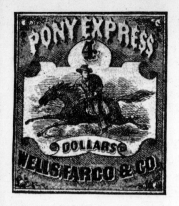

THE FASCINATION OF STAMPS

(Top left) Stamp of the Pony Express, which linked California with the Middle West. "Buffalo Bill" and "Wild Bill" Hickok were among the daredevil riders employed by Wells, Fargo & Co. *(Top center and right)* Two stamps out of the "Postal Zoo"—the proboscis monkey of Borneo and the koala of Australia. *(Bottom right)* The world's rarest stamp, a one-cent black-on-magenta stamp of British Guiana, dated 1856. It is valued at $50,000; no other copy is known to exist.

THE DIFFERENT TYPES OF COLLECTORS

What types of stamp collectors are there? Where do you begin? How do you advance? Two major and two minor distinctions can be made. First of all, there is the novice and the expert. A novice may be one of two types, a beginner or an amateur. An expert may be advanced or a specialist. What is meant by these four terms: beginner, amateur, advanced and specialist?

THE BEGINNER

First of all, let's consider the beginner. He may be a youngster or an adult who has, unknowingly, watched many interesting stamps being thrown away, never realizing what they could mean to him. Such a person might well begin collecting the stamps of his own country. A youngster starting to collect might do better to begin with foreign stamps. First of all, they are very reasonable in price. The majority of them cost one or two cents per stamp and may be purchased in large packages containing 100, 200 or 500

stamps each. Some will be duplicates, but they may be traded with other beginning stamp collectors. Youngsters may also be interested in collecting United States stamps that are in everyday use.

THE AMATEUR

The second type of novice is the amateur. The beginner soon becomes the amateur, who may be defined as the person who asks everyone he knows to save stamps for his collection. By this time, he has probably purchased a catalogue to help him identify his stamps and find out their value.

THE ADVANCED EXPERT

In the next stage of stamp collecting, the amateur has advanced to the point where he is an expert, cognizant of the many types of stamps, variations in the edge, in the face side of the stamp, and in the back or gummed side. These three things are important in classifying and distinguishing one issue from another. Stamps cannot be unmistakably identified by saying "Oh, that has a picture of Washington or Lincoln on the face."

THE SPECIALIST

The fourth and last type of stamp collector, the specialist, has progressed through the various stages mentioned and is now ready to concentrate on one phase of stamp collecting. Countries are issuing so many stamps today that there is a strain on the pocketbook. It therefore becomes necessary to limit the field of collecting. The specialist will select one type of stamp, one country, a certain issue, and collect them in all the variations. Just the fact that one saves a special type or issue does not however make him a specialist. He should study his collection and try to find something new in the field which he is collecting. In this way he may make an important contribution that will help other experts in his particular phase of collecting.

WHAT YOU SHOULD KNOW ABOUT THE STAMP ITSELF

PERFORATIONS

The edge of the stamp has been perforated so that persons can easily tear the stamps apart. When stamps were first issued they were printed in sheets and did not have the perforations. This made it necessary to use shears to cut them apart. Then one day someone used a common pin and punched holes between the stamps so that they could be torn apart. Machines now do this in one process by making holes between the stamps that have been printed in one sheet.

Some stamps have no perforations. These are called imperforated stamps. In some special issues there are stamps that are imperforated. This is not a mistake but is done for various purposes. However, almost all the stamps now possess perforations.

How Perforations Vary. Perforations are not all the same. You may purchase at little cost a gauge that measures these perforations and shows how many perforation holes there are along the stamp's edge in a space of two centimeters. The perforations found most commonly gauge 10, 10½, and 11 to the two-centimeter space. However, there are those that gauge 8, 9 and 12. Then, too, perforations may vary on the same stamp. We must consider both vertical and horizontal sides of a stamp. You may find one gauging 10½ horizontal and 11 vertical or vice versa. There are many such combinations.

THREE TYPES OF U.S. STAMPS

United States stamps are printed in three forms: coils, sheets and booklet panes. Coils are imperforated on the opposite sides. Coils are found in stamp machines. They are not issued in sheets, but in rolls; they have straight edges on two sides (either vertical or horizontal).

Booklet panes come from booklets of stamps. These may be bought in any post office and they come in sheets of six stamps each. The outer edge of the six stamps does not have perforations. To the collector, stamps such as these are more interesting; they must be in a pane of six to prove their origin. They are in the denominations of one and three cents.

THE OUTER EDGE OF THE SHEET

Another edge is the outer edge of the sheet, which contains many different kinds of markings. Of what significance are they and why are they there? The marks are printed there to facilitate handling, checking and keeping records of all those issued. One finds plate numbers in the corners of a sheet. When a stamp collector speaks of a plate block he is referring to the four-corner stamps which have the plate number (on the outer margin) attached to a block of stamps. One may find dots, lines, engravings of all sorts, and center lines which divide the sheet into four sections. They are usually there so that the post office clerk can readily see where to tear off twenty-five from a sheet, or any number of stamps desired, without counting out every stamp. On foreign stamps you are apt to find the denomination of the stamp printed in larger figures so that the clerk's job is made easier in finding the necessary denominations.

THE FACE OF THE STAMP

Let us now take a look at the face of a stamp. The important thing here is the centering. Centering refers to the position of the printed part or picture on the face of the stamp. Does it fall exactly in the center of the perforations or edges of the stamp? When perforations were first used, there were no machines to see that the perforations fell exactly between the printed parts of the sheet. Sometimes many sheets were wasted because the perforations cut the stamp in two. Almost every stamp was "off center." Today the electric eye is used to make sure that the printed portion of the stamps comes exactly between the perforations, thereby making them well-centered stamps and consequently more attractive. However, even now there are sometimes issues that are badly centered, thus detracting from the appearance of the stamp.

ERRORS THAT ADD VALUE TO STAMPS

There are misprints, errors, flaws and other mistakes in printing stamps. The sooner the errors are found, the fewer the number issued; and thus it increases the scarcity of the stamp and its value to collectors.

Some stamps require two printings because more than one color is used. This has sometimes resulted in the centers being inverted or turned upside down because the sheet was inverted when it was set on the printing press. One of the most famous examples of this type of error is the twenty-four-cent United

States airmail stamp of 1918 showing an airplane flying upside down.

Errors and oddities may result from overprinting. When there is a change in postal rates and not sufficient time to print new stamps, stamps of one denomination may have a figure designating the new denomination printed on them. An example is the overprinting of "Molly Pitcher" on the regular two-cent United States stamp in commemoration of her work at the Battle of Monmouth. This method eliminated the engraving and printing of a new stamp.

One thing to remember: Governments and individuals have been known to produce errors intentionally, in order that they may make a personal profit from stamp collectors. It is in many cases hard to determine that this has actually happened, but whenever it has been proved by experienced stamp collectors, it has been noted in the catalogues.

CANCELLATIONS

Cancellations affect the face of a stamp. Today the cancellations are more or less standard. However, when stamps were cancelled by hand stamp or pen, one finds interesting and odd cancellations. One type is the bull's-eye cancellation, which looks like rings on a pistol target. Stars and other various marks, if clear and not heavy, increase the interest of the stamp itself. Pen cancellations, used before hand stamps, are usually just a cross or an X. However, in some cases the postmaster placed his initials on the stamp to indicate that it had been used.

TYPES OF WATERMARKS

Now let us turn the stamp over and look at the back or gummed side. Stamps have gum on their backs so they may be stuck to an envelope or package. What else does the back tell us? A major point of interest to be noted is the watermark. This is the result of printing stamps on paper that had an imprint made on it when the paper was manufactured. Actually the paper is made thinner where the

THE ROMANCE OF THE AIRMAIL. In the top row: *(left)* ferrying gold; *(center)* Panama Canal; *(right)* Pan-American clipper. In the bottom row: *(left)* modern plane over ancient pyramids; *(center)* plane over Great Wall; *(right)* zeppelin over Russia.

watermark appears. There are many variations. For example, United States stamps have what we call single-line and double-line watermarks—that is, the letters of the watermark are of single or double lines. Watermarks may be inverted; but this is so common it does not add appreciably to the interest of the stamp, if at all.

How does one locate watermarks? Some may be seen with the naked eye. Another alternative is to place the stamp face downward on a dark surface and put some benzine on it. This will make the watermark apparent if there is one. Benzine is used since it will not destroy or damage the most delicate stamp or injure the gum on mint stamps. This is important since an unused stamp in good condition must have all of its gum and not be marred in any way.

BUILDING A SPECIAL COLLECTION

What special collections are possible? They are limited only by your ingenuity and the extent to which you wish to pursue stamp collecting. Specialization means hunting, searching, and observing. This should not be laborious but a constant source of pleasure, possessing all the qualities of any other recreational pursuit. You become more conscious of stamp designs, and come to appreciate the artistic qualities of stamps as well as their physical characteristics and markings.

One could go on endlessly listing possible specialized collections. However, the attractive designs of the issues of the last few years make the formation of topical collections most interesting. Here are a few examples:

Animals
Music
Games
Historical events
Stamps of one color
People and their dress
Ways of living
Statues and memorials
Dancers
Art
Commemoratives
Airmail
Industry
Plant life and nature
Tools and implements
Famous people
First-day covers
Church life
Transportation

From this list it can be readily seen that there are stamps that appeal to every interest: nature, music, art, dance, drama, ways of life, people, history and events of all kinds.

Men of art and science appear on left: *(top)* Rodin and Byron; *(bottom)* Goya and M. and Mme. Curie. Natives of far-off lands are shown on right: *(top)* Cameroons and Surinam; *(bottom)* Belgian Congo.

SPECIALIZING IN STAMPS OF ONE COUNTRY

The more usual form of specializing is to collect the stamps of one country or a nation and its possessions. This will enable you to comprehend the events and history of the country collected much more clearly. Such a collection will show not only the history of the country, but also the dates when certain machinery came into use, when new devices and inventions entered into the pattern of society, and how the country grew.

Two of the most common types of specialization are the collecting of British stamps and those of British possessions, or United States stamps. This seems natural to us because we belong to an English-speaking country.

Other special collections might include European nations and their colonies, Asia, Africa, South America and stamps of the various island groups.

VARIATIONS IN SPECIAL COLLECTIONS

Within special collections there are variations. Let us look at the United States stamps for an example of what is meant by these variations. There are the regular collections of used or unused United States stamps. Then there are

precancels—stamps canceled by the post office before they are sold. They have the city and state printed across the face of the stamp. There is a line above and below the city and state. For example, one might look like

Boston   or   RICHMOND
Mass.   VA.

Individuals or firms sending out large volumes of mail may obtain a special permit for the use of these stamps. This helps the post office by eliminating the need to cancel every piece of mail that is sent out. Precancels are stamped in sheets in one process; it is really an overprint.

THE CARE OF STAMPS

Many collections lose some of their value because the collector is not aware of the care that should be given to stamps, and of the materials and tools to use. Advice for best results follows.

REMOVING STAMPS FROM ENVELOPES

Should you remove used stamps from envelopes or packages? If so, how? It is not wise to remove stamps of early issues from envelopes or wrappings. Leaving them on the paper proves that they are authentic if the envelope with the post mark (cancellation) is left intact.

With the more modern stamps, it would be cumbersome and impractical to leave them on the envelopes. However, if there is an odd cancellation or it is a first-day cover, it is best not to remove the stamp. If stamps are to be removed, tear off a good margin of the envelope with the stamp to make sure the perforations are left intact, and soak for a short time in cool, clear water. After the stamp has become loosened, remove it from the paper and place it on a blotter, first flattening it out to dry. This prevents tearing the stamp or the perforations, or causing thin spots to appear in the stamp itself. All of this is important if its value is not to be destroyed.

Envelopes and wrappers present a problem. Should you save the entire envelope or wrapper? Some collectors do just that, but it requires a good deal of storage space. If the stamp is to be removed, cut a square at least 1½ inches, with the stamp in the center. Do not cut out just the stamp itself.

MATERIALS AND TOOLS NEEDED

A list of the materials and tools required in stamp-collecting appears below. What these are, and how to use them, will be discussed in the following paragraphs.

Materials
Album
Catalogue
Hinges and/or shields
Benzine
Blotters

Tools
Tweezers
Perforation gauge
Medicine dropper
Black tray

KINDS OF ALBUMS

An album is essential if stamps are to be kept in good condition. There are many kinds on the market. A loose-leaf type of album is the most practical because it allows for continuous expansion without transferring and rehandling of the stamps. This tends to keep them in a better condition. Many individuals make their own loose-leaf albums. This can be done by lining off the pages and lettering in the name, date, and catalogue number of the issues.

USING THE CATALOGUE

The mention of the word "catalogue" brings up the next point, the stamp catalogue. The catalogue describes every stamp in existence, and also gives its price and a picture of it. Such a book is very valuable because it helps you to identify and evaluate your stamps. Scott and Gibbons are among the companies that put out stamp catalogues.

HOW TO USE HINGES

Another precaution must be taken in the care of unused stamps. The gummed back should not be soaked off or even marred. Therefore, hinges to mount stamps are another essential too. Fold the hinge so that as small a surface as possi-

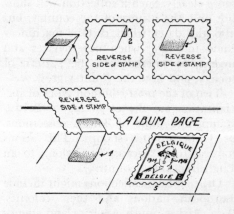

ble will be hinged to the back of the stamp and the remainder used to stick to the album.

CELLOPHANE TO PROTECT YOUR STAMPS

In recent years, cellophane and acetate products have been introduced. Stamps may be enclosed in cellophane and hinged to the album. This eliminates

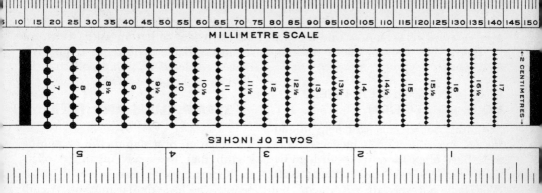

Showing a standard gauge used to measure stamp perforations. Millimetre and inch scales included.

sticking the hinge to the stamp itself, and provides a shield for the stamp. Two precautions must be observed: (1) Leave sides or top open in order that air may reach the stamps—this prevents deterioration. (2) Investigate the possibility that these products will discolor stamps or cause them to deteriorate. A stamp company or an advanced collector could probably give advice about the use of these new products.

HOW TO HANDLE STAMPS

For the proper handling of stamps you need a pair of blunt-nosed tweezers. If you fail to use them, the oil and moisture found on your hands may leave marks on the stamps. Blunt-nosed tweezers also prevent stamps from being marked or torn while being handled.

TOOLS FOR STAMP IDENTIFICATION

Two tools necessary for stamp identification are: (1) a gauge to measure the perforations; (2) a black tray used for discovery of watermarks. In addition to the black tray you need a dropper and some benzine to bring out the watermarks, as already explained.

HOW TO DEVELOP AND ENLARGE A COLLECTION

The method by which you develop your collection depends upon how far you have progressed. Therefore, various ways and means of enlarging a collection will be discussed so that you may choose whichever meets your needs.

BUYING STAMPS IN QUANTITY

If you are just starting a collection, probably the most economical approach would be to buy large lots of stamps. There are several types of mixtures, titled "United States Only," "Foreign," "High or Low Values," "Late 19th Century," or "Early 20th Century" and so on. Other examples are: Bank Mixtures, which contain stamps of high denominations, and Mission Mixtures, which usually contain stamps of foreign countries.

Another source that a beginner is likely to use is variety packets of different stamps. They are obtainable in all sizes, ranging from 15 to 100, 250, 500 stamps, etc., to a packet. A buyer of such a lot receives many stamps for a comparatively small sum.

From the standpoint of economy it is best to buy in large lots. If you use this method, you are bound to find yourself with many duplicates. However, almost everyone likes to trade or sell. You may increase the number of different stamps in your collection by trading with other stamp collectors. The sale of these duplicates will offset part of the initial expenditure.

It is a good idea to save every stamp. That is, of course, everything except the more common denominations of the present issue. Even then it would be well to keep the extra fine copies of all stamps that come into your possession. These may be given to beginners who are just starting a collection and need the common stamps.

ACQUAINTANCES CAN HELP YOUR COLLECTION

Another source that will help in adding to your collection is business associates. They often have stamps of high denominations on packages, and precancels. (You may not specialize in them, but they can be used in trade or sold to buyers in the stamp business.)

Friends and relatives can also be helpful in building up your collection. When you write to them, ask them to save the stamps you use, and, for your part, never send a letter with an ordinary stamp for postage. It is just as easy to buy commemorative stamps in the post office as it is to ask for a stamp and receive the common issue. Likewise, try to have friends and relatives use these stamps when writing letters or mailing packages to you. In a short space of time all these methods will bring in many duplicates which can be traded.

Stamps make excellent birthday gifts, since they can be purchased at various prices. A stamp here and there, received as a gift, slowly but surely adds to the collection.

AUCTIONS AND TRADERS

Another possible source of stamps might be an auction or an out-of-the-way antique trader. Old papers and letters often go up for sale. It is possible that they may be sold as old paper rather than for the value of the stamps that lie within the bundle. (I once picked up an old dresser for twenty-five cents. It had little value as a dresser, but in one of the drawers were some old newspapers. In olden days newspaper stamps were issued for use of mailing newspapers. This dresser contained eighty-five dollars worth of newspaper stamps.)

Finally, United States stamps may be purchased at face value through the Phil-atelic Agency, Washington, D. C., which will provide collectors with a list of stamps available upon request. This is a service rendered to stamp collectors by the United States Post Office.

STAMP CLUBS AND THEIR VALUE

Formation of a stamp club or joining a club that is already organized offers an opportunity to associate with other people who have similar interests. A club may subscribe to several magazines, acquire books and catalogues for the use of its members which would be too costly for an individual. Each member may call attention to articles written about stamps in magazines and newspapers which have been overlooked by other collectors.

THE CLUB AS A CLEARING HOUSE

The club can act as a clearing house in many ways. Individuals may pass on suggestions for improving collections, and help each other indentify stamps. Information on new stamps may be discussed and made available to all members. Another way in which a club can act as a clearing house is through the trading of stamps. Individual club members usually have different fields of specialization. Trading, creating a larger turnover, should then become fun, since all are not working toward the same goal.

DISPLAYING YOUR COLLECTION

A stamp club may hold exhibits, at which time everyone has an opportunity to display his collection. Then one realizes how much collections vary. In fact, variety is one of the great features of stamp collecting.

It is well to mention here that there are national and international stamp exhibits annually. The Chicago Philatelic Society, the Essex Stamp Club of Newark, the Garfield-Perry Stamp Club of Cleveland, the Collectors Club of San Francisco, and the Tulsa Stamp Club of Oklahoma are but a few of the sponsors of national stamp exhibits.

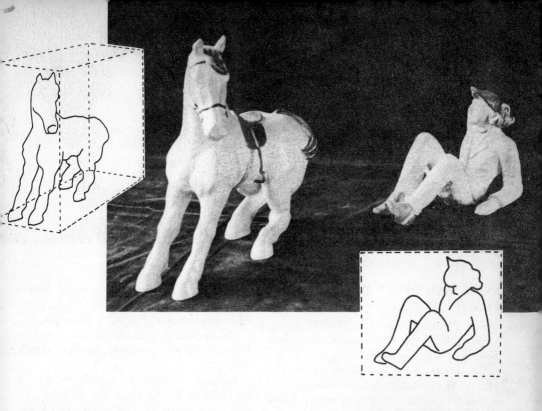

THE ART OF SOAP SCULPTURE

There is in most of us a fundamental urge to express ourselves through the creative arts. From earliest times self-expression through the art of sculpture has been attainable by only a few. The usual materials — marble, bronze and stone—were expensive to obtain and required the use of costly tools.

The introduction of white soap as a medium for carving, has, however, provided a simple and inexpensive way to gratify the "creative urge." The ease with which first carvings are created frequently spurs the ambition of the beginner to attempt even greater feats of achievement.

There are many interesting soaps on the market suitable for carving. However, large cakes of white all-purpose laundry soap are probably the most satisfactory because of their size and inexpensiveness. Some people prefer to carve from soap already colored. For instance, small figures carved from light green soap are effective and resemble jade. However, color may be added to white soap after the figures are carved. Almost any paint will do except the ones that have a water base; waterproof ink will likewise give pleasing results.

SUBJECTS FOR SOAP SCULPTURE

The following are some interesting subjects. Many others will suggest themselves.

Models of planes, ships, and small boats; figures of national type (a Dutch boy or girl, or a Chinese boy in national dress), or of occupational types (a sailor, a fireman, a cowboy) make interesting collections. Also, models of the flags of the United Nations. Carvings of the Liberty Bell, a Minuteman, Independence Hall, Washington, etc., are also attractive.

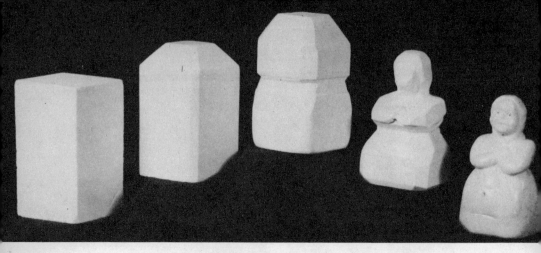

DETAILS SHOWING STEPS IN MAKING A WOMAN

HOLIDAYS OFFER INTERESTING POSSIBILITIES

For Thanksgiving Day. Models of turkeys, the Pilgrims and Indians, Plymouth Rock and the Mayflower.

For Hallowe'en. Pumpkins, black cats and witches riding on broomsticks.

For Christmas. Tree ornaments, Santa Claus, party favors, gifts.

For Easter. Eggs, rabbits and baby chicks.

For Lincoln's Birthday. The traditional log cabin, the fireplace before which Lincoln studied, and carvings of the Great Emancipator himself.

For Washington's Birthday. The cherry tree and axe, Washington's sword, his hat, etc.

A zoo, circus, barnyard or aquarium may also be made.

HISTORICAL AND ART SUBJECTS

If you are interested in going back to history for your subject matter, here are a few suggestions:

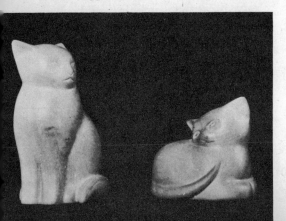

Egyptian. Jewelry, sarcophagi, hieroglyphic figures, statuary, bas-relief figures of votive images, Egyptian columns.

Greek. Coins, athletic figures, the Parthenon, Greek costume figures, Greek columns.

Roman. A basilica, the Pantheon, a caryatid, a Roman coin, a Roman column, a Roman arch, Roman brickwork, a model aqueduct, a model villa, the Colosseum.

Primitive Sculpture. Mask, totem poles, figures of gods, war clubs, sailing vessels, helmets, swords, shields, bowls, vases.

Modern Sculpture. Abstract, or conventionalized figures, free expression carving, models for marionette or puppet heads, etc.

OTHER IDEAS

Soap sculpture provides ideal entertainment and a simple, inexpensive creative activity.

For Children of All Ages. Soap carving contests for parties, classes; school or inter-school competitions; summer camp handicraft projects. Modeling in soap involves no waste, because shavings and carvings too can all be used.

For Hobbyists. Carvings for gifts, for home decoration, for table pieces and party souvenirs.

A SIMPLE CARVING PROJECT
The cat and mouse require no pattern. Use one-half cake of soap for each figure.

Soap sculpture is good therapy for convalescents and invalids. It provides relaxation and pastime for many otherwise tedious hours—with a minimum of equipment and inconvenience.

Other Uses. Soap sculpture has been widely utilized by professional designers for models of jewelry, buildings, landscape gardens, medals, plaques, anatomical and dental models, etc.

Soap may be also used to make blocks for printing posters, scarfs, handkerchiefs, table linens, book plates, greeting cards, etc.

WORKING HINTS

TOOLS

Knife, orange stick or cuticle stick, pencil, paper, pattern to be carved.

PREPARING THE SOAP

Scrape soap from one side of the cake, removing only enough to reveal a smooth, even surface.

Allow the soap to dry for about an hour before tracing the pattern.

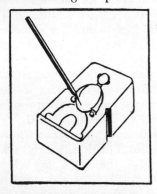

TRACING THE PATTERN

Blacken a sheet of paper by rubbing with a soft pencil. Place this, penciled side down, on the soap. Place the pattern over this, and trace with a pencil to obtain an image on the soap.

ROUGHING OUT DESIGN

In roughing out the design, care must be taken to cut away in small pieces or slices. Soap has a tendency to break if cut in large chunks.

JOINING A SCULPTURE TO A BASE

Cut a trench in both model and base, and stick a piece of toothpick in each with ends projecting. Next heat a piece of soap in a shallow pan of water. When the part near the heat reaches the consistency of jelly, fill the two trenches with the soap-jelly and press the two pieces together.

JOINING TWO CAKES

Scrape down the sides that are to be joined. Place smooth, scraped sides into a shallow pan of water over slow heat. Insert toothpicks where they will not interfere with carving. After thirty minutes, press the cakes together. Carving should not be started for another day.

POLISHING

Allow the model to dry for a day or two before starting to polish. Rub carefully all over with a paper napkin, proceeding cautiously so that projections or corners are not broken off. Next rub gently with the finger tips or the palm of the hand.

PROGRESSIVE STEPS IN SOAP CARVING

CARVING AN EAGLE

1. Take the cake of soap and with the knife cut off the raised edges and scrape off the lettering. This will give you a beautiful flat white surface on which to place the tracing of your design. Remember in all soap carvings that the chips are still soap and should be used.

2. Make a full size front view drawing of the eagle. Place a sheet of *pencil* car-

CARVING AN EAGLE

bon paper on the soap and your drawing on top of it, being careful to place the drawing so that it is in the proper position on the soap. It is sometimes wise also to place a tracing of the back view of the object on the opposite side of the soap, but if the front outline is followed carefully this is not necessary.

3. Holding the knife very much as if you were peeling a potato, cut out the outline of the soap about 3/16 of an inch away from the tracing, to allow for finer work later. When you have done this you will discover that already you have started a real piece of sculpture which is "beginning to take shape."

4. Caution: In roughing out the design, care must be taken to cut away in small pieces or slices. Soap has a tendency to break if cut in large chunks.

5. Holding the soap in such a position as to look down on the top of it, outline the top view of the head and cut straight down all around the outline to a depth of a little over ½ inch. You now have the main mass of the head blocked out.

Now outline the wings on the front, then on the side; cut in on the front until you meet the line on the side. Remove surplus soap.

Outline a V shaped wedge in the center of the eagle about ⅔ of the way down to note separation of the legs. Cut out the wedge about ¼ inch deep.

Outline the legs and claws, cutting away the excess soap.

Now, holding the cake of soap with the side toward you, outline the general profile of the piece from front to back. Note that it is narrowest at the head and thickest in through the chest. When you have removed the surplus soap, you will have the figure all blocked out.

6. Now round the eagle out by cutting around the corners. As you work, keep turning the soap around, always keeping the general shape of the piece in mind. Watch your high points and low points. The high points are those that jut out farthest from the surface of the soap. The low points are those farther in. On the eagle the high points are the claws and the chest in front, the wings on the sides and the tail in back. Carve from the highest point to the lowest. Proceed slowly to shape your model, observing if the planes and forms are correct. When you feel that the piece is about finished, you can smooth the rough surfaces with the edge of the knife. The details such as the eyes, the line of the beak, the claws and feathers can be marked in with the orangewood stick and the tip of the knife.

COLORING
You can add color to your carvings with waterproof ink.

Remove excess soap to within ¼" of line.

Round the figures, cut out arms, add hair, hands, shoes.

Smooth the figure, add small details. Polish by rubbing.

SQUAW AND PAPOOSE
Trace this drawing to obtain a pattern for soap carving.

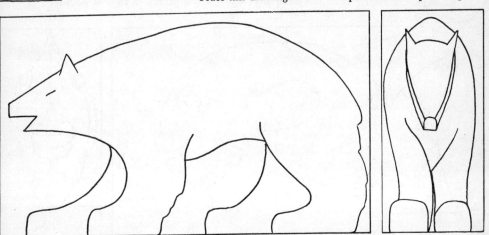

POLAR BEAR
Trace this drawing to obtain a pattern for soap carving.

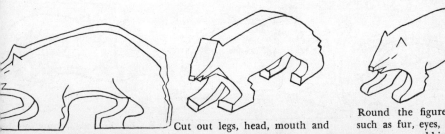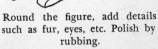

Cut out to within ¼" of line.

Cut out legs, head, mouth and ears.

Round the figure, add details such as fur, eyes, etc. Polish by rubbing.

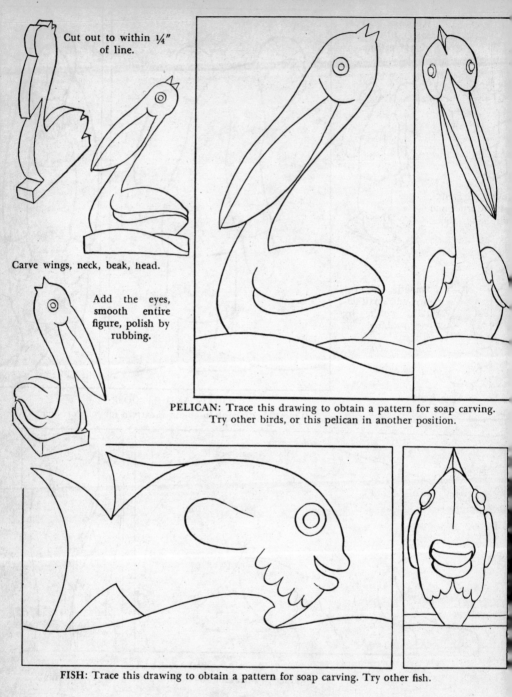

Cut out to within ¼" of line.

Carve wings, neck, beak, head.

Add the eyes, smooth entire figure, polish by rubbing.

PELICAN: Trace this drawing to obtain a pattern for soap carving. Try other birds, or this pelican in another position.

FISH: Trace this drawing to obtain a pattern for soap carving. Try other fish.

Cut out to within ¼" of line.

Cut out tail, fins, wave, mouth, eyes.

Round the body, streamline the tail, add details such as scales. Polish by rubbing.

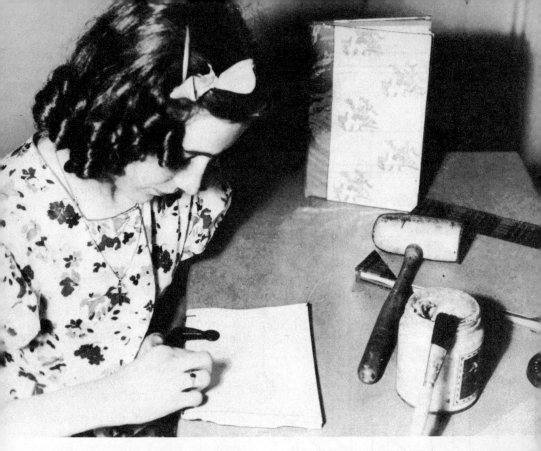

BOOK BINDING MADE EASY

Book binding is one of the oldest and most helpful of the crafts. It was brought to high perfection in the monasteries and many a monk spent a lifetime binding a single volume. Early writings were done on scrolls of parchment which were rolled when not in use. The frequent winding and unwinding weakened them and the parchment became cracked and torn. To prevent this, folio binding was devised. The scrolls were divided into large pages and laid on a board. Another board was placed on top and the edges tied together with a leather thong to hold the manuscript in place. This is the simplest form of book binding.

The basic techniques described in this chapter for binding magazines in a single volume may be used for making a scrapbook or rebinding a book as well. Nearly everyone owns a book that has outlived its cover. If it needs a new cover you might replace it with leather or marbleized paper. You will find directions for decorating. the leather in the Leather Craft chapter, and for making the paper in the following chapter on Paper Decorating and Portfolio Making.

Magazines of any consequence increase in value with time, so binding them is well worth while for interest and reference and perhaps for future barter. Very little is required in the way of materials and equipment, and once you have embarked on the enterprise you will want to store your magazines away each year in bound volumes.

EQUIPMENT

For the amateur bookbinder there are some specialized pieces of equipment which will be very useful although not all

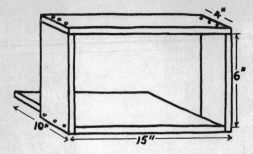

Fig. 1. Sewing frame.

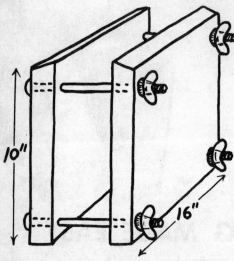

Fig. 2. Glue press and sawing clamp. Note beveled ends on one side of press.

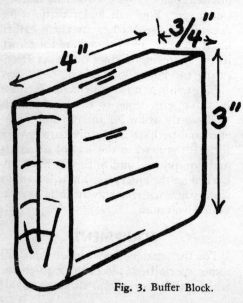

Fig. 3. Buffer Block.

of them are absolutely necessary. If the reader is in earnest about book binding he should either procure these articles from a bookbinder's supply house or make them. With the exception of a vise, all the special equipment we shall describe is easily made. The vise is the type found on a carpenter's work bench which should preferably have flat wooden sides capable of holding an object 12 inches long and 10 inches deep. The next piece of equipment is a sewing frame. An adjustable sewing frame may be bought or a simple one made from four boards as shown in the illustration (Fig. 1).

A gluing press is a great convenience although not absolutely necessary, provided the worker has access to a vise. This is also true of a sawing clamp. Figure 2 shows a single press which may serve for both the gluing press and sawing clamp, the use of which will be described later.

TOOLS

In addition to this equipment the worker should equip himself with a small carpenter's back saw, a straight awl, a buffer block (Fig. 3), a 2-inch carpenter's chisel, a flatheaded shoemaker's hammer, a pointed knife for cutting and scraping, a bone paper folder, two or three paper covered bricks to act as weights, a pair of shears, some 1 inch bristle paste brushes, some large bookbinder's needles and a thimble.

MATERIALS

Having the equipment and the tools, one now considers the materials for book binding. They consist of binder's boards (heavy cardboards used to reinforce book covers); covering materials such as leather, imitation leather, colored paper, bookbinder's buckram or any similar substance you wish to use for the cover; cloth tape about ¾ inch wide; decorative lining paper and plain white paper suitable for end sheets; plenty of torn pieces of newspaper to use as paste papers; pieces of wax paper with which to interleave the book during all gluing and pasting operations to prevent parts sticking together; paste rags; thick cord such as butchers use for tying meat; bookbinder's linen thread or some other strong white linen thread; transparent mending tape; coarse and fine sandpaper; ink eraser and art gum eraser; crash which can be bought from the bookbinder's supply houses under the name of super; strong muslin; a can of vegetable glue and a jar of photo paste. This completes the list of materials necessary both for repairing old books and for binding new ones.

PREPARATION

The magazine we shall use for demonstration is the *National Geographic*. The reader will find that this magazine has an ordinary paper cover glued on the back of the contents which can easily be torn off. The sections of the contents are stapled together with two staples, the ends of which can be turned up and the staples removed completely (Fig. 4). Advertisements form the several end sections which most bookbinders remove and discard. This leaves the sections that make up the contents or reading matter, generally ten in number. A section in any book is a single sheet of folded paper folded in a sequence of printed sheets and cut along three edges to the book size.

BOOK MAKE UP

A section is caused by the fact that in printing, paper is put on the book presses in standard sizes according to the ultimate size of the book and the capacity of the press. These are generally quite large sheets which after printing are folded in half, then they are folded in half again, etc., until the final multi-folded sheet is approximately the size of the page. The front, top and bottom of this folded sheet are then trimmed, making a section, the back of which is formed by the different folds of paper being one inside the other.

The reader can see that for the purpose of making the reading matter come out straight after all this folding the printer

places type upside down and every which way so that when the large sheet is printed on both sides and then folded, the type appears right side up and reads consecutively from page to page.

The number of leaves to a section are generally 2, 4, 8, 12 or 16. In printed pages this makes either 4, 8, 16, 24 or 32.

The reader has probably opened books which have been untrimmed, the leaves of which had to be separated with a paper cutter. Examining one of these books will demonstrate to the reader how the printer approaches his problem.

END SHEETS

Having removed the cover and the advertising of the magazine in question and removed the staples which bind the section together, we next scrape the glue and paper fragments from the back of the sections. Now take four pieces of plain or

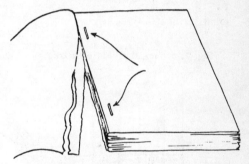

Fig. 4. Tear off paper cover. Scrape back clean. Remove staples shown by arrows.

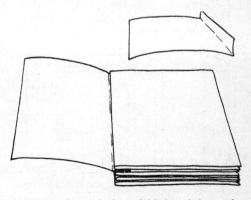

Fig. 5. An end sheet folded and inserted between first and second sections.

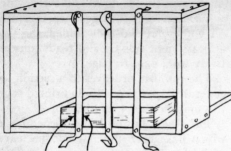

Fig. 6. Sections in sewing. Frame ready for marking at arrows.

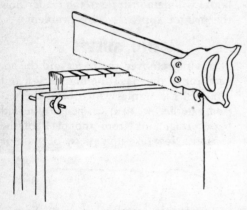

Fig. 7. Sawing the back at markings.

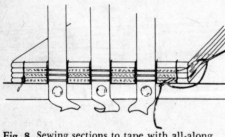

Fig. 8. Sewing sections to tape with all-along stitch. Kettle stitching at end.

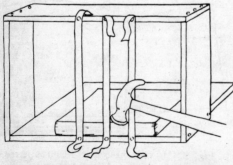

Fig. 9. Knocking down sections after sewing.

fancy paper exactly the length of a page but a half inch wider, fold this half inch flap and paste two pieces by this flap between the first and second sections (Fig. 5) using photo paste, turn the sections over and repeat this on the other side. This operation gives the prospective book two end sheets at both front and back.

If the paper is decorated, the decorated sides should face each other, since later on they will become the lining papers at each end of the book.

The magazine in question is generally bound in volumes of six numbers. Whether you are binding one number or six numbers into a volume, you use only four end sheets.

HOW TO SEW

Now lay the sections on the sewing frame. Square them up nicely and place a weight on top. Thumbtack three or four pieces of tape at intervals as shown in the illustration (Fig. 6) and with a ruler and pencil place a pencil mark on the back of the section directly outside of each piece of tape.

Remove the sections from the sewing clamp, taking care that you do not misalign them. Place the sections in the sewing frame and hold this in the vise, or else the sections may be placed between two heavy boards and held in the vise, and with the back saw make a one-sixteenth inch deep cut through the back of the sections where the pencil marks are. Then make an additional saw cut one-half inch from each end of the book (Fig. 7). Remove the sections from the vise and sawing clamp and place them front section down on the table beside the sewing frame.

We are now ready to sew the sections to the tape. This is accomplished by making stitches as shown in the illustration (Fig. 8). Take one section at a time. Sew this in place and then take the next section to sew on. Each time the reader must make sure that the sections are being sewn in sequence.

The simple method of sewing shown in

the illustration is called "all along." The method of turning the end stitches to return is called "kettle stitching." Kettle stitching should be done after each new section is added to the book. It holds the sections together and strengthens the ends of the book. The kettle stitching cannot be started until three sections have been sewn, as illustrated.

KNOCKING DOWN

After each section has been sewn in place it should be tamped down gently with the hammer at the back, on both sides of the tapes. This levels out the sections and prevents the book from being very much wider at the back where it is sewn than it is at the front where the leaves open (Fig. 9). Knocking down, as this is called, is particularly necessary when binding thick books.

After sewing, knocking down and finishing off the thread with a kettle stitch, remove the contents of the book from the sewing frame. Leave two or more inches of the tapes protruding on each side of the back. This is necessary to attach the contents to the cover. These projections are known as slips.

HOW TO GLUE

To strengthen the book, open it to where the first and second sections meet and, laying paste papers on the open pages so that only a quarter of an inch of the book near the backing shows, coat this quarter of an inch of exposed sections with photo paste. While coating, lay the first section on another book to keep the pages level (Fig. 10). Remove the paste papers and put a single piece of wax paper in their place. Close the book and put a weight on top. Allow this to dry. When the book is opened wide this prevents the end sections from coming loose and exposing the sewing and inside of the backing. It is only necessary to do this with the two end sections on each side of a book.

The sections should now be placed in a gluing press, back up, between two

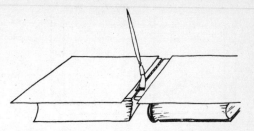

Fig. 10. Pasting first and second sections.

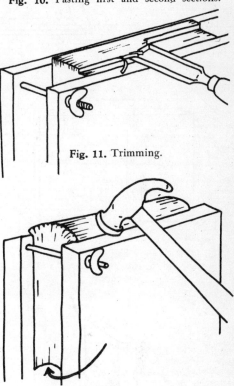

Fig. 11. Trimming.

Fig. 12. Rounding out back. Press up with fingers from below (see arrow).

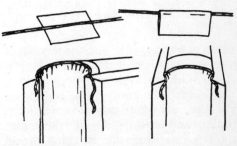

Fig. 13. Making and attaching headbands.

[111]

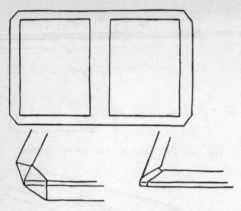

Fig. 14. A full binding and corner fold.

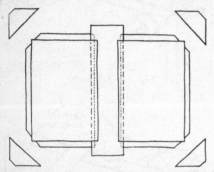

Fig. 15. Parts for a half binding. Glue backing strip to boards first. Cover and add corners.

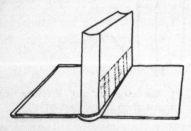

Fig. 16. Recasing, showing one end sheet glued in, other end sheet against contents exposing super-glued-over slips.

pieces of wax paper so that the wax paper overlaps the edges of the press to keep it clean. With vegetable glue applied sparingly, brush the entire back, going over the slips only where they are sewn to the sections and brushing the glue down into the saw cuts where the stitching thread goes through. Before going into this oper-

ation the sections should be perfectly aligned.

When vegetable glue has dried thoroughly, remove the sections from the gluing press and replace them so that the front of the section protrudes slightly from the gluing press. By slightly we mean a scant sixteenth of an inch.

TRIMMING

We are now going to trim the sections so that the edges are even and it is necessary that the sections be perfectly aligned at the back. There is a standard device used by professional bookbinders called a plow which the reader should investigate; most amateurs use the chisel we shall employ.

Take the two-inch carpenter's chisel and, holding the blade flat against the flat upper edge of the gluing press, trim the sections until they present an absolutely even appearance flush with the edge of the board (Fig. 11). Repeat this with the two sides which represent the top and bottom of the book.

Because of the fact that the book is thicker where it is sewn, we advise placing some heavy layers of cloth on each side of the sections before you clamp them in the gluing press preparatory to trimming. These thicknesses of cloth, preferably something in the nature of a blanket, will take up the unevenness in thickness between the front and back of the book. When you are cutting or trimming both ends of the book, cut from the backing toward the open edge.

SHAPING

After trimming, remove the sections from the gluing press and moisten the entire back slightly to soften the glue. This will take about fifteen minutes. Replace the sections loosely in the gluing press, using it bevelled side up. With the hammer round the sections out symmetrically by tamping the end sections down. This will give a convex appearance to the back of the book (Fig. 12).

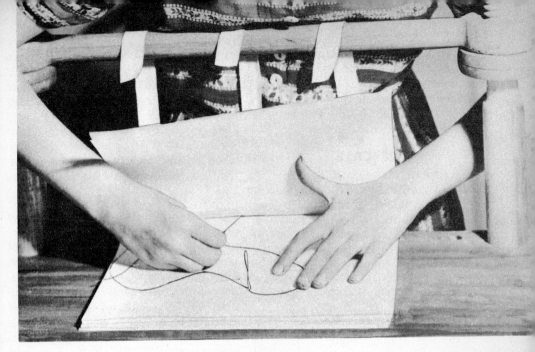

STITCHING
Showing the correct use of a stitching frame.

HEADBANDS

Headbands may be placed on immediately following this operation. Headbands are pieces of cord that have been glued in a folded piece of buckram. The method of making these and gluing them in place is apparent from the illustration (Fig. 13). Headbands add considerably to the wearing quality of a book. Vegetable glue should be used exclusively for this purpose.

THE SUPER

While the book is still in the clamp from tamping the back in place and placing the headbands, glue a piece of crash over the entire back within one-half inch of each end. Two to three inches of this crash should be allowed to overlap on each side. This overlap should later be glued down to the end sheets with the tapes or slips, as they are called, glued in between the crash and the end sheets. The crash is called the super.

FINE BOOKBINDING
A combination leather and decorated paper binding.

Wipe off all the excess vegetable glue and, placing a piece of wax paper on both sides of the book, place in the gluing press to maintain the shape of the book until the glue is dry. The book is now ready for the cover or case.

THE CASE

It is now necessary for us to make the case from the binder's boards and covering material. The boards should be cut one-quarter of an inch longer and one-eighth inch wider than the leaves of the book. This will permit a lap of the board on the top and bottom of the book of an eighth-inch and on the front where the book opens of an eighth-inch. At the back the board is kept almost flush with the leaves.

Sometimes a single piece of material is used to cover the entire case, as shown in the illustration (Fig. 14). This is termed a full binding. Other times, each board may be covered separately and then a separate strip used for the backing, as shown in the illustration (Fig. 15). The name of this style is a half binding In this instance, the corners are generally covered with the same material that is used for the backing strip.

FULL BINDING

We shall discuss the first method of covering the entire book with one piece of material. Lay the boards that have been cut to a suitable size on the backing material as shown. The corners of this material should be trimmed and the size of the material should be such that three-fourths of an inch can overlap the board. The distance between the two boards should be gauged by the width of the back of the book, which is held in place until the two boards are located. Allow room for closing the book.

The covering and folding operations while making the case should be done, as far as possible, with the contents inside the case. To make sure the contents are kept clean during these operations, we advise covering with a piece of wax paper. Another book approximately the same thickness on which to rest one side of the cover should be used while you are covering the boards with the covering material.

After you have overlapped the covering material on the board, score the cover where it will hinge in opening and closing. Use the bone folder for this purpose.

HOW TO RECASE

The next step is to place the contents in the case. Lay a piece of wax paper between the first and second end sheets of the contents and coat over the end sheet, super and tape thoroughly with vegetable glue. Place one side of the cover in place, shifting it around with the fingers until it is properly centered. Lay this side down, turn the contents over on it, exposing the other side of the case, and repeat the operation. The book should be carefully centered, the back tamped evenly and the grooves gone over with the bone paper folder before clamping in the glue press to dry.

If many books are finished in this manner they may be stacked with their backs alternating and the paper covered bricks used on top as weights. The books should be left to dry over night.

Upon opening the books for the first time, do so gently. Let them wear into flexibility gradually instead of straining the freshly glued material. New books are always stiff.

TITLING

Any necessary titles or identification marks may now be lettered on the cover or back with drawing inks, preferably in black or carmine. If the book cover is dark and library identification numbers are desired, paint white tempera in the area letters are to occupy before applying ink. Labels made in this way can be protected with white damar varnish.

The reader should now have a volume that will give him joy for a good number of years, both because of its contents and because of the creative effort he has put into it.

PAPER DECORATING and
PORTFOLIO MAKING

PAPER DECORATING

Decorating paper as covering material for portfolios, books, boxes and other similar purposes is a creative and useful craft. The accompanying illustrations show quite a few examples of this type of paper decoration. It is wise for you to equip yourself with various grades and textures of paper beforehand. Procure some pieces of tracing paper, tissue paper, bond paper, both soft and hard finished drawing paper, charcoal paper, kraft paper, oatmeal paper and any other type to which you may have ready access. And, of course, you will require waterproof ink.

BUTTERFLY METHOD

The simplest method of decoration is the butterfly method. In this type of decoration a piece of paper such as that used for school crayon work is folded down the center. A few drops of waterproof ink, in any color desired, are then placed in this fold. The paper is laid on the table, the two halves on each side of the fold brought together and the fingers pressed on the outside of the paper to move the ink around between the facing leaves. Work the fingers from the center of the fold towards the outer edges of the paper, open the paper again with a rapid motion while it is still wet and pin the

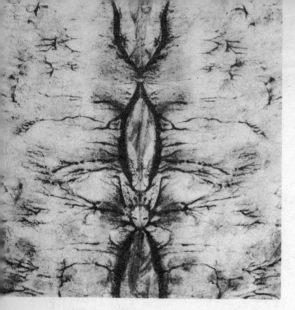

BUTTERFLY DECORATION

corners down on newspapers so that it may dry. The result will be something similar to that illustrated. You never get the same result twice. Variations of this can be made with one or more colors or by thickening the ink with a little bit of office paste.

CRACKLE

A second method of making a cover paper is to take a piece of soft paper and crumple it very thoroughly in the hand. Stretch it out again and wrinkle it again several different times. Now smooth it out on the table and paint one side in a light color of waterproof ink such as yellow or leaf green. Allow this to become damp dry, turn the paper over and paint a darker color on the other side. The darker color will seep through the

cracks in the paper and give a mottled effect on the side on which the lighter color has been painted. This, of course, is the finished side which you will use outermost in your book covers.

COLOR

There are very interesting color possibilities in both analogous and contrasting harmonies to be brought out by this work. For instance, if blue is used with the yellow paper, where the blue soaks through strongly it will appear as blue green. Where it does not soak through so strongly it will appear as a lighter green. A variety of effects are obtainable with this type of work, depending on the texture of the paper, the amount it has been crackled and how wet or dry the first color is before the second color is applied on the back. Experiments will prove interesting.

WATER-PRINTING

A third manner in which handsome cover papers can be made is also illustrated. This method is called water-printing and has been done on both paper and textiles in various media such as oil color as well as in waterproof inks.

To get this result, inks are mixed either with linseed oil, such as the purified linseed oil bought in artist materials stores, or Japan dryer. Mix half ink and half of whichever liquid you wish to use. Place them both in a small bottle and shake thoroughly. You must have a different bottle for every color of ink you wish to use. While the solution is thoroughly shaken up, drop a few drops onto a dishpan full of water.

You may use one color at a time or several colors, depending on the effect that you wish to get. Only experiment will determine this to your complete satisfaction.

The heavy part of the material sprinkled on the water will sink to the bottom, leaving a light film of color on the top. This can be made into fantastic

CRACKLE DECORATION

cloud-like effects by stirring with match sticks or bits of paper and blowing on the water.

When the swirled color looks interesting, drop a piece of paper onto the surface of the water quickly. Pick it up immediately before it sinks into the water and lay it on its back on spread out newspapers. Pin down the edges to prevent curling.

CRACKLE AND DRIP

The crackle-and-drip method of making cover papers is one of the most fascinating of all. The work can be done on any paper, but architect's tracing paper is the most suitable because it is easily crackled and has a hard surface which gives a clean cut effect.

Take a sheet slightly larger than the portfolio or whatever object you ultimately wish to cover with the paper. Wrinkle the paper very thoroughly in your hand, straightening it out and wrinkling it again several times until all the wrinkles seem to be uniform. Then flatten it out on a desk or table and sprinkle it as you would clothes, allowing drops of water to be speckled all over it. Next take a blotting paper and remove the excess water.

Now, while the paper is still moist, let fall on it drops of waterproof ink in either black or colors, allowing plenty of space in between each drop. The moisture of the paper will invite the ink to run down the cracks, giving a marbleized effect.

You can put only one color on at a time, allow this to dry, re-moisten the paper and then use a second color, or you can use several colors together while the paper is wet the first time. Each process gives a slightly different effect.

SPLASH TONE

This effect is obtained by pinning the paper down, wetting it shiny wet with clear water and then letting drops of waterproof ink fall on it from a height.

SPLASH TONE

CRACKLE AND DRIP

The drops splash and seep into interesting patterns.

MOUNTING

When papers made by the previously outlined methods are used for practical purposes it is likely that the user will want to protect them in some way. This is best done by giving them a coat of white shellac. If the papers are used on a book cover or portfolio, they should be mounted in place before shellacking. Vegetable glue or drawing-board paste are the best substances possible for this mounting.

It is well to use thin papers when the papers are intended for envelope lining or first sheets in book binding and similar purposes. Heavy papers are best for coverings.

THINGS TO DECORATE

Once you have learned how to decorate paper in interesting colors and design, you will want to put this skill to practical use. There are a number of projects you will want to make for the home that are

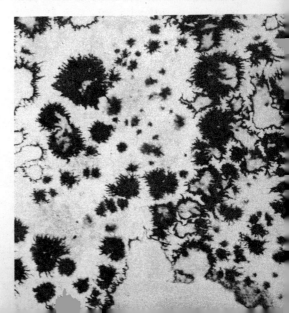

too large to cover with a single sheet of paper, such as a screen, waste basket, card-table top, coffee table, etc. This can be overcome by making several sheets in the same mixture of paints or inks so that each sheet is decorated in the same colors. Usually, the same colors and designs will be found on the outer edges also. By matching them, you may be surprised to find some interesting new motifs.

There are many useful projects to be made from one sheet of decorated paper. To be specific, cardboard boxes covered with marble paper make interesting cigarette or letter boxes. An oatmeal box covered with bright paper will become a holder for knitting if a heavy card is added for a handle. Decorated papers are also used for book binding, note book covers, table mats for parties, utility boxes for wardrobes, etc.

HOW TO MAKE A PORTFOLIO

One of the most useful projects that can be made from a sheet of decorated paper and a piece of heavy cardboard is a portfolio. The one described here is of medium size. If you are making one large enough to hold sketches or artists' papers, just change the dimensions and follow the same instructions.

MATERIALS NEEDED

Two stiff cardboards (binders board) 17 by 22 inches. One strip of unbleached muslin 7 by 45 inches. Two sheets of fancy paper decorated with ink, each 18 by 24 inches. One can of vegetable glue. One stiff brush, 2 inches wide, for spreading glue. Two pieces of leather or cloth for corners, size 5 by 5 inches. One piece of same material for backing, 5 by 25 inches. One 60-inch length of cloth tape. One sheet of lining paper, 21 by 36 inches.

SIZE

The size of the finished portfolio is first to be considered. The most useful sizes are as follows: (1) 11 by 14 inches, in which may be kept the standard 9 by 12-inch drawing papers and some slightly larger; (2) 17 by 22 inches, probably the most useful size (a half-sheet of Bristol or illustrator's board fits in this, which is generally 15 by 20 inches and known as plate size); (3) 20 by 26 inches, which size holds a standard sheet of charcoal paper, approximately 19 by 25 inches; (4) 23 by 31 inches, which will hold a sheet of show-card board, which is generally 22 by 28 inches; or a full sheet of Bristol board or illustrator's board approximately 20 by 30 inches.

The best material for the sides of the portfolio is binders board. If this is not procurable, news board or straw board runs a close second. The larger the portfolio the heavier should be the board to insure rigidity.

BACKING

Figure 1 shows the start of the portfolio making. We shall assume that this is to be a portfolio 17 by 22 inches in size. A strip of cloth 7 inches wide and 45 inches long is thumb-tacked on a board. This cloth may be any cheap material such as unbleached muslin. No matter what kind of material it is, it should be strong, since practically all portfolios are discarded after wear because the back has finally given way. The material should be dampened very slightly and then a coat of vegetable glue spread over it with a stiff bristle brush.

ASSEMBLING

We are now ready to place the 17 by 22 inch boards in the position they will occupy for the life of the portfolio. Make sure when this is done that points 1, 2, 5 and 6 are lined up with a straight edge, as are also points 3, 4, 7 and 8. The distance between points 2 and 5 must equal the distance between points 4 and 7. This distance, in this case 3 inches, is the extent to which the finished portfolio will be able to expand as more and more drawings are put into it. In a small portfolio it may be 2 inches or less; in a large portfolio it may be 4 inches or more. Three inches will do nicely for our purpose. Because the strip of cloth is 7 inches wide, this gives us a 2-inch overlap on each side, which margin insures the cloth having a good grip on each board.

Press the board firmly in place, remove the thumb tacks from the cloth and fold it down as shown at Fig. 2. Since the cloth is 45 inches long and the extreme length of the board is 22 inches, when the cloth is pasted down the center of the portfolio there will be a slight overlap.

COVERING

We are now ready to cover the portfolio with the cover paper. Cut two sheets of the decorated paper 18 by 24-inch size. Lay these sheets face down on the table before any vegetable glue is applied. Measure exactly where these cover papers will go and clip the corners to facilitate overlapping as shown in Fig. 2.

Now coat one sheet of the cover paper at a time with vegetable glue and paste it in place, making sure that all wrinkles are smoothed out and that the pasting is done evenly and neatly. Any excess vegetable glue may be wiped off with a damp cloth. The cover paper is then overlapped as shown at Fig. 3.

CORNERS

We are now ready for the backing-cover and corners. This material should be of cloth, imitation leather or real leather. The backing and corners receive the most wear.

For small portfolios gaily colored cretonne is a popular material. Imitation leather is dignified and will wear well.

For the backing and corner material let us presume we are using leather. Cut two squares of 5 inches each. Then cut each of these squares along the diagonal, which will give you four pieces, each the shape of a right angle triangle. Place these pieces under the corners of the portfolio as shown at Fig. 3. The method of overlapping and gluing these corners in place with vegetable glue is shown at Figs. 3A and 3B.

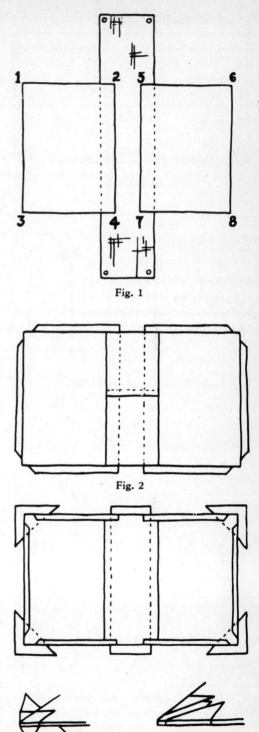

Fig. 1

Fig. 2

Figs. 3, 3A, 3B

[119]

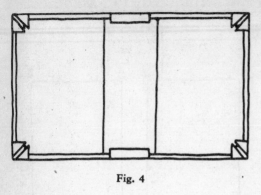

Fig. 4

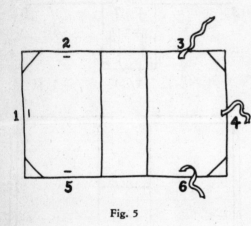

Fig. 5

pasted in place and the finished portfolio minus the tape and the lining paper will appear as at Fig. 4 when viewed from the inside.

TAPES FOR TYING

We are now ready for the tape and the lining paper, which finishes our product. Place the opened portfolio on a table with the outside up as shown in Fig. 5. Make six deep cuts with a penknife one inch in from the edges of the portfolio, as shown at 1, 2, 3, 4, 5 and 6 of Fig. 5. These cuts should be slightly longer than the tape to be used is wide.

Cut the tape 10 inches long and push it through the cuts with the penknife. Three inches of the tape is then securely fastened with vegetable glue to the inside of the portfolio. Considering that the cut for the tape is one inch in from the edge of the portfolio, when the portfolio is closed 6 inches of tape remain with which to tie it.

LINING

A suitable lining paper is then pasted over the entire interior of the portfolio, as shown at Fig. 6. This lining paper should be of a size so that a half inch of the cover paper, corners and backing, show as a border all around the lining paper when it is pasted into place. In the case of the portfolio we have just completed, the size of the lining paper would be 21 by 36 inches.

FINISHING

For extra wearing quality the entire outside of the portfolio may be given a thin coat of shellac. In some instances, where it is not desirable to change the texture of the backing and corner material by shellacking, it is better just to shellac the cover paper. This is done before the backing and corners are put on. Shellacking the cover paper will add greatly to its wearing qualities and also to the appearance of the portfolio. If each step has been done neatly we now have a handsome portfolio.

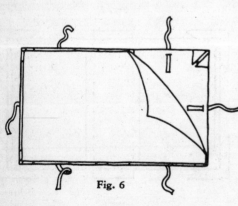

Fig. 6

When each corner is finished as at Fig. 3B, about an inch of the leather should be overlapped on the inside of the portfolio. The backing-cover, which is a strip 25 inches long by 5 inches wide, is then

FINGER PAINTING FOR THE FAMILY

Finger painting is a light-hearted, relaxing pastime which has a way of growing on one who dallies with it. It has many interesting possibilities, but it is sheer good fun to begin with.

Although you can really "make pictures" by this method—some of which you will doubtless view with pride and satisfaction—there is no long apprenticeship to serve before you acquire a technique. It is not just for those who have

had preliminary art training. Indeed, if you have done any drawing or painting, forget about them for the time being, and do not try to carry over into this new medium what you have previously learned. Even though you may think that you have no talent for design or composition, if you putter with finger paints for an hour or two you will feel your imagination stirring and ideas will begin to come.

PAINTS AND PAPER

Commercial finger paints are sold in all arts and crafts shops and they can be ordered from art supply houses. They come in a wide range of colors, which is an advantage if you have never learned to mix paints.

There is also a glazed paper on the market, especially prepared for finger painting. A beginner can use heavy wrapping paper for his first essays in this gay and happy-go-lucky art.

You will need a smooth, hard surface to work on—a table, or a tray or board.

The paints are soluble in water and however much you splash them about they will do no permanent damage, unless you are using a polished table for a working surface, in which case, cover it with oilcloth.

STEPS IN FINGER PAINTING

First, wet the paper all over with a sponge, then smooth it out on the table. Rub out all the wrinkles and air bubbles with the palm of your hand, working from the center to the edges.

Put on several daubs of paint, according to the color you are going to use to start with, and cover the entire surface of the paper by rubbing the color over it with your hand. You are now ready to paint.

It is a good plan to work with only one color at first, preferably a dark shade, so that the lines and markings will show more clearly. Work with your fingers, the ball of the thumb, the side of the palm, or even with your elbow. If you use the tips of the fingers, be careful not to scratch the surface of the paper with your nails. Do not "sit tight" while you work but let your body "go" with your hands.

You might, at first, limit yourself to manipulation, to get the feeling of how to handle your paint. Repeating one motif over and over, as in the accompanying paintings, is a good way to do this. Study your picture when it is finished and see if it reminds you of anything. Perhaps by making a few changes here and there

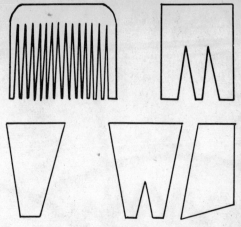

TOOLS FOR FINGER PAINTING

you might be able to find a subject or theme. If the lines run up or down, they could be worked into a clump of trees or a group of buildings. If you have a series of dots, touch them up to look like a string of beads, and then try to outline a dressing-table and a perfume bottle to make a composition.

The paints do not dry very quickly, so you can change your mind and rectify your mistakes. If you find you have made a mis-stroke, simply smooth it over and begin again. If the paint begins to dry, add a little water.

Later, when you have become adept and want to make finer lines than you can achieve with your fingers, use a pointed instrument, or a blunt needle. For a series of very small lines, try pressing a piece of frayed cloth into the paint. A comb made of cardboard is also a good tool. With it you can make swirls and all manner of odd designs, and you can repeat them more truly than you could with your fingers, if your design calls for repetition.

PAINTING A PICTURE

After you have practiced all the tricks of manipulation you can think of, it is time to try a picture. The first one may come more by luck than by taking thought. If you haven't an immediate inspiration, don't sit and ponder, just make an imprint on the paint surface with your palm, a leaf, or a spray, or perhaps a

MARINE SCENE

To make this picture—first try to get an interesting background effect by adding several different colors of finger paint to various points on the paper. Add a little water and blend them together by using the forearm. Next add the fish and starfish by simply pressing down on the spot with the arm which will remove the paint and leave a body of a fish. Add fins and tail with the forefinger. The starfish is made with the thumb. Superimpose another color onto the fish if you want to contrast them with the background. The seaweed is added last with the tips of the fingers and nails.

geometric object, and see what you can develop from it. Make some bold tracery with your fingers here and there at random and then try to pull them together with a central idea.

If you want to draw scenery and have perspective, to make certain objects look "near," draw the far-off things first, and gradually bring the other things toward you, making them larger.

Very soon you will want to paint in more than one color. The practice with finger paints is different than with water colors or oils. You do not mix your colors on a palette and apply them, you mix them right on your paper by putting one on top of the other. If several colors are used and repeatedly erased, they become muddy and lose their identity. The thing to do to prevent this is to cover the entire sheet with your over-all or predominant color and "mop up" spots where the other colors are to go. A face tissue or a paper towel comes in handy for this.

Perhaps you already have a picture in mind. You cannot sketch it on the paper first and then follow the outlines. So you make your sketch on a separate piece of paper and mark out areas on your "canvas," indicating where the different colors are to go. Then refer to your sketch when drawing in the outlines of your picture.

HOW TO DESIGN YOUR PICTURES

By this time your artistic sense will have become sharpened even though you have never thought much about composition and design before. You will want to make pleasing pictures, with a sense of balance and colors that harmonize. There are a few fundamental laws of design which will help you to achieve good results in a very short time. The most important ones are these: In finger painting, as with more serious work, you can get three-dimensional effects, particularly where one line crosses another, or if the paint is thick. When using several colors, there will be lines of blending colors where two colors meet.

In planning your design try to make the space areas pleasing. They must be in proportion to the size of the picture you are making, neither too large nor too small.

RHYTHM

Rhythm is an important element in design. You can get the effect of movement by repetition and by changing sizes and shapes. For instance, if you have mountains in the background, lead up to them with foothills that become smaller in the foreground, or else graduate the size of your trees.

PROPORTION

Proportion is another consideration. Everything in your picture should be properly related with respect to size and color. Colors, shapes, lights and darks, must also be harmonious. Without emphasis, your picture would be dull and lifeless. There should be one main center of interest. This can be accomplished by making the most important figure or object larger than the others or by grouping a number of smaller objects around it. By using stronger color in the main area, emphasis is also given.

BALANCE

Finally, your design must have balance; all lines should give the impression of leading toward the center of the picture rather than away from it. The weights of dark and light areas should be equal. If you use a color mass at one side of your picture, use the same color at another spot in a different tone if you prefer.

FORMS

Choose a form or forms with which you are familiar at first. It is better to create a design of your own from real objects than to copy pictures or designs made by somebody else. The history of design and ornament tells us that artists of consequence were always strongly influenced by the familiar natural forms surrounding them.

REPEATED MOTIF MAKES FINGER PAINTING

By considering both mass and form at the same time, you will soon learn color combinations and how to use them. A color wheel would be helpful in learning color relations. Perhaps you will enjoy yourself more, however, if you learn by experimenting.

PRACTICAL USES FOR FINGER PAINTINGS

There are many things you can do with finger painting besides making pictures and wall decorations. It can be applied to materials other than paper—wood, and beaverboard, to mention only two. Trays, coasters, bookends, and even furniture can be decorated in this way. If you do go in for finger painting on wood, and the wood is soft, give it a coat of clear shellac first, and then rub it smooth with steel wool or sandpaper. This will serve as a filler for the wood, and keep the paint from seeping in. Cover the design when dry with a coat of thin spar varnish. Paint the edges of the wood in an enamel of a harmonious color. This final varnishing will also make the painting permanent. Orange shellac will give an antique effect.

BASKETS AND SCRAPBOOK

You can make greeting cards, invitations, party favors, etc., on thin cardboard. When using cardboard, wet surfaces on both sides before doing your paintings.

Glazed chintz can be painted for curtains, screen covers, etc. Since the paints

DECORATED BOOK ENDS

are soluble, however, fabrics decorated in this way cannot be washed.

Lampshades are ideal objects for finger painting. Use thin bristol board or white drawing paper soaked in linseed oil. This will give a transparent effect.

Glass will take this kind of paint, so it might amuse you to decorate the mirrors in your room or some of the window-panes. Try making a "stained glass" window. Even the bottles on the side table can be touched up.

A very practical use is to make book jackets for the books you handle all the time, or perhaps for a borrowed book, to keep it fresh.

Last but not least, you can entertain your guests by inviting them to try their hands at this naïve art. You can make a good game of it by checking their first attempts with your own. Then, if you have long-ago memories in common, each of you might paint a scene and see whether the other can guess it.

When you have created a masterpiece or only a minor work, give it time to dry thoroughly, and then press it with a hot iron to keep it from curling.

PAPER PULP MODELING and CRAYON CRAFT

PAPER PULP MODELING

To do paper pulp modeling all you need is a bucket of water, a number of old newspapers, some flour paste and paints for decorations. There are numerous projects that can be made from paper pulp, the only limitations being that they must be more or less solid and not possess too detailed features.

HOW TO MAKE MODELS

First tear newspapers into small strips and put them in a bucket of water to soak. For best results, allow them to stay overnight, or at least for five hours. When ready to use, pull apart, mix and tear until a clay-like pulp is obtained. Squeeze the water out of the pulp, add paste or flour to clean water and mix with the pulp to produce a clay-like consistency.

Your clay or pulp is now ready to model. First take enough to cover the entire dimensions of the figure you wish to model. In other words, if you wish to make a figure of one of the girls illustrated in the photograph, include head, arms and body. Do not model the head and arms separately and try to attach them. Begin with a solid body and remove pulp a little at a time until the features appear.

When finished, allow it to dry slowly and thoroughly in the air It will take several days at least, as paper holds moisture and will even absorb it from the atmosphere on a rainy day.

DECORATING THE FIGURES

You will want to decorate the figures when they are thoroughly dry. Use a good tempera paint and allow one color to dry before adding another. When finished, put it away for a day to dry and cover with a coat of shellac.

Paper pulp modeling need not be limited to making small figures. It is an excellent medium for making relief maps, model railroad scenery, puppets, etc.

STEPS IN CRAYON CRAFT

(Left) Draw design with wax crayon. *(Center)* Brush over it with tempera or water color. Result—a rich batik effect. *(Right)* When dry, glaze with clear shellac or protect with a coat of liquid wax.

CRAYON CRAFT

This is a method of creating a rich batik effect on cardboard or heavy paper. It is useful for decorating paper plates, poster-making or, even as a magic trick.

The principle involved is to draw a design on a smooth dull surface paper or cardboard with wax crayon and paint over with tempera paint that has been diluted with about one-third water. The paint adheres to the background but will run off the design as the wax in the crayon resists water. Thus you have a bright design on a plain background.

Consider first the color you wish for the background and use only the colors for the design that contrast well with it. Complete the entire design before adding the paint.

Use the sharpened ends of your crayons and, if they become blunt, sharpen them with a knife. Press down heavily and evenly and keep your lines to an even width. Remember to use light bright colors with a dark background. White should not be forgotten; it shows up white where the paint is added.

PAINT HINTS

Test the background paint for color and consistency before using. For best results you should add a little water if the paint is thick. Brush the paint on the background with short, quick strokes; don't drag the brush. It is better to use a one-inch flat brush for this purpose than one with a point. Use the paint generously. For repeat designs use a stencil.

FOR THE PARTY

You will want to use this method to decorate paper plates for your parties. It is an excellent way to tie your party theme in with the decorations. As a part of the program of a party for youngsters, the guests would enjoy decorating their own plates. If you make a particularly attractive plate you wish to keep, glue two plates to the underside for thickness and add two or three coats of shellac for strength and to protect the design.

POSTER-MAKING

Crayon craft is also used in poster-making. Make the design on drawing paper, add background paint, then mount on heavy cardboard.

A MAGIC TRICK

A magic trick is done by printing a message or a word on white paper with a white crayon which will not be apparent to the audience. When painted over with a background color, it will show the word "Welcome," "Merry Christmas" or whatever is suitable for the occasion.

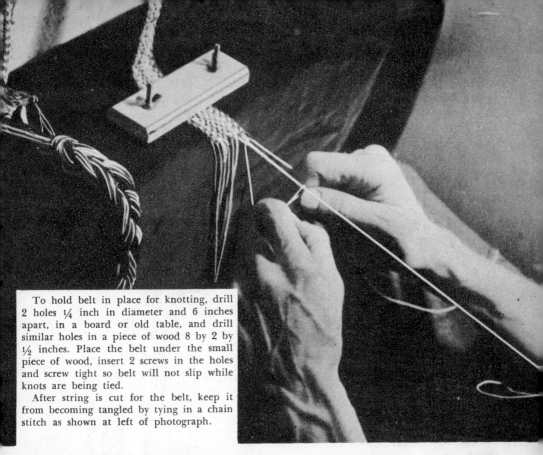

To hold belt in place for knotting, drill 2 holes ¼ inch in diameter and 6 inches apart, in a board or old table, and drill similar holes in a piece of wood 8 by 2 by ½ inches. Place the belt under the small piece of wood, insert 2 screws in the holes and screw tight so belt will not slip while knots are being tied.

After string is cut for the belt, keep it from becoming tangled by tying in a chain stitch as shown at left of photograph.

SQUARE KNOTTING – A USEFUL CRAFT

Square knotting is a most useful accomplishment, for there are so many things one can do with this comparatively simple technique. How or by whom the square knot was originated is not known, but sailors the world over have used it for ages for practical purposes and also for fashioning novelties in their spare time, during long voyages. There is a close relationship to the old-fashioned work known as macramé. This word—said to be Arabic—was used to describe ornamental braids and strips which grew to be elaborated into bags, table runners, and other decorative and useful objects. There is no reason, in the nature of it, why it could not be made in greater widths, but it is particularly suitable for belts, braids, and similar things.

In this chapter, which will serve to start you on your way as a square knotter,

will be given only one example of its application—how to make square knotted belts. But, if you learn to do this, all things in the way of square knotting will be possible to you.

EQUIPMENT AND MATERIAL

Some device is needed to hold taut the two centre strands of cord around which the knotting is done. Figure 1 shows a piece of one-inch dowel with a hole through which a cord is passed to tie around the waist, and a notch on the diagonal for holding fast the two strands of cord, the foundation for your work. The second type is made from a block of wood about two and a half or three inches long, about two inches wide, and at least an inch thick. Bore holes opposite each other about half an inch from the edge on two sides. These carry the cord to tie around the waist. In the middle of the block put a large nail or a hook (curtain hook) that can be bent back so as to grip the two centre cords tightly. Get someone to hold your cord while you are getting started, then pinch it in a drawer, hook it over a peg, a nail, the bedpost, or whatever is convenient for you.

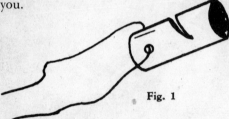

Fig. 1

Cable cord (about No. 12), or unpolished seine twine of equal thickness both work up very well in square knotting. For some articles, as you go on with this craft, you may wish to use a finer ply cord, but it will be easier to master the principle by using the thicker strands to begin. A cord as heavy as No. 36 is suitable for a man's belt.

A pronged metal buckle can be used to finish a belt, or two rings or squares of metal or plastic lashed together with a leather thong. How to use either of these types of buckle will be described in detail later.

MAKING A SQUARE KNOT IN ONE OPERATION

Square knots are always tied in groups of four strands. To tie the knot, separate the first four strands on the left from the others, and hold the middle two taut as described above. Now take the fourth strand—the one on the right—and make a loop about two inches long. Place it on top of the two middle strands (the taut strands), holding the end of the loop with the right thumb and forefinger. Put the thumb and first finger of the left hand down through the top of the loop that extends over the two middle strands, and reach down and under the middle strands; catch the end of the loop where the fingers are holding it, and pull it

through until it is tight (Figs. 2, 3, and 4).

Now take the first strand, or the one on the left, and pull it all the way through the double knots. You are now ready to separate the two knots. Reach under the two loops with the left hand, take hold of the small loop underneath, and hold the long string on the right with the right hand. Pull back and forth until the knot is separated.

Take the cords below the first part of the knot and pull the first half of the knot up tight. Then pull the strings

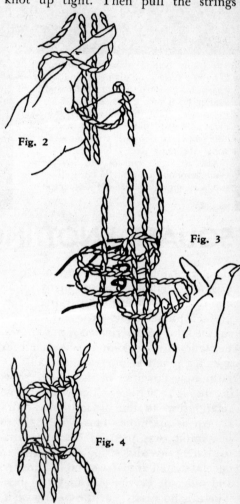

Fig. 2

Fig. 3

Fig. 4

below the second part of the knot until it is tight against the first half of the knot. Practice the knotting until you have a clear picture in your mind of every step of the operation.

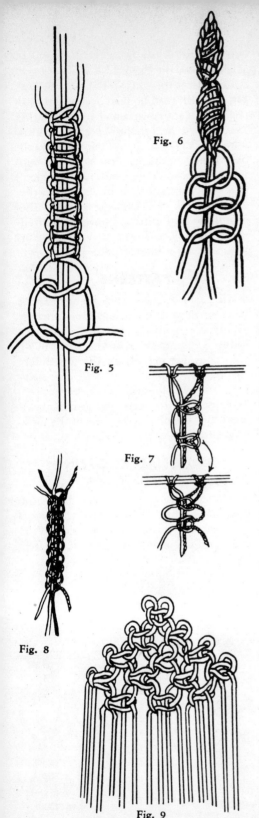

Fig. 6

Fig. 5

Fig. 7

Fig. 8

Fig. 9

THE HALF-KNOT

In making patterns, a series of half knots is sometimes used. To make a half-knot, hold the two middle strands taut. Loop the right strand across them. Carry the left strand over the right one and under the two middle strands, then up and over the right strand again. (Fig. 5.) Pull it up and you will have your half knot. Figure 6 shows a pattern variation made by half-knotting several times with the right strand, and then several times with the left, resulting in a curl or spiral effect.

THE HALF-HITCH

What scouts and sailors refer to as the half-hitch is really the same principle as buttonholing. One strand is held out taut, another strand is carried under it, leaving a loop. Carry the end of the loose strand over the taut strand and down through the loop, drawing it up tight. The diagonal pattern in Figs. 15 and 16 are examples of the half-hitch or buttonhole knot.

THE PICOT

Figures 7 and 8 illustrate the picot, another pattern variation. To make a picot effect, begin about half an inch from your last knot. Make a square knot at this point, then push it up along the taut strands to join the last knot you made. This will give you a small loop or picot on each side of the double strand.

MAKING A BELT

First, take the waist measure. For a plain belt you must allow three and a half times your waist measure for each strand, and, if you are using a pronged buckle, about three inches more to go through the buckle and "keeper." One end of the belt, however, must have loops, and at the other end the cords must be cut. The way to allow for this is to measure off *seven* times the waist measure (plus the extra inches), cut it off, and double it once. That will give you two strands of the necessary length—three

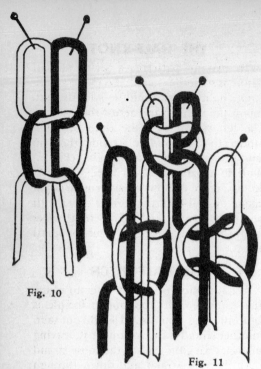

Fig. 10

Fig. 11

explained above. You can have as many as you wish—the procedure is always the same. Set up the cords for the start as in Fig. 10, each cord hooked over a nail or a peg. Fasten your two center strands in the "holder." Make a square knot. Below this knot, to the left, hook another strand over a peg. Working now with the two new strands and the strands nearest them, make another knot. Do the same on the right side (Fig. 11). Continue with the rest of the cord until you have the desired width (Fig. 12). Then go on with your belt, making whatever pattern you wish.

PATTERNS

All patterns arise from the sequences you use in your knotting. Once having mastered the initial technique, you can follow any pattern or devise patterns of your own. Figures 13, 14, 15 show different pattern possibilities, and the half-knot, half-hitch, and picot have been explained. With these you can make a great number of designs. One of the most interesting variations is explained below.

DIAGONAL KNOTTING

In Figs. 16 and 17 are shown examples of attractive pattern variations by use of diagonal knotting. To do this you begin with the first strand on the left side. With each cord in succession make a half-hitch

Fig. 12

and one-half times the waist measure. You need at least four strands for every knot, the width of the belt depending upon the number of strands and the ply of the cord.

Study Fig. 9. We are going to start from this pointed "end" to make our first belt. This belt pictured has sixteen strands, or eight double strands, as

Fig. 13

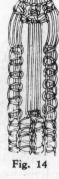

Fig. 14

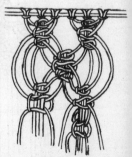

Fig. 15

or buttonhole knot over the first strand, which must be held taut in the bias position. When you reach the centre strand, begin at the right side and follow the same procedure until you come back to the centre cord again. Make a knot with the two outside cords. Continue knotting, working from the centre towards the left, and then going back and working out to the right edge. As you see, this makes a very effective pattern.

FINISHING WITH A LOOP OR "KEEPER"

When your belt is long enough, and you are ready to make the loop, bring the centre to a point (Fig. 18) by dropping two strands at a time, until you reach the middle. Then divide your strands from the point as in Fig. 19. Knot one side, as in Fig. 20, working at a right angle to the belt, and bring these strands to a diagonal to form the belt loop. The point should be on the same side (the top towards you) as the point in the belt itself. Now (Fig. 21) bring the strands from this belt loop around, and knot them to the loose strands with square knots. This joins the belt loop to the belt. When you have made the final knots tight, cut off the strands and turn the belt loop inside out before putting the belt through the buckle. After finishing the loop or "keeper" and trimming the ends of the

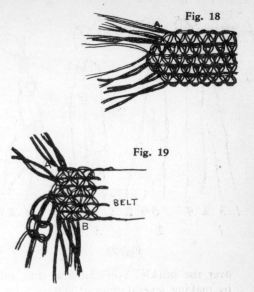

Fig. 18

Fig. 19

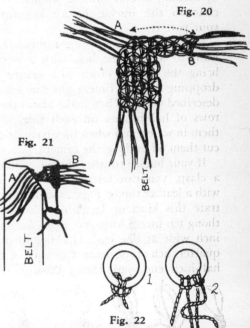

Fig. 20

Fig. 21

Fig. 22

Fig. 16

Fig. 17

cords, use duco cement to keep the cord from fraying where it has been cut. Soaking the ends in water before cutting also prevents fraying. After each washing, put on some more cement.

BUCKLES

You can begin a belt at the buckle end, if you like. Fig. 22 shows one way of doing this—by buttonholing your strands

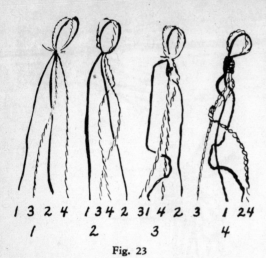

1 3 2 4   1 3 4 2   3 1 4 2 3   1 24

1   2   3   4

Fig. 23

over the buckle. You can also start off by making several rows of square knots close to the buckle before beginning your pattern.

If you are using a pronged buckle and want to finish your belt with a point, bring the strands down to a centre by dropping two at a time, right and left, as described above. Then make about three rows of half-hitches on each side, soak them in water, and when they have dried, cut them off and use the cement.

If your buckle consists of rings without a clasp, you can fasten them together with a leather thong. Figs. 23 and 24 illustrate this kind or fastening. Cut your thong ten inches long and about one-half inch wide at one end, tapering to one-quarter inch at the other. Cut a slit in the half-inch end, pull thong through one

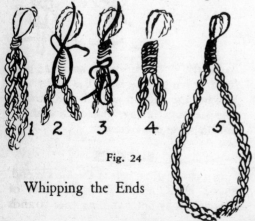

1   2   3   4   5

Fig. 24

Whipping the Ends

ring, and draw the whole strand through slit, thus attaching it to the ring. To tie, place the two rings together, and pull the thong under the ring to which it is not attached, then up through it, over both, and down through the first ring. Again bring it under both and up through the second ring, over the top of both rings and down through the first one again. You now have two loops around the rings. Bring the thong up between the rings and over the double loops from top to bottom, and under the first ring again. Now bring it up through the first ring and over the top and under the loop just made between the buckles. Cord may be used instead of a leather thong. Attach it as shown in Fig. 25.

In case you are using rings, having begun by looping your cords around one end, you will have to do the same when you come to the other end of your belt. Draw your strands from the back of the buckle to the front, then thread them down to the back again; turn buckle over and make a row of square knots on the under side, tight against the buckle. Soak the knots in water, dry, trim, and finish with a touch of cement.

A BRAIDED LANYARD

Measure off as much cord as the finished length of your lanyard. Suppose it to be sixteen inches. You will need, then, for your work, two cords two and one-half times that length, or two pieces of cord or twine forty inches long. Double your two strands and tie the loop ends with a piece of string, so that they can be hooked over a nail or a peg while you are braiding.

THE BRAIDING PROCESS

Spread out the four strands and cross 3 over 2 (Fig. 23). Next bring 4 *under* 2 and 3 and back *over* 3. Hold in place with left thumb and forefinger. Then bring 1 *under* 3 and 4 and back *over* 4. Again hold it in place with thumb and forefinger and continue braiding by bringing 2 *under* 4 and 1 and back *over* 1. Next

| Fig. 25 | Fig. 26 | Fig. 27 | Fig. 28 |

take the outside cord on the left, which is 3, and bring it *under* 1 and 2 and back *over* 2. The braiding is continued by taking the highest outside strand, bringing it under the two nearest ones and back over the second one. In other words, the sequence is always under two strands and back over one.

WHIPPING THE ENDS

When the braiding is completed, bring ends and loops together as shown in Fig. 24. Remove the small string around the loops and ravel out one small strand; wind this strand around the lanyard above the loops, as in the first step shown.

Next cut a piece of braiding cord fourteen inches long. Make a three-inch loop at one end of it. Hold the lanyard in the left hand and lay the loop over the binding strand, the ends away from the loops of the lanyard. Begin winding the whipping cord as tightly as possible. Continue until you have a three-quarters of an inch or an inch whip, then thread the strand through the extra little loop. Pull it up close, then pull the ends of the small loop down half way under the whip. Cut both ends close to the whipping.

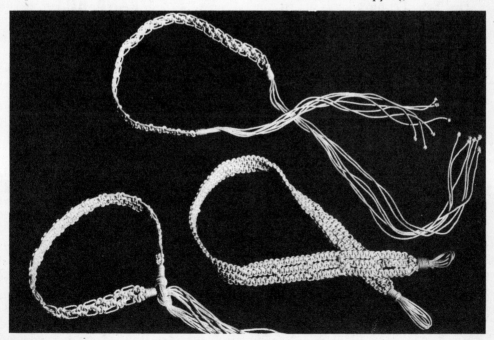

KNOTTED BELTS
Showing belts made with six, eight, and twelve strands.

TWELVE-STRAND BELT

Cut 12 strands of cord No. 30-36 three times the length of measurement of waist plus six inches for loops on the ends. Hold strands together by whipping about an inch below the loops as follows:

DIRECTIONS FOR WHIPPING

Cut a piece of cord twelve inches in length and make a loop at one end so that there are three inches on one side (see B in Fig. 25) and eleven inches on the other side. (See A in Fig. 25.) Hold the belt in the left hand with the loop about four inches above the fingers and lay loop of extra piece on top with loop in opposite direction from those of belt. (See Fig. 25.) Then take the eleven-inch strand in the right hand and begin winding around the belt as tightly as possible. (See Fig. 26.) Continue until you have an inch or more of whipping and then thread the end of the strand through the loop. (See Fig. 27.) Pull up on B until A is drawn half way to the top. Cut both ends close to whipping. (See Fig. 28.)

You are now ready to knot the belt.

First Row. Tie three knots in first row. There are twelve strands and four strands are used in tying each knot.

Second Row. Ignore first two strands and tie two knots with the next eight strands. Ignore last two strands.

Third Row. Take first four strands and tie a series of six knots. Repeat with second four strands and again with the last four strands.

Fourth Row. Repeat second row.

Fifth Row. Repeat third row.

Continue repeating second and third rows until belt is completed. To make the loop on the end, take the six strands on right side of belt and bend them around to form a loop to match the one on the opposite end of belt. Make a whipping with a soft thin string and tie close to the other strands of the belt. Cut off loose ends close to the whipping on each side. Cover by whipping again with a piece of heavy cord about twelve inches long. (See directions for whipping.)

EIGHT-STRAND BELT

Measure eight strands No. 30-36 three times length of waist measurement plus 24 inches for extra string for tying. Cut two strings twelve inches in length for whipping. Make a whipping twelve inches from one end to hold string together. (See directions for whipping.) Tie ends to the back of a chair and the belt is ready to knot.

First Row. Tie a knot with center for strings, ignoring the two outer ones on each side.

Second Row. Tie a series of two knots on first four strings and two knots on second four strings.

Third Row. Tie a series of two knots on center four strings, ignoring the two outer strings on each side.

Continue repeating second and third rows until belt is completed. Finish belt by whipping strings together as you did in the beginning. Tie a tight knot on the end of each string to keep them from raveling. If the knots become loose, add a drop of clear cement to the bottom.

SIX-STRAND BELT

Measure 6 strands No. 30-36 cord three times the length of waist measurement plus twenty-four inches for ties in the front. Cut two pieces twelve inches in length for whipping. Whip strands together twelve inches from one end. (See directions for whipping.) Tie strand to back of chair and belt is ready to knot.

First Row. Tie a knot with first four strands on left.

Second Row. Ignore first strand and tie a knot with second, third, fourth and fifth strands.

Third Row. Ignore first two strands and tie knot with third, fourth, fifth, sixth.

This completes the pattern. Repeat first, second, and third rows until belt is completed.

Finish belt by whipping strings together as you did in the beginning. Tie a knot on the end of each string to keep them from raveling. If the knots become loose, add a drop of clear cement to the bottom.

NETTING FOR FUN AND PROFIT

Netting is a simple handicraft—invaluable for making all kinds of hard-to-find equipment for fishing, active sports, gifts and household uses. Sailors and fishermen are adept at this art, but you too can easily learn to rival their remarkable skill and speed.

Along the coastlines from the North Pole to the South and all around the globe, men, women and children have been making and mending fish nets for ages. There was no literature on netting years ago—a son learned by watching a father, a daughter from her mother and neighbor from neighbor.

This chapter gives simple directions and illustrations for setting up and start-

ing a net and you will find detailed instructions for making various attractive and useful netted articles, such as hammocks, fish nets, nets for basketball and badminton, shawls and shopping bags.

EQUIPMENT NEEDED

A. **Netting Needle,** on which the cord or twine is wound.

B. **Gauge.** The exact gauge width to be used is given for each pattern in this chapter.

A and B may be cut or whittled from any thin, hard wood approximately the size illustrated in patterns A and B. The netting needle is slightly narrower than the gauge.

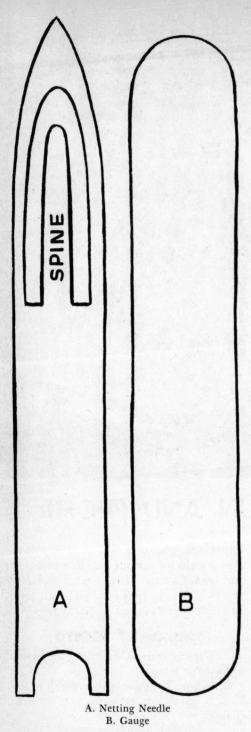

the loops, when completed, can be anchored around the nearest stationary object and reach to the person working. As the work increases, the length of the loop is shortened.

D. **Ball of Twine.**

Note. In some of the patterns appearing later in this chapter, it is suggested that a tongue depressor be used for gauge, cut to $\frac{1}{2}$, $\frac{3}{4}$, or $\frac{7}{8}$ inch width. This refers to a regular wooden tongue depressor such as is used in all hospitals.

GLOSSARY

Hitch. (Referred to in this chapter as "single hitch.") Method of securing a

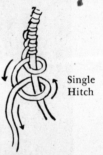

Single Hitch

rope to another object or stationary rope.

Clove Hitch. See Fig. 22 and Fig. 34.

Reeve. To pass the end of a rope through an eye or opening.

Seize. To put on a seizing, that is, bind one rope to another, a rope to a spar, etc., with small stuff (Fig. 5).

Small Stuff. Any small cord or line.

HOW TO MAKE NETTING

1. Fasten the twine to the spine.

    A. Wind as in Fig. 1.

    B. Turn the needle over and repeat.

    C. Continue until the needle has been filled leaving $\frac{1}{4}$ inch at tip of spine free.

2. From the loose end of the twine on the needle make a loop twice as wide as the gauge (B, page 139).

    A. Tie this loop around anchor loop. (C, page 139).

    B. Place the knot X of loop in the middle of the left side.

A. Netting Needle
B. Gauge

C. **An Anchor Loop of Thread** (not illustrated). This is made by doubling a length of thread and knotting the ends. The length should be sufficient so that

SPINE

A

B

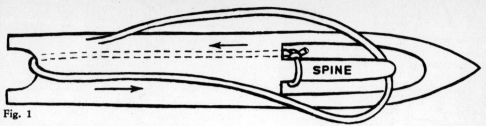

Fig. 1

SPINE

C. Hold gauge in left hand exactly in the position shown.

D. Holding needle in right hand pass through loop from r to l as
• shown in Fig. 2.

3. Using the gauge as shown, pull down twine to position Y. The gauge is used to measure the space of the mesh.

4. Hold the twine firmly to gauge at Y with thumb, as shown in Fig. 4.

A. Loop twine down and around to the left as shown in Fig. 4.

B. Pass needle under 1st two strands, over 3rd and 4th, as shown in Fig. 4.

5. Figure 5 shows the knot before being pulled hard and tight as in 6.

6. Do not remove the thumb from Y in Fig. 5 until the knot has been made tight by pulling toward right hip as in Fig. 6.

A. If the knot slips, it has not been correctly tied.

7. Remove the gauge and place the new knot on the left, as in Fig. 7.

A. Finish knot as in Figs. 2, 3, 4, 5 and 6.

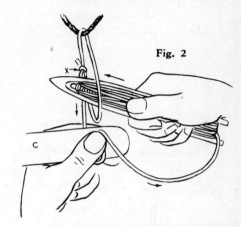

Fig. 2

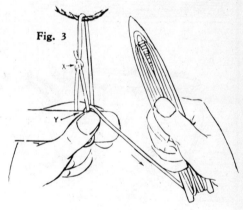

Fig. 3

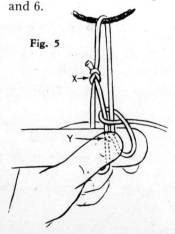

Fig. 5

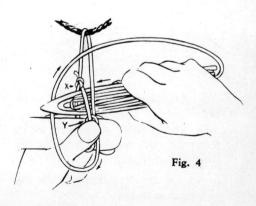

Fig. 4

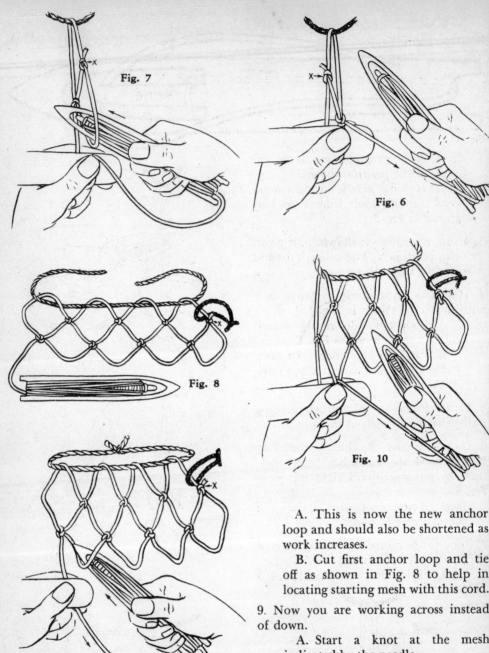

Fig. 7

Fig. 6

Fig. 8

Fig. 10

Fig. 9

A. This is now the new anchor loop and should also be shortened as work increases.

B. Cut first anchor loop and tie off as shown in Fig. 8 to help in locating starting mesh with this cord.

9. Now you are working across instead of down.

A. Start a knot at the mesh indicated by the needle.

10. Finish the knot as in Figs. 2, 3, 4, 5 and 6.

A. Continue working across to right until row is completed.

11. When you have completed the row of meshes, change the needle to the left hand, the gauge to the right hand as in Fig. 11.

B. Repeat until the desired number of meshes have been made.

C. The number of meshes to be set up depends on the size of the net you plan to make.

8. Thread a heavy cord through the top row of meshes as in Fig. 8.

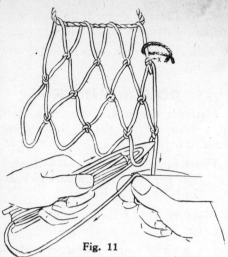

Fig. 11

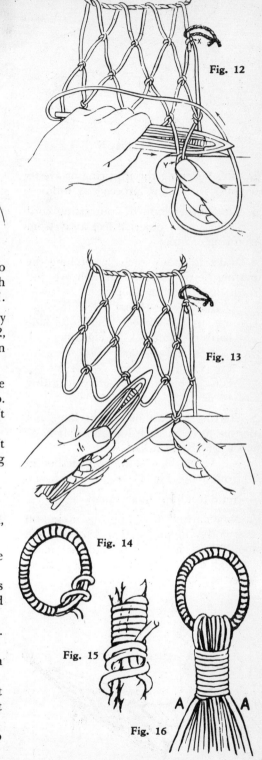

Fig. 12

Fig. 13

A. Working this row from left to right, start a new knot at the mesh indicated by the needle, as in Fig. 11.

12. Remember to hold the twine firmly with the thumb at Y as shown in Fig. 12, while you make in reverse the operation shown in Fig. 4.

13. Complete the knot by pulling the twine tightly downward toward left hip.

A. Continue working to the left until row is completed.

B. Repeat alternate right and left rows until desired length of netting is completed.

HAMMOCK OF SEINE CORD

Materials Required. Strong seine cord, and a gauge 2½ inches wide.

1. Fasten iron ring to bedpost. (If unable to obtain iron ring, make eye thus):

A. Wind cord several times around fingers or piece of cardboard 4 inches wide.

B. Slip loops off and seize (Fig. 14).

C. To seize:

1. Wind twine close and firm around loops (Fig. 14).

2. Pass end of twine under last few turns which have been left slack (Fig. 15).

3. Make turns taut, pull end to remove slack and trim.

Fig. 14

Fig. 15

Fig. 16

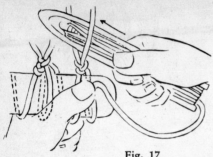

Fig. 17

2. After fastening the iron ring or eye to bedpost with loop, proceed as follows:

3. Tie another loop of contrasting cord this time, to an object 2 feet away from iron ring or eye.

4. Make 12 loops, each 2 feet long, by passing netting needle through eye and through contrasting loop.

    A. Pass a 24-foot cord through eye, leaving 12-foot lengths for side cords of hammock (a, Fig. 16).

    B Seize loops and cords close to eye (Fig. 16).

    C. Remove loop of contrasting cord.

5. Starting at bottom of first loop, net double mesh in each loop, so that hammock will be 24 meshes wide.

    A. Double Mesh: two meshes in one loop (Fig. 17).

6. Net 8 feet of ordinary mesh.

7. Now narrow to 12 loops by taking off every other mesh. (See Fig. 18.) Net each loop 2 feet long from body of hammock through a second iron ring or eye 2 feet away, (as done in Step 4 above).

8. Reeve 12-foot side cords through outer meshes of hammock and fasten to eye.

9. Seize loops and cords close to eye (Fig. 16).

DOLL HAMMOCK

Materials Required. Cotton rug yarn, or a heavy twine. Use ¾ inch gauge (tongue depressor).

1. Fasten eye or ring to bedpost with cord.
    A. For eye, see Hammock of Seine Cord, Step 1, A, B and C.

2. Make 20 loops 6 inches long, through eye (Fig. 16).

    A. Seize loops close to eye (Hammock of Seine Cord, Step 1 C).

3. Starting at first loop, net 22 inches of mesh.

4. Net row of loops 6 inches long from body of hammock through second eye or ring (as done in Step 2 above).

5. Seize loops close to eye (Fig. 16).

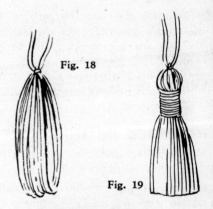

Fig. 18

Fig. 19

TASSEL TRIM

1. Wind several loops of twine around fingers or piece of cardboard, 3 inches wide.

2. Slip off loops and tie at top (Fig. 18).

3. Seize below heading (Fig. 19).
    A. Seizing Step 1 C, Hammock of Seine Cord.

4. Cut loops at bottom and trim.

5. Fasten at head of hammock.

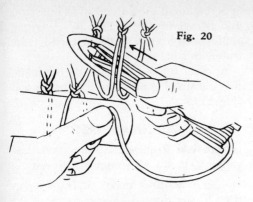

Fig. 20

LANDING NET

Materials Required. A strong, lightweight cord. Use gauge ¾ inch wide, or tongue depressor.

1. Chain 80 meshes.

When a chain is spread out there will be two rows, each row ½ the number of meshes chained.

    A. Set up 40 meshes on contrasting string and fasten to bedpost.

2. Net mesh to desired depth. The net illustrated is 24 meshes deep.

3. Taper off bottom by reducing number of meshes. To reduce: Net two meshes at a time by sliding needle through two

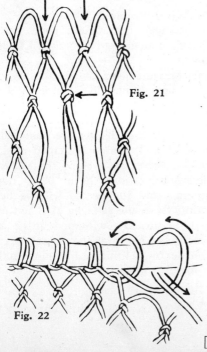

Fig. 21

Fig. 22

loops instead of one and finish knot (Fig. 20) in the following order:

    A. Reduce one in first row (near the middle).

    B. Take off every 3rd mesh in second row.

    C. Take off every 2nd mesh in succeeding rows.

4. Tie last few meshes together with cord. If a more pointed net is desired (such as a butterfly net), take off fewer meshes in a row. This will taper off the net more gradually to form a point.

5. Join sides with knotting (Fig. 21) as follows:

    A. Lay outer edges of mesh parallel.

    B. Place middle of cord for knotting at top of net with equal length side cords hanging free.

    C. Knot each side cord to adjoining mesh of net.

    D. Knot cords together.

    E. Continue C and D, trying to keep knotting meshes same size as netting meshes, to bottom of net.

6. Clove Hitch to frame (Fig. 22).

Note: If a hoop is used for frame, meshes can be worked directly on the hoop as follows:

    1. Set up desired number of loops on hoop with evenly spaced Clove Hitches (Fig. 23).

    2. Net from loops as above (Step 2).

LANDING NET FRAME AND HANDLE

Materials Required. Pole 9 inches or more long by 1½ inches in diameter, for handle. Two lengths of wood 22 inches long, ¾ inch wide, for frame. Drying press, board with double row of nails, outlining shape for arms of frame (Fig. 24).

1. Soak 22-inch lengths of wood in hot water or steam until pliable.

    A. Fit between row of nails on press and dry (Fig. 24).

2. At one end of handle cut triangular

wedges 3 inches long by thickness of the arms (Fig. 25).

3. Fit arms to handle (Fig. 26).

A. Cut small notches close to end of arms (Fig. 26 A, B).

B. Fasten waterproof leather thong or strong cord from notches a to b.

4. Finish by rounding off bottom of handle, sandpapering smooth and varnishing.

5. Screw small eye to end of handle and attach carrying cord (Fig. 26). A strong well-forked branch might be used for the frame and handle.

An oval frame can be made by steaming and shaping one length of hardwood (Fig. 27).

CIRCULAR NET

Materials Required. Strong cord. Use gauge ¾ inch wide (tongue depressor).

1. Use a hoop or make circle of heavy rope in size desired.

2. Set up loops on hoop with evenly spaced Clove Hitches (Fig. 23).

3. Net mesh from each loop, stopping a few inches short of center of hoop.

4. Finish net as instructions, step 3, for landing net. Tie off as soon as mesh can be joined at center.

5. Join sides with knotting (Landing Net step 5).

6. Seize rope handles to opposite sides of hoop.

A. Seizing step 1C, Hammock of Seine Cord.

LAWN TENNIS NET

Materials Required. Dreadnaught, or other strong, light weight cord. Use a 1¾ inch wide gauge for mesh 1¾ inches square.

Net Measurements. 36 ft. wide by 3 ft. high—Single Court. 40 ft. wide by 3 ft. high —Double Court.

Note that the tennis net and other play nets in this chapter are made with square meshes. Diamond shaped meshes would confuse the eyes of the players. These illustrations have been done assuming that the needle will be held continually in the right hand. The work should be turned (or flopped) at the end of each row. However the entire net can be made by holding the needle in the left hand, if desirable.

1. To net square mesh:

A. Start with loop tied to bedpost.

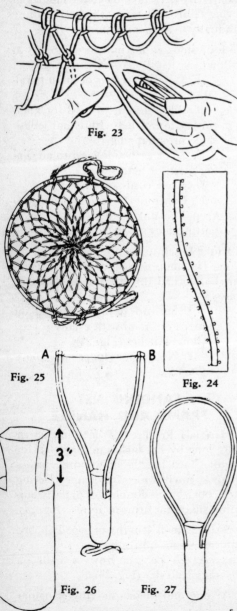

Fig. 23

Fig. 25

Fig. 24

Fig. 26   Fig. 27

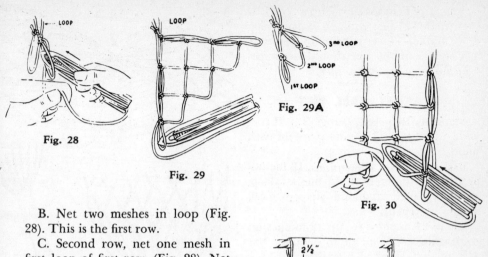

Fig. 28

Fig. 29

Fig. 29A

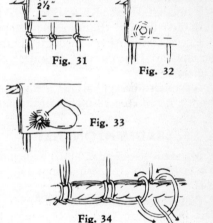

Fig. 30

Fig. 31

Fig. 32

Fig. 33

Fig. 34

B. Net two meshes in loop (Fig. 28). This is the first row.

C. Second row, net one mesh in first loop of first row (Fig. 28). Net two meshes in second loop (as in step 5, A, Fig. 17, Hammock of Seine Cord).

D. Third row, net one mesh in first loop, one mesh in second loop, two meshes in third loop (Fig. 29A).

E. From there on continue to net one mesh in each loop until the end of the row, then net two meshes in the last loop. (Your net will now begin to look like Fig. 29.) Continue this until you have 3 feet of meshes in row. (This represents the height of the completed net.)

Note: The following steps F, G, H and I square up the lower corner and begin to add the necessary width to the net, which would otherwise grow fan shaped.

F. At end of next row slide netting needle through 2 last meshes and make one knot (Fig. 30).

G. At end of next row net two meshes in last loop.

H. At end of next row slide needle through last two meshes and make one knot.

I. Continue G and H until you have 36 feet of meshes in row, more if a longer net is wanted.

J. At end of each row thereafter slide needle through last two meshes and make one knot.

K. Tie last two meshes with cord.

2. Sew piece of canvas or duck folded two or three times, to make a 5-inch-wide binding, along top of net (Fig. 31).

3. Reeve heavy rope or small galvanized wire cable through binding.

4. Make eyelets at ends of binding for cords to hold binding taut.

A. Punch hole at end of binding (Fig. 32).

B. Sew around hole a few times to strengthen (Fig. 32).

C. Sew above strengthening and through eyelet (Fig. 33).

5. Seize heavy rope to bottom of net with Clove Hitches (Fig. 34).

Note: For additional strength the net may be taped on the sides and along the bottom.

Standard Tennis Court Measurements:
Single—27 feet wide by 78 feet long
Double—36 feet wide by 78 feet long
The top of the net should be 3 fee
6 inches from ground, at posts.

BASKET BALL NET

Materials Required. Gauge 1⅞ inches
wide, winding cord around twice for each
mesh.

Basket Ball Net Dimensions. 13 meshes
around circumference, 3½ meshes deep,
with 7½ inch diamond shaped mesh
(when stretched).

Chain 24 meshes. Set up 12 meshes on
contrasting cord and tie to bedpost. Net
3½ meshes deep. Knot sides making
13th mesh around (Landing Net, Step 5).

Reeve drawstring through bottom
mesh. Clove Hitch to ring (Landing Net,
Fig. 22).

A standard basket ball net is suspended
from a metal ring 18 inches in diameter.

BADMINTON NET

Materials Required. ⅞-inch wide gauge
for ⅞-inch square mesh (tongue depressor).

Badminton Net Dimensions. Single—18
feet by 2½ feet. Double—21 feet by 2½
feet.

Instructions for making a Lawn
Tennis Net should be used for making a
Badminton Net.

The top of the net should be 5 feet
1 inch from ground at posts. Badminton is played with a "shuttle" or "bird,"
made of 14 to 16 feathers 2¼ inches from
tip to cork (spreading 2½ inches at the
top, firmly fastened with thread), stuck
into a cork 1 inch in diameter.

Standard Badminton Court measures:
Single—17 feet by 44 feet. Double—
20 feet by 44 feet.

SADDLE BAGS

Materials Required. Knitting worsted
or pearl cotton. 1 ball black, 1 ball green
or any 2-color combinations. If pearl cotton is used, stiffen, as described below.

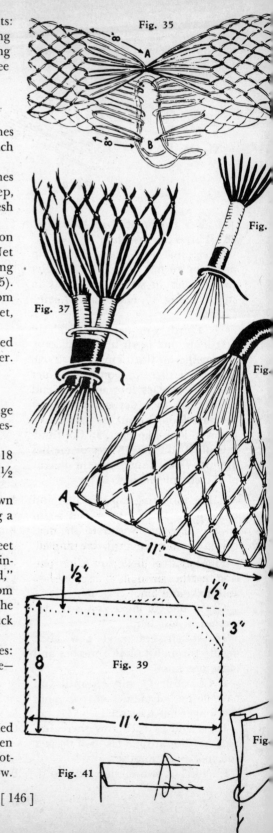

Fig. 35

Fig.

Fig. 37

Fig.

Fig.

A

11"

½"

1½"

3"

8

Fig. 39

11"

Fig.

Fig. 41

Use ½ inch gauge (tongue depressor cut to size).

Solution for Stiffening Net. 1 teaspoon sugar thoroughly dissolved in ⅔ cup hot water. When cool enough to handle, dip net in solution until saturated, wring out gently and block by placing it in a circular position on a flat surface until dry.

USING BLACK WOOL:

1. Chain 38 meshes of wool.

    A. Set up 19 meshes on contrasting string and tie to bedpost.

2. Net 16 inches of mesh.

3. Lay mesh flat.

4. With netting needle pick up each mesh at end with loops 8 inches long (Fig. 35).

    A. Repeat Step 4 at other end.

5. Using green wool, repeat Steps 1, 2, 3 and 4.

6. Handle—

    A. Fasten one set of black loops to one set of green loops (A, Fig. 35).

    B. Double mesh over and repeat A with two remaining sets of loops (B, Fig. 35).

    C. Starting at joining of one set of loops, seize (Step 1, C, Hammock of Seine Cord) green loops for 2 inches with black wool (Fig. 36).

        1. Seize black loops with green wool for two inches.

    D. Repeat C on second set of loops.

    E. Lay handles parallel. Mesh should be folded in center and flat for bags.

    F. Holding black handles together seize with black wool for 2 inches to make black section of handle on green bag.(Fig. 37).

    G. Seize green handles with green wool to make finished green section of handle on black bag (Fig. 37).

7. With mesh flat, weave up sides of bags with matching wool, leaving 3-inch opening on one side of each bag (Fig. 38).

8. Reeve 11-inch length of matching wool across bottom and fasten at A and B (Fig. 38).

9. Bag lining (make two).

    A. Cut piece of black rayon taffeta 12 inches by 16 inches and fold to make pocket 12 inches by 8 inches with ½ inch seam allowances (Fig. 39).

    B. Cut off corners 1½ inches wide by 3 inches deep on one side (Fig. 39).

    C. Fold ½ inch seam allowance (Fig. 39). Round stitch side seams (Fig. 40).

        1. Round stitch: Pass needle through edges at right angles to material (Fig. 40).

    D. Fold down top and bias corners ½ inch and sew (Figs. 39 and 41).

    E. Fit lining into mesh bag and fasten to meshes at opening and at top.

SHAWL WITH RUFFLE

Materials Required. Light or medium weight wool yarn, and a ½ inch gauge (tongue depressor cut to ½ inch).

1. Chain 128 meshes.

    A. Set up 64 meshes on contrasting string and fasten to bedpost.

2. Net enough mesh to form a square when laid flat.

3. Ruffle.

    A. Weave contrasting string

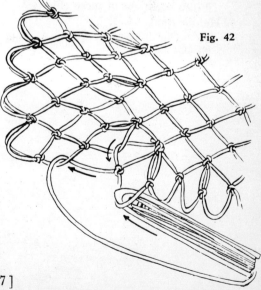

Fig. 42

through mesh a few inches from end of square and fasten to bedpost.

B. Tic wool to last mesh on left.

C. Net double mesh in each loop across (see Hammock of Seine Cord, Step 5, A).

D. Net next 3 rows in regular way.

E. Wind yarn double on netting needle for last row of mesh to give a double yarn finish.

4. Repeat ruffle on 3 other sides.

A. Link ruffle at corners by sliding needle through last mesh of adjoining row before netting next row of ruffle (Fig. 42).

SHOPPING BAG

Materials Required. Cotton rug yarn. If very heavy articles are to be carried, use strong twine. 1 ball orange, 1 ball green or any 2-color combination. Use ½-inch gauge (tongue depressor cut to ½ inch).

1. Body of Bag.
    A. Chain 32 meshes.
    B. Set up 16 meshes on contrasting string and tie to bedpost.
    C. Net 30 inches of mesh.

2. Make two pieces of mesh.

3. Lay 2 pieces of mesh flat and parallel.
    A. Join by weaving twine through adjoining loops of mesh (Fig. 43).

4. Handle (make two).
    A. Cut 9 lengths of green twine 20 inches long.

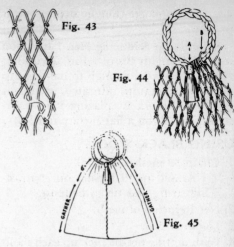

Fig. 43

Fig. 44

Fig. 45

B. Tie together at one end.

C. Divide into three and braid into flat braid.

D. Seize braids together (Hammock Seine Cord, Step 1 C) 3 inches from end.

E. Open up last 3 inches of braid and trim for tassel.

5. Tie tassel of one handle to one end of mesh at center (A, Fig. 44).

6. Lace loops of mesh close and tight to braid handle with green twine (B, Fig. 44).

7. Repeat Steps 5 and 6 above with second handle at opposite end of mesh.

8. Lay mesh flat, handles together (Fig. 45).

A. Measure 6 inches from handles, gather remaining meshes and fasten securely (Fig. 45).

LOVELY DOLLS ANYONE CAN MAKE

Doll making is an age-old craft enjoyed by adults as well as children. There are literally hundreds of methods of making dolls, ranging all the way from dressing the lowly corncob or clothespin to modeling and glazing a fine porcelain head. In this chapter we are going to give you directions for several novel ways of making character dolls that can be used for storytelling or added to your collection.

FACES FOR CHARACTER DOLLS

Any character doll can have the same body pattern, as usually, you want them near the same size if you are making a collection. But the faces must be differ-

ent. This is how you can create interesting faces.

Model a head the size you wish for your doll from modeling clay. Be sure the face has distinct features—rounded cheeks, nose, mouth, depression for eyes, etc. (Fig. 1 A). Next cut off the back of the head just behind the ears and lay the model in a small cardboard box *with face side up* (Fig. 1 B). Mix some plaster of paris with enough water to make it the consistency of heavy cream and pour over the model until it is covered at least one inch thick.

When the plaster is dry, tear off the box from the sides and remove the modeling clay with your fingers. You now

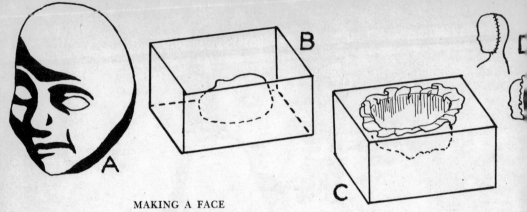

MAKING A FACE
Fig. 1. Showing the various steps in making a face by the
mold method.

have a negative mold. Paint the inside with shellac or varnish to make it water-resistant.

To make the face, use three pieces of cloth that have been dipped in thick starch or paste. One piece—the first one you use—should be thin silk or fine material, as it will be the face itself. The other two pieces are used to add strength, and a piece of soft knitted material such as found in a white sock is suitable. Dip each piece separately into the starch, remove excess with the hand and push firmly into the mold. Allow it to dry thoroughly before removing (Fig. 1 C).

After the face is removed, stuff the back firmly with cotton and sew on to a cloth head that has been properly shaped (Fig. 1 D). You now have a face with features and are ready to create the character you have in mind. First give it an overall

coat of paint (water color or tempera) in flesh color. Add a little rouge to the cheeks. Paint in the eyes, mouth and other features. Make the wig of yarn or artificial hair, as described below.

The same mold can be used over and over again. The advantage of having it is to add contour to the face. Each doll will appear different, according to the way it is painted.

HOW TO MAKE WIGS

Wigs can be made from various kinds of materials such as yarn, theatrical hair or paper. It is simpler to make the wig on a separate piece of material that has been cut and shaped to fit the top of the head, and add it to the doll when finished.

If you are using yarn or theatrical wool, sew it to the material first, at a line where the hair is to be parted. Add a

CHANGING FACES
Fig. 2. Faces may be changed by adding different features, changing colors and wigs.

[150]

little glue or paste to the rest of the cloth and allow the under part of the hair to stick fast to it.

Yarn is a very satisfactory substitute for hair. If you are making a wig for a small head, it should be raveled into thin strands and the ends glued into place. For long hair, cut the yarn into longer lengths and sew it to the covering material in a straight line along the center. Draw yarn down over sides of head and braid ends as shown in the photograph of "A Simple Doll."

Sheep's wool is excellent for making wigs for old men or women. The theatrical hair comes in various colors and is most satisfactory for making wigs, if available. Wigs are sometimes made from paper if a doll is to be used for story telling or display purposes. They are cut from construction paper to fit the head and usually shaped to a Dutch bob. The ends are cut into ½-inch strips about ¼ inch apart and edges curled around a pencil or small stick.

DOLL PROPORTIONS

In designing a doll, proportion the body as suggested in the chapter on drawing. The simplest rule to follow is to make the body eight heads high. The body and neck are three times the length of the head, and the legs and hips are four times as long. These proportions, however, can be varied for different characters.

HOW TO MAKE A BODY ARMATURE

If you are making a wire armature for the body, it should be made first and the head modeled later. Armatures are easily made and they will allow you to animate the doll into any pose or position. Here are directions for making a simple armature:

Cut a piece of medium-weight wire twice the length of the doll you wish to make (8 inches is a good height) and allow ½ inch at each end for the feet. Bend the wire together to form two

A SIMPLE DOLL
This doll was made from a sock, cardboard and yarn.

equal lengths with loop at one end. Twist the wire twice near the top, forming a loop for the head. The head should be ⅛ the length of the wire. Twist the wires again at the waistline and separate the two remaining ends to form the legs. Bend ½ inch forward for the feet. Cut another piece of wire long enough to form the shoulders and arms of the doll (see Fig. 3 A). Slip this wire halfway through the body wires just below the neck. Twist around center wires once to hold in place. Bend to form shoulders and twist ends into a small loop for hands.

Now wrap the body with rag strips ½ inch wide and add pieces of cotton as you wind to help shape the body. After the wrapping is completed, hold the ends of rags in place by sewing with needle and thread. This completes the armature (Fig. 3 B). Add the head after the face

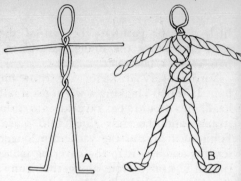

AN ARMATURE

Fig. 3. (A) Wire armature for a doll, and (B) the armature covered with rag strips.

ANIMATED DOLLS *(Left)*
The bodies of these dolls are built over a wire armature. They will stand and assume any pose.

has been completed and wig added. Stuff it with cotton and force it down over the wire loop of the armature and sew securely onto the body.

The hands and feet can be made from white knitted material cut to shape and sewed together with a running stitch. Turn right side out, stuff with a little cotton and sew onto armature. Cover feet with shoes made from a black kid glove and add a little flesh-colored paint to hands to give them a natural appearance.

After the doll is dressed it can be bent to stand, sit or assume other poses.

APPLE DOLLS

Apple dolls originated during the early pioneer days when materials were scarce. They are made by paring a large firm apple and sculpturing a face in the raw fruit.

Hollow out two depressions for eyes, shape the cheekbones and sculpture the nose and mouth. Make a wire armature for the body and leave a straight piece of wire about 1 inch at the top for the head (do not loop it). Force the wire up through the center of the apple and hang it over the stove or radiator to dry. This will take several days.

While it is in the process of drying, pinch the face into any shape you want it. It is extremely hard when dry and there

will be tiny wrinkles over the surface that will give a life-like character to the face. Add tiny beads for eyes, paint the mouth red, and rub a little rouge on the cheeks for color. A coat of clear shellac will preserve the face indefinitely.

Apple dolls are most suitable for making characters such as fishermen, mountaineers, old men or women, Indians, etc. They are more effective if a headdress such as a hat or bonnet is added. A little raveled yarn or theatrical hair can be added around the edge of the headdress. The head, when dry, is about the size of a walnut, so make the body in proportion, or about seven times the length of the head.

DOLLS CARVED FROM WOOD

Dolls carved from a single block of wood are easy to make and are excellent for use in doll houses. Take a piece of pine 1 by 1 by 4 inches and shape the body as shown in the photograph. Note that the legs are cut in one piece with only a small groove between them, and the feet protrude about 1/8 inch in the front. It is not necessary to carve the arms.

Small hands can be carved from wood with 1/8 inch arms and attached to the bottom of the sleeves. Make the sleeves full at the bottom, gather them and insert the arms. They will stay in place if a little glue is added to the wood and

[152]

thread in the gathers pulled quite tight and fastened in place with several back stitches.

STORYTELLING DOLLS

These dolls (Fig. 4) will delight children who like to dramatize their stories. The body is made of a piece of heavy cardboard 8 inches long and 2½ inches wide. The head, feet, and arms are made from white knitted material (a white sock will furnish ample material). The head should be one-eighth the length of body. Stuff the head with cotton and sew it to the top of the cardboard body. Next cut and shape two feet from same material, stuff and sew to legs. Finally cut two pieces of cloth and sew them together and sew to the cardboard which forms the upper part of back of body. This will serve as two arms, which are left empty for inserting the fingers of the child who will play with the doll. The thumb and little finger will fit into the sleeves to become the doll's arms. Thus the doll can be animated for illustrating action stories.

OLD AMISH DOLLS
These dolls were carved from wood. They are shown in native costumes.

Dress the doll in paper costumes according to the character of the story. The front of the dress is complete, but the back must cover only from waist down (Fig. 4, bottom). The upper part is left open in order to insert the hand. Use paper clips to fasten skirt together.

DANCING DOLLS

These little dolls (Fig. 5A) can trip the light fantastic not on a ballroom floor but on a table top. They are excellent for teaching children rhythm and how to keep time with music.

To make a dancing doll, cut a piece of heavy cardboard exactly the size of the body pattern shown. Next, cut some knitted material for legs and be sure the size of the pattern will fit your fingers. Sew the *front* of the stocking to the bottom of the cardboard and leave the back open for inserting the fore and middle fingers. Cut the costume (Fig. 6) from paper (if you do not have decorated paper, add some color with a brush) and

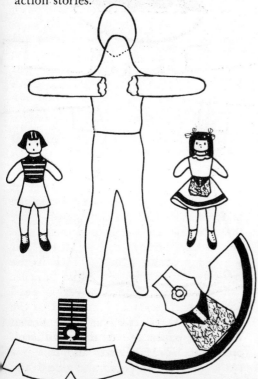

STORYTELLING DOLL
Fig. 4. The central figure is the back of the body of the doll. Note the cloth of the arms is attached about halfway up the back for the thumb and little finger to be inserted, giving movement to the arms. The basic pattern for the costume for both boys and girls is the same excepting two V-shaped cuts are made in skirt to form legs for the trousers.

COSTUMES

Fig. 6. Three costumes you can make of paper for finger puppets.

paste to the front of the body (Fig. 5D). Add the headdress and the doll is ready for its first performance. The doll dances when the fingers move (5E) to the rhythm of the music.

COSTUMES FOR CHARACTER DOLLS

Many costumes are made from paper or cloth like those shown (Fig. 7). They may be made to dress flat cardboard bodies like paper dolls, or cover wire armatures described in this chapter. Various kinds of paper can be used such as colored construction paper, fancy wrappings or crepe paper. Here are a few suggestions:

Indian. Make costume from brown wrapping paper and decorate with colored crayons. Make hair and shoes of black construction paper and glue to the

[154]

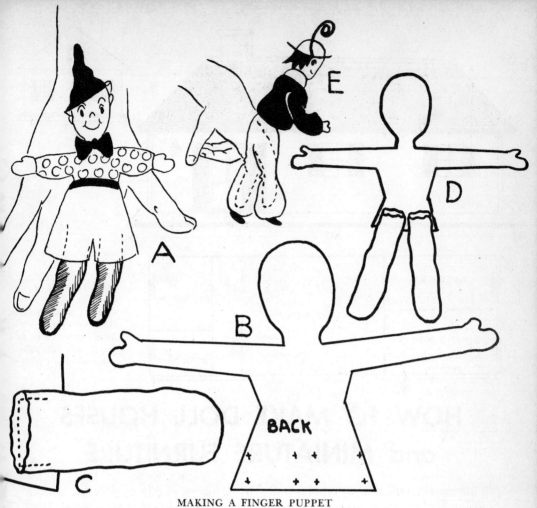

MAKING A FINGER PUPPET

Fig. 5. (A) Dancing doll finger puppet. (B) Puppet pattern showing placement for legs. (C) Details of leg stitched to body. (D) Both legs stitched to body. (E) Fabric-costumed finger puppet in action.

body. Cut a red feather and yellow headband from construction paper and add any color fringe to jacket and trousers.

Girl. The dress and hood are made from fancy wrapping paper. Make shoulder ruffles, flounce on skirt and waist and edge of bonnet, from border cut from paper doilies.

Soldier. Make costume from red construction paper. Cut hat, boots and belt from glossy black paper. A silver or gold buckle will give a final touch.

Pierrot and Pierrette. These costumes may be made from fancy wrapping paper such as white crepe paper with decorations added with black tempera paint.

Make the ruffs at the neck of white crepe paper or paper napkins.

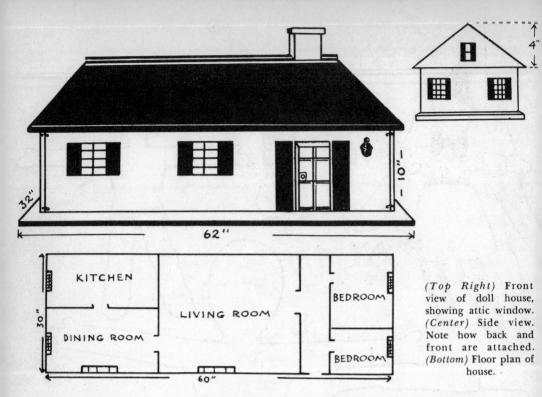

KITCHEN

LIVING ROOM

DINING ROOM

BEDROOM

BEDROOM

32"

62"

10"

30"

60"

4"

(Top Right) Front view of doll house, showing attic window. *(Center)* Side view. Note how back and front are attached. *(Bottom)* Floor plan of house.

HOW TO MAKE DOLL HOUSES and MINIATURE FURNITURE

This chapter tells how to build a doll house any father would enjoy making for his little daughter, and then how to furnish it. The house itself is just the right size for the average family of dolls. It has five rooms with a hall at one end and plenty of room for an attic in which to store extra properties when not in use. The living room is in the center with two rooms on one side that may be used as a bedroom and nursery. The other two rooms with hall between are suggested for a bath and kitchen.

MATERIALS AND DIMENSIONS FOR DOLL HOUSE

Framework, 40 inches of soft wood 1¾ by 3/16 inches. Base, walls, roof, ceiling, and floor, plywood 3/16 inch thick. Base, 32 by 62 inches. Front and back walls, 2 pieces 10 by 60 inches. Side walls, 2 pieces, 10 by 30 inches. Peak of roof, 2 pieces, 4

by 32 inches. Moldings, door and window frames, 42 inches thin strip wood. Door, 4 by 8 inches. Windows, 4 by 5 inches. Attic window, 2 by 3 inches. Two hooks for attaching front of house to side walls. Celluloid for windows.

MAKING THE DOLL HOUSE

The entire front and back are removable so that the doll house can be furnished and changed from time to time. These are held in place with small metal hooks when the doll house is not in use.

First build a skeleton frame the dimensions of the house with strips of wood. Cut four corner posts the height of the house and join similar strips to the top and bottom to make a frame for the roof and floor. Nail the lower strips to the foundation before adding the walls and roof. Fasten the strips together with small nails and glue.

Cut out windows and doors before you nail walls to framework.

If you prefer to work on the flat pieces, add celluloid for windows, window and door frames and blinds before nailing walls in place. You can also add the base boards, wall trims and doors.

Put the celluloid for windows between the frame and wall.

Strong glue will hold strips for moldings, windows and door frames in place, or you may use ½-inch brads when necessary.

Wood from cigar boxes makes excellent window shades and shutters. Use ½-inch brass hinges to hang door and fancy brass-headed tacks for door knobs.

It makes a more finished-looking house if, after the walls are in place, you put ½-inch quarter-round molding at outer top edge of foundation. This forms a groove for removable walls and holds them in place.

For floor and ceiling, 3/16-inch plywood is used. Cut it to fit the rooms you have built and nail to framework. The first floor should be nailed to a heavier board used as a foundation.

Cut two pieces for the roof; then nail to the roof joists. The chimneys are cut at the bottom to fit the roof and are glued on.

HOW TO DECORATE THE DOLL HOUSE

Now for ways to decorate the doll house. Use oil house paint on the outside in white or any color you may choose. The same type of paint is used on the chimney, window frames, shutters, etc., only in contrasting colors. If you want a brick chimney, outline the bricks with narrow white lines.

The interior can be painted with show-card colors. They are vivid and easily applied. You can tint the walls or paper them with real wallpaper.

LIGHTS FOR THE DOLL HOUSE

If you wish to wire the house for lighting, it can be done simply by using Christmas-tree light fixtures. As these come with lights on a string and all must be lighted in order to work, distribute them one in each room and the others on the outside of the house.

ACCESSORIES FOR THE DOLL HOUSE

After the doll house and its furniture are made, you will want accessories to lend the "lived-in" touch. This can be achieved very simply or you can spend many hours on details, such as patchwork quilts for the beds, tablecloth and napkins, hooked rugs, fancy drapes, etc. However, there are a few fundamental furnishings that we wish to suggest:

In general, bedspreads and bureau covers are attractive when made from batiste and edged with narrow lace. Table mats for the dining room can be cut from a lace-paper doily which has a design of small circles. Red and white checked kitchen towel can be made from an inexpensive handkerchief, towels, wash cloths and bath mat from a striped bath towel. A tiny comb and brush are cut from heavy silver paper. A pink button with a fluff of cotton on top makes a dainty puff box. Small inexpensive brooches can be used as picture frames with the picture pressed in the openings.

DOLL HOUSE RUGS

Cut discarded silk stockings in narrow rings. Loop rings together as shown in the illustration. Crochet the strip of rings into a rug as follows: Chain 5, then single crochet (1 stitch on needle; draw working thread through this stitch, making 2 on needle; draw thread through these 2 stitches) into this chain, going around and around until the rug is the size for your doll house. You will have to put 2 single crochet in some of the stitches to make the rug lie flat.

The stockings may be dyed if you like, and your rug may be of one color or with contrasting border. The width of rings depends on kind of fabric—rings cut from sheer stockings are wider than others.

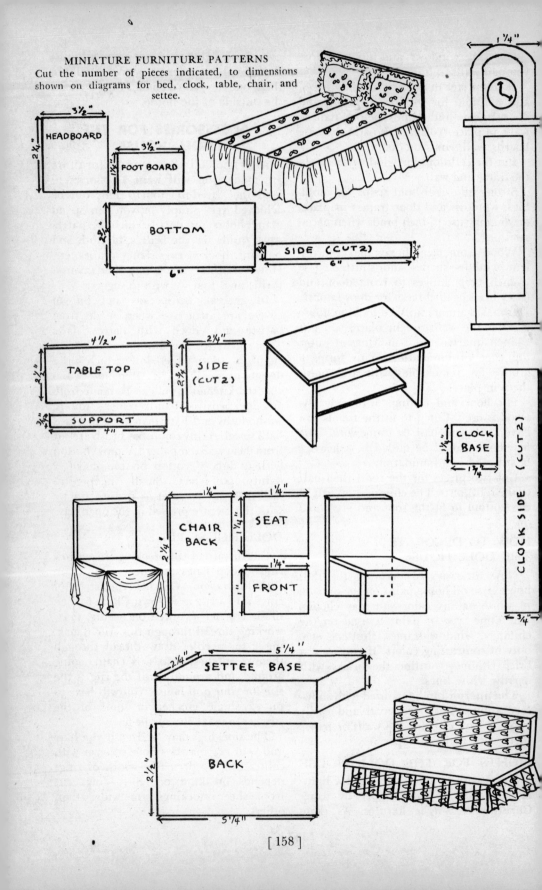

MINIATURE FURNITURE PATTERNS

Cut the number of pieces indicated, to dimensions shown on diagrams for bed, clock, table, chair, and settee.

HEADBOARD — 3½" × 2½"

FOOT BOARD — 3½" × 1¼"

BOTTOM — 6" × 2¼"

SIDE (CUT 2) — 6" × ½"

TABLE TOP — 4½" × 2½"

SIDE (CUT 2) — 2¼" × 2½"

SUPPORT — 4" × ½"

CLOCK BASE — 1¾" × 1¼" × ½"

CLOCK SIDE (CUT 2) — ¾"

Clock top — 1¼"

CHAIR BACK — 1¼" × 2¼"

SEAT — 1¼" × 1¼"

FRONT — 1¼" × 1"

SETTEE BASE — 5¼" × 2¼"

BACK — 5¼" × 2½"

WALL OF TROY

MAKING RUGS AND TABLE MATS
Don't throw away torn silk stockings—they'll make fine rugs for doll house or your own bedroom.
Use checked oilcloth for table mats with Wall of Troy or pointed edges.

Large rugs for home use may be made by the same method.

OILCLOTH MATS

Mats for the doll house or breakfast table are easy to make from oilcloth in a small checked design with straight or diagonal-shaped checks, as illustrated. The straight check forms a "Wall of Troy" edge when cut out; the diagonal check, a pointed edge.

To make mats for the doll house, cut them rectangular in shape, about ½-inch larger all around than you want them to be when finished. Then carefully snip away edges to the finished shape. When cutting a blue and white checkered mat, cut away all the white or all the blue material as you snip along the edge of a line of checks.

HOW TO MAKE MINIATURE FURNITURE

Doll furniture can be cut from cigar boxes. First decide if you want to make it in the colonial or modern style and keep to the same period in every room.

Patterns. The patterns should all be drawn to the same scale. First draw the pattern on heavy paper and cut around the outline. Take the pieces and fit them together to see if they are the right size. Lay the paper patterns on the cigar box

wood and mark around them with a pencil. Remove patterns and saw out the pieces with a coping saw. For accuracy, saw exactly along the pencil line.

A good scale to follow in making doll house furniture is one-twelfth the size of real furniture. Keep in mind the fact that empty spools are useful as stools, tables or stands.

Since there is little strain on the furniture it can be held together with glue. After it is assembled, smooth it thoroughly with fine sandpaper.

Decorating the Furniture. For best results, decorate the furniture with oil paints. However, show-card colors may be used if given a coat of shellac to keep the paint from wearing off. Tiny edgings of gold or silver paint will give daintiness to the furniture. Tiny flowers cut from a seed catalogue can be pasted on the bedroom furniture for added interest and color.

Finishing the Furniture. The furniture is also attractive when finished in the natural wood. This is done by giving it two or three coats of clear shellac, rubbing it down each time when dry with fine sandpaper or steel wool. Polish with floor wax; many cigar boxes are made from fine tropical woods, and if so, you will want to preserve its natural color and grain.

(Left) Plain dyeing of lingerie.
(Above) Four designs for guest towels.

DECORATING TEXTILES AS A HOBBY

Decorating textiles is a fascinating craft that may be both amusing and profitable. Once a person understands the art of dyeing and adding interesting designs for decoration, no materials will be thrown in the rag bag without close scrutiny as to quality and possible uses. If draperies or spreads become faded, the color can be removed with a bleaching solution and vivid colors added to make them look like new. The same applies to dresses, blouses, scarfs and other wearing apparel.

PLAIN DYEING

Before we talk about the different methods of decorating textiles, a word should be said about plain dyeing. Many attempts at dyeing have been unsuccessful because of carelessness, and not conforming to rules. Here are a few simple rules that must be followed:

1. Dip garment in cold water and wring out thoroughly.

2. White or light-colored fabrics will tint best.

3. The water used should be as hot as the hands can comfortably withstand.

4. After adding dye to the water, stir thoroughly thirty seconds.

5. The piece to be dipped should be clean and preferably damp.

6. Keep the article immersed until desired shade is achieved, swirling constantly through the dye solution.

7. If the article dyes too dark, rinse with cold water while wet. If too light, dip again in a stronger solution.

8. Wring excess moisture from article. Rub in the hands for a minute and roll in a towel to dry.

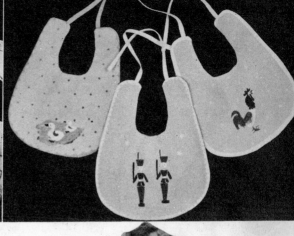

(Above) Luncheon mat and napkin to match.
(Top right) Three designs for babies' bibs.
(Right center) Monograms or initials make
an attractive design (see Lettering chapter).

BATIK—DYEING WITH DESIGNS

If one wishes to decorate a portion only
of a fabric, this type of work is usually
termed batik. Batik is the original Javanese method of decorating fabrics. In
traditional batiking, hot wax is applied to
the fabric where the dye is not to touch.

TIE-DYEING

A simple division of the batik field is
tie-dyeing. To tie-dye, a piece of fabric
is wrapped in sections with cords that
have been previously soaked in melted
paraffin and beeswax. To facilitate the
wrapping with the twine, pebbles of suitable size are placed in the fabric first.
The fabric must be very tightly bound
with this wax-soaked cord. The portions
of the fabric that are exposed are then
painted with dye or ink in whatever color
selection the artist wishes. One or two
colors may be used without unwinding
the cord and rebinding, or for a more
bizarre effect one color may be used, the
fabric released from its bindings, re-
bound in a different manner and then
a second color used. There are an end-
less number of applications of this simple
principle.

CRACKLE BATIK

Crackle batik is another very simple
form of dyeing. It is accomplished by
painting the entire piece of cloth with

STENCILED SLEEVE PATTERN: This
pattern can be stenciled in one or two colors.

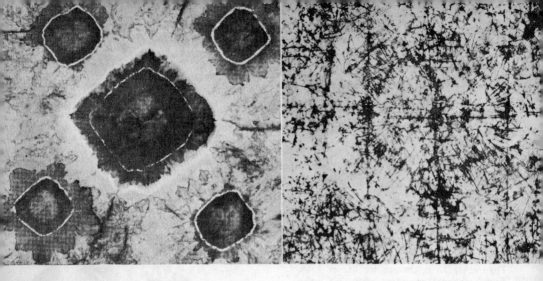

melted wax, allowing the wax to cool and then crackling the stiffened fabric uniformly. This is done by wrinkling it in the hands like a piece of paper. Now paint both sides of the fabric in any color of waterproof ink or dye which you may choose. The ink will soak through where the wax is cracked and leave a spiderweb effect on the fabric. The wax may be removed by washing the entire piece in gasoline, benzine or carbon tetrachloride or by placing it between two pieces of blotting paper and four or five layers of newspaper on the outside of them and pressing with a hot iron. The wax will melt and be absorbed by the blotters. Do not place the newspaper right next to the fabric as the print will come off.

Repeating this crackling several times with different colors of waterproof inks increases the effect.

BATIK WITH WAX

We shall first outline the traditional Javanese method of batik. For pictures and designs applied to cloth and similar articles, it is necessary to outline the design with wax first so that the colors cannot run past the wax outline. The Javanese use an instrument called a *tjanting* for this purpose. A *tjanting* looks for all the world like a miniature tea kettle on the end of a stick. Hot wax is scooped up in the *tjanting* and the end

or spout is then run along the lines to which wax is to be applied. These instruments are available from some art supply houses.

Most modern batiking is done by applying the wax with brushes. The dye also is generally applied in this manner. If only one application of wax is made, white lines will separate all the colored areas in the finished work. If the design is to be one in which the colors meet, wax must be applied and removed and new wax outlines applied to block out each color area separately as the work progresses.

To explain more fully this method, if green were to be used in the design, the entire piece of fabric would be painted with wax, except where the green dye were to take; the article would then be dipped in the green dye or the green dye painted on it and this allowed to dry. The wax would then be removed either by washing with a solvent, as previously mentioned, or else by pressing between blotters. New wax would then be applied to all parts of the fabric except where the second color, such as brown, were to be used.

This tedious process would go on as many times as there were colors. Each time the wax were removed from the fabric, the article would have to be restretched on its frame. Such a frame is made of stretcher strips, such as artists' canvas is stretched on. The strips must be wound around with muslin to facilitate pinning the work.

BATIK WITHOUT WAX

And now we may repeat what makes the decoration of fabrics infinitely easier when waterproof ink is the coloring matter used. This fact is that *on the majority of fabrics no wax outlining is necessary.* On textiles such as crepe and unbleached muslin, waterproof ink in colors may be applied just as though you were painting on paper. The ink will not run.

Steps in Batiking. First, secure a large white blotter and outline the design on it with pencil. With a few strokes of wax crayon in different colors spaced wide apart, indicate where the different colors of the design are to go. The blotter should be thumbtacked to a large drawing board or table and the silk crepe stretched on the blotter with pins. It will be found that the crepe is transparent enough to permit the design to show through, just as if you were looking through tracing cloth.

Now dip your brush in the first color of ink that you wish to apply and begin painting. Paint light colors first. As you paint, press the crepe down with your fingers on each side of the area you are coloring. Do not put too much color on your brush at a time, but should this be unavoidable, holding the crepe flat against the blotter will cause the blotter to absorb any excess that runs through the crepe.

It is a curious fact that the cheap silk crepes are more satisfactory for this process than expensive silk crepes. This is because the cheap crepes are filled and this filling aids in discouraging the ink from running. If you wash a crepe of this type before applying the inks, it will not be as satisfactory as when you paint on it while it is fresh and new. Do not apply the second color while the first color is still wet. These simple precautions are all that are necessary to do competent

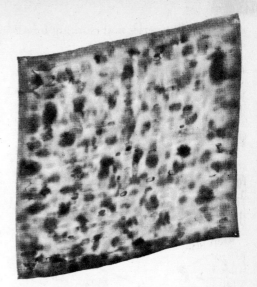

A simple blend. The cloth was first dampened.

batik work with inks by the direct painting method.

DECORATING CLOTH WITH TEXTILE COLORS

Nearly all craft supply houses and some department stores carry sets of textile colors containing the primary colors and enough penetrating and extending solution to decorate several yards of cloth. If you are planning to decorate in several colors and have a limited number of designs, it is more economical to buy the colors in sets.

Textile colors are easy to use, can be washed, or dry cleaned, and are non-fading. Designs may be as simple or as intricate as desired, with a single color or ranging through the entire spectrum. Colors are often more interesting if they are mixed and blended from the primary colors.

THINGS TO DECORATE

There is no end to the possibilities of things to make. You can decorate a handkerchief or guest towel with a single monogram, or execute a large wall-hanging with an intricate design of many colors. Textile colors may be applied to almost every fabric such as rayon, silk, cotton or linen, which makes it possible to decorate draperies and clothing for all occasions.

HOW TO DECORATE

There are only five simple steps, as follows: (1) Wash the cloth. (2) Mix your colors. (3) Apply to fabric. (4) Dry thoroughly. (5) "Set" with hot iron.

Step 1. Wash the Cloth. Eliminate all size or filler, as it is sometimes called, from the fabric you are planning to use. This is done by washing in warm soapy water, rinsing thoroughly and pressing (Fig. 1).

Step 2. Mix Your Colors (Fig. 2). First mix color with thinner or extender. Practically any type of mixing dish may be used. Many like to use old dinner plates, putting the colors around the edge of the plate and the extender in the center. Small saucers for each color may also be used.

Don't hesitate to mix one color with another. Many unusual and interesting color combinations can be easily secured by mixing the colors regularly supplied.

Step 3. Apply to Fabric (Fig. 3). The application of textile colors varies with the various techniques used. However, there are a few general points to keep in mind.

1. Always use a white blotter under the fabric. This takes up any excess color. Stretch the cloth tightly to your drawing board with scotch tape or thumbtacks.

2. These colors are very concentrated —you need ever so little color on your brush. Charge the brush sparingly—then stroke it across a cloth or paper to remove excess color.

3. Rather than use one heavy application, go over an area several times, without recharging the brush, in order to obtain the desired intensity of color.

4. Use a firm stroke in applying the color.

Step 4. Dry Thoroughly. Allow the finished work to dry thoroughly before setting the colors (Fig. 4); twenty-four hours is the ideal drying time, even though the colors will appear dry in a few minutes. Your attention to this simple detail will increase the fastness of your work.

Step 5. "Set" with Hot Iron. The setting of the colors is simple, but must be done thoroughly. The colors are made wash-fast by applying plenty of heat— ironing for at least three minutes at 350° F. as explained below, will do it:

1. After the colors dry (see Step 4), place a dry cloth over the design—face up—and press the decorated portions with a hot iron (Fig. 5).

2. Turn the material over and press the back.

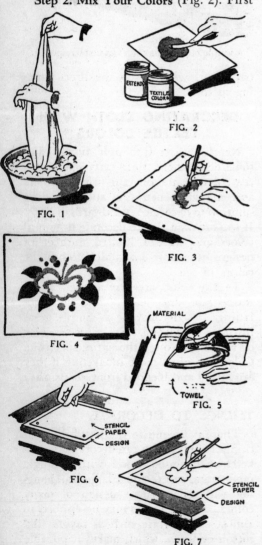

FIG. 1

FIG. 2

FIG. 3

FIG. 4

MATERIAL

TOWEL

FIG. 5

STENCIL PAPER

DESIGN

FIG. 6

STENCIL PAPER

DESIGN

FIG. 7

[164]

3. A dampened pressing cloth may then be used as desired.

Note. For heat-sensitive fabrics such as rayon, on which high temperatures must not be used, a warm iron, 280° F., for a longer period is recommended.

HELPFUL SUGGESTIONS

White and light-colored cottons, rayons and linens are ideal for decorations with textile colors, and if the simple directions are followed they will launder and dry-clean successfully. Textile colors are also used on silk, wool, felt, nylon, etc., with beautiful effect. The nature of these materials, however, is such that they require careful handling, and light washing, if any, should be given. It is common practice to dry-clean such fabrics. Due to the great variance in wools this fabric is the least desirable to use. It is recommended that a small piece be used for experimentation before proceeding.

Textile colors, being transparent colors, are most effective when they are used on light or medium backgrounds. If a dark background is desired, however, it is better to print or paint the design on light-colored material and then paint the dark background around the design. If a dark-colored material must be used, add white to the colors to make them opaque enough to cover the dark background. The white, being opaque, does not penetrate the fibre of the fabric sufficiently to give entirely secure anchorage, therefore it will not be as washable as the other colors.

The storing of mixtures is not recommended. Mix only enough quantities of colors with extender for each project. (Professional users sometimes carry mixtures over for several days in order to avoid any variance in colors on large projects. In such cases the mixtures should be thoroughly stirred daily.)

ADDING COLOR WITH STENCILS

Applying a design to cloth by using a stencil is perhaps the easiest method and the most effective. Make a careful tracing

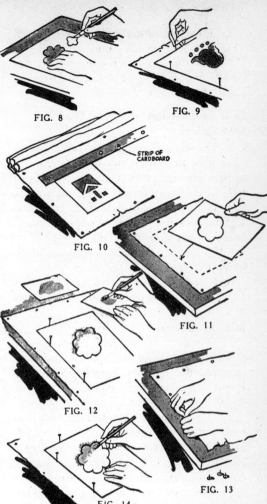

FIG. 8

FIG. 9

FIG. 10

STRIP OF CARDBOARD

FIG. 11

FIG. 12

FIG. 13

FIG. 14

of your design onto a piece of stencil board or thin cardboard. If you are using two or more colors in your design and they are close together, it may be necessary to make a stencil for each color. Use a sharp knife for cutting out the stencil. A complete circuit is cut around all the traced areas on the stencil and the design piece removed. The colors are applied to the cloth with stencil brushes (round or flat) using a circular motion over the cut areas. The beginner should follow the step-by-step directions given below:

First Wash and Press Your Cloth.

If It Is One-Color Stencil:

1. Fasten the stencil paper to the design with tape or thumbtacks (Fig. 6).

2. Trace the design with a hard pencil (Fig. 7). Stay on the lines.

3. Cut the stencil on the lines with a stencil cutter (Fig. 8), sharp knife or razor blade.

If It Is a Design of More Than One Color:

1. Draw a right angle, or put 2 pieces of tape or pins at right angles, where the upper left corner of your stencil paper falls (Fig. 9). Always place your stencil so that the upper left corner fits into this. For borders, use a strip of paper or cardboard as a guide (Fig. 10).

2. Trace each color on a separate piece of stencil paper.

3. Place stencils together and hold up to the light to be sure the various parts of your design fall into place.

Mix the Colors:

1. To every color add extender. It makes the colors go farther and improves the working qualities. A good proportion is an approximately equal amount of each.

2. To make a color lighter, add extender until the desired hue is obtained. Suggestion: If you wish the color lightened only slightly, add extender to the color; if a very light tint is desired, start with extender, and add color—it saves on color. (White will also lighten the colors, but will cut down washability.)

3. To make a color darker, add black (a little goes a long way).

Apply the Color:

1. Stretch the cloth and fasten to heavy cardboard or drawing board (Fig. 11).

2. Work the color into the brush, then stroke across a cloth or paper to remove excess color (Fig. 12). *Remember*—all you need is a very little color on your brush.

3. Place stencil in position on the previously washed, dried and pressed cloth (Fig. 13).

4. Allow your brush to hit the stencil about ½ inch from the opening and sweep across the opening, always toward the center (Fig. 14). Repeat the stroke

until you have the desired intensity of color.

Another method of application is stippling. Hold the brush vertically and use an up-and-down motion.

5. For extra brightness, go over the design again—without adding more color to the brush.

6. Always hold your stencil firmly on your guide lines or fasten it with scotch tape or thumbtacks. Hold the stencil down firmly with the fingers to prevent color getting underneath the stencil.

7. If the color thickens too much, add a little thinner but remember to keep the consistency as thick as heavy cream.

Dry Thoroughly and Press.

If these simple directions are followed, your finished work will be highly resistant to sunlight, laundering, dry cleaning.

Additional Working Hints

If you plan to reuse your stencils at a later date, clean off all color with textile cleaner before filing.

Use good stencil brushes. If possible, have a stencil brush for each color. This insures clean, brilliant results.

Attractive results are produced by shading the color from darker edges to a lighter center.

Artistic effects are also produced by going over the outer edge of the stenciled area with a second rim of analogous or related color. For instance, if any area has been stenciled with yellow-orange, then go around the outer edge of this area with a straight orange color or a grayed red.

Small areas are stenciled more rapidly and thoroughly if the brush is held vertically and applied with a stippling motion. This method is easier, too, with fabrics that are thin and sleazy.

Thin, transparent surgeon's rubber gloves are a convenience when doing considerable work with colors.

Fine line details such as outlining, veins in leaves, etc., may be added to the stenciled design, using a ball-pointed pen or a toothpick to apply the color.

BLOCK PRINTING WITH LINOLEUM

Wood cutting and printing is an old art. Linoleum block printing is comparatively new, starting with the discovery of linoleum. Picture printing, impractical before the introduction of linoleum block printing, can now thrill the hearts of all. The thrill that comes with the crispness of the first hand-made print, and the interest registered upon the face of the amateur artist is proof enough that this is a worthwhile activity.

USES OF BLOCK PRINTING

There are many uses of block printing. Fundamentally, it is printing and may be used wherever a printed subject occurs. Some of the more common uses are for greeting cards, book covers, tickets, monograms, programs, banners, flags, badges, textile printing, book plates, place cards, book markers, etc. To this list may be added many other uses. Spe-

cific directions for printing on textiles are given at the end of this chapter.

TOOLS

The tools used for linoleum block printing are commonly called linoleum cutters. They are made in several sizes. The smaller cutters are called veiners. The larger cutters are called gouges. You require about six cutters: a small U-shaped veiner, a V-shaped veiner, a small gouge, a ⎵-shaped gouge, a large gouge—and a knife. Art and craft supply houses generally sell these in sets.

Some cutters are made like pens, so that all the cutters will fit the same handle. The cutters are tightened in the handle with a set screw and a screw driver, the better handles having a steel collar to hold the cutter firmly. The handle should be of sturdy construction and designed to fit the palm so as to feel

comfortable in the hand. Cutters and handles that are too flimsy should not be considered.

A most worthwhile contribution to the various types of linoleum cutters is a tool which is drawn toward you when cutting. This cutter is known as the linozip. The linozip cutters are made in four sizes to match the conventional type of linoleum cutters. They are made in the same way as the "push" type cutters and fit into the same handles.

With the linozip cutter you can sketch very freely on the linoleum in the same way you sketch with pen or brush, because the tool is held and used like a pen or pencil. Such a tool will largely eliminate the danger which exists when a tool is pushed away from the user. All the thrusts are underhand and not toward the free hand.

The linozip is used as a sketch tool and is very useful in doing large areas and backgrounds. The prints on this page and page 169 show examples of the kind of work possible with the linozip cutter. In many ways it complements the use of other tools.

A worthwhile accessory to the line of cutters is a stencil knife. This is used for cutting the large pieces of linoleum to size for use. A knife with a good size handle and a short blade is best.

The linoleum cutters, the stencil knife, and linoleum may be procured from your local stationer, school supply house or art dealer. Usage will determine your selection of tools of your craft.

FACTS ABOUT LINOLEUM

Linoleum for block printing is known as Battleship Linoleum. It is manufactured in thicknesses up to one-fourth inch. It is usually a natural brown, but may be had in almost any color. The brown is best for cutting. Battleship Linoleum should not be confused with cork carpet which is like it in appearance but much coarser and softer. If the surface of the linoleum is not perfectly smooth it may be worked down by using a very fine sand paper. For large, bold areas or a new type of handling, cork carpet may sometimes be used to advantage. Never use a linoleum with a pattern.

Weather conditions will change the consistency of linoleum, and will influ-

ence its handling. In cold weather it becomes hard and will easily crack. In such cases it must be warmed before using.

Many of the linoleums in this type are waxed. This must be removed, as wax is repellent to ink or tracing with carbon paper. Remove the waxed surface with turpentine or heat, and clean with art gum.

MOUNTING LINOLEUM

Linoleum cuts that are to be printed in a power press or a hand jobber must be type high which is thirty-one thirty-seconds of an inch in height. This includes the combined thickness of the wood and linoleum. The better blocks are made from five-ply, laminated wood and three-eighths inch linoleum. In some cases the linoleum is white surfaced to facilitate drawing and cutting, and to harden the surface so that longer runs may be had from the cut. It is always wise to select a well-made block when you contemplate printing any number of copies.

Mounting may also be done in the school or home shop. Use a good quality glue, spread it evenly on the plywood and on the burlap back of the linoleum. Then put it in a press or weight it down to dry. Place newspaper above and below the blocks to catch the glue that may ooze out, and allow to remain under pressure for at least twelve hours.

When blocks are to be printed on hand press, or by hand, it is not necessary to mount the linoleum on wood, unless the linoleum is very thin or the plate very large. Many people mount linoleum on cardboard or plywood for hand work.

CUTTING LINOLEUM TO SIZE

When buying linoleum in bulk, you are confronted with the problem of cutting it down to the size on which you wish to work. Place the large piece of linoleum on a table, after it is room temperature, measure with rule and square (a 12-by-18-inch steel square is fine), follow the lines with a small veiner and then cut with a stencil knife. Hold the knife steadily and cut

to a consistent depth, always cutting from one side of the large piece to the other. Now, grasp the whole piece in both hands and break. The burlap still joins the linoleum, and this may be cut with either knife or shears. This method is used for ordinary work. For more accurate work, a vertical cut all the way through the burlap is used, but this is more difficult to do.

BRAYER, INK AND SLAB

The hand brayer used in block printing is a rubber roller with a handle. It is used for spreading the ink in an even surface on the block in preparation for printing. A four-inch brayer is wide enough for ordinary work, but for larger work a larger brayer is better. Block printing brayers are inexpensive in comparison with the gelatin printer's brayer. Gelatin brayers are rather hard to handle and need frequent replacing because climatic conditions, as well as heat and cold, will change their consistency.

The most practical and least difficult

to handle is a water soluble, block printing ink. This ink is sold in one and one-half ounce and four ounce tubes, in all colors. It is a true water color ink and can be washed with water, making it so much more practical for use. The ink may be mixed and toned, is adaptable to most papers, dries quickly and looks well.

When the print is to be permanent, use an oil ink. A job black or half-tone ink is very satisfactory. This ink requires a special cleanser—gasoline or benzine.

When inks become too sticky, or weather conditions affect them, provide yourself with a reducer. Reducers may be had for both water color and oil inks.

For spreading the ink before applying to the surface of the linoleum cut, procure a flat non-porous surface about 12 by 18 inches in size. The best material is a marble slab. Old bureau or table tops are excellent. If marble cannot be had a piece of plate glass will do, or a piece of enameled hardwood has been found satisfactory. The ink is rolled out on this surface with the brayer until it is spread evenly. The slab is also used for thinning or mixing ink.

THE PRESS

In order to print the linoleum block, it is necessary to apply pressure to the block, which may be done in many ways. Some print well by using a vise or an improvised wash-wringer with rubber rollers. It is even possible to procure results by stepping on the block. For more accurate results it is well to own a press. An old-fashioned book press with a large wheel and screw will give you excellent service. Such a press should be fitted with a sliding work board made from plywood to facilitate the work.

There are now several presses on the market which have been especially designed for block printing. They are small, light and inexpensive and will do the job well where only ordinary prints are made.

OTHER NECESSARY MATERIAL

Pencils. Use a soft pencil (H B) for original sketching and blackening the paper for transferring. A harder (2 H) pencil for fine lines, layouts and outlining, and a hard (6 H) for transferring to the linoleum. A fine point mimeograph stylus is used when you want accuracy and precision in the traced line.

Paper. Use a good quality white paper to make the sketch. A smooth surfaced paper is best because it will transfer more readily. Drawing paper has too coarse a tooth. Carbon paper should be of good quality either blue or black. Printing papers should be of absorbent quality; Japanese rice papers are the best, but you will find many good results are obtained on inexpensive poster stock. The author uses ordinary newsprint for proofs and finds it excellent.

Triangles. For squaring paper, a 45° or 60° celluloid triangle is handy. For squaring linoleum a 12-by-18-inch steel square is used. For corner squaring of linoleum and wooden mounts, use an

ordinary carpenter's square. (Refer to illustration on page 174.)

As you become interested in your hobby you will provide yourself with sharpening stones, special lettering pens, waterproof ink, shears, etc.

Each person will use those materials which will help him most in creating what he desires to express.

MAKING A LINOLEUM BLOCK PRINT

The steps in making a linoleum block print are as follows: (1) the drawing or sketch, (2) transferring to the linoleum, (3) cutting or engraving, (4) printing, and (5) mounting for display purposes and framing.

Sketch the drawing on good, tough, white paper, have the paper square, and complete drawing before transferring or engraving. In case of lettering, or drawings with right and left sides, as in people doing things, the drawing must be reversed, if not so drawn. In reversing a drawing, place it against a window, and trace, or place the drawing on a piece of carbon paper with the carbon coated side up, and trace. Tracing can be avoided by making your drawing on thin transparent paper such as onion skin or transparent bond paper.

When the drawing is completed trace it on a piece of linoleum about one inch larger than the drawing. Fasten the drawing and the carbon paper to the linoleum with thumb tacks, placing the thumb tacks outside of the drawing, or in parts of the drawing which are to be white on the print. The reason for this is that the holes made by thumb tacks are noticeable in the print. Use carbon paper because it will not rub off as easily as pencil or chip off like ink or paint. Now you are ready to begin cutting or engraving the block.

In engraving, the first tool to use is the U-shaped veiner or V-shaped veiner, depending on the nature of the print you are doing. The first cutting to be done is the outlining with one of the two

named tools. When all outlining is done, the larger parts which are to be white may be gouged out with any of the gouges, all depending on the size and the nature of the print you are doing. After this preliminary work, detail may be added with the U-shaped or V-shaped veiners. When the print is completed, cut it square with the stencil knife. Test corners of linoleum with triangle or square, and the engraving is then ready for printing.

In freehand sketching, work directly on the linoleum with brush or pencil. Begin at once with such tools as you may want to use in expressing your idea. Freehand sketching with carving tools requires much more skill than carving from a tracing on the linoleum.

Squeeze a little water color printing ink on the slab and roll it out with a brayer until the brayer is entirely covered with ink of the same consistency all over the roller. Roll ink over the linoleum block, using pressure over the entire surface, making sure that the ink is spread evenly over the entire engraving. Place the inked block on a piece of paper. Then place under press and apply pressure, release, and your print is made. Care must be taken that the block is under the center of the press, directly under the center of pressure. Take care in padding, so that there is a reasonable stack of printing paper in the press when prints are made. When there are high spots on the print, that is, black parts which should not print, the block should be cleaned and the black parts removed. Another reason why a print may not come out clear cut is that you apply too much pressure. Correct pressure is most important in hand printing. It must be gauged by the amount of black in a print. A print with a lot of white requires little pressure, while a block with large black areas requires more pressure. Skill in

hand printing will be acquired through experience.

Use color in your printing, both in backgrounds and ink. Much interest can be aroused in this way.

The prints should be thoroughly dried before handling. Do not place them in piles, but spread them out individually, so that air can reach the printed surface.

For display purposes, mount prints on sturdy stock in correct color and spacing. This will do much to enchance the appearance of your work.

Good prints should be framed in plain black frames with clear glass, with or without margins, depending on the nature of the subject.

METHOD OF HOLDING THE
LINOLEUM CUTTERS

Fig. 1. For thin sketch lines where little pressure is needed for freehand work.

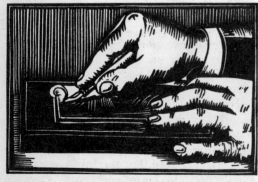

Fig. 2. For heavy lines and deep cuts, where more pressure is needed; for routing and all large work.

HOW TO HOLD THE TOOL FOR CUTTING THE BLOCK

Methods of doing things vary with people. Different people will hold engraving tools in different ways and get results, but for beginning any craft it is well to know a few accepted methods. The following are two ways of holding tools for most work.

For sketching and thin line work, which is not cut deep in the block, use the method as shown in Fig. 1. Always have the light falling on the linoleum so that there will be no glare; also hold block so that your free hand is in back of the surface you are cutting. This method gives you more freedom and should always be used for detailing and for intricate small lines. With this you have a lot of freedom but not so much pressure.

The way to hold the tool for most work is shown in Fig. 2. Here the tool is gripped firmly in the palm of the hand and guided with the forefinger. This is used where deep, consistent cutting is required. It is a good method to insure accuracy and firmness. Always cut away from yourself, holding the block with the flat of your free hand. By turning the block and the tool, all types of lines and corners may be handled.

Use the smallest cutter for the initial cut around traced lines. Do not cut out line, but alongside of lines. Lines have thickness which must be preserved to carry out the original plan of your drawing.

The tool should be held at about a 45-degree angle, holding the cutter steady, so that it will not dig deeply below the surface and break out ugly lines. A good rule to follow is never to dig in below the upper edge of the cutter.

When cutting a straight line, develop enough skill so that it can be done with one steady thrust, thus showing itself true. Usually each stopping place will show. In cutting a small square use four separate cuts, moving the block for each thrust rather than turning around corners. The grip shown in the second illustration is used for routing and large work.

A good craftsman will always see that the tools of his trade are in good condition and will not work with dull tools and loose or flimsy handles.

PROPER WAY OF CUTTING

When ink is applied to the block, the cut-out parts of the linoleum should be cut low enough to escape contact with the brayer. Narrow spaces should be cut, but never so deep as to go through to the burlap backing unless you are working on a mounted piece of linoleum. The sides of the cuts should be slanting and not vertical. This makes the engraving stronger. Follow the method of cutting shown in Fig. 7. Avoid cutting as shown in Fig. 8.

Sometimes the background may be enhanced by the ridges between the gouge cuts that pick up ink as the roller goes over them and deposit it on the paper. Such accidents add to the interest of the medium and teach you how to secure better effects.

You will want to know how the cutting you are doing will print. There are a few ways of finding out without soiling the block with ink while still in the engraving process. One is to make a rubbing

DIFFERENT SHAPES OF ENGRAVING TOOLS

Fig. 3. (1) the U-shaped veiner, used for outlining and detailing—most valuable tool in any set; (2) the V-shaped veiner, used for finer lines, more delicate work, and for sketching when doing a freehand cutting; (3) the small gouge, used for cleaning out and routing. This tool is used after outlining has been done with tools number 1 or 2; (4) the ⌞⌟-shaped gouge, used for cleaning out—indispensable for cutting borders and letters of a large size; (5) the large gouge, used for larger surfaces, in cleaning out and routing. Should be used for large white portions and when the work with number 3 or 4 becomes tedious. This tool is used very much in cleaning out white surfaces on posters and backgrounds on lettering.

CROSS-SECTION OF THE BLOCK

Fig. 4. Showing what kind of a cut each tool will make.

CUTS OF THE DIFFERENT TOOLS

Fig. 5. How they will show when printed. The small circle is a complete turn with the U-shaped veiner, the five-pointed star is five cuts with the V-shaped veiner, and the large circle with large gouge.

FIVE BORDERS AND AREAS

Fig. 6. Done with the five different tools. Notice how the tool may be used for different effects and how different cuts may be made with the different tools.

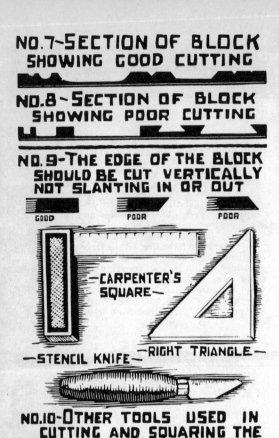

NO.7-SECTION OF BLOCK SHOWING GOOD CUTTING

NO.8-SECTION OF BLOCK SHOWING POOR CUTTING

NO.9-THE EDGE OF THE BLOCK SHOULD BE CUT VERTICALLY NOT SLANTING IN OR OUT

GOOD   POOR   POOR

—CARPENTER'S SQUARE—

—STENCIL KNIFE—   —RIGHT TRIANGLE—

NO.10-OTHER TOOLS USED IN CUTTING AND SQUARING THE BLOCK—

Fig. 11. *(Left)* Single line with U-shaped veiner. **Fig. 12.** *(Right)* Single line with V-shaped veiner.

of the engraving. You have done this with a coin or on embossed lettering on a book. Merely place paper over the cut portion and rub over it with a soft lead pencil. If a piece of carbon paper, carbon side up, is placed under the paper when the rubbing is made, an exact reproduction of the print will appear on the reverse side of the rubbing. Another way is to fill the depressions with white talcum powder.

CUTTING THE OUTSIDE OF THE BLOCK

When the engraving is completed, it is necessary to cut the block square. Cut with a stencil knife (Fig. 10), and always cut vertically. Test the corners with a carpenters' square (Fig. 11). Slanting cuts, in or out, are never satisfactory.

Accuracy and skill are so much a part

of good craftsmanship that it should always be the aim of the artist to work carefully, using the best tool in the most practical way.

SINGLE LINE CUTTING

In engraving, the beginner will find the single-stroke white line easier to do, as well as giving him better results. For this first attempt, use the U-shaped veiner and your print will be like the one in Fig. 11. This can be done with the V-shaped veiner, as shown in Fig. 12. Further detailing and line can be added with white-line cutting. Thus results as shown in Fig. 13 can easily be accomplished.

Shading and texture are necessary to more fully suggest your ideas. First this is done with an accented stroke to show light and shade, and thus, through experimentation, you will more fully dis-

Fig. 13. Engraved with both U-shaped veiner and V-shaped veiner, a good way to do cutting for quick results.

cover what can be done by using different strokes with the various shapes. Thus, very fine and delicate white lines may be cut with no limitation, and all will print easily. Contrast these with the strict limitation of the black line on the white background.

Do not limit yourself to only white on black or black on white. Try both and develop a technique which will be suitable to all your needs. This usually is made up of both strokes.

BACKGROUND TECHNIQUE

Background technique should be developed early in block printing. By so doing you will avoid having prints which are unbalanced because of too much white.

EXAMPLES OF BACKGROUND TECHNIQUE

Figs. 16-21. These are all done with the U-shaped, or V-shaped veiner; the U-shaped is the more suited to line work.

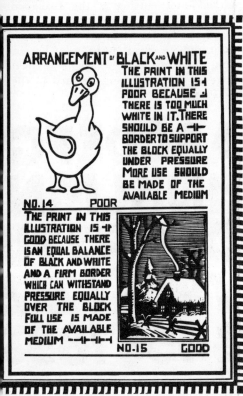

USE OF BORDERS

Figs. 14-15. Much originality may be exercised in the use of borders. After you master the art of cutting and printing, borders may be omitted if the block is planned to withstand pressure without them.

USE OF A BACKGROUND IN A PRINT

Fig. 22. You can very easily see how the design and balance were enhanced by this treatment. In printing, the block will be much firmer with this kind of cutting.

The linozip cutter is an excellent tool to create new, free backgrounds. Use both the large and small sizes. Prints showing linozip backgrounds may be found on pages 168 and 169.

LETTERING: SINGLE STROKE AND SINGLE STROKE SHADED

Lettering is an important phase of the craft, since in the ability of cutting well-

SINGLE-STROKE ALPHABET

Fig. 23. A white-line alphabet cut with the U-shaped veiner.

ABCDEFGHIJ
KLMNOPQR!
STUVWXYZ&
1234567890?$

SINGLE STROKE SHADED

Fig. 24. To bring out still more character, add serifs and gouge out the shaded parts. The single-stroke, white-line alphabet may be developed in numerous styles and adaptations.

designed and legible letters lies the utility of the medium.

All letters for printing purposes must be cut in reverse so that the finished print will read in the conventional left-to-right manner.

For an elementary alphabet, use the single-stroke alphabet shown in Fig. 23. This is easy to do and will look well. To gain more solidity in elementary lettering, shade the single-stroke alphabet with the same tool as shown in Fig. 24.

In early lettering, advertising, and labeling, always avoid a fancy letter. Rather work for a bold, firm, legible letter of character.

For freehand lettering, the linozip cutter may be used. This tool will produce results quickly where a free-style letter

is desired. All lettering must be carved in reverse.

HOW TO CUT BLOCKED LETTERS

The single-stroke letter and white-line letter are not adequate for all your purposes. You can develop a simple block letter, that is a letter which will be cut in relief, printing in black on white and very effective. For such a letter, begin with the bold blocked letter shown in Fig. 25.

Cutting the block letter is entirely different from the white letter or single-stroke letter. In the white letter a single stroke will make a member, while in the blocked letter each member of the letter must be cut with four strokes.

The tool used more extensively for blocked-letter cutting is the U-shaped veiner. This is used in all steps in cutting a letter under less than an inch in size, and in the first two steps in larger letters, while the small gouge, the ⌴-shaped gouge or the large gouge is used in the last step.

ABCDEFG!
HIJKLMN
OPQRSTU
VWXYZ Z
3456789&

BLOCKED ALPHABET

Fig. 25. Always cut the letters as bold as your work will permit. As to spacing and arrangement, follow the same principles as in any other lettering exercise. Avoid large spaces between letters in all cases. Later serifs can be added and the letters may be shaded or decorated. For most work this alphabet will do very well.

LINOLEUM

HOW TO CUT BLOCK LETTERS

Fig. 26. First cut the block for each space. The cut-out line between the letter blocks will in this way be your space between the letters; second, cut out the shape of the letter which was not cut out in cutting the line above and below; and third, gouge out the spaces within the letter shape, which must be wider.

HOW TO HAND-BLOCK TEXTILES

Once you have learned to cut a linoleum block you will not want to limit yourself to printing only on paper. There are textile paints on the market now—thick enough to be rolled out on a piece of glass with a brayer and transferred onto the block for printing. The colors are fast so do not hesitate to decorate fabrics that must be washed or dry cleaned.

This method of decoration is particularly appropriate for hangings or drapes.

PRINT YOUR OWN APRON

This apron has been printed in an attractive peasant design. Note that every other block reverses colors.

VARY YOUR DESIGN

Printing on textiles with blocks of various sizes and shapes creates interest and appeal.

There is no limit to the size of the block you can cut and do not worry too much if each print is not perfect. If some parts are hazy or lighter in color it usually adds to the interest of the design.

Other projects such as blouses, luncheon mats, aprons, kitchen curtains, shopping bags, beach accessories, etc., are easily made. Keep in mind that all the prints need not be of one color. Certain designs are more interesting if every other print is made with a different color.

The following steps are suggested for printing with textile colors:

Cut the design on a linoleum block (Fig. 27). "Fused Gray" blocks are best for this purpose. They have a light gray non-glare surface which contrasts with a black undercoating, making cutting easy.

Preparing the Color. Mix the following with a palette knife on a piece of glass: 2 parts textile color, 1 part extender, 2 parts hand-blocking extender.

Applying the Color. 1. Spread the mixture evenly on the glass by means of a brayer (Fig. 28). The mixture should have the "tacky" quality desired for hand blocking. If the mixture becomes too stiff, add a little extender.

2. Roll the brayer which is now charged with color over the block until it has an even coating of color (Fig. 29).

3. Apply the color to the fabric by placing the block face down on the cloth and pounding with a mallet or hammer (Fig. 30).

4. With larger blocks, place the underpadding, cloth, and inked block on the floor. To produce the prints, step onto the block and rock the foot back and forth a few times. This method will provide the most even prints with larger blocks.

Or, perfect impressions can be readily produced by pressing a cold electric iron over the back of the block (Fig. 31).

Impressions of a linoleum block design may be run off on a regular press, if one is available.

5. Clean the block with turpentine.

Fig. 27. Cutting the design.

Fig. 28. Spreading the mixture.

Fig. 29. Rolling the brayer.

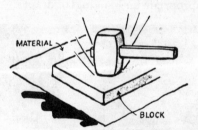

Fig. 30. Applying color to fabric.

Fig. 31. Securing impressions with cold electric iron.

WORKING WITH LEATHER

Working in leather is one of the most practical of hobbies because of the useful and lovely things which even a novice can make, often within a few hours. After making one or two small articles, you will feel confident enough to go on to larger things.

In leather working, as in all crafts, the chief thing is to understand your tools and to learn how to handle them well.

It is always good practice to begin with as few tools as possible, and then add to them when you have developed some skill, and have got the feeling of the work "in your hands." Quite often, as you have doubtless noticed, very expert workmen will be found doing intricate and exacting jobs with one or two homely, unconventional tools, perhaps of their own making, whereas a beginner might feel that he had to set himself up with

a dozen or more fancy gadgets although having only a sketchy notion of how to use them.

MINIMUM TOOLS FOR LEATHER WORK

With the following tools, you will be able to do almost any kind of leather work.

Fig. 1. Spoon and tracer.

The modeler, consisting of spoon and tracer, will serve for tracing and tooling designs on your leather. The tracing end comes in handy for other things, too—drawing lines, etc.

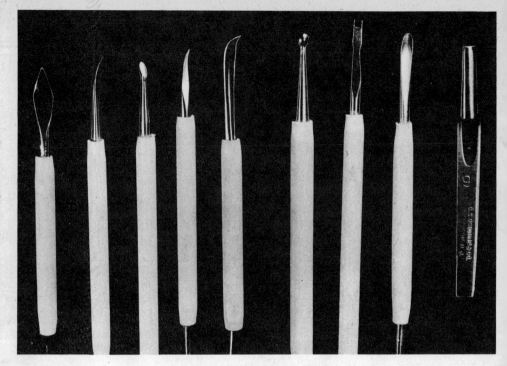

MODELERS
Showing the types of modelers used in leather work.

Fig. 2. Cutting knife

This is the same type of cutting knife used for chip carving and other kinds of woodwork—a fine utility tool, and good for cutting leather. You can, however, use a scissors for cutting out, if you prefer.

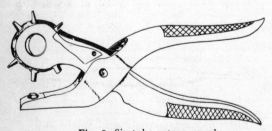

Fig. 3. Six-tube rotary punch

The rotary punch makes holes of several sizes—for lacing, and for putting in eyelets and snap fasteners.

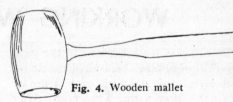

Fig. 4. Wooden mallet

A wooden mallet is recommended for some of the operations you will find yourself doing.

Fig. 5. Eyelet setter

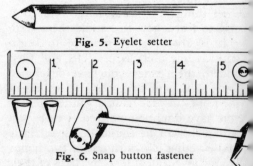

Fig. 6. Snap button fastener

A number of useful leather articles require eyelets, so get an eyelet setter.

A snap-button fastener, shown in Fig. 6, is indispensable. There is a six-inch steel rule, as you see. It is for measuring and marking off the leather.

In addition to these things, you will have to have a working surface. A hardwood board in a size large enough for cutting out handbags, book covers, or portfolios, makes a good portable work table. Keep one side smooth for tooling, and on the other do your cutting and pounding. (If there is a glass slab around, you can use that for a tooling surface.)

MATERIAL AND SOURCES

The kind of leather you use will depend, of course, upon the kind of article you are going to make. Calf skin, cow hide, steer hide, goat skin, morocco—these are some of the most important kinds. If you are going to do tooling, specify this when buying your material. Some kinds of leather are too heavy or not properly processed for this purpose; you will be on the safe side if you buy English kip, calf skin, cow hide, and goat skin.

Leather is sold in whole, half, or quarter skins, and in remnants, and it is priced by the square foot. Kid skin and soft leathers and a shaved leather known as "skiver" are often used for lining. For lacing the best thing to use is goat skin. It comes in many colors, to match the dyed leathers. There is a composition lacing, slightly cheaper, but use goat skin if you can get it, for it is more durable and better looking.

Handicraft supply stores usually sell leather, and in most large cities there is a leather district where you can buy wholesale or retail. Many of the small shops in these quarters do a tremendous business by mail.

MAKING A KEY CASE

We have chosen a key case as our first project because it involves almost all the operations used in leather work. After you have made one of these, you will be able to forge ahead into advanced work.

The first thing to do is to cut a paper pattern. The size is a matter of your own taste and convenience. There are two points especially to be noted (Fig. 7). The marks on both sides of the key plate indicate that you must allow some material here for the fold-over—one-quarter inch on each side. Also allow for the overlapping of the ends. Rounded corners and a scalloped edge for the overlap make a nice finish.

Lay your paper pattern on the leather. You can use a little rubber cement on the corners to hold it in place. Learn to be economical in laying on your pattern. Leather scraps can be utilized for buttons, book markers, and small purses, but don't cut into your material until you have figured how to get the most out of it.

Put your ruler on the edge of the pattern and draw an outline with a pencil or with your tracer. Cut it out with a knife or a pair of scissors. If you use a knife, hold the steel rule firmly at the outline while you cut; this will guide and steady your knife and give you a clean edge.

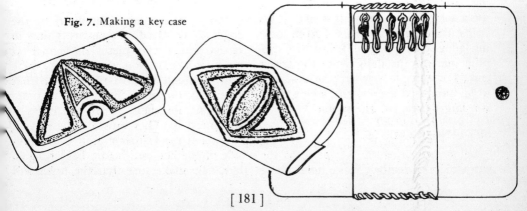

Fig. 7. Making a key case

Next cut an extra piece of leather on which to amount your key-plate. (Key-plates, by the way, can be purchased at craft stores. They hold from three to six keys.) The leather mount should be about three-quarters of an inch wider and an inch and a half longer than the plate. If you like, you can make it long enough to be laced in at the bottom. This will make the case a little firmer.

TOOLING

Draw a design on paper and transfer it to the right side of the leather for tooling. If you haven't an idea at the moment, perhaps you can find a decoration that appeals to you somewhere else in this book. But it's best not to make an exact copy of anything. You'll enjoy your work more if you put some imagination into it.

Wet the leather all over on both sides with a sponge. The design draft will adhere to the damp hide while you are tracing it. Use the tracer end of the modeler, and impress the design firmly into the leather. (If it dries while you are working, wet again, and go all over it, front and back, each time.)

The first step in the actual tooling is to deepen your outlines with the tracer. Next, with the spoon held sidewise, follow the outline—the edge of the tool should rest in the dent. Press down and away from the outline towards the center of the background. Go around the whole outline this way, to throw the design into sharp relief and then go over the background area with the spoon. When making your outline deeper with the tracer, use a sort of push-and-pull stroke. This keeps it even and prevents it from looking gouged in places. If you are stippling part of the design, use the tracer end. For any place where the design is to be impressed deeply, and where there is a larger area, use the spoon.

SETTING EYELETS

Before attaching the key-plate to the extra piece of leather, make holes along the top edge with the rotary punch (the small hole) where it will be laced into the case proper. Place the key-plate on the mount and make a pencil mark where the eyelets must go. Then punch the holes. Push the metal eyelets through from the plate to the back of the mount. Then turn it over, use your eyelet setter, and flatten it out by giving the end of the setter a blow with the mallet.

Mark the place where the snap fastener is to go, punch the holes, and put in the button part first. The fasteners come in four parts. The hollow metal piece which fits over the snapper is put over the larger end of the snapsetting device, after pushing it as far as it will go through the hole in the leather and into the button. Cover the button or the end of the mallet with a piece of leather or cloth to avoid scarring the button. Give one smart blow with the mallet to set the button. The button usually goes on the right-hand side of the case.

Fold over the lap and make sure that you have marked the right spot for the other part of the fastener. You will see how it has to go, and also that the smaller end of the setting device is made to accommodate this part of the fastener. Use the little steel gadget that comes with the ruler. Place it over the snap projection, and give a blow with the mallet. A second blow here is liable to flatten out the fastener, so try to gauge your stroke nicely.

Your key case is now all finished but the lacing.

STITCHING OR LACING

You must first punch holes along the edges to be laced. If you are going to lace together two pieces of leather of equal thickness, you must "skive" them down enough towards the edge so that when glued together they will be no more than one thickness. Trim the edges if they need it. They must not be ragged.

Cement the leather mount to the outside of the key case before beginning to lace. To make sure that the holes will

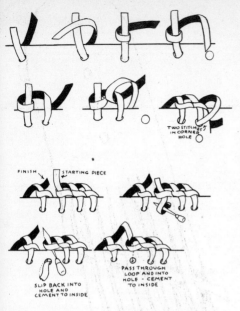

FINISH   STARTING PIECE

SLIP BACK INTO
HOLE AND
CEMENT TO INSIDE

PASS THROUGH
LOOP AND INTO
HOLE - CEMENT
TO INSIDE

TWO STITCHES
IN CORNER
HOLE

Fig. 7A. Detail showing how to start and end lacing. Work from left to right.

match, make a pencil mark for them, and work from that point in punching the rest of the holes.

Use your steel rule and a pencil or the tracer to draw a line for your holes. The depth of the lacing depends on the article—the size and the wear and tear it may have. One-eighth or three-sixteenths of an inch from the edge will be about right for fine work. The holes should be one-eighth of an inch apart.

A tool which is helpful here, but not absolutely necessary, is a three- and four-pronged marker, or a tracing wheel. Either of these will make marks to guide the rotary punch so that your holes will be evenly spaced. (If you want to invest in an additional tool, there is a gauge punch which is very useful. It marks the place for the next hole, as it punches.)

Figure 8 shows ten ways of lacing leather. There are still more lacing stitches, but these are the most important. The most commonly used are the Single Strand Running Stitch (No. 1), the One-Strand Spiral or Whip Stitch (No. 3), the Loop Stitch (No. 9) and the Saddle Stitch (No. 10). If you do much leather work you will eventually need to know all ten.

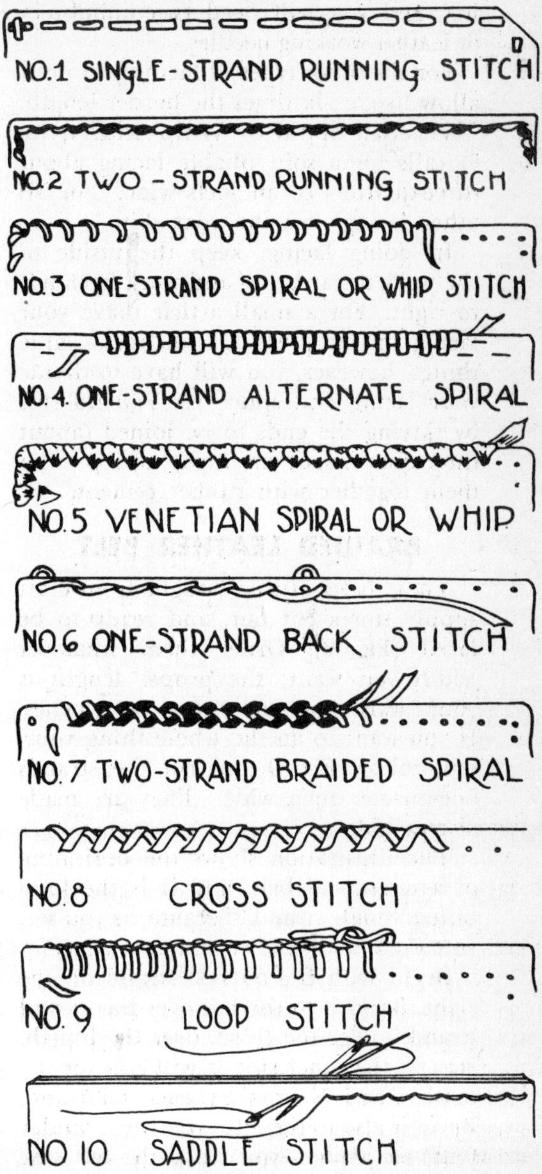

NO.1 SINGLE-STRAND RUNNING STITCH

NO.2 TWO-STRAND RUNNING STITCH

NO.3 ONE-STRAND SPIRAL OR WHIP STITCH

NO.4 ONE-STRAND ALTERNATE SPIRAL

NO.5 VENETIAN SPIRAL OR WHIP

NO.6 ONE-STRAND BACK STITCH

NO.7 TWO-STRAND BRAIDED SPIRAL

NO.8 CROSS STITCH

NO.9 LOOP STITCH

NO 10 SADDLE STITCH

Fig. 8. Stitches used in leather work.

The amount of lacing needed varies with the different stitchings, the depth of your border, and the thickness of the leather. For the Single Running Stitch allow about one and three-quarters times the border measurement; for Spirals about two and a half times.

The Saddle Stitch takes two and a half

times your measurement. You can use waxed linen thread for this type of stitching, and you will need two upholstery or leather working needles.

For the other types of lacing you must allow five or six times the border length.

Venetian Spiral or Whip Stitch (No. 5) calls for a soft, pliable lacing about three-quarters of an inch wide. For all other lacings use the goat skin.

In doing lacing, keep the inside of the work towards you and work from left to right. For a small article, have your lacing in one piece. If you make large things, however, you will have to divide your lacing and splice it. You do this by skiving the ends to be joined (about three-quarters of an inch) and pasting them together with rubber cement.

BRAIDED LEATHER BELT

These belts can be bought from craft supply stores cut out, and ready to be laced (Fig. 9). Order them whatever width you want; the proper length is your waist measure plus ten inches. If you want to do the whole thing yourself, follow Fig. 9 and cut the strands one-quarter inch wide. They are made of cow hide.

The illustration shows the beginning of a ten-strand belt, and it is the kind called "single-strand" because, as you see, you work with one strand at a time.

Begin with the outside strand on the right. Braid it to the left over the second strand, under the third, over the fourth, etc. At the other side it will go over the tenth strand. Next take the second strand. Braid it also to the left, over three, under four, etc. When you reach the left side with strand two, take the first strand, and bring it under the second, in line with the other strands. Continue in the same way, braiding the outside strand at the right through all the strands to the left, and at the left always bring the preceding strand under it. The strands should be only slightly slanted and they must be kept parallel or the belt will not be straight.

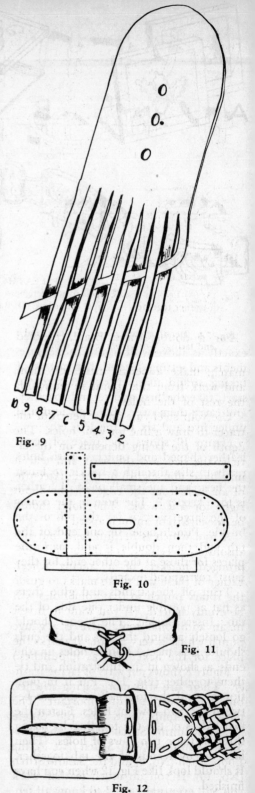

Fig. 9

Fig. 10

Fig. 11

Fig. 12

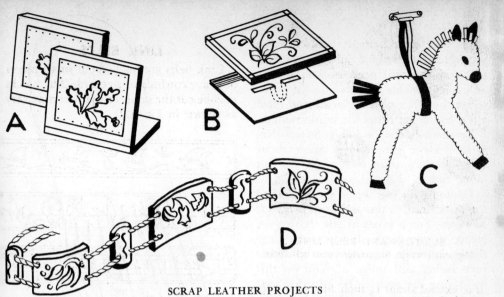

SCRAP LEATHER PROJECTS

Fig. 13. (A) Leather leaves glued to wooden book ends. (B) Buttons, made by cementing 2 pieces of leather together. (C) Lapel ornament. (D) Belt made from leather pieces strung on cord.

For a double-strand braid, proceed exactly as above with regard to measurements and setting up, and then instead of taking strand number one at right to start, take the first and second together, and carry them over three and four and under five and six to the left, etc.

Figure 10 shows one piece of scrap leather shaped and punched with holes ready to slip through a buckle to finish the belt; and the small piece of leather is the "keeper." The hole in the center of the large piece is for the pin of the buckle. Punch holes in one end of the tab and then double it and mark the places for those at the other end, for they must correspond exactly.

Trim off the strands and glue them as flat as possible under one side of the tab. Insert buckle. The keeper should go loosely around the tab and the ends should just meet. Punch holes in the ends, as shown in the illustration and tie them together (Fig. 11). Put it in position around the top half of the tab between the two rows of holes. Fasten the two halves of the tab together by lacing through these two rows of holes. Then lace the oval ends of the tab together. It should look like Fig. 12 when you have finished.

BOOK ENDS

Leather cutouts make an excellent decoration for wood. We have shown only a pair of book ends (Fig. 13A) but the same type of decoration may be applied to wooden boxes, wooden book covers, plaques, etc.

Use thin leather such as calfskin or sheepskin. First stain and finish the wooden object to which the design is to be applied. Cut away the edges and turn them down while the leather is still damp, with your modeling tool. Allow the leather to dry thoroughly and cement in place on the wood with rubber cement.

BUTTONS

Leather buttons (Fig. 13B) are made by cutting two pieces of leather (a top and a bottom piece) to the shape and size you wish for your button. Also cut a small strip of leather 1/8 by 1 inch to use as a hook for sewing the button in place.

Decorate the top piece either by tooling in a design, or cutting out a design from contrasting colors of leather. The cutouts can be pasted on with rubber cement.

Next punch a small hole in the center of the second piece, fold the small strip in half and push loop end down through hole from wrong side of leather, allowing

BUTTONS AND BELT LINKS
Use small scraps for buttons and belt links.

it to extend about ⅛ inch. Spread out the two ends as shown in the illustration and cement to the bottom piece of button.

When dry, cover the entire piece with rubber cement and cover with the top piece that has been decorated.

LAPEL ORNAMENTS

Leather lapel ornaments (Fig. 13C) may be made from scraps of soft leather such as kid or suede. The horse shown in the illustration is cut from two pieces of leather 3 by 2 inches. They are sewed together with a heavy waxed thread with an overcast stitch. Stuff with cotton or kapok.

To fasten to the buttonhole, cut a triangular piece of leather about 1 inch wide at the base, cover back with rubber cement and roll into a tight roll. To this, sew two narrow strips of leather about 2 inches long and attach the other end to the horse.

LINK BELTS

Link belts are made from small pieces of heavy cowhide or steerhide. The blocks may be cut the same, or the sizes may vary as shown in Fig. 13D.

DESIGNS FOR TOOLED LEATHER BELTS
Fig. 14. These may be traced and enlarged for tooling. As you become more proficient in tooling, you should develop your own designs.

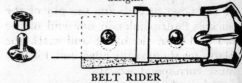

BELT RIDER
Fig. 15. (*Left*) Double rivet. (*Right*) The rider, with rivets fastened.

FINISHED BELT
This belt was made of cowhide. Add rider and attach buckle with rivets.

Draw a design to fit the block, and transfer it to the leather. Tool on the background and punch two holes at each end. If the blocks are wide, you will need to punch an extra hole. Lace together with heavy cord, being sure the cord passes *underneath* the block. Tie a knot in the end of each cord and add a drop of rubber cement to end of each knot to keep it from fraying.

LEATHER BELTS

Belts are made from heavy cowhide or steerhide. It is usually more economical to buy the leather already cut in strips. Craft companies carry them in all widths.

First decorate the belt by tooling on it one of the designs shown in Fig. 14, or your own design. Next, add a rider (Fig. 15), which is a strip of leather ¼ inch wide, to hold end of belt in place. Attach the buckle by punching a hole for the tongue to slip through about ½ inch from end. Pull leather through buckle and bend back on underside of belt.

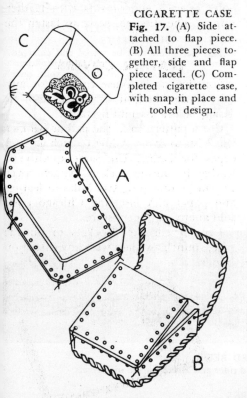

CIGARETTE CASE
Fig. 17. (A) Side attached to flap piece. (B) All three pieces together, side and flap piece laced. (C) Completed cigarette case, with snap in place and tooled design.

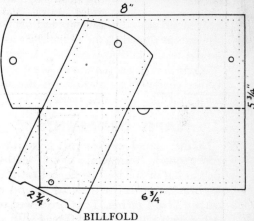

BILLFOLD
Fig. 16. The pattern shows both pieces, the smaller superimposed over the larger.

Fasten in place with 2 rivets as shown in Fig. 15.

BILLFOLD

Calfskin will serve excellently for this project (Fig. 16). Draft a pattern so that the small side of the large piece is ½ inch larger than a dollar bill all the way around. Cut leather. Punch a small hole in center to allow corner to fold. Apply design to the part you wish decorated, and model.

Cut small piece for coin pocket. Now thin the edges with sharp knife. Cement to lower left-hand corner of large piece as indicated in the drawing. Be sure to put on snaps before billfold is assembled. A lining can be added if desired.

Lace edges together and lace with any stitch described earlier in this chapter.

In drafting the pattern, allow ¼ inch on all sides for seams, add snap before lacing. Cut leather with a sharp knife and smooth with modeler or edger all edges not included in lacing. Tool your design (17C). Punch holes ⅛ inch apart along the edges, being sure the holes match on edges you wish to join. For additional strength, line with thin leather or skiver.

Join edges with rubber cement, add snap and tie four corners with a piece of string to hold in place and proceed to lace.

KNIFE SHEATH

First cut paper pattern for two pieces (Figs. 18A, 18B) to fit your knife and allow ¼ inch for seam. Use heavy cowhide or steerhide for your leather.

Cut leather with a sharp knife and with a modeler or edger smooth all edges not included in lacing. Tool in design (Fig. 18B) before lacing leather together. Lace together with any stitch given earlier in this chapter.

Cut slits with sharp knife and add holes at each end of slits with leather punch. The slits will serve to fasten the sheath to your belt.

LEATHER COVERS

For this project, use calfskin or any thin leather and, if decorated, tool in lesign before assembling parts.

Cut a pattern to fit the pad or booklet you wish to cover. Allow ¼ inch around edges for lacing. Use same quality of leather for inside pockets. Attach cover to pad by punching two holes in leather and paper and inserting Chicago posts sold at any stationery store.

Cement edges of pockets to outside piece, punch and lace with any stitch you prefer.

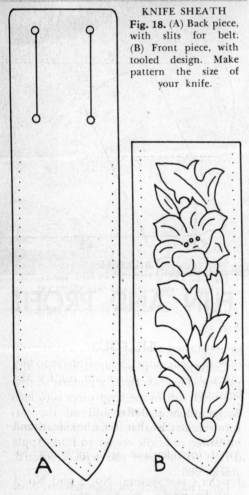

KNIFE SHEATH
Fig. 18. (A) Back piece, with slits for belt: (B) Front piece, with tooled design. Make pattern the size of your knife.

A   B

CIGARETTE CASE

For best results, use calfskin to make this cigarette case. Cut a paper pattern for three pieces—back, front and side (Fig. 17B) to fit a package of cigarettes, allowing enough leather on one of the long sides to come over the top for a flap.

[188]

METAL CRAFT FOR FUN AND PROFIT

Anyone who wishes to make useful and attractive articles of metal can easily do so in his own home workshop. With a little patience and inventiveness, you can develop the skill to make not only metal craft projects, but many of the tools and some equipment as well.

TOOLS AND EQUIPMENT

First of all you will need a work bench. If you haven't a strong table or bench that can be used, a hard wood stump cut to table height makes an excellent work bench and will deaden noise of hammering. A vise is useful, but beginners can do simple projects without one. However, there are a few simple tools you will need to get started and if they are not already in your tool cabinet, you will have to buy them. Here is a minimum list for the beginner:

Ballpein hammer (8 oz.)
Rawhide mallet (flat face one side, round other)
Anvil (old flatiron will serve for beginners)
Jeweler's saw (several No. 2 and No. 3 blades)
Files—half round
Soldering iron
Shears—curved and straight
Dividers (6-inch)
Drill (a nail will do in a pinch)
5 Crotch awl for outlining designs
Pliers

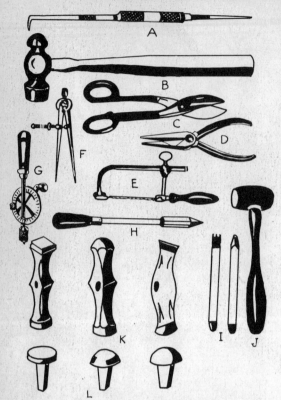

TOOLS FOR METAL CRAFT

Fig. 1. (A) Scriber; (B) ballpein hammer; (C) tin shears; (D) pliers; (E) jeweler's saw; (F) dividers; (G) drill; (H) soldering iron; (I) punches; (J) mallet; (**K**) combination hammers; (L) stakes.

METALS AND THEIR USES

About twelve metals and alloys are available in most cities. Of these, only seven are commonly used by the beginner. These seven and their various uses are:

Copper. Copper is a nonferrous metal, that is, it becomes soft when heated to red heat and plunged into water. When heated, it can be bent into various shapes, and lends itself to almost any type of decoration that can be worked on metal. It can be chased, etched, or stamped with equal ease.

Pewter. An alloy of tin, pewter is the easiest metal to work because it is soft and easily shaped. It is difficult to solder

because of its low melting point, so is suitable for trays and other projects cut into one piece.

Silver. A very expensive metal, silver is easily decorated. It is used largely in jewelry making.

Aluminum. Sheet aluminum that is commercially pure and designated by the number-letter 2S or 3S should be used. It is best suited for trays, plates or articles that do not require soldering.

Tin. Tin can be cut, soldered or riveted into useful household gadgets such as cookie cutters, cups, etc.

German Silver. An alloy of nickel, this metal cracks easily. It has a soft finish and is often used for jewelry as a substitute for sterling silver.

Brass. Brass is brittle and cannot be easily stretched. It must be annealed often while working to avoid cracking. It is frequently used as a contrasting metal on copper.

HOW TO WORK IN METAL

The techniques of working in metal may be divided into two general heads. preparing and working the metal; and decorating the project. First, we will consider the processes involved in preparing the metal.

FILES

Fig. 2. Files are used to finish edges off smooth and also for decorating metal. They come in various shapes, as shown above. The craftsman needs an assortment of files in different sizes and shapes in order to fit them to small cutouts and curves.

CUTTING

Hand or tin snips are used to cut sheet metal up to a thickness of 32-ounce copper and 20-gauge brass. Use a cold chisel or saw for curved or difficult places.

SAWING

Sawing is best done over a V-shaped vise fastened to the end of the table. For cutting out detailed design or making overlays, a jeweler's saw is used. Mount the blade in a frame with the teeth pointing toward the handle. The teeth may point toward the outside or toward the handle, depending on the direction you are cutting.

If inside cutting is to be done, drill a hole just large enough to insert the saw blade at a point on your pattern, fasten to frame and saw along the outline. It is important that the blade be drawn taut to prevent breakage.

Hold the metal firm on the table or in the vise with your left hand and saw with your right. The saw handle is below the metal. Move the saw up and down with

CORRECT WAY TO HOLD JEWELER'S
SAW

very little pressure and a steady speed. The cutting action should take place on the downward stroke.

TRANSFERRING DESIGN

The simplest method is to polish the metal and transfer the design with a piece

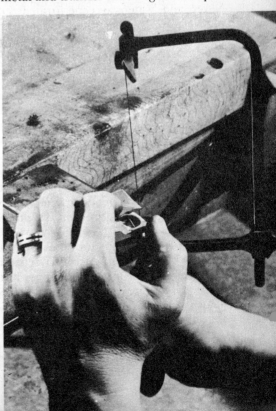

of carbon paper. A more accurate way is to first heat your metal over a clean flame and rub a cake of beeswax over it. Trace the design on thin paper and then cover the back over an area slightly larger than the design; the design is then carefully oriented on the cooled waxed metal and the design gone over on the original lines with a hard pencil. The outline can then be scratched permanently into the surface with a scriber, the wax remelted and wiped off.

ANNEALING

To anneal copper, as silver, heat to a dull red over a gas stove or by means of a blowtorch. They can be cooled rapidly by quenching in water or pickle. Brass must be cooled slowly. If aluminum is used, heat only to a dull pink.

PICKLING

After annealing, the metal is cleaned in a pickling solution. Make this up in a stove crock or glass container. The solution is 4 to 10 per cent solution of sulphuric acid in water.

Caution: The water should be room temperature or colder, and the acid should be poured slowly into the water. Never add water to concentrated sulphuric acid. If kept covered, the solution will not deteriorate with age. The metal is left in the solution until it is bright. Remove with copper tongs, rinse in water and wipe dry.

SHAPING

1. To Flatten. Lay metal on smooth hard surface such as an anvil or old flatiron. Pound with a relatively soft mallet of paper, leather or wood.

2. To Curve. Again use mallet and shape over any rounded surface. It may be a piece of pipe, wooden jig, table leg, etc.

3. To Bend. Draw a line across the metal at the point at which it·is to bend. Lay over wooden form and hammer it to shape. If you are bending a long strip, hammer one end and then the other until the entire edge is formed.

HOW TO SOLDER

For elementary work, soft solder is used, which melts at about 414° F. It can be purchased on a spool, like wire. For metals that oxidize at room temperature, you will need a reagent called flux. This usually comes in two-ounce cans and is in the form of a resinous-looking paste.

An electric soldering iron of 65-watt capacity is the most convenient means of soldering. When the tip gets hot, touch it to the solder on all four sides. This is called tuning the iron. Be sure the two pieces of metal to be soldered together are perfectly clean. To join, heat each surface and melt solder on it and allow to cool. Join together and heat again until both sides fuse, and hold firm until it hardens.

Hard solder requires intense heat which melts both the metal and solder. It is used mostly for joints or seams to make them invisible.

RAISING

This is the shaping of metal by hammering it into a wooden mold or sand box. This is the simplest method of shaping metal and is used largely for making plate ashtrays and other projects from disks. The molds must be made from hard woods and cut to the exact shape of project. Place metal on top of mold and hammer down first with mallet and then with hammer. Always start with the base line and then sides. It is important to hammer over the same place on the block and keep the disk moving around with the left hand so that the hammer strikes a different part of the metal each time.

DECORATING METAL

Etching. This is perhaps the simplest method of decorating metal. The literal translation of etching means "eating away." In metal work, the eating away is done with acid. First the metal must be thoroughly cleaned and design transferred with carbon paper or a scriber, as described earlier. Next, the design which is to remain raised must be covered with

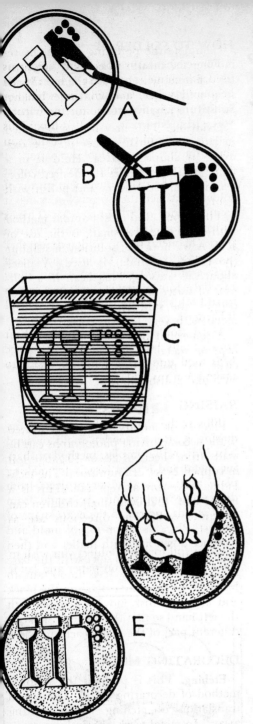

STEPS IN ETCHING METAL COASTER
Fig. 3. (A) Cover design with asphaltum varnish. (B) Trim for clean edges. (C) Etch in acid solution. (D) Remove asphaltum varnish. (E) Completed etched coaster design raised from background.

a resist. There are several available, but the one most commonly used is black asphaltum varnish thinned with turpentine. Carefully paint the part of your design you do not want eaten away by the acid, and allow to dry thoroughly. Then turn your metal over and coat the back.

A basic formula for etching solution is one part of concentrated nitric acid and two parts of water. The acid is poured slowly into the water and the solution kept in a glass dish or crock. *Caution:* Use this solution out-of-doors or in a well-ventilated room. In case of burn, wash area in cold water and cover with baking soda.

The length of time required for etching depends on strength of solution or the depth you wish your design. It may be five minutes to one hour. Remove the metal from the solution from time to time with a glass rod or wooden paddle—never with the hands. When finished, wash with cold water. Then remove asphaltum with turpentine and rag.

Line Chasing. This is the term given to designs in metal made by marking the metal with various-shaped blunt chisels. There are many different shapes. Some are used for giving curved or straight lines, others for background effects in different shadings, stippling, etc. A beginner can do quite creditable work with only six or eight tools and can make or acquire others as the need arises.

A straight line chaser is the one most commonly used. Place the metal on a smooth hard surface and hold the tool nearly vertical, leaning slightly away from the direction you are going to chase the line. Strike the tool one short, sharp blow. Move the tool forward about half its width and strike again.

By moving the tool forward only half its width each time, the previous mark in the metal helps to guide the tool for the next mark, and creates a continuous line. A chasing hammer is generally used, but an ordinary carpenter's hammer may be employed for this work.

Spotting. This means creating a ham-

HOMEMADE TOOLER

Fig. 4. These toolers may be made from ¼-inch dowel stick. Six inches is a good length.

mered effect on the surface of metal. The usual hammers for this work are the spotting, planishing, or silversmith's hammers, all of which have highly polished faces. Always begin hammering near the outline of the design and work out.

Piercing. This is the sawing out of backgrounds of designs and smoothing the edges with various files. This type of decoration is effective on jewelry, paper, knives, bracelets, etc. It is accomplished by drilling a small hole in each unit that is to be removed in order to insert the saw blade. Fasten the saw blade to the jeweler's saw and cut around the design.

Embossing. Embossing means raising the design either on the surface of the metal or on the back. It is accomplished by laying the metal on a soft surface, such as linoleum; hammering embossing tools or various-shaped hammers may be used.

FINISHING

There are a number of ways of finishing metals. If you want a bright surface, the common method is to use a buffing wheel. First use a stitched muslin wheel with tripoli (a kind of limestone). Start the polishing motor, touch the wheel with the tripoli stick for a moment and then press the metal against the wheel until a high polish is attained. Replenish the tripoli from time to time.

The wheel should revolve at a high speed toward you, and the polishing is done below the center of the wheel. Always polish from the center of the work toward the lower edge. Never allow the wheel to touch the upper edge of the work as it is liable to strike it from your hand.

Complete the polishing process by removing the muslin wheel and substituting a flannel wheel. Wash the metal with soap and water, and continue buffing. Substitute jeweler's rouge for the tripoli.

Oxidizing. This may be accomplished in two ways. First, copper may be oxidized by simply heating. Hold it in a flame until it becomes the desired color, wax it while still warm and polish with a soft cloth.

The second, and most popular method with the home craftsman, is the use of acid. A warm or hot solution of sulphur (potassium sulphide) is used. A piece about the size of a lima bean in a half-pint of water is sufficient. In the case of copper, the solution is applied to the metal with very fine steel wool.

A somewhat permanent finish may be kept on metal by adding a thin coat of clear nail polish that has been thinned with nail polish remover.

REPOUSSÉ

Plaques or jewelry such as illustrated in the accompanying photographs can be made from sheets of 28- or 30-gauge foil in copper, brass, or aluminum. The technique is known as repoussé. This is a simple craft that even small children can do quite well. The directions are as follows:

1. Cut foil to size of object you wish to make. Draw a design on paper and lay it

DESIGN FOR PLAQUE

Fig. 5. The metal is attached with ¼-inch brass nails to a wooden plaque.

REPOUSSÉ PLAQUE AND PIN

The pin in the shape of a horse's head was made on a square piece of foil, and tooling done before the background was cut away. Fill in back with plastic wood and press in a small safetypin before it hardens. The plaque was first tooled and fastened to a finished piece of wood with small nails.

over the metal. Trace around the design with a pencil and bear down enough to transfer the design to the foil. Remove paper and again trace around the design with a sharp tool so the lines are distinct and there are no breaks.

2. Decide which part of the design is to be raised and which is the background (to be lowered). Make a thick pad of newspapers and place the metal on it right side up. You are now ready to tool.

3. The tool you use may be a leather tooler (tracer on one end and spoon on other), an orange stick, or you can cut a ¼-inch dowel stick to shape suggested in Fig. 4. First press down the background by using modeling end of tool. Then turn the metal over and press down on design from underside. Repeat until the design stands up quite high in relief.

ANTELOPE PLAQUE

To make this handsome plaque (Fig. 6), cut a piece of thin copper 30 or 33 gauge 4¼ by 5½ inches or any size you choose. Trace and enlarge. Transfer pattern to tracing paper. Lay pattern on metal and transfer design by tracing around the edges with a scriber or any sharp-pointed instrument. Remove the design and again go around the lines with the same tool to make them very distinct.

REPOUSSÉD WALL PLAQUE

Fig. 6. This design unit is planned for tapped metal or repousséd wall plaque.

[195]

Now place the metal on a soft pad of newspaper or cloth and proceed to lower the background and raise the design. (See preceding directions for Repoussé.)

Mount the finished piece on a piece of wood or cork cut about ½ inch larger than the metal all way around. Hold in place with small brass nails.

GIRAFFE BOOK ENDS

To make giraffe book ends, cut two pieces of wood 6½ by 8 by 1 inches and shape the top as shown in Fig. 7. Next cut two pieces of thin copper (30 gauge) to the same dimensions. Tool in the design as directed in Repoussé instructions.

Add two small pieces of wood 6½ by 3 inches to back of each book end at the bottom so it will stand upright. Attach the tooled metal pieces to the face of each book end with small brass nails.

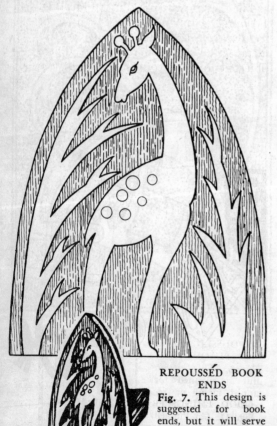

REPOUSSÉD BOOK
ENDS
Fig. 7. This design is suggested for book ends, but it will serve equally well for a wall shelf or door stop, etc.

DESIGNS FOR ETCHED BRACELETS
Fig. 8. You can transfer these or other designs to your bracelets by following the simple instructions for etching given earlier in this chapter.

BRACELETS

There are two main parts to the making of a bracelet: making the design and shaping. The steps necessary for etching designs on metal have already been discussed, and a variety of designs are also presented herewith. Select one—or create your own. Now we come to shaping the metal.

Bending a Bracelet. The simplest way to shape a braclet is to make a bracelet bender as shown in the accompanying illustration. Cut a strip of heavy copper or some other heavy metal (18 gauge) 10 by 1½ inches. Bend one side into a half-circle with a 1½-inch radius and bend back the end at the base ¼ inch to make a small groove. To bend a bracelet "blank," insert one end in the groove of the bent end and bend it all the way around the circle. Your bracelet is now shaped on one side.

Remove the blank from the holder and slip other end into groove and bend it in the same way. If the bracelet needs to be a bit smaller to fit the arm, push ends together with the hands.

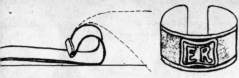

SHAPING A BRACELET

Fig. 9. Shape a piece of heavy metal as shown on the left. Insert and bend first one end of bracelet, then the other. Finish shaping with wooden mallet over another mallet head or anything round.

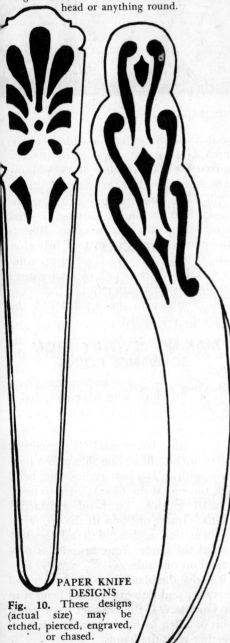

PAPER KNIFE DESIGNS

Fig. 10. These designs (actual size) may be etched, pierced, engraved, or chased.

PAPER KNIVES

Select one of the accompanying designs (Fig. 10) and transfer carefully on tracing paper. Now cover the metal with carbon paper and transfer design, being sure the design is 1/8 inch from each side of metal.

Punch a small hole in the edge of each design unit about 1/8 inch in diameter. Insert saw blade, fasten in jeweler's saw, and saw along all edges until cutouts are removed.

Next, file the edges smooth and finish with emery paper. Cut out the handle and blade and file the edges. With some extra filing, the edge of one side of the blade can be made sharp for cutting paper.

ATTRACTIVE PROJECTS FROM SCRAP METAL

The accompanying illustration (Fig. 11) presents nine projects that can be cut from scrap copper, pewter or silver. Use metal 18-20 gauge in thickness. These objects can be decorated either by the

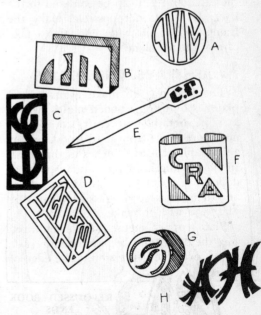

GOOD THINGS FROM SCRAP METAL

Fig. 11. (A) Pin; (B) letter holder; (C, D) pin; (E) letter opener; (F) napkin holder; (G) cuff link; (H) pin.

etching or piercing process, both described earlier in this chapter.

If the designs are to be pierced, cut them out before removing the edges of the metal, as it is much easier to work with a larger piece.

In planning a monogram pin, remember a pin must be attached to the back. Place the letters in a position where both the catch and pin can be soldered to the back. If this is not possible, make the frame of the pin wide enough to take care of the problem.

ASHTRAYS AND PLATES

The best way to make ashtrays and plates is by using wooden molds, which may be obtained at craft stores. The molds are made from hard wood, preferably maple at least 4 inches in thickness. In the middle is carved a hemispherical depression about ½ inch or 1 inch deep, and diameter according to size of tray or plate you wish to make.

Place copper metal disk of required size (these may also be purchased in craft stores) over the depression. (The edge of

the disk should extend a trifle over the edge.) Aim for the center of the depression with the round face of the doming mallet shown in the accompanying photograph. Give one firm blow, driving the copper into the mold. Rotate the disk ½ inch or so and strike again. Repeat this operation, rotating disk slightly after each blow of the mallet. Continue pounding metal with each face of mallet until disk fits perfectly into mold.

Now emboss on the molded disk the design of your choice.

MAKING JEWELRY FROM SOUVENIR COINS

The suggestions and instructions given here are for those who have collected a few valuable coins and would like to mount them so that they will make attractive ornaments as well as remind them of far-off and long-ago things.

A LINK BRACELET

A bracelet (Fig. 12), can be made from five or six coins and a foot of soft wire. Silver or copper wire are the best if you

Fig. 12

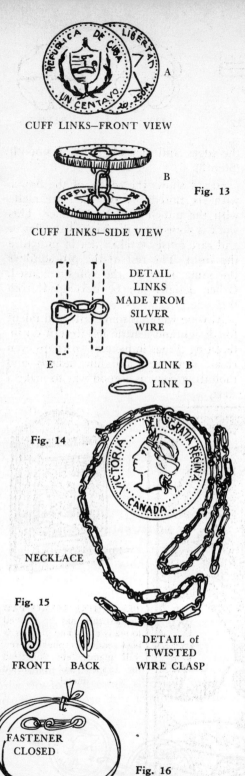

CUFF LINKS—FRONT VIEW

CUFF LINKS—SIDE VIEW

Fig. 13

DETAIL
LINKS
MADE FROM
SILVER
WIRE

LINK B
LINK D

Fig. 14

NECKLACE

Fig. 15

FRONT   BACK

DETAIL of
TWISTED
WIRE CLASP

FASTENER
CLOSED

Fig. 16

SOFT WIRE

can get them. The tools illustrated in Fig. 18 are all you will need.

Drill two holes in each coin, make round wire links with the pliers, and join the coins together. Put on an extra link at each end to catch the fastener (Fig. 15). The fastener is then shaped and sprung together, after which it is attached to the last link on the other end of the bracelet.

Figure 16 shows how to close the bracelet. The wire must be stiff enough to hold its shape without solder. All of the sharp edges on the fastener, the links, and the holes in the coins can be smoothed with the small file and fine steel wool.

CUFF LINKS

To make the cuff links (Fig. 13) four coins are needed. The two for the front should be approximately the same size but not necessarily the same design. The other two should correspond in the same manner.

Bore two holes about three-sixteenths of an inch apart (Fig. 13A) in each coin to allow link (C) to be attached with the flat end on top. One link is needed for each coin. A long narrow link (D) is used to join them in pairs (E). They are very attractive and they meet the three major requirements for a good piece of jewelry —usefulness, decorativeness, and rarity. Rarity will certainly be admitted of a bracelet which serves as a reminder of distant scenes and battles long ago.

COIN NECKLACE

The necklace in Fig. 14 is made by drilling a hole at the top of a coin and attaching a round link such as was used to connect the coins in the bracelet. A piece of chain can be bought or the more ambitious craftsman can make his own. If you elect to do this, solder the links, for you will probably make them of finer wire. A fastener similar to that used in Fig. 12 is suitable.

Special care should be taken to close the links which are not soldered and to smooth the edges to avoid having them catch in the hair or the clothes of the wearer.

STEP 1

STEP 2

STEP 3

Fig. 17

STEP 4

STEP 5

FLOWER NECKLACE

This kind of jewelry can be made from small disks or squares of silver, aluminum, copper, or even tin. The disks or squares can be beaten with the round end of the hammer and used without decoration or they can be made into three- or four-petal flowers.

The four-petal flower (Fig. 17) is made by filing the notches at four even spaces (Step 1) and then shaping the edges. The lines running toward the centre are cut with the pointed end of the file. All this is done with the file while the coin is held in the vise. By using the little anvil which is usually in front of the vise and beating the tin with a hammer, you can turn up the edges, and then file them off smooth (Step 3).

Step 4 shows the centre of the flower with six raised places which are made with the punch and the hammer. This work is done from the back of the flower and care must be taken not to puncture the front. The rest of the procedure is the same as when the coins are used. Other designs can be developed from this one.

Anyone who has some taste and talent for design and a little leisure can do interesting things in metalry—perhaps even create some new and fine designs—and mounting coins is a good way to make a start.

TELEPHONE MEMO PAD
Design unit may be applied to many other fine projects as book ends, scrapbook cover, wall plaque, etc. Suggested for tapped and repousséd metal.

ANYONE CAN DRAW

Through pictures we have a universal language. The efficiency of an artist depends on his recollections of line, mass, and color. An artist often interprets rather than makes a true representation of a subject, and he finds no subject too common for his pencil.

ARTIST'S EQUIPMENT

Elaborate sketching equipment is not essential to the aspiring artist. A tablet of tracing paper makes an ideal working surface. The pages may be removed from the pad or kept intact and the drawings referred to at a later date. A kneaded eraser and several pencils will be needed. Pencils marked H to 6H have hard lead and are used for making faint and thin lines. Pencils marked HB to 6B are soft

and black. H-HB and 4B pencils are used for general sketching.

DRAWING WITH YOUR EYES SHUT

Anyone can draw. If you do not believe it, try drawing with your eyes closed.

Suppose you start drawing a rooster. Make some zigzag lines for the beak and the comb, a curved line for the back and several indented curved lines for the tail. Swing a curved line around to the beak for the under part of the body. Extend two straight lines down for the legs. There are four front toes and a small one at the back if you want to be accurate in adding the feet.

Now open your eyes, make any embellishments such as a wing and eyes.

Perhaps this will be the best rooster you ever drew because you were not afraid to draw. Next try drawing with your eyes closed—a fish, a flower, a house, or any object that comes to your mind.

DEVELOP YOUR ABILITY TO OBSERVE

To make a shift from practicing drawing outlines and shapes, you will have to cultivate the "seeing eye." You should look at anything and everything, no matter how familiar the object is to you. Pretend you are seeing it for the first time. Ask yourself how it differs in size, form, and texture from others of the same kind. You will be amazed at the variety you will discover among the everyday things around you!

Take for example the woodwork that runs around your room. See how the light plays on it, making highlights and some sharp shadows, while other shadows are soft and almost lost in the wall.

Now look at the faces of those around you. Did you ever realize that no two faces are exactly alike? Perhaps you have seen examples of trick photographs where the photographer matched two rights or two lefts of faces, with the result that the face was entirely different from the original.

The next time you are out of doors, take a good look at the trees. Notice how the branches hang in overlapping layers. For detail, look to see if the leaves grow in pairs, groups of threes, fours, and so on. Perhaps they are in clusters or whorls at the ends of the branches. Now look at their size and shape—no two leaves are exactly alike. However, all have strong similarity because they belong to the same tree.

While you are developing your ability to observe, look at the flowers that are in bloom. Count the number of petals and note their coloring. You will find the outer edges are of a deep shade graduating to a lighter color toward the center. Measure the stem and decide the distance between the leaves and the flower. Are the leaves alternate or opposite on the stem? Finally, are the stems straight in general as in the hollyhock or do they have a tendency to hang over, as in many of the shrubs? When you go back into the house, look at the objects in your room. Compare them in size and see if you can judge the difference in their measurements. How would you make them appear to stand away from the wall? Can you shade to indicate the direction from which the light is coming? You can give them depth by making the parts furthest away dark and gradually shading off to lighter as they come toward you. Dark areas next to light areas give sharp contrasts and help much in achieving the appearance of solidity.

AN EASY DRAWING LESSON

Remember your "trained eye" will be your most valuable asset when you draw. Let's begin by drawing a water glass. Perhaps you never really observed one before. Bear in mind the fact that you need not make your picture an exact facsimile, but you will want to draw it so that anyone looking at it will recognize it as a tumbler. It will be your own interpretation of the way it looks to you.

Before you begin, however, you will want to know something about form, light, and shade (texture).

FORM, LIGHT, AND SHADE

Form is achieved by a series of lines joined one to the other to obtain an outline of the object. They may be verticals, horizontals, or curves. The weight of the line depends upon the character of the subject.

The direction of the light on a subject will influence the highlights, shadings, and cast shadows. When a subject is placed in the path of light and another subject is placed between it and the light source, light will be eliminated from that portion of the surface, resulting in shaded sections or cast shadows.

Since you are starting with a water tumbler as your subject, first you ought to hold one in your hand and observe it.

It has a round top, a round slightly tapered body and a round base. Feel the texture with your fingers. It is very smooth and hard. Hold it to the light. You can see through its surface and so it is not opaque, but is very transparent. These are its characteristics, and these characteristics, which can be felt and seen, must be transferred to your pencil and be expressed on paper.

Hold the tumbler at eye level, slowly raise it above the level of your eyes; now lower it until you are looking down into it. This performance will show you how a circular object appears in different positions.

Your eye is like the lens of a camera; when focused properly, it will give you distinct images which can be converted into artistic impressions.

With practice, you will soon cultivate the habit of observation which is so very necessary in the art field.

Place the water tumbler on a table. Now look at your subject hard. Is it twice as tall as it is wide or only half as tall? Establish the proportion in your mind. Look at the top and the bottom. You find two circles. Are they full circles or are they ellipses? Draw the lines that will make the two sides. Add the curved lines for the top and the bottom of the tumbler. Now that you have your outline, consider what is happening to the glass at this moment to make it interesting. It has an appearance of roundness resulting from light on its surface. Indoors, lights and shadows will depend upon windows or electricity for their source.

In Fig. 1, the mass form was sketched in a free scrawling line. The outline was then drawn in to give recognition to the subject. The light source was determined and the shading and shadows were placed.

Loose and rapid scratches and scrawls were used to make the illustrations in Fig. 2. This technique is often used as a preliminary step for more detailed illustrations.

HOW TO DEVELOP A STILL-LIFE DRAWING

After you have finished drawing the tumbler, you might try a still-life composition. Look around for a subject—perhaps in your eagerness to learn to draw, your dishes are still on the table. Let's pretend there is a bowl of flowers, a plate, and a spoon on the plate. For interest, you might add a linen napkin and lay it over the edge of the plate.

Now consider each article in relation to the other. Think of size, shape, texture, and color. Look at the objects until you have all the characteristics fixed firmly in your mind.

THE FIRST SKETCH

Start by lightly sketching in the largest mass first, which is the bowl of flowers. Study the placement and the proportion of the plate in the foreground. Block it in. Next, sketch in the napkin that overlaps the plate and the spoon resting on the rim of the plate. Always work from the top of the composition outward and down. After the first rough blocking-in of your sketch, stop and look at it and

A WATER TUMBLER
Fig. 1. A scrawling line was first used to achieve the form of the tumbler.

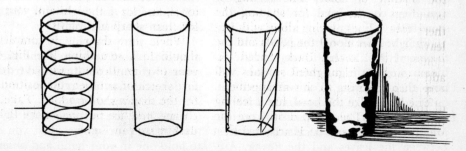

EARLY STEPS IN DRAWING

Fig. 2. These shapes were quickly drawn with the strokes and scrawls shown at the left.

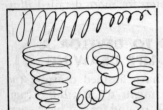

check it from all angles. Don't erase, just pencil over the light lines. Your outline sketch should resemble Fig. 3.

MOVEMENT

Now you should consider your sketch for what is known as movement. A table line is established and the object should rest on this table surface and not appear to float in space.

Before you begin to round out the composition, there are these character-istics to consider. The bowl, the plate, and the spoon have a definite solidity in appearance. They appear as still masses placed on a surface. The flowers move upward and out, thereby giving a feeling of activity. The napkin is not crisp and freshly folded, but has been used and crumpled in an informal manner.

SHADING AND COLOR

At this point you are ready to put in the shading or color. The feeling of roundness is the goal for shading the bowl. Heavy lines playing along with fea-thery light lines model the petals and the leaves of the flowers. Dark shaded sec-tions touching highlighted sections will add crisp contrasts to this arrangement.

The plate, like the bowl, has a feeling of roundness. The sharp drop from the outer rim into the plate is accented by a

very black area graduating from gray to white.

The spoon has a hard, shiny surface and catches well-defined highlights and shadows. The modeling of the spoon is aided by a series of fine lines used for middle tone.

The napkin is composed of irregularly curved flowing lines with a middle tone shading under the soft folds. There are no sharp edges and to keep the feeling of softness no dark accents are introduced. Irregular masses of dark and middle tone shading placed under the bowl and the plate help to keep these objects in place.

Keep in mind while sketching, that your picture should indicate the source of light and from which direction it is coming. Also, the picture should show whether you are looking at the subjects at eye level, above or below eye level. Remember to balance your dark and light masses against each other. Make use of a variety of lines, using bold heavy strokes for accents, fine lines for middle tones, and leave the white of your paper for clean sharp highlights.

When your drawing is completed, it should look something like Fig. 4. For your own amusement, we have drawn a first sketch of another composition ready for the shading to be added. Take a pen-cil and practice putting in the light and dark masses in Fig. 5.

[204]

A STILL-LIFE OUTLINE
Fig. 3. Draw your first sketch lightly, so you may correct it later without making extensive erasures.

THE FINISHED STILL LIFE
Fig. 4. Movement and shading complete the outline drawing.

HINTS FOR ORIGINAL COMPOSITION

Now that you know something about form and texture, how would you like to make an original composition? Here are some hints that will help you:

DEVELOPING A COMPOSITION

Composition is the art of balancing light and dark areas in a given space.

Select an interesting subject such as "Under the Sea," "the Farm," "City Life," etc.

Close your eyes and make a mental image of the major elements involved. In Fig. 6, an underwater marine scene was selected as the subject to be developed. The elements were fish, air bubbles, water, and vegetation. A simple imaginary fish was sketched in a given area. The fish was then surrounded by wavy lines suggesting water. Air bubbles were introduced and marine vegetation was

added for balance. For additional interest, several more fish, wavy water lines, and air bubbles were sketched in to develop a varied and balanced composition.

For your second attempt you might try drawing a jungle. Draw the trees any

FILL IT IN YOURSELF
Fig. 5. By applying the principles explained in the text, you should be able to fill in details of movement, form, and texture.

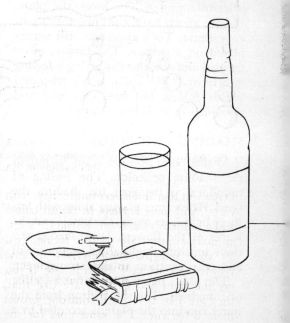

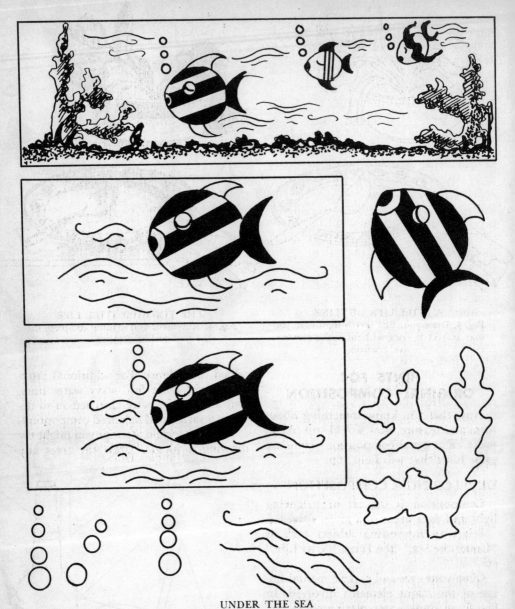

UNDER THE SEA

Fig. 6. Air bubbles plus wavy lines to indicate water lend balance and interest to this simple composition of fish, vegetation, and sand.

shape you like and intermingle them with vines. Add some flowers in bright colors and a palm or two. Next, introduce a few animals appropriate to this locale. Just let your imagination run riot because very few people have seen a jungle. If you say the trees and animals are like that, they are like that until someone proves them otherwise! The same goes for the marine scene, for how many people have been five miles under the surface of the water, especially off the coast of New Guinea?

Now, to get back to the more serious side of drawing. Sometime you will want to get an easel and do some sketching out of doors. This will require some knowledge of other techniques used by the artist, so we are giving you a few suggestions for your notebook. If you want to develop a landscape. there are many things you will want to know. The following hints will help you get started:

DISTANCE AND PROPORTION

Suppose you decide to draw a landscape, with a hill, a tree, and a house. To determine the proportion of the objects to be sketched, compare the height of one object (tree) against the height of another (hill), by closing one eye and holding a pencil horizontally in front of the eye that is open. Raise the pencil so that it is in line with the hill. Does the tree appear to be above the pencil line? If so, you know that the tree is higher than the hill. Sketch it so. If the tree appears below the line of the pencil, sketch it lower than the hill.

Distance can be determined by this method. Holding your pencil perpendicularly in front of your open eye, you can judge how close or how far that particular tree is located from the house. Hold the pencil in line with the tree; if the house appears to remain away from the line of the pencil, it should be sketched away from the tree, either to the left or to the right. Holding a pencil in a horizontal, perpendicular, or slanting position in front of your eye will enable you to compare distances and proportions against each other.

DRAWING TECHNIQUES

Technique is the manner in which the appearance of an object is executed. Artists develop mannerisms in handling a pencil and so, although the same subject may be sketched by several artists, each rendition will be different in technique. Lines can express texture, movement, and tonal qualities of a subject. A good picture can be attained by using line alone. There are many techniques of applying line tones. Make use of:

TRIANGLES AND CIRCLES
Fig. 7. Simple geometric shapes may be combined into entertaining pictures.

[207]

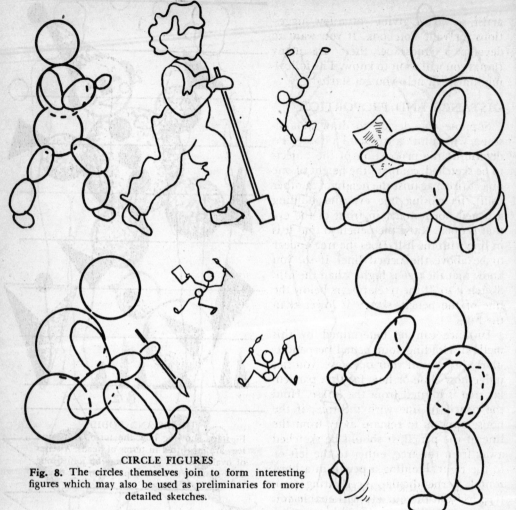

CIRCLE FIGURES
Fig. 8. The circles themselves join to form interesting figures which may also be used as preliminaries for more detailed sketches.

Soft broken lines—quick preliminary sketching
Hard slick lines—defining sharp accents
Blurred lines—diffused objects, distance
Fine soft lines—delicate subjects, middle tones
Rough lines—blocking in large masses
Make it a habit to study objects for characteristic line traits.

DRAWING WITH CIRCLES AND TRIANGLES

How about doing a little trick drawing by using circles and triangles? It is very easy and a good way for children from seven to seventy to start, as the results are always amusing. This is how you do it

(Figs. 7 and 8):
Starting with a circle for the head, attach a larger circle to the lower part of the one you have made. Add four small circles to the large body circle to represent the arms and the legs. Triangles for the hat, hands, and feet embellished with circles of varying sizes will result in an active clown figure.

Three triangles, two for the sails and one for the hull, will start a boat sailing across your drawing tablet.

A pert bird is composed of three circles (head, eye, body) and four triangles (tail, wing, feet, and beak).

Flowers of circles and triangles will introduce ideas for a garden bouquet.

Using triangles and circles in simple

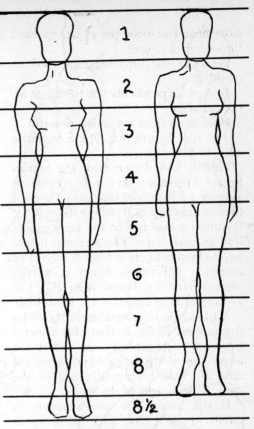

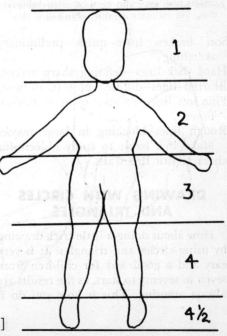

sketching is fun and can be considered a shift from unconscious doodling to conscious sketching.

Study Figs. 7 and 8 and then begin to work out your own characters.

HOW TO DRAW FIGURES

No aspiring artist can draw for any length of time without some knowledge of figure drawing.

The simplest way to draw a figure is by action lines or "sticks." For practice, strip down photograph characters from magazines to stick construction, keeping the original lines of action. Rhythm, movement, and mood can all be expressed through stick figures.

Perpendicular lines suggest growth or reaching.

Broken perpendicular lines suggest action, conflict.

Horizontal lines are quiet, peaceful.

The stick figures (Fig. 9) are of course only the first step.

Finally, how do we draw the human figure? The easiest way is to proportion a figure into units of one size. They are usually drawn in ovals or egg shapes.

Almost every part of the body can fit into an oval shape. The accepted height for the human figure is 8 heads high. The magazine illustration figure is usually elongated to 8½ heads (Fig. 10). The average child of 4 years is 4½ heads high.

A little rule to remember in sketching the human figure is that the distance from the finger tips of one hand to the finger tips of the other hand when the arms are held horizontally will be the same as the height of the figure.

If you keep these measurements in mind, you will have little difficulty in drawing a figure with correct proportions.

PLANES OF THE FACE

Fig. 11. A face drawn by the plane method creates an appearance of greater solidity than the ordinary profile or full-face view.

FACE DRAWING MADE EASY

Planes of the Face. Blocking in planes produces a solidly constructed head and is very helpful in deciding where dark and light shadings are to be placed in relation to the light source. Planes closest to the light will appear very light and those receding from the light source will be in middle or dark shadow.

The plane of the forehead slopes upward and backward and then turns to the side to become the temples.

The plane of the face is divided by the nose and is broken on each side by a line from the cheekbone to the center of the upper lip forming the jaw (Fig. 11).

Head Proportions. From a straight front view the average adult's head is three inches more in measurement from the top of the head to the base of the chin than the distance across the widest part of the face. Looking at the head from a profile view, the length of the face from the top of the head to the base of the chin compared to the distance from the brow to the back of the head is 1½ inches longer.

DRAWING THE FACE

To draw the face, first block in its contour. With your pencil indicate the hairline. Now divide the remaining space below the hairline into three equal parts.

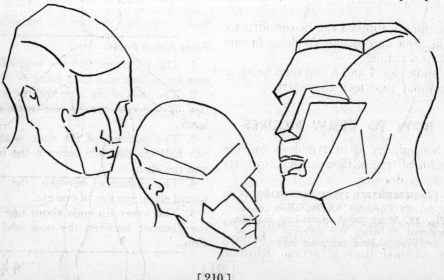

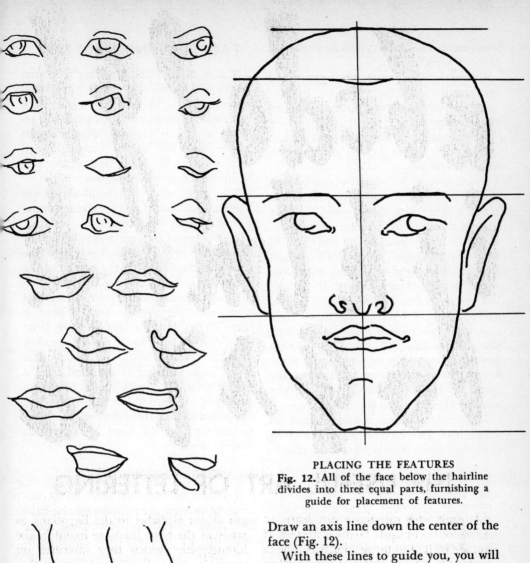

PLACING THE FEATURES

Fig. 12. All of the face below the hairline divides into three equal parts, furnishing a guide for placement of features.

Draw an axis line down the center of the face (Fig. 12).

With these lines to guide you, you will find it very easy to place the features.

Facts About Faces:

1. The eyebrows and the tops of the ears are in line with each other.

2. The base of the nose and the lower tips of the ears are in line with each other.

3. The position of the nose is about one half the distance between the brow and the chin.

4. The distance between the eyes would equal the size of one eye.

5. The lower lip ends about one half the distance between the nose and the chin.

DIFFERENT FEATURES FOR DIFFERENT EXPRESSIONS

Fig. 13. Many facial expressions may be achieved by using the different types of eyes, mouths, and noses shown.

abcdefgh
ijklmnp
oqrts

THE USEFUL ART OF LETTERING

Anyone who can write can learn to letter, for no unusual talent is needed. If you are willing to invest sufficient time to master the fundamentals as presented in this chapter, you will enjoy richer returns on your investment than can be derived from many similar investments in the allied arts. No artist's background is complete without a working knowledge of the basic alphabets and the tools best suited to their production.

For steady employment few occupations offer the opportunities enjoyed by poster artists who are able to do good lettering at a commercial speed.

STORY OF THE ALPHABET

The history of lettering makes fascinating reading. Historians ascribe the origin of our alphabet to the Egyptians, as many of the basic lines are found in the hieroglyphics which they inscribed on stone. In time the Phoenicians further simplified these forms to be used in their commerce. Later the Greeks developed the same forms into the Greek alphabet still in use today.

It was the Romans, however, that followed the thin and wide forms, and the old Roman capitals are considered the finest form of lettering today.

Undoubtedly the most beautiful lettering that has been preserved from the Middle Ages is to be found in the old monastery books with their hand-lettered pages combined with beautifully decorated initials, generally at the beginning of each page or paragraph.

OLD ENGLISH TEXT

One of the most difficult alphabets to print is the Old English Text. It is used mostly for religious purposes, or at Christmastime for greeting cards and posters. However, the letterer will spend hours inking in the letters because of the satisfactory results.

ROMAN LETTERS

Roman lettering is composed of both capital and small letters. Since they are used more frequently than other types, the capitals should be memorized by every artist. Copying the alphabet is the best method of learning the proportions and curves of each letter. Next fit the letters into different words in varying weights, making some in light weights, others bold and heavy.

THE LETTER AND ITS PARTS

While there is a wide variation in the form of both type and drawn letters, depending on the tradition followed, it is customary to use certain terms to describe their parts. The spread terminals of the main strokes are known as serifs. In the lower-case alphabet (small letters as opposed to capitals) the vertical strokes are known as ascenders and descenders, a distinction based on whether the stroke rises or goes below the line. For example, the vertical strokes in the lower-case *b, d, h, k, l,* etc., all have ascenders; the lower-case *g, p, q,* and *y* all have descenders. Fillets are the threadlike lines which connect and decorate the bolder strokes in some alphabets.

PRINCIPLES OF GOOD LETTERING

Good lettering requires careful attention to its spacing. When the style of the letter character has been determined, the attention of the designer should be focused on the balance between letter mass and background space. An even distribution of dark and light gives a pleasing sparkle to the finished work.

HEIGHT OF LETTERS

Many of the letters in the Roman alphabet are triangular in form, some are circular in shape, while others are rectangular in character. For this reason, if the tips of the triangular letters, or the tips of the arc of rounded letters merely touch the top or bottom of the guide line, they may appear smaller than their neighboring letters. To offset this, the artist must extend such parts of letters either above or below the guide lines.

CORRECT LETTER SPACING

Good spacing is more important than good lettering. Many beginners who can make a fair alphabet have trouble with letter spacing. If an effort is made to equalize the space between the letters while learning their construction, this should be avoided. A page of lettering properly done has an even tone over all. With this in mind, study your finished work and correct any light or dark spots that may exist.

Using a "yard-stick" to measure the width or distance between different letters seldom produces pleasing results and is generally detrimental to legibility. The experienced letterer achieves correct spacing intuitively. Such work is "optically equalized." These simple suggestions offer the beginner a good starting point:

1. Different letters and dividing areas seldom occupy like spaces.

2. Words read better when the spaces between the letters are less than half the space occupied by the letters themselves.

3. For convenience, letters may be divided into three classes: *Regular,* E-H-I-M-N and U; *Irregular,* A-F-J-K-L-P-R-T-V-W-X-Y and Z; *Circular,* B-C-D-G-O-(P)-Q-(R)-S-& and ?.

4. Ugly gaps between irregular shaped letters can be avoided by fitting them closer together according to their shape.

5. Circular and irregular shaped letters should cut into the spaces between them and the letters adjoining their curved or irregular sides, the amount thus taken from the "dividing" areas helps compen-

sate for the extra space created by the form of the letter.

6. Letters can also be grouped as *Narrow,* B-E-F-I-J-L-P-S-T-Y and ?; *Normal,* C-D-G-H-K-O-Q-R-U-V-X-Z and &; and *Wide,* A-M-N and W.

7. Compressing a wide letter to make it fit into a space that suits a narrow or a normal letter causes it to appear blacker than the rest of the letters. And stretching a narrow letter into the space of a wide one makes it appear lighter than the rest.

Good and Bad Spacing. The accompanying chart illustrates how different combinations should be spaced. The full space as it appears between two straight letters is shown by the stippled block marked "A." Block "B" illustrates the dividing area between two circular letters. Note how the letters cut into it. Block "C" shows how the area appears between a circular and a straight letter. Block "D" shows the area between an irregular and a straight letter. Block "E" shows the area between an irregular and a circular letter.

Note that the extra space at the top and bottom of a circular letter approximately equals what the letter cuts out of the dividing area—and the irregular letters offer a similar example that requires closer fitting to compensate for their shape. The examples shown here illustrate how the different combinations work out in use. In the word "Spacing" letters of the same size and shape are spaced both ways. Note how legibility and unity are destroyed by the mechanical arrangement.

The yard-stick spacing of "Minatown" shows what happens when letters are all fitted into like areas with the same distance between them. Note how spotty the different letters look, especially the M, A and W and how unrelated the irregular letters appear. By making the M, N, A, O and W wider and fitting the irregular letters optically an even tone is obtained.

The word "Blooming" illustrates bad and good arrangements of the same letters. When good lettering appears uneven, spotty, or is hard to read, you will find the spacing at fault.

DEVELOPING YOUR SKILL

Rough letters should be sketched first in order to develop a fluency in style. This can be done with a soft pencil and drawing paper. A ruler and triangle are also necessary. A carpenter's pencil provides an excellent lettering point for the beginner. With it he can practice making both the narrow and broad sides of the letters. By using a broad, narrow point he can demonstrate which parts of the letter are to be wide or thin.

HOW TO INK IN LETTERS

After you have mastered the problems in spacing and are familiar with the different alphabets described by us in this chapter, you will need some practice in inking in the letters. This is best done with a lettering pen.

CORRECT LETTER SPACING

BLOOMING

THIS IS A SPLENDID ILLUSTRATION OF "YARD-STICK" SPACING *NOT EASY TO READ*

BLOOMING

HERE AN EFFORT HAS BEEN MADE TO "OPTICALLY" EQUALIZE THE AREA BETWEEN SAME LETTERS

OPTICAL
SPACING
MECHANICAL
SPACING

Note the improvement in legibility effected by the optically equalized spacing above.

Simplified spacing guide for different letters.

Fit the letters of a word together according to their shape, with the area between them pleasingly balanced, and you will have units that lend themselves to good layout

" OPTICALLY FITTED LETTERS " NOT CRAMPED - **GOOD UNIT** 7

MINATOWN

"YARD STICK SPACING" LETTERS + SPACES OF LIKE WIDTH - **POOR UNIT** 7

MINATOWN

TOO BLACK   DARK   TOO BLACK   LIGHT   DARK   TOO BLACK   DARK

A B C D

& J K L ¢ M

R S T W

$ 1 2 Y 3 5

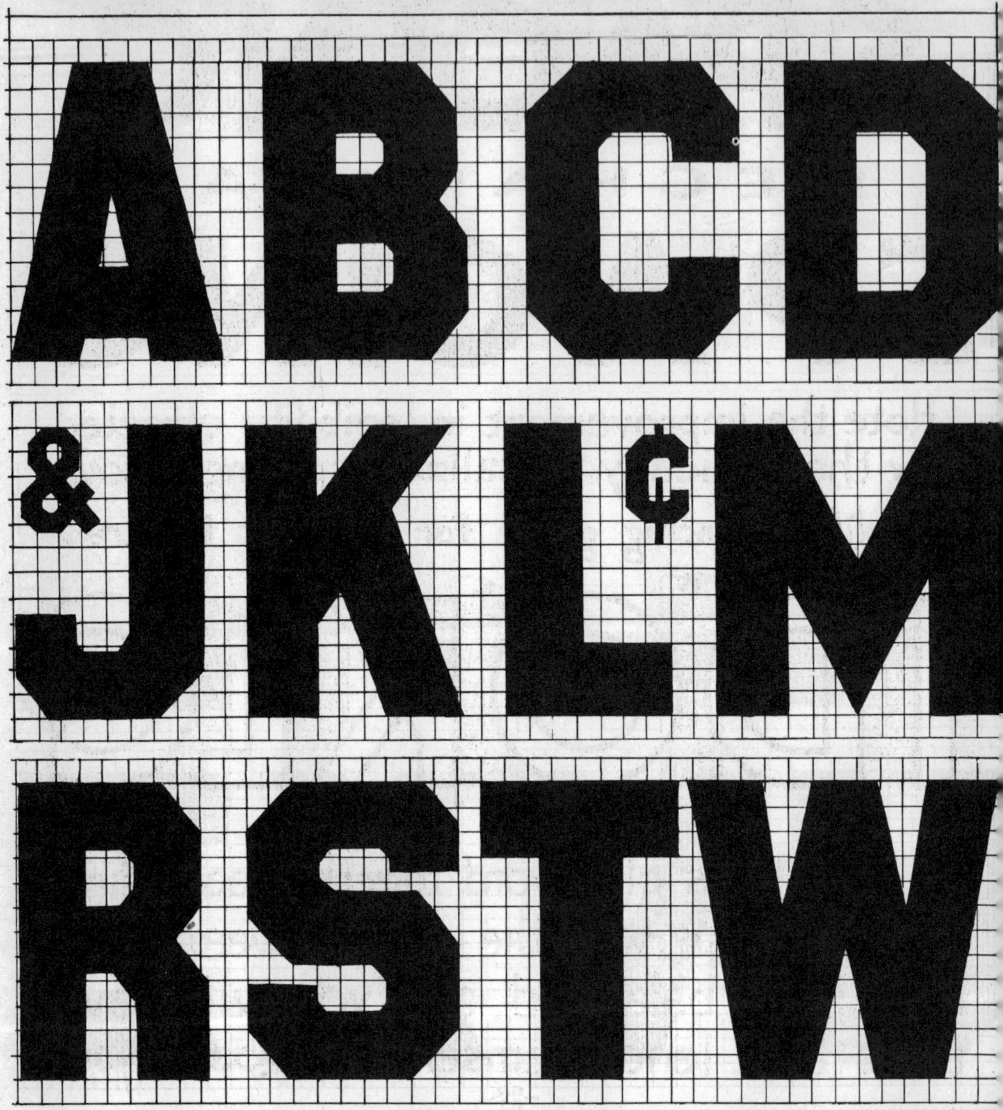

LETTERS TO BE FIRST SKETCHED WITH A PENCIL THEN

EFGHI
NOPQ
UVXZ
64798

A RULE OR T-SQUARE WILL BE HELPFUL
FILLED IN WITH A BRUSH OR PEN

Segregating the alphabets into
THREE *BASIC* GROUPS
Simplifies the Study of Lettering—

Gothic ABCDEFGH
Gothic
abcdefgh

All letters composed of uniform width elements are classified with the Gothics
Before this simplified classification was adopted, Text letters were known as Gothic

---

Romans ABCDEFGJ
Roman
abcdefghi

All letters composed of thick and thin elements are called Roman

---

Text ABCDEFGH
Text
abcdefghijkl

Includes all styles of Old English Text, Church Text, Cloister Text,
Black Text, German Text, Bradley Text, Gordon Text and others.

In the creation of new alphabets these illustrations
will help to show how variations or modifications
of the =Serif= changes the appearance of a letter

iniiinnnnnnrrr

roman *roman* gothic texts
ROMAN *R* GOTHIC Text

Black Text

A B C D E
F G H K L
I J M N O P
Q R S T
U V X W
X ? & Z

CLASSIC

A B C D
I J K L
Q R S T
X Y Z ?
4 5 6 7

This beautiful alphabet was fashioned from letters carved on the base of Trajan Column, Rome-114 A.D. J, U, W, &, ? and numerals not found in original characters.

ROMAN

EFGH
NMOP
UVW&
$123
890¢

ALL ARTISTS, ARCHITECTS, PENMEN AND SHOWCARD WRITERS SHOULD LEARN
THIS ALPHABET; FOR LARGER LETTERS USE A BRUSH.

abcdefgh
ijklmno
r s m n
pqrrstü
u
vvwywxz
12345¢ $6789¢

ABCDE
FGHIJL
MNOPQ
RSTUW
VX s&k YZ
BvL

Lettering Pens. Lettering pens come in different widths, but it is easier to learn the different strokes with a rather fine point. If you use such pens you cannot help knowing where the narrow and wide part of the letter will come.

The pen is held firmly between the forefinger and thumb with the side of the hand resting on the table. By holding the pen horizontally, the line becomes thin or narrow. Vertical strokes produce thick lines. If the letters are large, such as those used on posters, you should ink in the outline with a lettering pen and paint in the center with a lettering brush.

LETTERING FOR DESIGNS

Good lettering is widely used in working with the crafts, no matter what medium is employed. The use of monograms or a single letter is one of the favorite means of decoration of the beginner. In order to fit monograms or letters into a given area, the craftsman must sometimes also create new forms and shapes.

Lettering for design purposes can be changed from the triangular, circular, or square forms of the original alphabet. You use the basic lines and curves, but add variations. For instance, a white line drawn through the center of each letter will divide the dark area and add interest. The line can also be made zigzag, of small dots or a close double line.

Decide if your letters are to fit into a square, circle, or triangle. Choose the type of letter best suited for the design and shape the outside to fit into the area. The middle letter can be superimposed on the other two, or used to join them together.

The grouping of two letters only is a new trend which is more artistic than the old style of intertwining complicated initials. The craftsman will find initials or monograms particularly useful for decorating wood, metal, leather, cloth, plastics, and paper.

A SEED COLLECTION

ADVENTURES IN INDOOR GARDENING

Gardening indoors can be much more extensive than just having a few potted plants about and seeing that they are watered, or ordering a window box from the florist, all set up with petunias and trailing vines.

To start with a bare window sill and plot and carry out a garden scheme is a real adventure, beset with hazards, expectation, and surprises, just like gardening on a larger scale.

COLLECTING SEEDS

A good way to begin miniature gardening is by collecting seeds. Collect any and every kind of seed. You never can tell what you are going to want, once you begin, and you will soon find yourself in communication with other small-time growers, making exchanges and swapping experiences. There is a strong guild feeling among gardeners just as among fishermen, and the same urge to narrate, compare, and rival.

Get a number of small glass bottles and label them. Your friends will be glad to save you a few seeds from each of their packets. Enlist the services of rovers and hikers and get some seeds that fall from plants growing in fields and woods. Get some fruit seeds. The difference in seeds is a study in itself. Some are large and beautiful and shiny.

HOW TO START A WINDOW GARDEN

When you have accumulated a good assortment of seeds it is time to start the window gardening. Any box of suitable size and shape for your window sill will do. You needn't buy one. You will need another box, too—a shallow one—for cuttings or for plants for resetting, for you will shortly be able to share some of your garden products with friends and colleagues.

Fill the bottom of the window box with small pebbles and sand for drainage. Cover this over with good earth from a garden that has been well fertilized, or with woods dirt. This is standard procedure for gardening either indoors or out. If you are in the city, you can buy dirt from a florist.

[223]

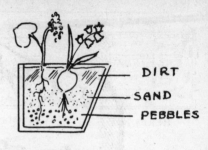

FLOWER BOX

CROSS-SECTION

You will have to plan your garden according to such light, shade, and sunshine as your window exposure will give, so you will need to know about the kind of plants that will take kindly to your location. To post yourself on this sort of information, send for seed catalogues. All the large growers get out beautiful books, many of them with colored plates. They make very interesting reading for anyone who loves plants and flowers. If you have a taste for names as well and like to roll syllables around, you will enjoy learning the formal names of some of the familiar garden flowers, as well as their local names in different sections and countries.

To encourage yourself by seeming to get somewhere quickly in this gardening venture, start growing a pumpkin or a gourd. You will not have to wait long for results, for these seeds sprout quickly and soon you will have a lusty blossoming vine.

Plant several seeds at intervals during a week and check their growth. Many will never reach maturity in your window, but you will have learned to recognize them and you can give them to your friends to transplant in their gardens. Some of these vines will grow in water, but you must have one or two at least in your window box.

At first you might find it more exciting to sow mixed seeds and to postpone scientific planning until later on. Mixed seed packets can be bought, but if you have a collection in bottles, mix your own. See how many you can identify before they bloom.

NATIONALITIES OF FLOWERS

An interesting side path for a gardener is to learn something of the origin of his own flowers and plants. Can you give your flowers a nationality? For instance, zinnias, very common in our gardens, are natives of Mexico. There they were field flowers, and the colors of the ordinary varieties—the bright yellows, reds, and oranges—are those we associate with the native dress. The zinnias have been cultivated and refined, however, so that certain merchants who specialize in the seeds can supply them in the most delicate and rare shades. Blue phlox, eupatorium, and many other plants are field flowers in their native spots and garden flowers by adoption.

Poppies are attributed to China, tulips and hyacinths to Holland, and many of our herbs had their beginnings in England and France.

THE HERB GARDEN

If you would like to have a special feature with a practical side, grow an herb garden in your window. You can grow ten kinds together in an average sized box. Your friends will appreciate jars of flavoring herbs for the kitchen shelf and bags of sweet herbs will please the fastidious for bureau drawers, clothes-presses and linen cupboards. Some of the fragrant herbs have homely virtues, as well, such as discouraging moths. A favorite and cleanly sweet scent for a clothes-press which will keep it free of marauders is composed of lav-

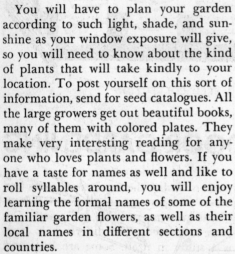

[224]

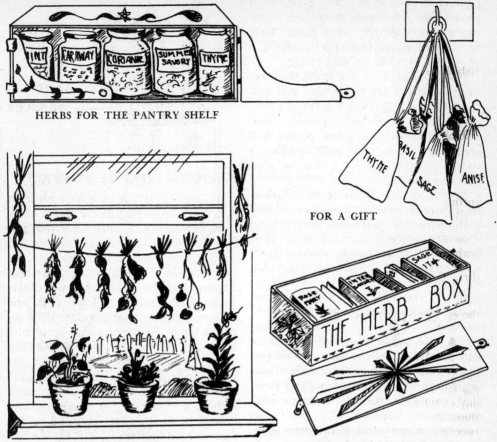

HERBS FOR THE PANTRY SHELF

FOR A GIFT

GROWING AND DRYING

ONCE IT WAS A CHEESE BOX

ender flowers, whole cloves, and gum camphor.

You needn't mind breaking off stems from your herb plants, for others will soon grow in their places. The new shoots spring up from the roots. When the plants are full grown you can pick them and hang them up to dry. Your seed catalogues will give you many useful points about herb growing.

The most common flavoring herbs are: Sage, basil, balm, sorrel, savory, thyme, parsley, mint. The aromatics: Rosemary, lavender (both flowers and leaves), sweet marjoram (leaves), thyme.

DISH GARDENS

Here is another indoor gardening specialty. If you are impatient and want to see something green in very short order, get a sponge, wet it, and set it in a dish in which a small amount of water is kept to be sopped up by the sponge. Cover the sponge with flax seed. It will be green in three days.

If you can wait a little longer, use radish seed and have a showing of green in five days. The tiny plants will have sturdy, shiny leaves. Grass seed, too, grows in this way. Avocado seeds will come to life in an egg cup, but they will take their time about it.

If it appeals to you to have a number of little garden spots in your room, some of the following lowly vegetables can be used:

Carrots. Cut off the top and three-quarters of the lower part of the bulb and place it in a dish surrounded by pebbles to hold it in place. Cover with water. Soon fernlike branches will begin to grow from the top. Some people have been heard saying that this is, indeed, a very good thing to do with carrots!

Horse Radish. Slice and insert the slices in wet earth. They will sprout and will show foliage suggesting a tropical plant.

Practically everybody knows from school days that a sweet potato will sprout in water, very soon sending a trailer over the side of a dish or glass and showing buds.

Save seeds from your fruits — grapefruit, apples, oranges, and lemons—and plant them in a small pot or bowl of good dirt. Before long you will have little plants with shiny leaves, suitable for a table decoration, a fruit salad to feast the eyes.

A GARDEN IN A BOTTLE

To make a novelty garden in a bottle or a jar, put enough pebbles and sand on the bottom (in this case, the side it rests on) to take care of drainage, and cover them over with rich dirt. With a pair of tweezers or a long thin stick, plant seeds in different spots and watch them grow. This is only the basic idea. You can elaborate as much as you like. Wet the sand and earth before putting them into the bottle. The plant needs both air and moisture, and the best way to regulate the atmosphere is to perforate the lid or cap and keep the jar or bottle covered to prevent evaporation. A tiny spray will serve as a watering can when your garden does need more moisture.

POTTED PLANTS

You will have noticed that florists keep potted plants in very small pots. Most people without experience with house gardening think they are favoring their plants by repotting them. The small pot is better, however, because it binds the roots of the plants, and this stimulates them and makes them bloom. If there is too much soil, the plants become lazy and

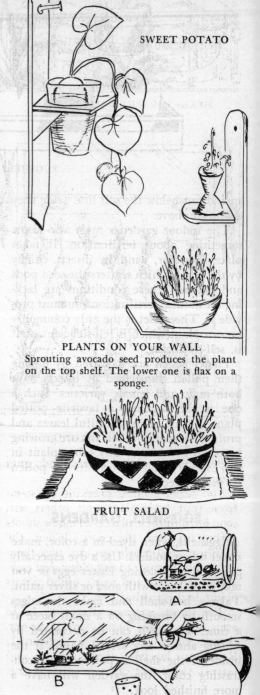

SWEET POTATO

PLANTS ON YOUR WALL
Sprouting avocado seed produces the plant on the top shelf. The lower one is flax on a sponge.

FRUIT SALAD

BOTTLE GARDENS
(A) Plant in a round jar. (B) Planting seeds in a milk bottle.

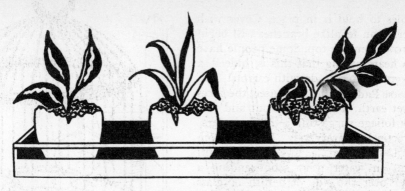

EGGSHELL GARDENS

spread out below the soil line while they diminish above.

The indoor gardener must also know something about fertilization. It takes place by water, wind, or insects, chiefly by the wind, which scatters the seed pods and pollen. Where conditions are lacking for natural fertilization you must provide it. The violet is the only commonly known plant which is self-sufficient, that is, self-fertilizing.

Plants which are fertilized by having their pollen transferred by insects have both male and female varieties. Such a one is the begonia, a favorite potted plant because of its beautiful leaves and profuse flowering. When you are growing begonias indoors, or any other plant in this category, you can transfer the pollen by using tweezers.

EGGSHELL GARDENS

Eggshells, when dyed in a color, make novel flower-holders. Use a dye especially prepared for coloring Easter eggs or you may cover them with gold or silver paint. Take a half-shell and make the edges smooth by breaking off a small piece at a time. The shell can be decorated by adding almost any artists' paint. If the inside of the shell is painted in a contrasting color, the garden will have a more finished look.

Since an egg has rounded ends, it will not stand upright without some support. One of the simplest ways of eliminating the problem is to cut a circle of card-board about two inches in diameter and paint it in a color to match the egg. In the center, place a half-teaspoon of soft plaster of paris and set the egg on it before it dries. Add a little color to the plaster after it dries and the egg is firmly in place.

A row of eggshells set on a narrow strip of wood (see illustration) makes an attractive window decoration. The shells are held in place by adding a small cushion of plastic wood where the shell is to be placed. Force base of shell into plastic wood before it hardens.

Each shell holds a single flower. Fill the shell with gravel (you can buy bird gravel at a pet store) to hold flower in place. Only everlasting flowers that retain their shape and color when dried are suitable for planting. Select a flower that has a stem two or three inches long and force it down into the gravel. For interest, add two or three tiny green leaves. These may be made from crepe paper attached to a piece of thin wire, or several pieces of club moss will serve the purpose.

Eggshell gardens make attractive place cards or party favors. A fresh flower may be used for special occasions by pouring a little water over the gravel.

TERRARIUM

Cut three pieces of glass 15 by 10 inches, two pieces 10 by 10 inches, and one 16 by 11 inches for a cover. The large pieces will form the two sides and bottom

A TERRARIUM

BIRD CAGE HANGING GARDEN

of the terrarium, and the small pieces the two ends. Fasten together with metal ¼-inch strips cut from copper or zinc. Do not use tin, as it will rust. Bend the strips along the center so they will fit around the edges of the glass. Hold in place with cement. Bind all the corners and edges around the bottom with the metal and add another strip around the top of the terrarium.

After the terrarium is completed, cover the bottom with a layer of small pebbles or tiny stones. Next, add a half-inch of leaf mold mixed with sphagium moss to hold moisture for the plants. Spread a thin layer of wood soil on top. You are now ready for planting.

WHAT FLOWERS TO PLANT

Any small plant or flower is suitable for planting in a terrarium. Tiny maidenhair ferns and partridge berries are especially beautiful. Choose plants that are hardy, and be careful not to injure the roots while transplanting them. The nature-lover will want only wild flowers and plants found in woods or along a stream. Almost any plant will grow if the terrarium is placed in a window where there is sunlight part of the day.

If you plant flowers that bloom early in the spring, they will begin blooming soon after Christmas. Many of these flowers have beautiful foliage that add charm to the terrarium even when not in bloom. Among these are the hepatica, striped wintergreen, violet, and anenome. You will want some trailing arbutus in one corner and clumps of tiny ferns. Search the woods for some club moss to add dark, green foliage, and if your terrarium is large enough you may even use tiny cedars or maples. Be sure to include wintergreen and partridge berry, for their red berries give a spot of color.

WHEN TO PLANT

The best time to make a terrarium is in the early fall before the plants have been injured by frost. After the planting is completed, add enough water to dampen the soil and be sure all dirt is washed from the leaves. Place the large piece of glass over the top to keep the water from evaporating. It will not be necessary to water the terrarium more than once a month.

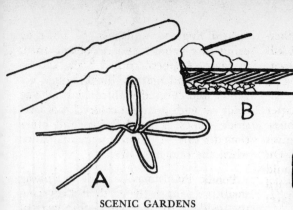

SCENIC GARDENS

(A) Make armatures for figures from hairpins—build them up with self-hardening clay or plastic wood. Paint with poster colors and cover with shellac.

(B) Place pebbles in dish and cover with rack to hold figures and scenery.

(C) Trees are made of wire covered with green crepe paper. Stem and leaves are dipped into melted paraffin to preserve them.

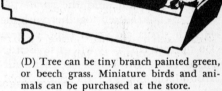

(D) Tree can be tiny branch painted green, or beech grass. Miniature birds and animals can be purchased at the store.

(E) Fishing scene. Use mirror for lake. Make trees of green crepe paper dipped in wax. Add painted stones around pool.

HANGING GARDENS

If you have a bird cage and no bird for a tenant, you can convert it into a hanging garden. Give it a coat of semi-gloss enamel in white or any color you choose. Make a box to fit the bottom of the cage, about 1½ inches in height and paint the outside in a matching color. Line the bottom with small pebbles and cover them with leaf mold and woods dirt. Around the edge, plant ivy or any other vine that will hang down over the edge of the cage.

You may fill the center with almost any flowers that are suitable for growing in porch boxes. If they require sunlight, hang the cage in the window or on the porch. It is unnecessary to make a box for the bottom of the cage if you do not want a variety of flowers or plants. If the cage is large enough, place a single plant in the center and paint the pot green or white. This arrangement will give you an opportunity to change the flowers according to seasons.

SCENIC GARDENS

A scenic garden is an attractive project for adults and children as well, and many effective scenes may be produced.

THE CONTAINER

A cake or pie pan or baking dish from the ten-cent store provides the container. This may be painted black both for looks and, in the case of the tin, to prevent rust. Or a shallow box or a hollow log may be used. All containers, if possible, should have small holes punched or drilled in the bottom for drainage; otherwise excess water is apt to sour and kill the roots. Gardens will live, however, without drainage holes if watering is done judiciously.

On the bottom of the container scatter a layer of loose pebbles and small stones. This makes the drainage better and gives the roots something to cling around. On top of this, put your earth, which should first be gone over to remove all hard lumps, sticks, and stones. Fill to the level of your container and you are now ready to build your garden.

SCENES FOR YOUR GARDEN

Gardens can be so varied, it is possible here to suggest only a small number. One of the following may please you, or you may easily originate your own.

1. Duck pond — ducks, chickens, pigs under a tree at edge of pond.
2. Fishing village — with sailboats in stream and miniature houses on banks.
3. Fairy spring — fairies at edge of pond.
4. Japanese garden — bridge, pagoda, figures.
5. Desert scene — a pyramid, camel caravan at oasis.
6. At the edge of the forest — deer at a stream to drink.
7. Beside the brook — rabbits under a tree at brook.
8. Mermaids by a stream.
9. Boy fishing in stream — with dog.

HOW TO MAKE SCENERY

Miniature mountains and boulders can be made from coal clinkers, which are so porous and of such grotesque shapes that they are interesting in themselves. Some of the depressions may be filled with earth, and seed planted. The mountain may be tinted all the colors of the Grand Canyon. Small tubes of oil paints with a one-inch paint brush and some turpentine are the materials needed and the suggested colors are Chinese red, cerulean blue, and chrome yellow medium and black.

New England walls can be built by using tiny pebbles and cementing them in place. A stucco gabled house can be built of kindergarten blocks glued together and covered with cement, all one color or with a bright-colored roof. Art stone comes in many colors and other cements can be painted with oil paints when the cement is dry.

Ponds. Ponds may be made by sinking small pie pans in the earth and covering the inside of the pan with a thin layer of white or blue-green cement into which small pebbles are stuck while the cement is damp, to represent rocks on the bottom. The sides and edge are covered with cement and pebbles and larger flat stones. Some of these are cemented to keep them in place; others may lie there loose. The soil on these loose stones should be planted with grass seed, ferns or moss so that the point at which the pan and the earth join is completely hidden.

Plants and Trees. As a suggestion of plant life for your garden, here is a simple list, but individual ingenuity will evolve many more.

Moss and small ferns and palms cost very little and can be bought from any florist or greenhouse, but it is more fun to find them in the woods.

Bird seed, grass seed, parsley and carrot seed are all usable.

Sprigs of any tree will remain alive and fresh looking for quite a while if merely stuck into the soil where trees are wanted.

Any short, stubby plant with many branches may be used for a tree.

Matches and small twigs or reed such as is used in basket weaving can be laced together to make fences, arbors, trellises, bamboo houses, log cabins, bridges and gateways.

People and Animals. Farm animals, dolls and small figures help greatly in completing the scene. These may be bought in the ten-cent store, as may Japanese figures and bridges if it is desired to have a Japanese garden.

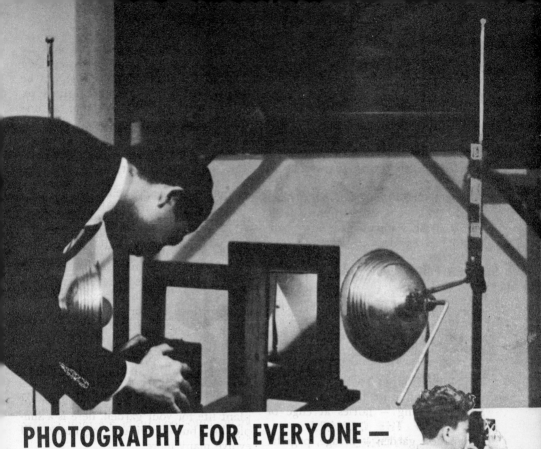

PHOTOGRAPHY FOR EVERYONE —
and How To Make Your Own Apparatus

Photography is a striking product of our modern age — born and bred in the last century. Hidden in seclusion as a virtual "black magic" process for the first half of its young life, it was not taken up by the populace until little more than twenty-five years ago. However, its most phenomenal growth has been written during the past ten years. During that time it has become one of the most extensive hobbies in the world, to say nothing of the growth of its importance in almost every phase of modern life and industry.

There is scarcely an occupation — artistic, scientific, or industrial; hardly an activity — manual, physical or social, in which photography cannot and does not play some part. It is this universal application of the subject plus its un-

Taking pictures is an enjoyable hobby pursued with success by children as well as adults.

mistakable appeal to every type of person that makes it so important from a recreational point of view.

PHOTOGRAPHY FOR ALL

Photography combines in a delightful way two such widely separated activities as art and science. For recreational purposes, no extensive study in either of these fields is necessary, and yet individual leanings in either direction may be completely satisfied. For the person who possesses neither manual nor intellectual ability, satisfaction is still attainable.

[231]

To frustrated artists and thwarted scientists, photography is the way out, since its drawings are so easily made and its technical processes so simple that visible evidence of ability and work well done is easily forthcoming. And yet to talented artists and expert scientific workers, photography presents unlimited opportunities and a still unexplored realm.

Even to those to whom photography is only of secondary interest, its place is valued because of its ability to correlate and aid other primary interests.

Within this great field there is a place for the energetic extrovert who can exert himself to the full extent of his physical powers and a place for the moody introvert who may concern himself with the quiet and intellectual phases of the subject. From early childhood to old age, photography has the ability to hold the enthusiast interested and occupied in the varied stages of its processes and forms of activity.

HOW THE CAMERA WORKS

The camera is a light-tight box with a hole that can be opened by means of a shutter to admit light which reacts on silver-coated film within. The opening or hole is adjustable. The smaller the opening, the sharper the image and the longer the film must be exposed. With the small-est opening, the image will be sharp regardless of distance between camera and object. As the opening is enlarged, the exposure time must be shortened, and sharpness is localized according to the set focus. Example: If focus is set for 8 feet with a full opening, the only area in sharp focus will be within the limits of 7 to 9 feet.

SHUTTER SPEED

The shutter speed must be in relation to light. If you are using the smallest opening F (focus) 16 and your object is in full sunlight, set your shutter for 1/100th of a second. Indoors, you should also use a fast film with a rating of 100.

If it is a medium-bright day, the opening should be F8 and the shutter speed 1/50th of a second. Film, 100 rating.

On a gray day, use the full opening F4.5 or F3.5 and set the shutter for one-half or one full second. Film, 100 rating.

Indoor Portraits. For indoor portrait work, it will be necessary to use artificial light. Foto-flood bulbs are most satisfactory.

HOW THE IMAGE IS FORMED

The word "photography" comes from the Greek "to draw with light." Once that idea is firmly fixed in the mind, the study of photography is half mastered. Optics, that branch of the subject which concerns itself with the formation of the

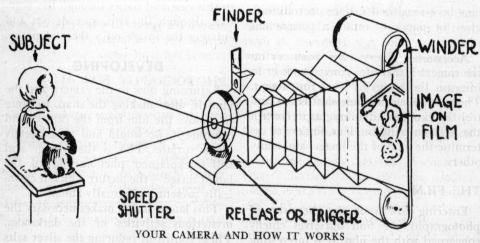

YOUR CAMERA AND HOW IT WORKS

image by the lens, uses light for this purpose. Chemistry, that branch concerned with the retention of this image, also uses light as its prime factor.

Let us consider first the formation of the image. This is usually achieved through the use of a camera, descendant of the "camera obscura" of the Middle Ages. In basic construction this consists simply of a light-tight box with an opening at one end for the entrance of a light, and opposite this a surface on which the passage of light forms the image.

Light rays from the subject converge at the opening in front of the camera and, since light travels in straight lines, the top of the subject appears on the bottom of the film, thus giving us an image which is upside down and reversed from right to left. This may be accomplished with no more than a pin-hole, but since this limits the quantity of light entering, camera lenses are more frequently used.

The Lens. The lens permits of shorter exposures — snapshots. Specially formulated lenses are often used for purposes of increasing the size of the image or increasing the angle of the view.

The Box. The light-tight box may be a simple one of cardboard, or it may be a collapsible leather· bellows for compactness or a metal tube as used in miniatures. The image surface may be oiled paper or ground glass to allow you to view the image before snapping, or it may be a sensitized surface on celluloid, glass, or paper to retain a permanent picture.

Accessories. Every other accessory on the camera is there for convenience or to increase the scope of the instrument. These accessories include shutters to control the exposure, diaphragms to control the light entering the lens, finders to determine the field of the image, and many others.

THE FILM

Entering now upon the chemistry of photography, we find ourselves chiefly concerned with the film. It is interesting to note that scientists were able to obtain images long before they were able to retain them, which must have been most exasperating. It is the action of light on silver, turning it black, which is the phenomenon underlying most of modern photography. If we coat a piece of celluloid with silver salts, place it in the camera and make an exposure, we will get an image of our subject on the film.

The Negative. A little thought now will cause us to realize that since light turns the silver black, we will obtain a reversed image of our subject. All black parts of the subject will scarcely affect the film, if at all, and all white parts will be black. This then gives us an image which is reversed in tone as well as upside down and reversed from right to left. This apparently is not a truthful nor usable picture.

But we had the forethought to make this negative on a transparent celluloid base. If now we turn this negative around, place it in contact with a sheet of paper also coated with silver salts, and throw a light through it, the light will give us an image on paper which will be the reverse of the negative — a positive.

Possessing this negative has advantages. In the first place, any number of copies may be made of the same picture. Secondly, it permits of enlarging. Enlarging is no more than the use of a camera backwards. The light is at the other end in this case and passes through the negative, through the lens, spreads out and enlarges the image on a sheet of paper.

DEVELOPING

Returning now to the camera and the film. If, after making the snap, we were to remove the film from the camera and examine it, we would find a completely blank surface. This is the strange and still unexplained phenomenon of the latent image — the picture which is chemically present and visually absent.

This latent image makes necessary the mysterious activities of the darkroom. These consist of reducing the silver salts

1. Two pictures are spoiled if you forget to advance the film and make a double exposure on one section. Acquire the habit of always winding your film to the next number as soon as you have made a picture.

2. At left, holding the camera level resulted in a good picture. At right: tipping the camera upward made vertical lines converge, so that the building seems to lean backward. Rather than tip the camera, take the picture from farther away.

3. A poorly chosen background can often mar an otherwise good picture—especially in the case of an informal portrait. How much better the picture on the left than the one on the right! The sky itself makes an excellent background.

4. At the left: the subjects were carefully located in the finder and a fine picture resulted. At the right: careless or too hasty sighting through the finder spoiled what would have been a good shot.

5. The picture at the right was spoiled by tipping the camera sidewise. The whole scene seems to be "running downhill." Unless you are trying for an unusual effect, hold your camera level.

THESE COMMON PICTURE-MAKING

6. The blurred snapshot at the right shows what happens if you do not hold the camera steady while tripping the shutter. A similar result follows if the shutter speed is not fast enough to "stop" the action.

7. The image at right is blurred because the shutter speed was not fast enough to arrest action from a broadside position. Such moving subjects can be caught, even with ordinary cameras, if not too close and taken from an angle.

8. When using a focusing camera, be sure to set the lens at the correct distance mark. The blurred picture at right is out of focus. The focus was incorrectly set for a distance beyond the subject.

9. A dirty or misty lens does not see clearly, as illustrated at right. To remove dust or moisture, wipe the lens carefully with lens cleaning paper. Occasionally, use lens cleaning fluid. Never take the lens apart.

10. Be careful not to let any of your fingers project out over the lens. The picture at the right shows the penalty for this common error.

ERRORS ARE EASY TO AVOID

IDEAL LAYOUT FOR DARKROOM
From left to right: print box, developer, hypo, and water.
On wall above pans: light box and cabinet for photographic supplies.

to a visible form in a chemical formula known as a developer, and then making this image permanent by means of another formula known as hypo — a fixing bath. This is required for films, prints and enlargements and constitutes one of the most fascinating of operations.

THE DARKROOM

The darkroom of course is, in most cases, not totally dark. Sensitized films and papers are sensitive to varying colors in varying degrees. Most of them are not sensitive to red and therefore it is safe to handle these in a room lit only with a red light. With some material, yellow, orange, or green are the safe lights. And with some there is no safe light. All this naturally reasons that no light other than the safe light or the light of the controlled exposure may fall on the image surface.

That, in brief, explains the photographic process. There are other phases of the subject, such as toning, coloring, color photography, infra-red, etc., but these require specialized discussion.

In the above résumé, the importance of light in photographic operations has been emphasized and it is safe to say that assuming standard chemical processing, the technical quality of the photograph is determined by the quality and quantity of the light falling upon it. Pictorially, composition and subject matter as well as the arrangement of the lighting determines its quality.

MAKE YOUR OWN APPARATUS

Much of the photographic equipment may be constructed entirely in the home. Purchased commercially, this would be quite expensive, but a little ingenuity, a little knowledge of photography and craft, some old lumber, materials, and tools will result in surprisingly efficient

[236]

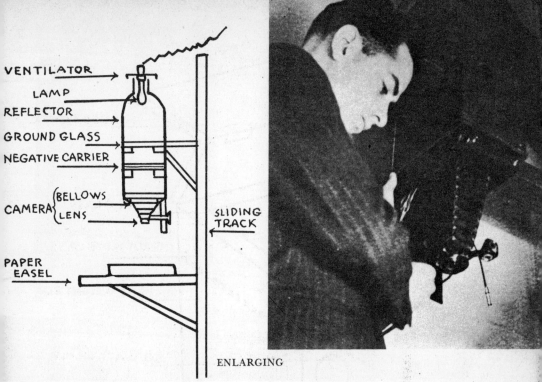

ENLARGING

apparatus. Enlargers, printing boxes, trays, safelights, and other accessories present few problems to the home workshop. Of course, as one becomes more experienced, finer equipment may be desirable. For those who wish to make their own apparatus, the following plans are suggested.

ENLARGER

As illustrated, top to bottom, the various parts of the enlarger are described below:

The Ventilator. The ventilator consists of a tin beer can soldered to the top of the reflector, over which is suspended the cover of a shoe-polish can as a light trap. The lamp and socket hangs from this cover. As a necessary part of the ventilating system a series of holes are drilled near the ground glass and covered with a light trap.

The Reflector. The reflector is metallic on two sides, consisting simply of two sheets of tin bent over two wooden forms shaped to a parabola. The other two sides of the reflector are of five-ply wood a half-inch thick.

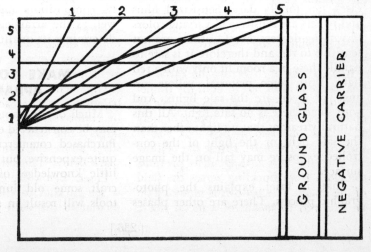

PARABOLIC
REFLECTOR
Divide sides as shown into equal parts, mark off points and join with curve.

[247]

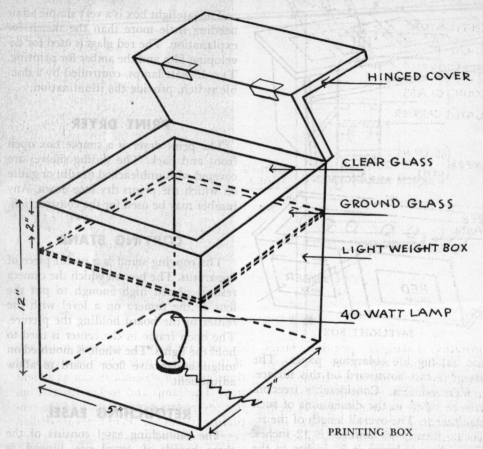

HINGED COVER

CLEAR GLASS

GROUND GLASS

LIGHT WEIGHT BOX

40 WATT LAMP

PRINTING BOX

2"

12"

5"

7"

Light. The ground glass used for diffusing the light rests on two shelves nailed to the sides about 8 or 10 inches below the lamp, which is a frosted 200-watt bulb.

Negative Carrier. Two inches below the ground glass, two more shelves are nailed in to hold the negative carrier, which consists of two sheets of clear glass between which the negative is sandwiched.

Bellows. An inch below the carrier a final ledge is built out to hold the framework for the bellows, simply a piece of opaque, rubberized cloth approximately 12 inches long and shaped to a 5-by-7-inch rectangular tube. Inside the bellows a coil-spring wire arrangement prevents the cloth from buckling across the field of the image. The bellows is mounted on an iron rod by means of a metal sleeve

which allows for adjustment by means of a thumb screw.

Lens. In the lower end of the bellows the lens is fixed in position. Almost any lens will do. In most cases the camera of the worker can be used in lieu of the bellows and lens.

Fastening and Painting. The whole apparatus is fastened to the wall with tongue-and-groove floor boards. This arrangement permits the sliding adjustment necessary in varying the size of the enlargement. A pulley with a counterbalancing weight facilitates adjustment by counteracting the weight of the enlarger. The interior should be painted silver above the ground glass, and dead black below. The exterior is all black.

Easel. Below the enlarger a flat board is set parallel to the enlarger (perpendicular to the wall) to serve as an easel

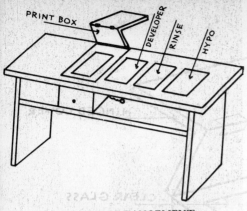

BENCH ARRANGEMENT

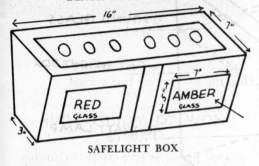

SAFELIGHT BOX

for holding the enlarging paper. The image is cast downward on this surface.

Measurements. Considerable freedom can be taken in the dimensions of such equipment. The overall length of the reflector illustrated however is 12 inches. The whole enlarger is 20 inches to the bellows, with inside dimensions 5 by 7 inches. The track is 7 feet long, the easel 18 inches square.

PRINTING BOX

The printing box is adequately described in the sketch. The wood used is five-ply, a half-inch thick. The hinged flap cover is lined with felt and the interior of the box painted silver. A red lamp in the box is very useful.

DEVELOPING BENCH

The illustration suggests a developing bench that may be made from an old table. The printing box, described earlier, is built in for convenience. Shelves below can be used for paper or storing of trays.

SAFELIGHT BOX

The safelight box is a very simple affair needing little more than the sketch for explanation. The red glass is used for developing film and the amber for printing. Two 15-watt lamps, controlled by a double switch, provide the illumination.

PRINT DRYER

The print dryer is a simple box open front and back. The sliding shelves are covered with unbleached muslin or gauze on which the prints dry face down. Any lumber may be used for the construction.

COPYING STAND

The copying stand is a useful piece of apparatus. The box on which the camera rests is placed high enough to put the lens of the camera on a level with the center of the board holding the picture. The open frame in the center is used to hold the lights. The whole is mounted on tongue-and-groove floor board to allow adjustment.

RETOUCHING EASEL

The retouching easel consists of the three boards of equal size hinged as

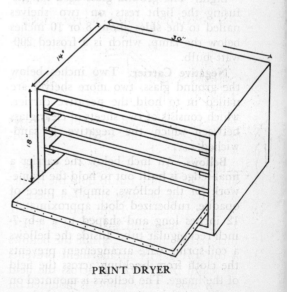

PRINT DRYER

shown. The center one is cut out to hold a 5-by-7-inch ground glass on which the negative is placed. The bottom back piece is painted white to provide a reflecting surface.

MISCELLANEOUS EQUIPMENT

Negative Dryer. An effective negative dryer is made of an open frame with wire strung across it. Wooden spring clothespins suspended from the wires hold the wet negatives.

Trays. Trays may be made of wood, lined with oilcloth and painted with asphaltum.

Tripod. A serviceable tripod may be made of three straight dowels fastened to a platform of flat wood. A ¼-20 bolt through the platform will hold the camera.

Pinhole Camera. A pinhole camera may be made as shown in the photograph by forming a light, tight box of card-by forming a light-tight box of cardboard. A piece of tinfoil is pierced with a No. 10 sewing needle and placed at one end of the box. A piece of cut film is placed at the other, and excellent still-life pictures may be taken.

Printing Frame. A printing frame may be made by simply fashioning a hinged

PINHOLE CAMERA

back from an old picture frame or by making the picture frame itself.

HOW TO MOUNT YOUR PRINTS

Good prints deserve careful mounting. Invest in some special mounting tissue which is coated on both sides with an adhesive substance. Cut it to fit your print. Press on back of print in two spots with warm iron, then place on mounting board. Cover face of print with clean photo blotter and press down with warm iron. Heat will cause adhesive to stick to print and mounting board.

THINGS TO REMEMBER

Keeping loading box free from dust.

Always hold film by outside edges.

Before shooting, check time, focus, and opening, according to light.

Don't forget to turn film after each shot or you'll double expose.

Always protect lens from direct light.

Keep developing tank and trays scrupulously clean.

Never allow hypo and developer to come in contact with one another.

Don't expose printing paper to white light.

Keep camera lens clean. Dust with soft tissue paper.

(A) COPYING STAND. (B) RETOUCHING EASEL

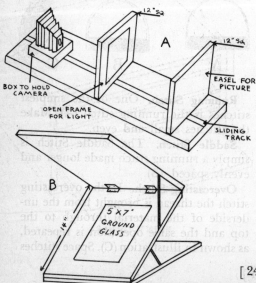

FUN WITH FELT FOR YOUNG AND OLD

"A fabric made of matted fibres of wool, fur, hair or cotton, mixed with glue and rolled under pressure." Webster describes in these few words a material that has become an important textile used in industry, in garment manufacture, garment trimming, etc.

Felt is easy to use. When cut, the edges do not ravel, so in the making of many articles it is not necessary to turn to the edges. It can be molded, shaped, and cut in the most intricate designs. You will be able to make many hundreds of attractive things with felt once you have mastered the simple instructions given here.

HOW TO SEW FELT

Felt is very easy to sew. As we said before, felt does not ravel and the edges need not be turned in except where desired. If you have a sewing machine, you can sew such things as handbags, purses,

etc., on the machine, the same as any other material. To get the handmade touch there are various types of stitches you can use.

A   B   C

Running Stitch. One of the simplest stitches is the running stitch (A). Make the stitches small and even.

Saddle Stitch. The Saddle Stitch is simply a running stitch made longer and evenly spaced (B).

Overcasting Stitch. In the overcasting stitch the thread is brought from the underside of the material through to the top and the same operation is repeated, as shown in illustration (C). Space stitches close or wide as best suited for the article you are making.

Blanket Stitch. The blanket stitch is similar to the overcasting stitch except that before drawing the needle entirely through the material, throw the loop of thread over the point of the needle (D). The spacing of the stitches can be wide or close as desired.

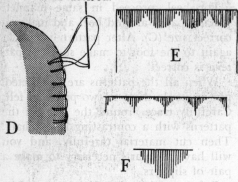

Scallop Stitch. The scallop stitch is a series of long and short stitches made to form a scalloped design (E). Either simple half-curves or more intricate designs such as illustration (F) can be made with this stitch.

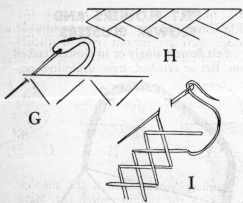

"V" Stitch. The "V" stitch is a series of zigzag stitches, used for sewing two pieces of material together, or for decorative purposes. This is similar to a running stitch, except stitches are placed in a zigzag line (G).

Feather Stitch. The feather stitch is like the "V", except each succeeding stitch starts in the center of the preceding stitch (H).

Herringbone Stitch. This stitch is best described by the illustration (I). It is a series of zigzag stitches crossing each other.

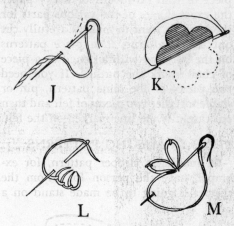

Chain Stitch. Make the first stitch any desired length. The second stitch starts in the center of the first and is placed parallel with it. Continue until finished (J).

Solid Stitch. This stitch is used for making solid flowers and other designs. Place stitches close together and follow any outline (K).

Buttonhole Stitch. Made the same as the blanket stitch, but very close together, commonly used for finishing buttonholes (L).

Lazy Daisy Stitch. Form loops and make tacks at the round ends. This stitch can be formed in all kinds of flowers and other designs (M).

MOULDING OF FELT

The first step in the moulding of felt is to stiffen the felt. Dissolve sugar in water until water is slightly tacky. Brush this liquid onto the felt, and let dry thoroughly. Then it can be bent or formed into any shape. You'll find that stiffening felt this way will help you create many things that would otherwise be difficult.

HOW TO MAKE PATTERNS

In making things of felt as of any other material, it is very often desirable to make a pattern before cutting the felt. If you are making a handbag, draw on a piece of thin cardboard or heavy paper the exact shapes of the various parts for the bag you want to make. Carefully cut out these patterns, then place patterns on the felt, and with a pencil or a piece of chalk mark the outline. If you need two pieces of the same pattern, pin or staple together two pieces of felt and then cut carefully the line marked on the felt.

STEPS IN MAKING PATTERNS

In making a slipper pattern, for example, have the person for whom the slipper is going to be made stand on a

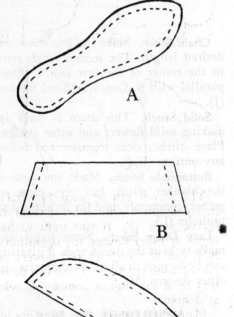

piece of paper in his stocking feet. Draw an outline of the foot on the paper. Then make another outline about one half inch outside the first line drawn, and cut on the second line. This will give

you a pattern for the sole (A). For the upper part of the slipper, place a piece of the pattern paper over the instep, and hold it firmly to the foot. At the juncture of the foot and the floor, draw a line. Remove pattern, draw a line one half inch outside this line, cut on the outside line, and you'll have a pattern for the top of the slipper (B).

For heel, proceed in same manner, placing paper around heel and marking correct size (C). After pattern is cut, fit again to the foot to make sure the pattern is correct.

When all the patterns are completed, pin or staple them to two pieces of felt. Carefully trace around the edge of the patterns with a contrasting color chalk. Then cut material carefully, and you will have the parts necessary to make a pair of slippers.

Before sewing the slippers together, you can trim them with fancy banding, flowers or other appliqué. Then stitch together with any of the stitches described earlier, most suitable for the purpose. Make patterns for other articles in a similar manner.

FELT FLOWERS AND FLOWER CLUSTERS

Felt flowers singly or in clusters tacked on, flat or crushed, have unlimited pos-

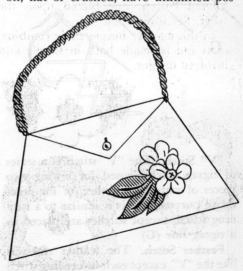

sibilities as trimmings. The simplest use of flowers and other appliqué is by tacking contrasting color flower appliqué on the object to be trimmed.

You can use any of the stitches shown below to sew the flowers together.

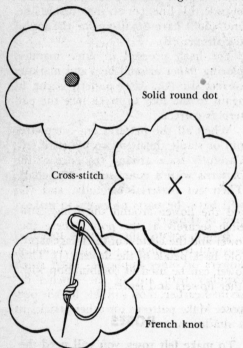

Solid round dot

Cross-stitch

French knot

Using contrasting color thread adds additional interest to the decorative scheme.

The next step is the use of different colored flowers, one placed upon the other. See illustration.

In this manner innumerable combinations can be made both in simple and involved designs.

HOW TO MAKE CRUSHED FELT FLOWERS

This is a very simple method of getting a third dimension into flower appliqué. Take any flower such as (A), fold it in half (B), then fold again (C). Stitch through the point of the folded flower (D).

Twist the thread twice around the point (D), stitch through again, and knot. Cut the thread. Unfold the petals and flatten slightly. It will appear as in illustration (E).

Use flowers of different shapes to get varied effects.

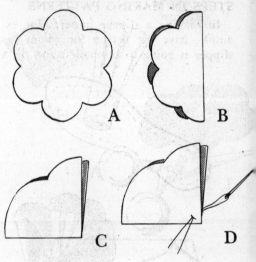

A   B

C   D

This flower can be used by itself or in combination with other flowers and leaves, as in (F). If you want to have larger or fuller flowers, the operation A, B, C can be used with two flowers, one placed upon the other. These two flowers may be of the same or contrasting colors as desired.

Plain circles of felt may be made into roses by sewing together as above, then turning over the edges (G).

Another type of flower that can be made is one with a heart in the center. Take about one inch of felt fringe and roll into a cylinder (H). Take any large flower and cut a small slit in the center (I). Draw the bottom of the cylinder of fringe through the slit about ⅛ inch;

[244]

fold the flower around the fringe and
stitch securely at the point where the
flower and the bottom of the fringe meet.
Fold back petals of the flowers (J). This
flower can be used in combination with
other flowers and leaves.

ROSES

To make felt roses, you will need the
following materials, their quantity depending on the number of flowers you
wish to make: heavy wire for stems; light
wire for leaves; felt—3 small petals, 4
medium-sized petals, 4 large petals, 1
leaf, and green crepe paper for wrapping
stems.

PATTERN FOR ROSE

E

F

G

H

I

J

CUT 4

CUT 4

CUT 3

CUT 1

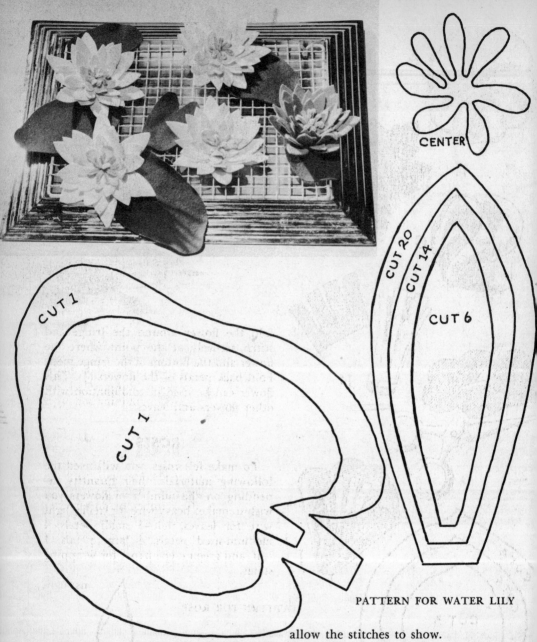

CENTER

CUT 20
CUT 14

CUT 6

CUT 1

CUT 1

PATTERN FOR WATER LILY

Cut heavy wire into lengths you wish for stems. Roll center of rose and wrap one end of wire around base. Spread out the cut ends to resemble stamens. Attach the petals by forcing the wire down through the blunt end and bringing them up tight against the center. Add small petals first and spread them around, then the medium size and finally the large ones. Secure them in place with needle and thread, being careful not to allow the stitches to show.

Reinforce the leaf by sewing a piece of thin wire to the back. Let the wire project far enough beyond the base of the leaf to wrap around the stem of the rose. Wrap the stem with green paper.

WATER LILY

Use white or pink felt for petals, yellow for center and green for leaves. To make the lily, you need 20 large petals,

POT-HOLDERS

14 medium size, 6 small ones, 1 center, 1 large leaf, and 1 small leaf.

First attach center to a piece of fine wire about 6 inches long. Pull top together with your fingers and wrap wire tightly around the base so the center does not show. Spread out the top so the cut ends look like stamens. Next, add small petals by pushing the wire through the blunt end and placing them at intervals around the center of the lily.

Continue adding petals, first the medium size and the large ones, in the same way until the flower is complete.

Sew each row to the previous row of petals to hold them in place. Make stitches at a point where the thread will not show. Add the two leaves when the flower is completed. Twist the wire into a knot and push it back into the felt as much as possible.

FELT POT-HOLDERS

A pot-holder is an excellent felt project, as felt is a good insulator of heat and two layers are ample to protect the hands from a hot handle.

The outline of any object is suitable as long as there are few appendages. Fruits of all kinds can be made in matching colors of felt, chickens or birds, a teapot, or leaves from different trees. Instead of cutting out the object itself, it is possible to cut the felt into geometric shapes and add the design to the center. Flowers, hearts, dishes, or fruit are appropriate for the kitchen. If you have wallpaper in the room, add a part of the motif as a decoration. Attach the design with a buttonhole stitch.

The approximate size of a pot-holder is 6 by 6 inches. Cut two pieces of felt to any shape you may desire. After the two pieces of felt are cut and decorated, take 2 inches of silk cord, form a loop and sew the pieces of felt and cord loop securely together at the top of the holder. Sew sides of the pot-holder together with the zigzag stitch.

APPLIQUÉ BELTS

Cut belt strips the width and length you need for your belt. Use either a straight or pointed end. Decorate the belt in any cutout design you may choose, being sure one design is placed exactly in the center of the back and matching designs on the other side as you go toward the front. Each side of the belt must be the same. Sew the cutouts onto the belt with the zigzag or buttonhole stitch.

Punch holes about ¾ inch from the ends of the belt and insert an eyelet to protect the felt from tearing. (See directions for setting an eyelet on page 182.) Eyelets come in different colors, so it is possible to match the color of your belt. Cut a silk cord 8 inches to 14 inches long, make a knot at one end and draw the other end through the hole. Sew the knot securely to the back of the belt just opposite the eyelet. Repeat same operation on other end of the belt.

Finish off the other end of cord by tying a knot about 3 inches from the end, thread on a wooden bead and tie another knot as close to the bead as possible. This will hold the bead in place. Cut off any string left below the knot and cover the end with cement or glue to prevent it from raveling.

BRIDGE TABLE COVER

Cut a piece of felt ¼ inch larger than the top of your bridge table. Then cut four strips of felt 3 inches wide and as long as each side of the table. Attach these to each side of the top piece with the zigzag stitch, then sew the corners together, using the same stitch. Rein-

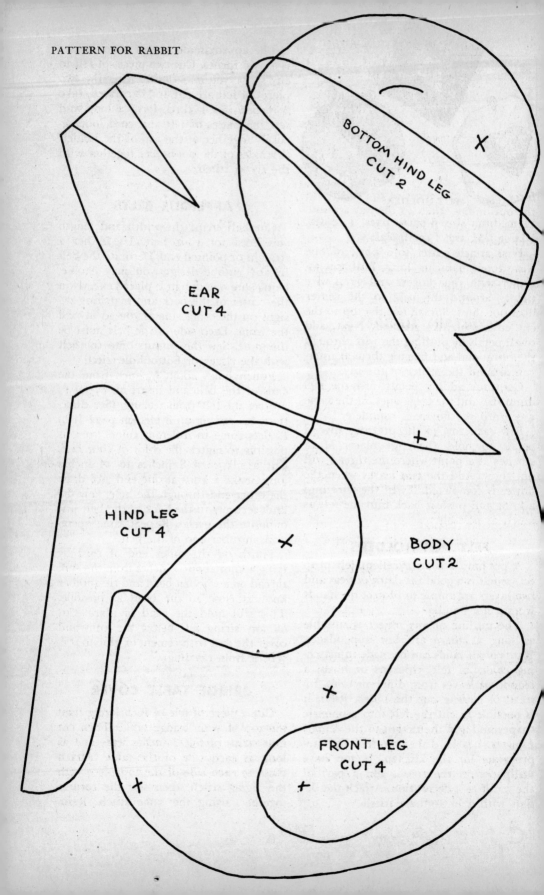

PATTERN FOR RABBIT

BOTTOM HIND LEG
CUT 2

EAR
CUT 4

HIND LEG
CUT 4

BODY
CUT 2

FRONT LEG
CUT 4

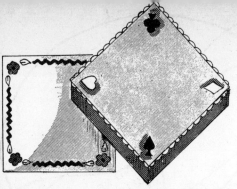

force the bottom edges of the sides with the buttonhole stitch all the way around.

Use a neutral color felt for the cover and decorate by adding a black spade and club and red heart and diamond. Apply these to each corner (see illustration) with upholsterer's cement, or sew to cover with the buttonhole stitch.

CURTAIN TIE-BACKS

Curtain tie-backs are usually about 24 inches long. They may be made with a solid band of felt, or a heavy cord on which felt cutouts are strung. The solid bands may be decorated by appliquéing along the center with the buttonhole stitch, or they may be attached with glue, since there will be little handling once they are in place. Sew two small metal rings on each end for hanging purposes. Add a large flower at one end to cover the rings (A).

Attractive tie-backs can also be made by stringing flower cutouts cut from various colored felts on heavy cord (B). This is done by cutting slits in the center of each flower large enough to allow the cord to slip through. Add an extra flower at each end of the cord and tie a tight knot to hold the flower in place. To use, put cord around curtain, draw curtain together and tie knot, allowing ends to hang down (C).

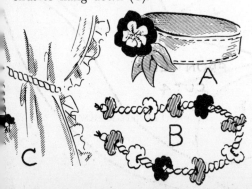

STUFFED RABBIT

Draft pattern to size you wish your rabbit, fasten to felt and cut out pieces. Fit body parts together and sew with an inside seam about 1/8 inch wide. Leave a 3-inch space near where one of the legs will be attached, for stuffing the animal. Turn right side out and add two small circles of felt for the eyes and embroider a mouth with yarn or silk floss. Add some broom straws for whiskers. The tail can be made from clipped ends of yarn.

Cut arms and legs and sew them together with an outside seam, using a running stitch. Stuff and attach to body before it is stuffed. An easy way is to sew on a button at the point they are to be attached.

The ears are made of two pieces of felt glued together. They are folded in at the bottom to give a natural effect.

Stuff the body with cotton, using a ruler or stick to push the cotton in firmly. Sew up the opening with needle and thread, using the overcast stitch.

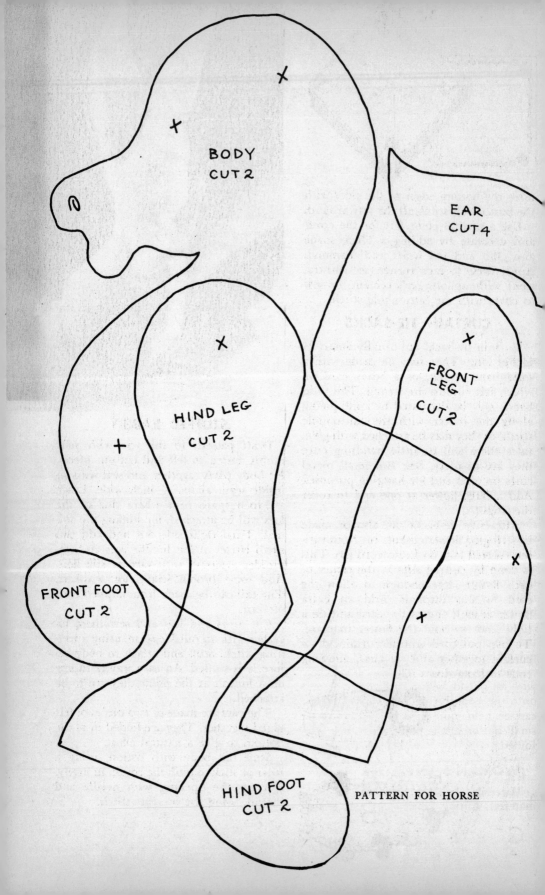

BODY
CUT 2

EAR
CUT 4

HIND LEG
CUT 2

FRONT
LEG
CUT 2

FRONT FOOT
CUT 2

HIND FOOT
CUT 2

PATTERN FOR HORSE

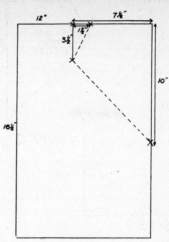

FIGURE A.

STUFFED HORSE

Draft a pattern to size of horse you wish to make and allow 1/4 inch all around for seams. Lay pattern on felt and cut out all the pieces before you begin to assemble them. Sew the body together with an inside seam excepting 3 inches on the underside, which must be left open for stuffing.

Turn the body right side out—add two small circles of felt for the eyes and embroider a mouth with yarn.

The mane is made with short pieces of yarn pulled halfway through the top of the neck with a darning needle and stitched together at the bottom so that the mane will stand up straight. After all the yarn is pulled through, trim the top to equal lengths. The tail is also made of yarn braided at the top and left bushy at the bottom.

Stuff the body with cotton and sew up the 3-inch slit with needle and thread, using the overcast stitch.

The legs and ears are sewed together with an outside seam, stuffed and sewed onto the body before it is stuffed. They can be held more securely by adding a small button at the point where they are joined.

WOMAN'S ENVELOPE BAG

Materials. Felt — 3/8 yard of 36-inch material. Lining fabric—3/8 yard. Tarla-tan or crinoline for interlining. One 10-inch zipper. Mercerized sewing thread.

How to Make Patterns. Use smooth brown paper, pencil, and ruler. Mark a rectangle 12 inches wide by 16 1/2 inches long (A). On top 12-inch edge measure over 7 1/2 inches; mark. Square a line down from this mark 3 1/2 inches; mark.

At the top 7 1/2 -inch mark, measure back 1 1/2 inches; mark. On side edge shown, measure down 10 inches; mark. Connect the 1 1/2 -inch mark with the 3 1/2 -inch mark and then over to the side 10-inch mark (broken lines indicate pattern).

Illustration B shows the bag section pattern and C shows the bag inset section pattern. D and E show where and how much allowance must be added to which edges.

The 1 inch allowed on edges of inset section provides for the fringe trimming.

Cutting Directions. *Bag*—1 piece by pattern. *Bag Inset*—1 piece by pattern. *Lining*—1 piece, 12 inches wide by 16 1/2 inches long. *Interlining*—1 piece of tarlatan or crinoline, 12 inches wide by 16 1/2 inches long.

Sewing Directions. 1. Clip in 1-inch-deep fringe 1/8 inch apart on edges of bag inset section (F).

2. Lap bag inset section 1/2 inch over edges of bag section, keeping fringe free. Baste and top-stitch close to inner edge

[251]

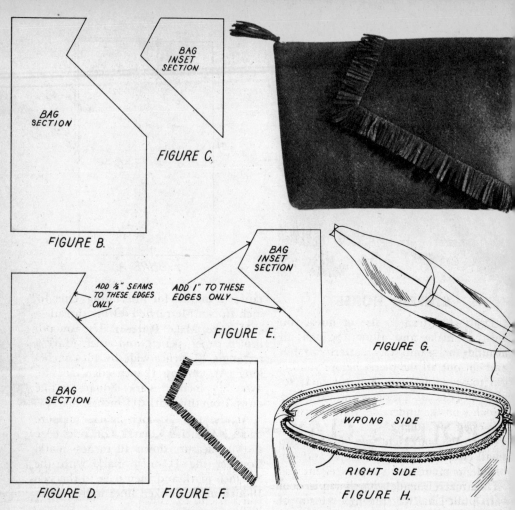

FIGURE C.

BAG INSET SECTION

BAG SECTION

FIGURE B.

FIGURE E.

ADD ⅛" SEAMS TO THESE EDGES ONLY

ADD 1" TO THESE EDGES ONLY

BAG INSET SECTION

FIGURE G.

BAG SECTION

FIGURE D.

FIGURE F.

WRONG SIDE

RIGHT SIDE

FIGURE H.

of fringe through all thicknesses.

3. Fold bag in half through the width, right sides together. Baste and stitch side seams. Press seams open, clipping in almost to seam line at bottom fold of bag.

4. With bag still wrong side out, fold a miter across each side seam (at bottom) as shown in G. Stitch across, forming each miter as shown.

5. With zipper open, baste zipper around top edge of bag, wrong side of zipper up, teeth of zipper back ¾ inch from raw top edge (H). Baste and topstitch ⅛ inch from teeth of zipper.

6. Turn in top edge of bag 1 inch, turning zipper up into position at same time.

7. Catch-stitch raw top-edge flat to bag with stitches invisible on right side of bag. Press.

8. Baste interlining to wrong side of lining piece.

9. Fold lining in half through the width, right sides together. Baste and stitch side seams. Press seams open, clipping in almost to seam line at bottom fold of lining.

10. Stitch miters across side seams (at bottom) same as for bag (Step 4).

11. Turn in top raw edge of lining 1¼ inches; press.

12. Slip lining into bag, right side out, seams matching. Slip-stitch top edge of lining to tape of zipper.

13. Cut a strip of felt 1½ inches long by 2 inches wide. Clip in 1½ inch-deep fringe (through width) ⅛ inch apart.

14. Twist unclipped part of strip around pull of zipper and whip-stitch securely in place.

POTTER'S CLAY—HOW TO USE IT

Modeling in clay is an excellent craft if you crave manual expression of some kind, but are not in the mood for a precise, fussy activity. There is a certain broadness and freedom about working in clay which appeals to the elemental in us. It satisfies the constructive instinct but does not bind us to small detail. Moreover, there is a wide market for well-modeled vases, small busts, etc. Ceramics is an advanced art and highly technical, but the potter's craft out of which it grew is simple and direct.

Clay to Use. Some amateur potters like to prepare their own clay, but commercial clay will be found much better for a beginning. It has already been subjected to all the necessary tests, particularly firing, and it will have the proper texture and consistency.

Wedging the Clay. The first thing to be done is to "wedge" the clay—that is, to get out the air bubbles by throwing it again and again onto a heavy board or slab. If you cannot do this yourself, call on a friend to lend a hand. Be sure that all the air has been expelled before you start to work it.

HOW TO WORK WITH CLAY

Slip Method. There are several ways of working clay. The Indians built up their utensils by piling coil upon coil. The coils were bound together with "slip." This is simply clay thinned with water to a paste consistency. If you are making small objects, which is advisable for a start, mix your slip in a saucer or a small bowl (Fig. 1). As the primitive potter moulded, shaping his bowls and jars, he covered the coils with this thin clay, thus binding them together.

In moulding such things as jars or bowls you will need a template (Fig. 2)

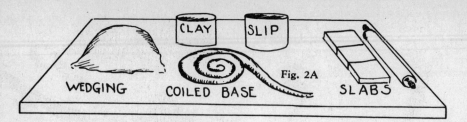

Fig. 2A

WEDGING   COILED BASE   SLABS

as a guide to make the sides of the vessel even. This can be made of stiff cardboard or of metal.

Templates may be cut to various shapes. Figure 3 shows three of them and the finished bowls when moulded. By using the coil method for building up bowls and jars, almost any shape can be attained if the change in shape is gradual. If a template is to be used over and over, it should be cut from a piece of three-ply wood.

Ball Method. Another method is to take enough clay to form the piece of pottery you have in mind. Make it into a ball or into some other form resembling

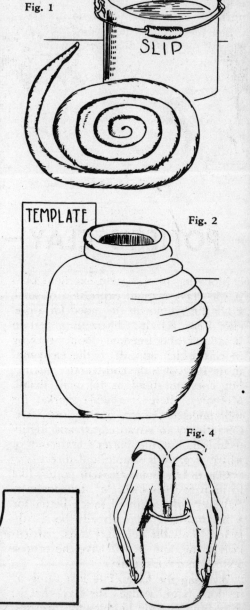

Fig. 1

SLIP

TEMPLATE

Fig. 2

Fig. 3

Fig. 4

[254]

the shape you are going to make. Hollow ware is fashioned by pressing the thumbs inside the ball of clay and "sculpturing" the outside with palm and fingers (Fig. 4). Do not have the walls of your hand-fashioned vessels too thick if they are to be fired in a small kiln, for the heat will not be sufficient to bake them properly.

In making a solid object, the ball or approximate form is made just as for hollow ware, and then the parts are cut away until the desired shape is arrived at.

Slab Method. When the "slab method" is used, the clay is rolled or patted to appropriate thickness for the object; the various pieces are then cut out and put together just as one would go about making a wooden box. The pieces are bound together with slip. You can use a brush—a stiff paint brush—for applying the slip.

Slip Casting. Sometimes the thinned clay or slip is poured into moulds and allowed to harden. The moulds are then removed. This is called "slip casting."

Plaster Reproductions. The sculptor's way of using clay is to have a wooden or wire framework called an armature, on which the clay is massed, to be modeled into a bust or figure. When finished, the sculptured clay is usually cast in plaster. From the plaster mould reproductions can be made by shellacking the mould inside and pouring in plaster.

HOW TO MAKE POTTERY

All of the methods described earlier are used for pottery, except the last one. Pottery is finished by firing and glazing to make it permanently hard and waterproof. The firing can be done commercially, and if there is a kiln conveniently near, you had better have your firing done there. No natural clay can be fired in an ordinary oven. For permanent baking, the temperature must reach 1500°, and most ovens are built to reach a maximum heating capacity of only 450°.

There are in the market electric kilns as small as 6 by 6 inches in size. These are used for testing purposes, and they would

DECORATE YOUR POTTERY
Unglazed pottery lends itself nicely to decoration with waterproof ink. Ink in design only if the pottery is white or a pleasing color. If you want to color the entire surface, dilute the ink and put on the background. Add designs later with undiluted ink.

be large enough for firing some of the pieces of pottery described here.

When your clay is soft and well wedged, make a simple piece of pottery for a start. Choose any form you like—a bird or animal or a little dish. Begin with a lump of clay and mould it, or use coils and slip and build up a little bowl.

When your piece is modeled, put it in a safe place where it will dry slowly to avoid cracking. If a piece of unfinished work must be left temporarily, it can be kept moist by wrapping it in a damp cloth and putting it in a tin box or can. Cracks or crevices can be sealed with clay to keep in the moisture. This makes a good "damp-box."

It would be just as well, for your first piece, to make something plain and rather flat in shape, for it will be less likely to break in the firing. If it comes out well after the first firing, glaze it, and have it fired again.

HOW TO GLAZE POTTERY

Bisque Firing. After the pottery is thoroughly dry it is placed in the kiln and fired to a temperature of 1500-1800°. This is known as bisque firing. The kiln may be filled to capacity, as it does not matter if the pieces touch each other. When the firing is completed, the kiln is allowed to cool and the pieces of pottery removed. You are now ready to add the glaze.

Glazes. The glazes come in powder form and are mixed with water to the consistency of cream. Apply them to the bisque with a small brush, using a short, even stroke. Be sure all parts are covered excepting the bottom, which does not show.

The pieces are next placed in the kiln on small stilts and care must be taken not to let them touch. If the glaze runs from the edges or becomes darker in the depressions, it means you have added too much glaze.

POTTERY PIN

FRONT OF PIN
Fig. 5

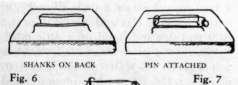

SHANKS ON BACK   PIN ATTACHED
Fig. 6   **Fig. 7**

Metal Pin Back

CLAY TILES OR BELT LINKS
STRUNG ON LEATHER OR CORD
Fig. 8

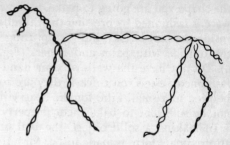

TWISTED WIRE ARMATURE
Fig. 9

Temperature. The usual temperature for firing glazes is 1900°. However, the time of firing varies with different glazes, so read directions on the package or catalogue. Turn off the kiln when it has reached the proper temperature and allow it to cool before opening the door.

HOW TO MAKE PINS AND BELT LINKS

By using the slab method, pins and belt links can be made, and these would be good to start with. The pin illustrated (Fig. 5) is cut from a piece of clay 1½ by 1¼ inches. Model a design on the front and make two clay shanks on the back (Fig. 6). The shanks should be ¼ inch apart. Attach them with slip. Fasten a metal pin-back between the shanks with cement, after the last firing (Fig. 7).

Attaching a Pin. A very easy way of attaching a pin is to make a groove across the back of the clay-modeled pin before it is fired. Then, after it has been fired and glazed, put a safetypin in the groove and cement it into place.

Belt Links. Belt links (Fig. 8) can be made by cutting out pieces 2 by ½ by ¼ inches and decorating them in the same manner as the pins. When they have been fired and glazed, string them together with cord or a leather thong.

HOW TO MAKE BUSTS AND FIGURES

Plasteline is a commercial clay mixed with grease to keep it soft. No water is

EASY TO SCULPTURE

Small figurines such as these are easy to sculpture. Animals can be glazed in any color, or two colors may be used. Squirrel on left is glazed in dark green. The one on the right has a gray body and black tail.

needed with it, but it cannot be fired. It is a good medium for experimental modeling—such things as a puppet head, a figure, or, if you are ambitious, you might try to do a portrait bust in miniature of a friend or of a well-known character. For a start it is well to try something rather bold and exaggerated.

Use an armature, attaching small pieces of plasteline at a time, so that they will adhere firmly and give a solid working foundation. A bottle loaded with shot or sand makes a good armature for a small head, but if you want to make a bust or an animal you will have to devise a framework with a fundamental relation to the figure you wish to produce (Fig. 9).

HOW TO MAKE A PLASTER CAST

If you get something you would like to keep, cast it in plaster. First, put down newspapers, for plaster is apt to spatter. Take a wide pan and half fill it with water. You will want enough plaster mixture to make a 2-inch-thick mould, so you must gauge it according to the size of your sculpture. Five pounds of plaster of paris will make two or three small casts. Add the plaster to the water by the handful or cupful. The mixture will look at first like soft custard.

Your cast will have to be in two pieces, so put a thick cord across the centre of the plasteline model, pressing it in a little so that it will not hurt the modeling, but will stay in place when you pour the plaster. The ends of the string must come below the figure on the armature.

When the water has soaked up the plaster, stir it round and round slowly until it begins to "boil." Do not stir rapidly because you do not want any air bubbles in your mould.

When it has boiled for a minute or two and seems to be showing signs of thickening, pour it over the figure. Hold the armature over the pan, and be sure you get the plaster well into eyes, ears, wings, etc., so that you will have a good reproduction. The mould should be at least two inches thick, and you must make it extra thick where a feature is prominent.

Round off the plaster and let stand for about a minute, then pull the string out, so that the mould will be divided in two. Let it stand, then, until it has dried. You can use small pieces of metal instead of strings to divide the mould. Place them along the line you wish to cut and remove them just as the plaster begins to harden.

You may have to use a chisel to get off the mould. It should be a perfect negative of your figure.

MAKING THE REPRODUCTION

To get a reproduction of your sculpture from the mould, you can use plastic wood or papier mâché. In either case, soap or grease the mould lightly. For the papier mâché you will need some brown wrapping paper with paper towels or colored paper for alternate layers.

Soak the paper in water. Mix fish glue with fox paste and outline your mould with small pieces of paper wrung out of the water and coated with the paste. The first layer has the paste side up, the rest have the paste side toward the mould. Use a stiff paintbrush or a modeling tool to get the paper into corners and features, so that you will not lose the detail of your modeling.

Use about six or seven layers of paper. It is well to put on about three layers and then let them dry before going on. When it is all finished, let it dry for several days or a week, depending upon the weather. In humid weather it takes longer. When it has dried, remove it from the mould, paste the pieces together, and paint it.

If you want to experiment with making a plaster reproduction, try a small bas-relief first. If it goes well, and there is every reason why it should, you might do a small portrait plaque.

As we said earlier, there is no telling where a simple hobby may lead: we began with the most primitive of clay-working methods, and here we are already venturing in the domain of Lucca della Robbia and Benvenuto Cellini!

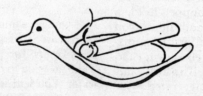

CARD TRICKS, MENTAL FEATS and MAGIC

Almost everyone enjoys watching a good performance of magic or card tricks. Skillful entertainers are always popular at parties or camps, or find a profitable field for their talents in theaters, at benefit shows, or on other occasions. And it is so easy to develop your ability as a magician! You do not have to be an expert in "prestidigitation"—the art of using your hands dexterously. All you need to do is master the simple tricks explained in this chapter and develop your native flair for showmanship, and people will soon be attributing marvelous powers to you. The equipment is very simple —a deck of cards or other inexpensive properties. Here, as in other crafts and hobbies, application is the secret of success.

An essential part of any showman's bag of tricks is his patter. In many tricks you must distract your audience's attention from what your hands are doing. For this purpose anecdotes, jokes, or entertaining stories are often useful. You should develop your patter as you practice a given trick, so that your timing may be perfect.

TRICKS WITH CARDS AND DOMINOES

THE QUEENS DIG FOR DIAMONDS

Taking the pack in your hands, separate from it the four kings, queens, knaves, aces, and also four common cards of each suit. Then, having laid the queens face upwards in a row upon the table, you commence telling your story, something like this:

"*These four queens set out to seek for diamonds.* (Here you place any four of the common cards of the diamond suit half over the queens.) *As they intend to dig for diamonds, each takes a spade.* (Here lay four common spades over the diamonds.) *The kings, their husbands, aware of the risk they run, send a guard of honor to protect them.* (Place the four aces half over the spades.) *But, fearing that the guard of honor might neglect their duty, the kings resolve to set out themselves.* (Here lay the four kings half over the four aces.)

"*Now, there were four robbers, who, being apprised of the queens' intentions, determined to waylay and rob them as they returned with the diamonds in their possession.* (Lay the four knaves half over the four kings.) *Each of these four robbers armed himself with a club.* (Lay four common clubs half over the four knaves.) *As they did not know how the queens might be protected, it was necessary that each of them carry a stout heart.* (Here lay four common hearts half over the four knaves.)"

You have now exhausted all of the cards with which you commenced the game, and they are ranged in four columns. Take the cards in the first of these columns and pack them together, beginning at your left hand, and keeping them in the order in which you laid them out. Having done this, place them on the table face downwards. Pick up the second column, proceed in the same manner, and so on with the third and fourth.

The pack is then handed to the company, who may cut them as often as they choose, provided they cut whist fashion. This done, you may give them what is termed a shuffle-cut; that is, you appear to shuffle them, but really you only give them a quick succession of cuts, taking care that when you have finished this flourish, a card of the heart suit remains at the bottom.

Then lay them out again as you did in the first instance, and it will be found that all the cards will come out in their proper order.

A CARD TRICK WITH A MATHEMATICAL BASIS

When you demonstrate this, it is necessary to keep talking so that your mathematically minded friends will not catch on to it too quickly.

Shuffle the cards well. Be sure that you have a standard pack of fifty-two cards, a bridge deck, without joker or any other extra card. You may invite one of your audience to shuffle, if you like. Then begin to lay out the cards face up in piles, thus: If the first card should be a four, of any suit, it makes no difference, begin counting (to yourself) with "four" and lay out cards, continuing to count silently until you have reached thirteen. Then begin another pack. The knave is counted as "eleven," the queen as "twelve," and the king as "thirteen."

Turn the packs over, giving a glib reason for doing so. If there should be an odd pile which will not count up to thirteen, say something to this effect—"we shan't need these for the moment, but they'll come in useful later on."

Now, supposing you have five or six piles, face downward on the table, invite your audience to select three packs to work with. Pick up the remaining packs and put them with the odd cards which you have put aside. Let one of the onlookers turn up the top card of two of the packs and then you can tell the audience what the top card of the third pack is.

You arrive at it thus: Suppose a four and a queen are turned up. The queen counts twelve, twelve added to four makes sixteen; to this (or whatever is the sum of the two upturned cards) you add ten. Say that we have now twenty-six (all of course in your head, while you continue to talk). Take the pile of discards, shuffle them, and rapidly (to yourself) count twenty-six, turning them up as though you were looking for something. When you have counted twenty-six, begin at one and count to the end of the pack. If you should have, say, eleven cards left, the concealed top card on the third pack will be a knave.

Manœuvre it so that the thicker packs are selected to work with, for, if there were only one card it would have to be a king, and if there were three, it would be a knave, and this would make it easier for the audience to catch on.

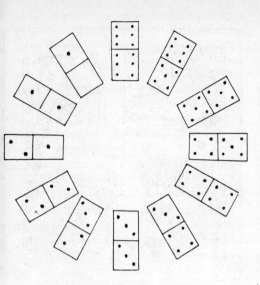

THE DOMINO ORACLE

This trick, to one not familiar with it, is certainly surprising.

Arrange twelve dominoes as shown in the illustration, and tell anyone present that if he will think of one of the dominoes and remember it, you will point it out to him. Now, supposing the double-deuce is the domino selected; you tell the person who has made the choice that you will count around the circle and, when you have counted twenty, including the number of spots on the selected domino, he must tell you to stop, and that your finger will then rest on the domino chosen.

The secret is this: You count carelessly around, 1, 2, 3, 4, 5, 6, 7, on any of the dominoes, but at the eighth count you always manage to point to the double-six, and after that you continue counting around *regularly to the right*. Be sure you remember this, for it is the key of the trick.

For example, as we have said before, we will suppose the double-deuce to be the chosen domino. We know the above instruction, and count and point at the dominoes promiscuously the first seven counts; but at the eighth count, we point at the double-six, and then continue to the right on the six-five, double-five, and

so on in succession until we arrive at the double-deuce, where we will be told to stop, because by that time we will have counted sixteen, with which if we add the spots on the domino selected, we will have twenty. This rule holds good no matter which domino happens to be selected.

It is perhaps, needless to say that you must not count out loud nor appear to be counting mentally, but let it seem as though you are only pointing at the dominoes at random. You must let the person who selects the domino do all the counting.

GUESSING THE ENDS OF A DOMINO LINE

Let a set of dominoes be shuffled together as much as any of the company may desire. You propose to leave the room and assert that from your retreat you will be able to tell the two numbers forming the extremes of a line composed of the entire set laid out according to the rules established for laying one domino after another in the draw game.

All the magic consists in taking up and carrying away, unknown to anyone, one domino (not a double) taken at random. The two numbers on it will be the same as those on the end of the two outer dominoes. Your experiment may be repeated ad infinitum, by taking each time a different domino, which, of course, changes the numbers to be guessed.

LIKE WITH LIKE, OR HOW TO KEEP A HOTEL

Pick out all the aces and picture cards, and then place any ordinary card upon the table. *"This card,"* you say, *"we will call a tavern."* You commence your story as follows:

"On a dark night there came four farmers to this tavern and asked for a night's lodging. As none of the landlord's rooms was occupied, and as he had four of them, he showed each of the farmers to one of the rooms, and went quietly to bed. (Here you place the four knaves

around the card which represents the tavern, and proceed.)

"Not long afterwards, four police officers knocked at the door, and requested also a night's lodging. As the landlord now had no chamber unoccupied, he put an officer in with each of the farmers. (Here you place the four aces upon the four knaves.)

"Presently four fine gentlemen came along and they, too, wanted a night's lodging. Our host was now in great embarrassment, but there was nothing left for him to do except to put a gentleman in each of the four occupied chambers. (Here you lay a king upon each ace.)

"Thus far matters went tolerably well, although not meeting with general approbation; but now came four fine ladies who also had to have a night's lodging. The landlord was now beside himself with perplexity. Indeed, he fairly lost his senses, for the stupid fellow actually quartered a lady in each of the already occupied chambers. (Here you place the queens upon the four other cards.)

"The ladies were highly indignant. 'Could he not have put us like and like together?' they asked. 'That is what he should have done, and not mix us up—police officers and farmers, gentlemen and ladies!

" 'Well,' cried the landlord at last, 'if you are agreed, I will lodge you like with like.' All readily consented, and soon all the farmers were lodged in one chamber, all the officers in another, and all the gentlemen in a third, and all the ladies in the fourth."

While you are saying this, you lay the four heaps upon one another and let the company cut them as often as they choose. But notwithstanding all their cutting, if you now tell them off in order from the bottom of the pack, and place them about the tavern, all the knaves will be in one heap, all the aces in another, and so on.

THE FOUR KNAVES

Take the four knaves, and upon the lower half of the first knave place the

upper half of the second, rectangularly; upon the lower half of the second knave, place the upper half of the third, also rectangularly; then the upper half of the fourth knave upon the under half of the third; and lastly, thrust the under half of the fourth knave under the upper half of the first, and the trick is finished.

THE MAGIC COURTS OF ZOROASTER

Sort the twelve court cards from the pack, excluding the aces, and place them in three rows, that is to say, with four in each row. Beginning with the fourth card in the bottom row on the right, take them up longways, that is, from the bottom to the top, one over the other, the knave of diamonds over the king of hearts, and so on, and offer them to someone to cut. It is a matter of indifference how often they are thus divided; only you must be particular to have them cut without shuffling.

Now, deal them out in four divisions, and, strange as it may seem, the king, queen, and knave of each suit will be found together.

The key to this inscrutable mystery consists in simply observing the following arrangement in disposing the cards at

first: place one of each suit in the upper row, beginning the next row with the same suit that you closed with in the first; and commence the third or last row with a court card of the same suit that terminated the second. By thus arranging the cards you will not have two of any one suit in any of the rows, either vertically or horizontally. The illustration shows exactly how the cards should be placed in order to perform the trick successfully.

If you follow the above directions in taking up the cards the result will be as described. Although this illusion is one easily performed, we never yet saw it practiced without exciting the wonder of the spectators, and the principle on which this is achieved, owing to the apparent consequence of the suits, has successfully baffled the calculations even of the finest investigators of this art.

MENTAL FEATS

THE FIGURE HE STRUCK OUT

Ask someone to write down secretly, in a line, any number of figures he may choose, and add them together as units; having done this, tell him to subtract that sum from the line of figures originally set down; then desire him to strike out any figure he pleases, and add the remaining figures in the line together as units (as in the first instance), then inform you of the result, whereupon you will tell him the figure he struck out.

Suppose, for example, the figures put down are 76542; these added together as units make a total of 24. Deduct 24 from the first line and 76518 remains; if 5, the centre figure, is struck out, the total will be 22. If 8, the last figure, be struck out, the total will be 19.

In order to ascertain which figure has been struck out, you make a mental sum one multiple of 9 higher than the total given. If 22 be given as the total, 3 times 9 are 27, and 22 from 27 shows that 5 was struck out. If 19 be given, the sum deducted from 27 shows 8.

Should the total be equal multiples of 9, as 18, 27, 36, then 9 has been expunged.

With very little practice any person may perform this with rapidity; it is therefore needless to give any further examples. The only way in which a person can fail to solve this riddle is, when either the number 9 or 0 is struck out, as it then becomes impossible to tell which of the two it is, the sum of the figures in the line being an even number of nines in both cases.

THE CERTAIN GAME

Two persons agree to take alternately numbers less than a given number, for example, 11, and to add them together till one of them has reached a certain sum such as 100. By what means can one of them infallibly attain to that number before the other?

The whole artifice in this consists in immediately making choice of the numbers 1, 12, 23, 34, and so on, or of a series which continually increases by 11, up to 100.

Let us suppose that the first person, who knows the game, makes choice of 1. It is evident that his adversary, as he must count less than 11, can at most reach 11 by adding 10 to it. The first will then take 1, which will make 12; and whatever number the second may add the first will certainly win, provided he continually adds the number which forms the complement of that of his adversary to 11; that is to say, if the latter take 8, he must take 3, if 9, he must take 2, and so on. By following this method he will infallibly attain to 89, and it will then be impossible for the second to prevent him from getting first to 100. For whatever number the second takes, he can attain only to 99; after which the first may say—"and 1

makes 100." If the second takes 1 after 89 it would make 90, and his adversary would finish by saying—"and 10 makes 100."

Between two persons who are equally acquainted with the game, he who begins must necessarily win.

THE DICE GUESSED UNSEEN

A pair of dice being thrown, to find the number of points on each die without seeing them: Tell the person who cast the dice to double the number of points upon one of them and add 5 to it; then to multiply the sum produced by it by 5, and to add to the product the number of points upon the other die.

This being done, ask him to tell you the amount, and having thrown out 25, the remainder will be a number consisting of two figures, the first of which, to the left, is the number of points on the first die, and the second figure, to the right, the number on the other.

Thus: Suppose the number of points on the first die which came up to be 2 and that of the other 3; then if to 4, the double of the points of the first, there be added 5, and the sum produced be multiplied by 5, the product will be 45; to which if 3, the number of points on the other die be added, 48 will be produced, from which, if 25 be subtracted, 23 will remain; the first figure of which is 2 and the second figure, 3, the numbers on the first and second dice.

TO FIND A NUMBER THOUGHT OF

1. Let a person think of a number, say	6
2. Let him double it	12
3. Add 4	16
4. Multiply by 5	80
5. Add 12	92
6. Multiply by 10	920

Let him tell you the number produced. You must then in every case subtract 320; the remainder is in this example 600; strike off the two ciphers and announce 6 as the number thought of.

ANOTHER WAY TO FIND A NUMBER THOUGHT OF

1. Let a person think of a number, say   6
2. Multiply it by itself   36
3. Take 1 from the number thought of   5
4. Multiply it by itself   25
5. Tell you the difference between this product and the former   11
6. You must then add 1 to it   12
7. Then halve this number   6

This must be the number thought of.

TO DISCOVER TWO OR MORE NUMBERS THOUGHT OF

This holds good only when each of the numbers is less than 10. Suppose the numbers are 2, 3 and 5.

1. Double the first number, making   4
2. Add 1 to it, making   5
3. Multiply by 5, making   25
4. Add the second number, making   28
5. Double this sum, making   56
6. Add 1 to it   57
7. Multiply by 5   285
8. Add the third number   290

Proceed in the same manner for as many numbers as were thought of. Then ask for the last sum produced, in this case 290. If there were two numbers thought of, you must subtract 5, if three, 55, if four, 555. In the above case you subtract 55, leaving a remainder of 235, which are the numbers thought of—2, 3, and 5.

When one or more of the numbers are 10, or more than 10, and where there is an odd number of numbers thought of: Suppose the numbers selected are 4, 6, 9, 15, and 16.

Let your audience add together the numbers as follows and tell you the various sums:

1. The sum of the 1st and the 2nd   10
2. " " " " 2nd and 3rd   15
3. " " " " 3rd and 4th   24
4. " " " " 4th and 5th   31
5. " " " " 1st and last   20

You must then add together the first, third, and fifth sums—54.

The second and fourth—46. Take one from the other, leaving 8.

Half of this is the first number—4. Take this from the sum of the first and second, and you have 6, the second number. This taken from the sum of the second and third will leave 9, the third number. And so on for the other numbers.

Where one or more than one of the numbers are 10, or more than 10, and where an even number of numbers has been thought of: Suppose the numbers thought of are 2, 6, 7, 15, 16, 18.

Let the person add together the numbers as follows and tell you the sum in each case:

1. The sum of the 1st and 2nd   8
2. " " " " 2nd and 3rd   13
3. " " " " 3rd and 4th   22
4. " " " " 4th and 5th   31
5. " " " " 5th and 6th   34
6. " " " " 2nd and last   24

You must then add together the 2nd, 4th, and 6th sums which will equal 68. And the 3rd and 5th, which will come to 56. Subtract one from the other, leaving 12. The second number will be half of this—6. Take the second from the sum of the first and second and you will get the first—2. Take the 2nd from the sum of the 2nd and 3rd, and you will have the third number, 7, and so on.

MAGIC TRICKS

THE BALANCED COIN

The illustration represents what seems to be an astounding statement, namely, that a quarter or other piece of money can be made to spin on the point of a needle.

To perform this feat, procure a bottle, cork it, and in the cork place a needle. Now, take another cork, and cut a slit in it, so that the edge of the coin will fit into the slit. Next place two forks in the cork as seen in the illustration. If you place the edge of the coin on the needle, it will spin round without falling off.

The reason is this: The weight of the forks, projecting, as they do, so much below the coin, brings the centre of gravity of the arrangement much below the point of suspension, or the point of the needle, and therefore the coin remains perfectly safe and upright.

THE BALANCED TURK

This stunt is based on the same principle as illustrated by the balanced coin, but it calls for a little handiwork on your part. A decanter or bottle is corked and in the cork a needle is stuck. On this is balanced a small wooden ball having a cork or wooden cut-out figure standing on top.

From the ball project two wires, bent to make a semi-circle and having at the ends two balls of equal weight. Push the balls and the whole will turn around on the needle, the figure standing upright all the while; twist it about from side to side as much as you like and it will always regain the upright position.

THE ERRATIC EGG

You can't use your breakfast egg for this. It must be uncooked or it won't work. Set up your simple properties as in the illustration. The problem is to transfer the egg from one wineglass to the other and back again without touching the egg or the glasses, or allowing anyone else to do so. To accomplish this, all you need do is to blow smartly on one side of the egg, and it will hop into the next glass; repeat this and it will hop back again.

TO LIGHT A CANDLE WITHOUT TOUCHING THE WICK

Let a candle burn until it has a good long snuff; then blow it out with a sudden puff; a bright wreath of smoke will curl up from the hot wick. Now, if a flame be applied to this smoke, even at a distance of two or three inches from the candle, the flame will run down the smoke and rekindle the wick in a very fantastic manner.

To perform this experiment smoothly, there must be no draught while the mystic spell is rising.

THE SPANISH DANCER

Here is a stunt featuring the principle of rotary motion. Take a piece of cardboard and cut out a little figure such as that in the illustration. Paste or gum it in an upright position to the inside of a watch-glass. Take a plate or a small tin tray, place the watch-glass holding the figure on it, incline the plate and it will, of course, slide down.

Next, put a drop of water on the plate, place the watch-glass on it, and again incline it. Instead of sliding it will begin to revolve. It will continue to revolve with increasing velocity, obeying the position and inclination of the plate, as directed by the hand of the performer.

The reason for this result is that, in consequence of the cohesion of the water to the two surfaces, a new force is introduced by which an unequal degree of resistance is imparted to different parts of the wine-glass in contact with the water, and consequently, in its effort to slide down, it revolves.

The drop undergoes a change of figure; a film of water, by capillary motion, is drawn to the foremost portion of the glass, while, by the centrifugal force a body of water is thrown under the hinder part of it. The effect of these actions is to accelerate the motion.

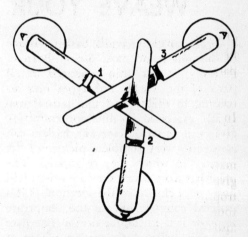

THE BRIDGE OF KNIVES

Place three cups or glasses—A, A, A—in the form of a triangle, their open sides up, and arrange three knives upon them as illustrated, the blade of No. 1 over No. 2, and that over No. 3, which rests on No. 1. The bridge so made will be self-supported.

WEAVE YOUR OWN BASKETS

Of all our native crafts, basketry is one of the oldest and most useful. Born of necessity, it has been practiced in all parts of the world. The types vary according to utility and the natural materials available in different countries. In fact, if you are observant, baskets can give you a very complete picture of the country in which they originated. The materials from which they are woven will give you a clue as to the location. Is it a tropical country, one in the temperate zone, or is it in the far north? The dyes also will indicate the native plants or minerals. The type of basket will tell you how it is to be used, as well as something about the industry of the country in which it was made. Finally, the decorative designs often depict scenes from history, religious symbols, festivals and customs of the people.

In this country, our American Indians have always been the masters of the art. They have experimented with suitable materials and dyes until they have become skilled craftsmen in all kinds of basket weaving. Many of our finest baskets come from the mountains in the South where such vines as honey-suckle, buck bush, wisteria, Virginia creeper, and willow grow in abundance.

MATERIALS AND EQUIPMENT

It has usually been our custom to weave baskets from materials brought in from other countries. Since these imported materials are smooth, long and ready to weave, this eliminates the task of cutting away the leaves and tendrils from vines and twining plants. Whatever material is used, the method of weaving is the same, and the same basic techniques are used in forming a basket.

KINDS OF MATERIALS

Reed. Most commonly used. Comes in all sizes. It comes shaped oval, flat, and round.

Cane. Comes cut into narrow strips and glazed. It is stronger than reed and harder to manipulate.

Rush. Made from native cat-tails. It can be dried and dyed to any color.

Splints. Strips of wood cut very thin into different widths. Usually hickory, oak, or maple.

Willow. Young shoots cut from year-old saplings. Can be used green or dried.

Vines. Honeysuckle, buck bush, Virginia creeper, wisteria, coral berry and many others.

It is necessary to have a quantity of runners on hand so that the worker may select enough of uniform length and size to make the basket.

Working Equipment. This should include a razor blade or sharp knife, scissors, string, sandpaper, a bucket, and plenty of water.

GENERAL DIRECTIONS FOR MAKING BASKETS

Woven baskets are built of two sets of runners: (1) the ribs which form the foundation on which the weaving is done; and (2) the weavers. The number of ribs required to make a basket varies from eight on up, depending on the size and shape of the basket and on the size of the vines used for ribs. The long runners should be saved for weavers. This will eliminate frequent joinings and will result in a smoother, more durable basket. The very fine runners should be saved for beginning the base of the basket.

Before using, soak the runners in warm water until pliable. This eliminates breaking and cracking. Frequent soaking during the weaving will facilitate the work.

CUTTING THE RIBS

The shorter runners may be utilized for the ribs, which must be uniform in size. In some baskets, the ribs are cut long enough to form the base, the side, and the border.

The distance between the ribs should not be more than one inch at the widest part of the basket when medium-sized runners are used. The smaller the runners, the smaller should be the distance between the ribs.

DIFFERENT TYPE WEAVES

A right-handed person will usually weave from left to right, while a left-handed person will weave from right to left. In these directions, "weaver No. 1" refers to the weaver farthest to the left, and "weaver No. 2" to the one second from the left. This will be reversed for the left-handed person, "weaver No. 1" referring to the one farthest to the right, and "weaver No. 2" referring to the one second from the right.

Single Over and Under Weave (Fig. 1a). Single over and under weave is made by placing one weaver behind any rib, bringing it in front of the next rib, and continuing around the basket. This

REED BASKETS
These baskets are easily made by working with reeds. At top is shown a garden basket, at bottom a fireside basket.

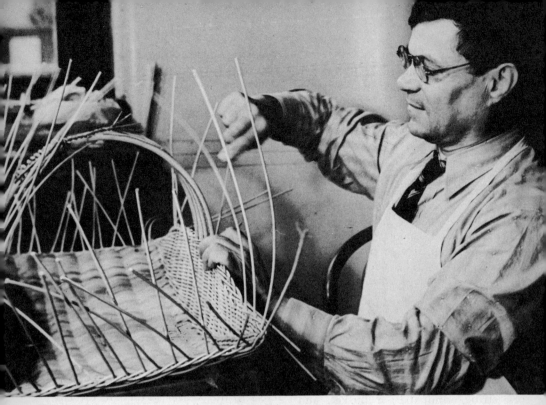

BASKET-MAKING IS EASY
In making a basket, first weave in the bottom, then the handles. You complete the two sides and then the ends.

weave requires an uneven number of ribs.

Double Over and Under Weave (Fig. 1b). This weave is the same as single over and under, except two weavers are carried as though they were one. This weave also requires an uneven number of ribs.

Pairing Weave (Fig. 1c). Any number of ribs may be used for this weave. Start with any two ribs, placing one weaver behind each rib. Weaver No. 1 is brought in front of one rib over weaver No. 2 and back of the next rib. Weaver No. 2 is brought in front of one rib, crossed over weaver No. 1 and back of the next rib. Continue around the basket. Variation of pairing weave may be made by going over a group of ribs instead of single ribs.

Triple Weave (Fig. 1d). Any number of ribs can be used for this weave. Begin with any three ribs and place one weaver behind each. Weaver No. 1 is brought in front of two ribs and back of one. Weaver

No. 2 is brought in front of two ribs and back of one, and weaver No. 3 is brought in front of two ribs and back of one. As each weaver is brought to the back, it crosses over the other two weavers.

Japanese Weave (Fig. 1e). This weave requires any number of ribs not divisible by three. It is an over and under weave made by bringing a weaver in front of two ribs and behind one. This weave can be varied by carrying two or more weavers as one.

Coil Weave (Fig. 1f). Any number of ribs may be used. Four or more weavers are placed behind four or more successive ribs and woven as triple weave until the point of beginning is reached. At this point, the order of handling is reversed, bringing weaver No. 4 in front of two ribs and back of one rib, weaver No. 3 in front of two ribs and back of one; then weaver No. 2, and weaver No. 1 are treated in the same manner. Now the weavers are back of the ribs from where they

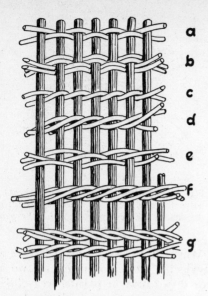

DIFFERENT TYPE WEAVES
Fig. 1. (a) Single over and under weave; (b) double over and under weave; (c) pairing weave; (d) triple weave; (e) Japanese weave; (f) coil weave; (g) arrow weave. Single over and under weave, pairing weave, and triple weave are used as foundation weaves. The other weaves are commonly used as decorative weaves.

started. Repeat for additional round, reversing the weavers at the point of beginning.

Arrow Weaving (Fig. 1g). Any number of ribs may be used. The first row is the same as triple weaving until the point of beginning is reached, when the weavers are reversed as in the coil weave. For the next row, the weavers are brought in front of two ribs and back of one rib, and under the weavers instead of over them. If more rows are desired, reverse again and weave the third row as the first. Finish the coil by bringing the right-hand weaver in front of two ribs and under the top two weavers to the inside. The other two weavers are finished in the same manner.

BASES FOR BASKETS

Wooden bases may be bought, but the person who wishes to make a distinctive basket will weave the base from the runners from which the basket proper is made. There are numerous bases; four of

the most commonly used are described.

The number of ribs used will be determined by the design selected, the size of the basket, and the size of the ribs used.

Base No. 1 (Fig. 2). Cut eight ribs the desired length, and, with a knife, make an opening one inch in length through the centers of half of the ribs. Insert the remaining ribs through the openings so that they lie side by side.

Tie the ribs in place with a string.

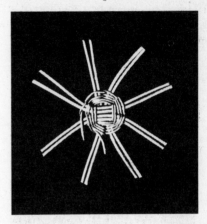

BASE NO. 1
Fig. 2. This is probably the most simple base, and the one easiest to make. Insertion of one group of ribs through the other gives balance.

(After the base is well underway, the string may be removed.) Select a very fine runner and double it around the inserted spokes (Fig. 3). Bring the back weaver to the front and the front weaver to the

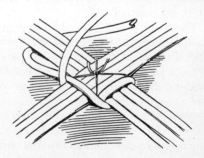

PAIRING WEAVE
Fig. 3. This shows the beginning of the pairing weave after a weaver has been doubled around a group of ribs.

[271]

back. This puts the weavers in place for pairing weave around the groups of four ribs.

Weave two rows of pairing weave. Then separate the groups of four into groups of two ribs each and weave three rows of pairing weave. Then separate the ribs into singles and continue the weaving according to the design of the basket. If the plain over and under weave is to be used in the basket, an extra rib must be inserted before the base progresses very far. This is the best method of starting this type of base when large ribs are used.

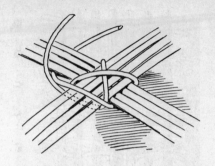

Fig. 5. The diagonal crossing of the weaver holds the ribs firmly in place. The ends of the weaver are now in position for the pairing weave.

Weave two rows of pairing weave and divide the ribs into groups of two and weave two rows of pairing weave. Separate the groups into singles and weave according to the design for the basket.

As in Base No. 1, if the over and under weave or any weave which employs an uneven number of ribs is to be used, an extra rib must be inserted in the base before the work progresses very far.

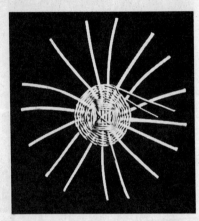

BASE NO. 2

Fig. 4. Starting the weaving about groups of four ribs, then about two, and finally about single ribs, gives smoothness to the base.

Base No. 2 (Fig. 4). After the design for the basket is selected and the size and number of ribs to be used are determined, divide the ribs into two groups of equal number.

Place one group over the other group so that the groups cross at right angles and the ribs in each group lie parallel. Place a weaver around the ribs and bring one end diagonally across the front to the lower right-hand corner.

Now bring the other end under one group of ribs and diagonally across in the opposite direction to the first weaver, forming a cross in the center (Fig. 5). This places the weavers in position to begin the pairing weave around the groups of four ribs.

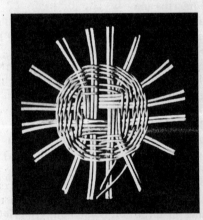

BASE NO. 3

Fig. 6. This base is more decorative and is often used for baskets open at the top.

Base No. 3 (Fig. 6). Four groups of four ribs each are placed over and under as in plain weaving. Double a weaver around any group and, holding the ribs in position on a flat surface, weave two or three rows of pairing weave to make the base secure. Then separate the groups of four into groups of two. Now weave several

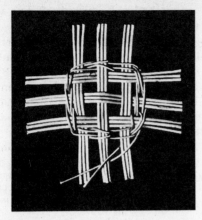

A CHANGE IN BASE NO. 4
Fig. 7. This is a variation of Base No. 4, using nine ribs in three groups instead of eight. Bases are often varied in this manner.

rows of pairing weave and then divide the groups of two into singles.

If a large basket is to be made, increase the number of ribs in each group. If a smaller basket is to be made, the number of ribs may be reduced. However, sixteen ribs is a good number to work with.

The ribs may be cut long enough to weave the base, sides, and borders, but in some baskets the base is made the desired size and extra ribs cut and inserted. For large baskets, one rib may be inserted on each side of each rib in the base. The original ribs are then trimmed off. This will double the number of ribs used.

Base No. 4 (Fig. 7). This base is the same as Base No. 3, except that six groups

TYPES OF BORDERS
Fig. 8. While the open borders, No. 1 and No. 2, are easier to do, the closed borders give a much more attractive and durable finish to the basket, and are not difficult when the ribs are pliable.

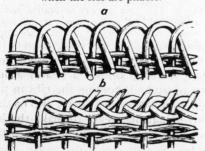

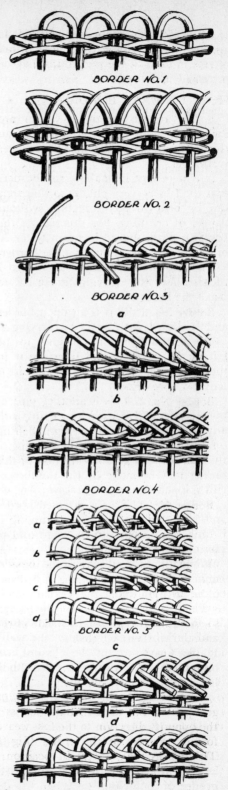

BORDER NO. 1

BORDER NO. 2

BORDER NO. 3

a

b

BORDER NO. 4

a

b

c

d

BORDER NO. 5

c

d

a

b

BORDER NO. 6

of three ribs each are used instead of four groups of four ribs each. The number of ribs in each of the six groups may be increased if desired.

HOW TO MAKE BORDERS

Borders are the ends of ribs woven into each other. This gives the basket an attractive finish and at the same time makes it stronger.

It is necessary in making the borders that the ribs be very pliable so that they can be bent in any direction without danger of breaking. For this reason, the basket is again soaked in warm water 30 or 40 minutes before starting the border.

The ribs should measure from 5 to 7 inches above the weaving in order to make the border.

Border No. 1. This is an open border and is started with any rib, carrying it to the right and bending it down to the left of the next rib and inserting it in the weaving far enough to be certain it will stay. (See Fig. 8.)

Border No. 2. This is another type of open border and is made by starting with any rib, bending it to the right behind one rib and inserting it in the weaving to the left of the next rib. Variation of this border may be made by the number of ribs skipped (See Fig. 8.)

Border No. 3. This is a closed border and is started with any rib, bringing it behind the next rib to the right and to the outside of the basket.

When all of the ribs are to the outside, begin with any rib and bring it in front of the next rib under the weaving made by the rib and to the inside of the basket. When all the ribs are to the inside of the basket, trim them off close to the weaving. (See Fig. 8.)

Border No. 4. This is also a closed border. Start with any rib. Bring it to the front of the rib on the right and behind the next rib and back to the outside of the basket (Border No. 4a, Fig. 8).

When all the ribs are on the outside, start with any rib. Bring it in front of the next rib to the inside of the basket (Border No. 4b, Fig. 8). When all the

ribs are on the inside, trim them close to the weaving.

Border No. 5. Start with any rib. Carry it behind the rib next to it and to the outside of the basket (Border No. 5a, Fig. 8).

When all the ribs are outside, take any rib, bring it in front of the rib to the right and to the inside of the basket (Border No. 5b, Fig. 8).

When all the ribs are inside, take any rib, bring it behind the rib on the right under the weaving done with the other ribs, to the outside of the basket (Border No. 5c, Fig. 8).

Taking any rib, bring it in front of the rib on the right under the weaving and to the inside of the basket (Border No. 5d, Fig. 8). Trim the ends of the ribs off close to the weaving.

Border No. 6. Begin with any rib. Bring it behind the rib to the right to the outside of the basket (Border No. 6a, Fig. 8). Each rib is then brought under the next rib and left resting against the second rib from where it started (Border No. 6b, Fig. 8). This will leave the ribs in an upright position on the outside of the basket.

Each rib is next brought over the rib against which it rests and follows it behind two ribs to the outside of the basket (Border No. 6c, Fig. 8). Each rib now follows the rib it is resting against in front of the rib and to the inside of the basket (Border No. 6d, Fig. 8). When all ribs are to the inside, the ends are trimmed close to the weaving.

HOW TO SHAPE THE BASKET

After the base is made, soak it until the ribs are pliable and turn them up to form the foundation of the basket. Do one row of weaving around the base, making a smooth edge on which the basket rests.

A basket may be shaped over a container. If so, the size of the container will determine the size of the base. Tie the container to the base with a cord, passing the cord between the ribs and around the bowl from top to bottom (Fig. 9). When the base is the correct size, turn up the

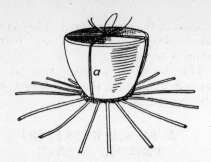

Fig. 9. Weaving over a container is an excellent method for beginners to use in learning how to shape baskets.

ribs, weave one row of coil and continue weaving as directed.

Any weave may be used to make the basket. When finished, weave one row of coil weave at the top and finish off the basket with any border desired.

HOW TO MAKE A HANDLE

For a handle, cut four runners 24 inches long. Insert these runners into the weaving 1½ inches apart, one inch above the base of the basket. Insert a weaver into the weaving by the side of one of these runners. Hold two runners of the handle close together with the weaver. This group is bound together in spiral fashion with the weaver for a space of 5

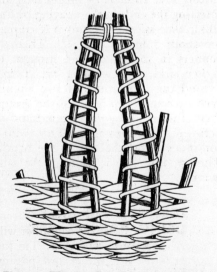

Fig. 10. The handles should be made of larger runners than the weavers. This shows a simple and substantial handle.

inches. The binding should be spaced one-half inch apart. (See Fig. 10.)

Bind this group to the other two runners inserted for the handle, wrapping the weaver around the two groups four times. Bring the weaver through the center and wrap two or three times. Then wrap the other group down to the place where the runners are inserted in the basket. This is repeated on the opposite side of the basket.

Next, bring the runners of the handles close together 3 or 4 inches above the last winding. Wind three times around the two groups with a single weaver. The weaver is then brought up between each runner of the handle and wrapped once around the winding. This may be repeated at intervals along the handle.

NUT BASKET MADE WITH DOUBLE OVER-AND-UNDER WEAVE

A very simple but dainty basket for nuts is easily made, and requires only a small amount of material: Six ribs each 15 inches long, and one rib 8 inches long, one very fine weaver or raffia, and 3 or 4 weavers 10 feet long. Three runners 22 inches long are used for the handle. To start the base, follow directions given for Base No. 1, page 271.

When the base is started, separate the groups and weave around each rib in turn with the same pairing weave for three rows, thus making a close center. Cut off the weavers and make the ends secure. Insert a new weaver and complete the base of the basket with single over and under weave.

When it is 5½ inches in diameter, soak the base until the ribs are pliable and turn them up at the edge of the weaving to form the foundation of the sides. After turning the ribs, insert a second weaver and continue weaving for 2½ inches or until the basket is as high as desired, using the double over and under weave. The sides should be fairly straight, or may flare a little. Finish the basket with Border No. 4, page 274.

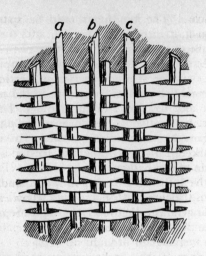

Fig. 11. Runners used for handles can be pointed on the ends in order to insert them easily in the basket. The handles should be inserted close to the ribs, and deep enough in the weaving to be secure.

To make the handle, turn the base up, insert the three 22-inch runners beside three separate ribs (Fig. 11), twist around each other, and on the opposite side of the basket insert the other ends of the

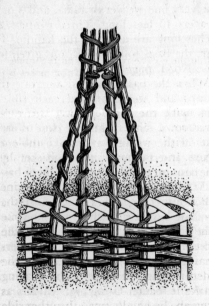

Fig. 12. The interlacing of the runners around the two groups in the handle is very similar to the method used in lacing shoes.

runners in the same manner. The handle can be shaped in any fashion desired while it is wet.

The size of this basket may be increased by cutting the ribs longer and making the base larger.

A SMALL BASKET IN PAIRING WEAVE

The base for this basket is made according to the directions for Base No. 3. The basket in the photograph is woven over a glass container which makes it very suitable for flowers. The container over which the basket is to be made will determine the size of the base. As soon as the base is started, tie the container to the base with a cord between the ribs and around the bowl from top to bottom (Fig. 9). When the base is the desired size, weave a row of coil weave to make a smooth edge on which the basket will rest. Soak the ribs until pliable and turn them up for the sides of the basket. Pairing weave is used in the basket in the illustration. However, any other weave may be employed. Finish with Border No. 4, page 274.

The handle for the basket is made by cutting four runners 24 inches long and inserting the ends in the weaving by four ribs in succession. Each runner is wrapped for about 5 inches (Fig. 12). Then the runners in the handle are brought together and two winders are twined around the two groups of two runners each by coming up between the groups, then crossing and going around and up between the groups again. This twining continues across the top of the handle. The opposite side is made in the same manner.

TALL FLOWER BASKET USING PAIRING AND TRIPLE WEAVE

This basket requires 16 ribs 32 inches long, and two or three runners 45 inches long for the handle.

To begin the basket, follow directions for making Base No. 2, page 272.

After center is started, separate ribs into groups of two and carry them as though they were a single rib until the basket is nearly finished, as directed. Pairing weave is used as the main body

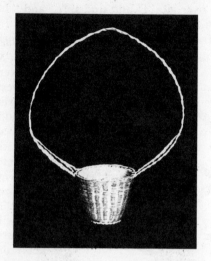

SMALL BASKET IN PAIRING WEAVE
Baskets intended for flowers need large handles, which will frame the blossoms and not crowd them.

of the basket. To add interest the weave may be varied.

When the base is about 4 inches in diameter, it is finished by bringing a rib in front of the one next to it on the right and up between the last row of weaving. When each rib has been treated in this manner, the base should measure about 5 inches in diameter.

With the base finished, the basket proper is ready to be made. Double a weaver around any rib and begin pairing weaving as described on page 270. Weave about 4 inches of pairing weave before changing the weave. The triple weave was used in the basket in the photograph.

Insert a third weaver and weave one inch triple weave. Turn the extra weaver to the inside of the basket and cut off. Change back to the pairing weave and weave 1½ inches. Change again to triple weave, inserting a new weaver, and

weave 1½ inches. Again turn the extra weaver to the inside, cut off, and then weave one inch of pairing weave.

At this point, the basket should measure 5 inches in diameter across the top. To make the basket flare, work from base up, keeping ribs straight for 4 inches, then gradually pull them apart enough to give the desired diameter of the basket at the top. Keep the weavers moist at all times to make them pliable. Soak the ribs at the top of the basket in warm water until they are pliable, and with flat pliers or fingers, bend ribs to right angle. Separate ribs into singles and continue pairing weaving for 1½ inches.

To make the border, bring each rib behind rib next to it and down to outside. Then bring each rib over rib next to it and down to the outside (Fig. 13). Cut ribs off close to the weaving.

Fig. 13. This border, with the ribs trimmed off on the outside rather than on the inside, can be used when the top of the basket is turned down.

To make the handle, insert two runners about 4 inches from the base of the basket with one rib between. Double a weaver, and fasten it in the basket by going around a rib and to outside of basket. With a weaver in each hand, twine them around one of the runners until the top of the basket is reached. Do the same on the other runner. When the top of the basket is reached, bring the two runners in handle close together and draw the winders through the edge of the weaving to make it secure. Using two winders as one, wrap the handle until the other side is reached, then repeat the same process. Make the ends secure and cut them off on the inside of the basket.

BASKET MADE WITH KNOT WEAVE

The knot weave is very decorative and easily done. It is usually made over a vase, bottle, or jar, as it is so fragile that it will not stand hard wear unless a support of some kind is used. Use ribs 10 to 12 inches longer than for the usual weaves, as this weave takes up quite a lot in working.

used in the next sets. Ribs "a" and "f" are tied around "c" and "d" in the following manner: Lay rib "f" over ribs "c" and "d"; lay "a" under "c" and "d." Bring rib "a" up over rib "f" and carry "f" over "c" and "d" and under rib "a," forming a loop with "f" by carrying it back over "c" and "d." Rib "a" is brought up over rib "f" and under "c" and "d," and up through the loop formed by "f."

In the knot to the right of the one just

Fig. 14. This drawing will serve as a guide in placing the different ribs around the basket. By tracing each rib up through the rows of knots, it will be seen that when an uneven number of rows is tied, each rib will be directly above the point from which it started.

Select a well proportioned vase, bottle, or jar and weave a base to fit the bottom. Soak in warm water and turn up the ribs for the sides of the vase. Weave several rows of plain or pairing weave before beginning the knot weave as in Fig. 14.

For tying the knots, start with any six ribs. Letter them "a," "b," "c," "d," "e," and "f," as in Fig. 14. Ribs "e" and "b" will not be used to tie knots in this set, but "b" is bent backward and "e" forward, out of the way and ready to be

tied, rib "e" will be used in the same manner as "a" was used, and in the knot to the left "b" will be used in the same manner as "f" was used. Tie the knots the same way around the container. Tie the knots up to the top of the container and finish weaving with any weave desired. Finish the top with Border No. 2 or Border No. 3, page 274.

For the basket pictured in Figure 15, three rows of knots are tied. The ribs are then divided into groups of two (Fig. 15).

Insert a weaver, and weave three rows of single over and under weave around the groups of two. Turn the weaver to the inside and cut off. Leave an open space of 1½ inches, insert a weaver, and weave

Fig. 15. The knot weave is a dainty weave that gives an artistic touch to the basket. It may be used in combination with any weave, and is sometimes used for the entire basket.

7 rows of over and under weave. Carrying two ribs as one, finish with Border No. 2, page 274.

The handle is made by cutting two runners and inserting the ends in the weaving beside two ribs in succession. Twine the runners about each other and insert the ends into the weaving on the opposite side.

TALL FLOWER BASKET OF SPLINTS AND HONEYSUCKLE

Weave a honeysuckle base for the basket, following directions given for Base No. 1.

Make this base about 2½ inches in diameter with an uneven number of ribs, such as 13 ribs, each 30 inches long. Honeysuckle is used for the ribs. Use honeysuckle weavers for the base and for the flare at the top, and oak splints ⅜ inch wide for weaving the sides. One large honeysuckle vine 24 inches long is needed for the handle.

After the base is made, soak the basket in warm water and turn up the ribs for the side. The weaving of the flared vase is begun as soon as the sides are turned. Weave 1 or 2 inches of pairing weave with honeysuckle, cut off the weavers, and make the ends secure. With the oak splint, weave the basket with a plain over and under weave. Continue with the splint for 9 inches, allowing the ribs to flare so that the diameter across the top will be 5 inches. Soak again and bend the ribs out and use the honeysuckle again as a weaver. Weave the pairing weave for 1½ inches, and finish the edge in accord-

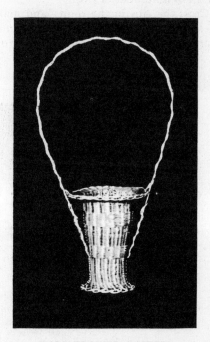

TALL FLOWER BASKET

The long lines of a tall basket may often be broken by the use of two different weaves. This type of base makes the basket rest flat on the table.

ance with instructions for Border No. 6.

The ends of the runner for the handle are sharpened and inserted on opposite sides of the base at the edge. A smaller piece of honeysuckle vine is used to fasten the handle to the edge of the basket at one side and then it is wrapped around the handle to the opposite side through the edge of the basket and made secure.

Various shapes and sizes can be worked out in these materials.

SANDWICH BASKET MADE OF SPLINT OAK

To make this basket, cut 16 splints 1 inch wide and 14 inches long for the ribs. Mark the center of each, and beginning at each end, taper the ribs to ¼ inch at center. Split all the ribs except one clear to the end, through the middle within 1½ inches of the center. The other rib is trimmed off to be the same size as the split ribs. This is done in order to have an uneven number of ribs.

Cross the ribs in the center and make them secure with a string to hold them in place for the weaving. Space an equal distance apart. Using splints ¼ inch wide, start weaving the center with plain over and under weave, going over or under the ribs which were split as one for the first five or six rows; then separating the ribs which have been split. There should be 31 ribs. Continue the over and under weave until the ends of the ribs are reached.

With a sharp knife, trim off all ribs even with the weaving. Holding a splint on the outside and another on the inside of the outer edge of the basket, bind off the edge with a splint by going over the outside edge between the last row of weaving.

For the handle, cut a splint about 21 inches long and 1 inch wide. Taper to a point at each end. Shape the basket by turning up the sides (see photograph of basket), and hold secure by tying with a cord until the handle is put in place. Insert one end of the handle about 5 inches between the weaving and a rib. Directly opposite, on the other side of the basket, insert the other end of the handle. Remove the cord which was used to shape the basket.

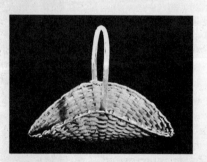

SANDWICH BASKET OF SPLINT OAK

Splints are desirable for heavy and durable baskets such as lunch baskets or clothes hampers. For a smooth finish, the splint used to bind the edge must be very pliable. It is easier handled when wet.

HOW TO MAKE FLIES AND FISHING RODS

Fishing flies are made to look like natural flies. Not from biology books but from direct observation the fisherman knows that flies have a cycle and that they are short-lived. They mate in the air over the water and lay their eggs on a limb or a leaf which eventually falls into the water, where the eggs lie and incubate for a year or more. Sometimes the "incubator" is eaten by the fish. When hatching time comes, the shell or covering breaks, the larvae develop and float to the top of the water, the new flies emerge to mate, lay eggs, and to fall on

the stream again for the hungry fish, continuing the cycle.

There are hundreds of kinds of flies, each of which has its day. The astute fisherman sometimes wades into the stream and gets some of the larvae which are about to hatch, so that he will know what kind of artificial fly to use that day. That is why there must be so many varieties of fishing flies in a good kit.

A fisherman observes what fly is on the water, selects one like it from his book or from the piece of sheepskin on his hat band. After the fly is attached to

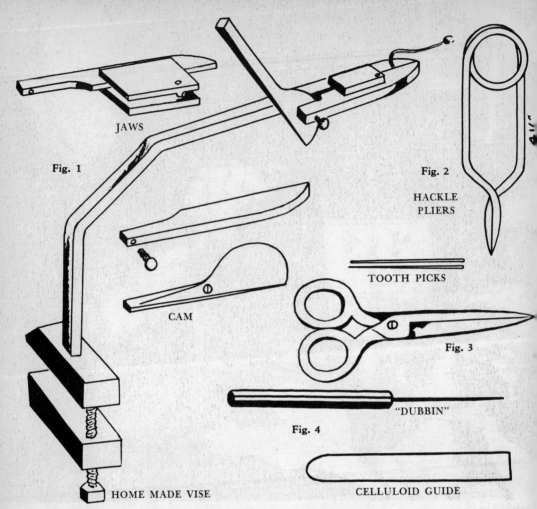

JAWS

Fig. 1

Fig. 2

HACKLE
PLIERS

CAM

TOOTH PICKS

Fig. 3

"DUBBIN"

Fig. 4

HOME MADE VISE

CELLULOID GUIDE

his line, he wades gingerly into the water, casts his line far over the surface, drags it a little, waits, reels it in, and repeats this over and over again, until a fish strikes, and the battle is on.

This chapter is intended only as a beginning in fly-tying and not as a complete manual. We have space to give only first principles. It will serve, however, as an excellent start on a highly skilled craft which is almost limitless in scope.

FLY-MAKING TOOLS

The vise illustrated in Fig. 1 was home-made. The parts and assembly (jaws and cam) are shown in detail in the event that someone should want to make one, but they can be bought from any supply house.

The hackle pliers (Fig. 2) were also home-made. A piece of 1/8-inch welding brass was used.

The applicators came from the first aid case, and the scissors is usually filched from a sewing basket (Fig. 3). The "dubbin" is a matchstick with a needle stuck in the end of it. The celluloid guide was cut from a shirt collar (Fig. 4).

These are the tools which a fly-tyer needs.

Besides the tools, he must have hooks and snells, which are short pieces of gut used to fasten the hook to the leader. The hooks vary in size from very small ones to those which are large enough to hold a bass.

Quills or parts of feathers are used for the bodies of the artificial flies. Rabbit fur, colored woolen yarn, chenille, and

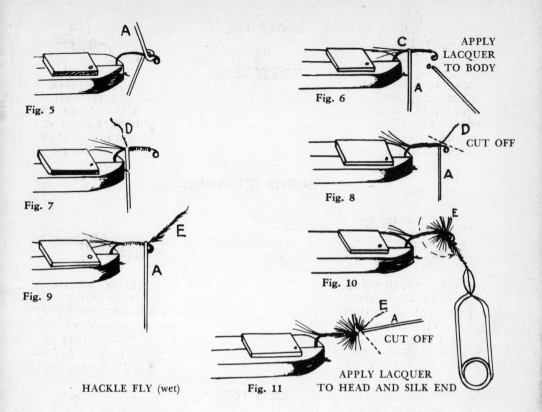

Fig. 5

Fig. 6 — APPLY LACQUER TO BODY

Fig. 7

Fig. 8 — CUT OFF

Fig. 9

Fig. 10

HACKLE FLY (wet)   Fig. 11 — CUT OFF / APPLY LACQUER TO HEAD AND SILK END

tinsel are also used for the body of the fly. Hackle, which is composed of feathers, is used for legs and wings.

Dubbin, a kind of wax, is used to make dry flies water-proof. Lacquer holds the body firm after it is wound onto the shank of the hook. There are hundreds of other materials which the artisan-devotees—the fly-makers—have learned to use, but those listed above will do for the beginner.

VARIETIES OF FISHING FLIES

Fishing flies are usually divided into five groups.

The dry fly, which is made to float on top of the water, is covered with wax and made as light as possible.

The wet fly is one that is made to resemble a submerged insect which floats under the water.

Bass flies are of the dry variety, much larger than the usual dry flies.

"Feather Streamers" look like "minnies," by which a fisherman means minnows, or small fish. These, of course, are wet flies, and they are dragged through the water like swimming fish.

The "Nymphs" are wet flies which are weighted so that they will go to the stream bed where the real larvae or nymphs are.

Besides these there are other subterfuges, such as a bass bug, and, most surprising, a mouse. Both of these are wet flies.

HOW TO MAKE A HACKLE FLY

A hackle fly is one of the easiest and simplest to make. It is a wet fly and therefore not to be waxed. This will be a good one to start with for an example of procedure.

To begin, fasten the hook into the vise (Fig. 5) and wrap the tying silk (A) spiral-

DRY FLIES

MARCH BROWN
TAIL—GROUSE
RIBS—BROWN SILK
BODY—BROWN FUR
HACKLE—GROUSE
WINGS—GROUSE

HARE'S EAR
TAIL—NONE
RIBS—YELLOW SILK
BODY—RABBIT FUR
HACKLE—YELLOW
WINGS—GREY

FEATHER STREAMERS

PARMACHENE BELLE
TAG—PEACOCK HERL
TAIL—SCARLET—WHITE
RIBS—GOLD
BODY—YELLOW FLOSS
HACKLE—SCARLET—WHITE
WINGS—SCARLET—WHITE

SILVER DOCTOR
TAG—NONE
TAIL—BLUE—GREEN—RED
RIBS—NONE
BODY—SILVER
HACKLE—BLUE—GUINEA
WINGS—BROWN—RED—BLUE

BASS FLIES

ROYAL COACHMAN

BROWN HACKLE

PARTS OF A FLY

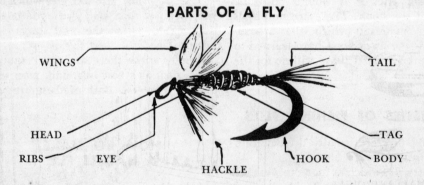

WINGS · TAIL · HEAD · RIBS · EYE · HACKLE · HOOK · TAG · BODY

ly around the body close enough to cover the part of the shank used for this part of the fly.

In Fig. 6, the tail (a few barbs with the barbules removed) is attached with the fly-tying silk and lacquer is applied with an applicator. In Fig. 7, a quill (D) or centre of a small feather is used to wrap the body. The silk (A) and the quill (D) are wrapped together to the eye end of the hook. Here the remainder of the quill (D) is cut off (Fig. 8). Lacquer is applied to make the head and, also to the silk, to hold it secure. Both A and B are then cut off. This completes a hackle fly without wings.

HOW TO MAKE A MALLARD QUILL

To make a fly with wings, start at Fig. 8, after the tail is attached (Fig. 8 repeated). Cut two pieces of feather, one from each of identical feathers in a pair of wings, if possible, so that they will be left and right wings on the insect. Attach a small amount of hackle (G) as illustrated in Fig. 12. The celluloid guide (Fig. 4) can be placed between the wings until the tying silk (A) is looped over the ends of the wings and hackle and drawn secure (Fig. 12). This is called a Mallard Quill, and it is a rock fly.

HOW TO MAKE OTHER FLIES

The dry flies illustrated in the full-page drawing are the March Brown and the Hare's Ear. Underneath each will be found the "dressing" for them. They are made like the wet ones, excepting for the use of the wax to waterproof them so that they will float.

The Feather Streamers or artificial minnows are made according to the methods given underneath the illustration.

The bass flies are well known, being the Royal Coachman and the Brown Hackle.

HOW TO MAKE A FLY BOOK

A fly book is very useful for carrying the flies and the leaders, which come in 15-inch pieces and must be tied together. The book illustrated in Fig. 13 is made of three sheets of aluminum 6 by 4½ inches. These are made into a book by using strips of leather for hinges. Bore holes in the aluminum and sew the leather to the metal with heavy thread. Then

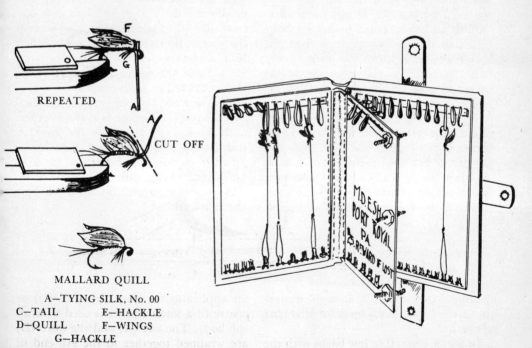

REPEATED

CUT OFF

MALLARD QUILL

A—TYING SILK, No. 00
C—TAIL   E—HACKLE
D—QUILL   F—WINGS
     G—HACKLE

Fig. 12. HACKLE WET FLY WITH WINGS. (Begin with Fig. 4)

Fig. 13. A HOME-MADE FLY BOOK. For snelled hooks with leather cover and metal pages.

[285]

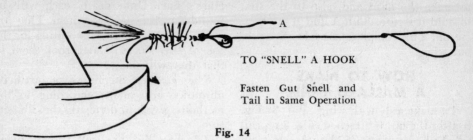

TO "SNELL" A HOOK

Fasten Gut Snell and
Tail in Same Operation

Fig. 14

bore holes ¼ inch apart at the top and bottom of each "page." Attach common hooks with thread and fine wire sewed through the bottom holes.

Both sides of the middle page can be used for mounting the flies. Rubber bands are strung through the top row of holes and the snelled hooks are attached as shown in Fig. 14. Carried thus they do not become snarled or brushed.

To allow for space between the pages, headless bolts are placed at the three points on the centre pages. Screw in nuts on both sides to hold them in place. A piece of heavy leather one-quarter inch wider than the metal at top and front was used for a cover. It was fastened to the first and third pages by boring holes in the metal one-quarter inch from the back edges. This leaves the leather cover loose from the metal excepting at the back and makes a place to carry leaders and extra hooks.

To prevent the contents from slipping out, a snap fastener was attached to each corner of the leather and each front corner of the first and third pages. Last of all, three small leather straps and snap fasteners were attached, to close the book.

The fly book is a cherished possession.

The fisherman usually has a strap on his belt from which the treasured "volume" hangs, so that he won't see it floating downstream after an arduous encounter with a strong-willed trout.

HOW TO MAKE FISHING RODS

For those who would like to make their own rods, Fig. 15 shows a kind that is most satisfactory. It is pentagonal in shape, made of five pieces of bamboo which are glued together lengthwise. This gives flexibility and strength. The guides and the tip are attached with colored silk thread which is wrapped around the rod. The ends are whipped under. (For directions on whipping, see page 135.) Then the whole rod is shellacked and varnished to waterproof it.

The reel and tapered line are attached to the handle. The line is made to taper, with the light end towards the hook. A transparent leader of about eight feet is attached to this, and the fly and hook go on the end of the leader.

A good automatic reel saves winding the line back.

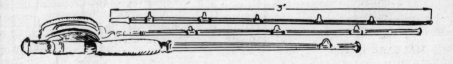

Fig. 15. THREE SECTIONS OF A NINE FOOT ROD

BUILD IT YOURSELF — Woodworking and Toys Anyone Can Make

Making things of wood is one of the most universally enjoyed crafts. Woodworking is easy to learn, and provides not only a rich field for creative self-expression but also a means of producing many practical and attractive objects for your home or for sale. This chapter gives you a concise background in woods, glues, tools, techniques, and painting, as well as plans and instructions for making such useful things as a folding bench ladder, a linen closet, book ends, a waste-paper basket, toys, and many more. With the basic information you will acquire here, you can proceed to make scores and scores of other things you will use and enjoy.

HOW TO SELECT WOOD

If you are not familiar with the various kinds of lumber available, it is suggested that you consult local retail lumber dealers. They can offer suggestions as to which species of wood or kinds of wood products will be best adapted and most economical to use in constructing specific articles.

Many American woods are naturally durable; that is, they possess special properties which make them resistant to decay and insect attack. Heartwood, the darker-colored lumber cut from the inner part of the tree, is always more durable than sapwood, the lighter-colored lumber cut from the outer part of the tree. Heartwood, therefore, is well adapted for use under decay or insect-producing conditions such as in fences, garden furniture, or wherever wood is exposed to moisture or comes in contact with the ground. Lumber used under exposed conditions is frequently treated with chemicals, which make it more durable.

All lumber, as it comes from the tree, contains a large amount of moisture. In order to adapt this lumber to good construction or for use in fabricating articles made from wood, it is necessary that it be seasoned, which simply means removing excess moisture. If unseasoned lumber is used, it will shrink and may warp and twist. Good workmanship, proper gluing, finishing, and decorating of articles made from wood is dependent to a very large extent on the use of properly seasoned lumber.

In ordering lumber, it is necessary to be familiar with the definitions commonly used in the lumber yard.

WOODWORKING TERMS

Yard Lumber. Lumber that is 5 inches or over in thickness, intended for general building purposes.

Structural Material. Lumber that is 5 inches or over in thickness and width.

Rough Lumber. Lumber undressed (not planed) as it comes from the saw.

Surfaced Lumber. Lumber that is dressed by running through a planer. It may be surfaced on one side (S1S), two sides (S2S), one edge (S1E), two edges (S2E), or a combination of sides and edges, (S1S1E) surfaced one side and one edge, (S2S1E) surfaced two sides and one edge, (S1S2E) surfaced one side and two edges, or (S4S) surfaced four sides.

Strips. Yard lumber less than 2 inches thick and under 8 inches width.

Boards. Yard lumber less than 2 inches thick, 8 inches or over in width.

Dimension. All yard lumber except boards, strips, and timbers; that is, yard lumber 2 inches and under 5 inches thick, and of any width.

Planks. Yard lumber 2 inches and under 4 inches thick and 8 inches or over in width.

Scantlings. Yard lumber 2 inches and under 5 inches thick and under 8 inches wide.

Heavy Joists. Yard lumber 4 inches thick and 8 inches or over in width.

Timbers. Structural lumber 5 inches or larger in least dimension.

TOOLS

The following list will serve as a guide for anyone who desires to accumulate a fairly complete set of tools for the home woodwork shop:

1 claw hammer, 13-ounce
1 screw driver, 4-inch
1 two-foot folding rule
1 crosscut saw, 22-inch
1 try and miter square, 6-inch
2 chisels, ¼ and ¾ inch
Coping or jig saw
1 marking gauge
1 jack plane, 11½-inch
1 ratchet brace, 8-inch sweep
2 auger bits, ⅜ and ¾ inch
1 oilstone
1 jackknife
Screw clamps

The growing interest in woodworking as a hobby and home industry has resulted in the development of power-driven woodworking tools and equipment which may be obtained at surprisingly low prices. Power-driven woodworking

WOODWORKING TOOLS COMMONLY USED

AUGER BIT

RULE, TWO-FOOT, FOUR-FOLD

CHISEL

SCREW DRIVER 4"

SMOOTH PLANE 8"

SIDE CUTTING PLIERS 6"

HALF ROUND CABINET RASP 8"

JACK PLANE 11½"

SCOUT AX

BLOCK PLANE 7"

COMPASS SAW 12"

DIVIDER 6"

LEVEL

PANEL SAW 22"-9 PT.

NAIL HAMMER 13 OZ.

RACHET BRACE 8" SWEEP

BACK SAW 12"

MARKING GAUGE WOOD

HAND DRILL

TRY AND MITRE SQUARE 6"

COPING SAW 6½"

NAIL SET

DRILL BITS

SHARPENING STONE 8" X 2" X 1"

SCREW CLAMP

DRAWING KNIFE 11½"

CABINET SCRAPER

SCOUT KNIFE

BENCH VISE 2"

HARDWARE FREQUENTLY USED

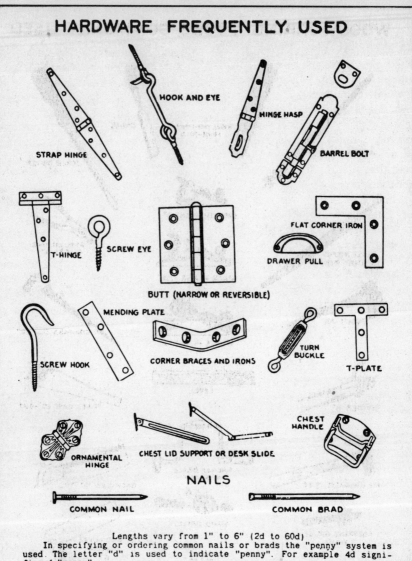

STRAP HINGE

HOOK AND EYE

HINGE HASP

BARREL BOLT

T-HINGE

SCREW EYE

BUTT (NARROW OR REVERSIBLE)

FLAT CORNER IRON

DRAWER PULL

SCREW HOOK

MENDING PLATE

CORNER BRACES AND IRONS

TURN BUCKLE

T-PLATE

ORNAMENTAL HINGE

CHEST LID SUPPORT OR DESK SLIDE

CHEST HANDLE

NAILS

COMMON NAIL

COMMON BRAD

Lengths vary from 1" to 6" (2d to 60d)

In specifying or ordering common nails or brads the "penny" system is used. The letter "d" is used to indicate "penny". For example 4d signifies 4 "penny".

To determine the "penny" size of nails or brads to use, multiply the thickness of the board holding the head of the nail by 8 and add 1-1/2 to the result. For example, when nailing through a 9/16" board, it is suggested that a 6d nail be used. (9/16 x 8=4-1/2   4-1/2 + 1-1/2=6).

To determine the length in inches of common nails or brads for a given "penny" (d) size, up to and including 10d, divide the "penny" size by 4, and add 1/2. For example a 5d nail measures 1-3/4". (5/4 + 1/2=1-3/4).

WOOD SCREWS

FLAT HEAD

ROUND HEAD

OVAL HEAD

Lengths vary from 1/4" to 6"
1/4" to 1" lengths increase by 1/8"
1" to 3" lengths increase by 1/4"
3" to 5" lengths increase by 1/2"

equipment saves time and enables you to turn out better work at less cost.

GLUES AND HOW TO USE THEM

In the home, as in the factory, glue is an indispensable item in the making of useful wooden articles. Glue, like nails or screws, is a fastener, but whereas a nail or screw fastens at one point only, glue, properly used, holds over the entire surface of a joint and can weld wood together so that the glued joint is actually stronger than the pieces of wood to which it is applied.

Glue suitable for wood joints and veneers is usually sold by hardware stores, paint stores, and by up-to-date lumber yards and building-supply merchants. Do not make the mistake of buying mucilage, paste, or cement which, although suitable for gluing paper, cardboard, or crockery, will not make a strong permanent bond on wood.

Dry powder waterproof glue is now sold in ½, 1 pound, and larger packages. It is quickly made into liquid glue by mixing with cold water, following directions printed on packages. This type of glue is specially suited to home-craft work because no heat is required in mixing or applying; the glue can be used for indoor or outdoor purposes. Joints of either hardwood or softwood, when properly glued, will be stronger than the wood itself. This type of glue is quick setting and water resistant. Commercially speaking, well-made glue joints are waterproof.

Liquid glue is sold in liquid form ready for use. Its strength is not equal to the other types described, but it is usually satisfactory for softwoods. It is not waterproof.

HOW TO PAINT

Decoration of articles for both inside and outside the home, such as bookcases, stools, folding screens, wall panels, and garden furniture, involves a consideration of some of the general principles commonly observed in painting. The use of attractive colors is, of course, highly desirable.

For benches and other outdoor equipment which must withstand the action of the elements, linseed oil paints are usually preferred. While they require from 12 to 14 hours to dry before a second coat may be applied, the serviceability of such coatings is superior to most other types. However, there is no objection to the use of a pint of spar varnish to a gallon of such paint, in order to increase its gloss and hurry its drying properties. Linseed-oil paints referred to are usually marketed under the name of exterior house paints. They come in a very wide range of colors.

In the case of porch furniture, wicker chairs, and other objects which are protected to some extent from the sun and rain, 4-hour varnishes, varnish stains, or varnish enamels may be used with excellent results if the wood is first primed with an elastic primer. While some people may prefer a clear varnish, others prefer varnish stains which stain and varnish the wood in one operation. Beautiful effects may be obtained with mahogany varnish stains. Two coats are usually sufficient over a primed area. For the most colorful results many people prefer the use of 4-hour enamels, which also come in a very wide range of colors.

If an exceptionally smooth and highly finished surface is desired on interior shelving or other objects which are built for the interior of a dwelling, the cracks should be filled with putty or crack filler and the surfaces given a priming coat of silica wood filler, which may be purchased in liquid form at any paint store. After the primer has been allowed sufficient time to become thoroughly dry and hard, varnish stain, color lacquer, or color varnish may be applied in one or two coats to obtain the desired finish. If the woodwork has a large number of knots present, it is often desirable to touch up the knots with a coat of aluminum paint. (Provided it is to be finished with paint instead of a clear coating.) In fact, aluminum paint may be used as a primer over many of these surfaces, especially if they are to be painted and exposed out of doors, with assurance that the top coats of finishing color will be more durable. After the first coat of color varnish or lacquer has been applied and allowed to thoroughly dry, it may be lightly rubbed with fine sandpaper to remove any imperfections before applying the final coat. A much smoother surface is thus obtained.

HELPFUL WOODWORKING SHOP SUGGESTIONS

A scriber or sharp-pointed instrument should be used to mark cutting lines on pieces to be sawed or planed.

Trace along the inner edge of a steel square when using it as a straight-edge.

Notch the edge of the lumber with a sharp knife before starting to saw in order to prevent the saw from jumping off the line.

When sawing a piece of wood to size, saw on the waste side of the line; otherwise the piece will be undersize.

When cutting a number of pieces of the same dimensions, always use the first piece as a pattern.

Always plane parallel to the grain of the wood.

When planing, use full-length strokes, removing the plane only at the end of the piece.

When planing the ends of boards, plane from the edges to the center or securely clamp a piece of wood to the edge of the board at the end of the plane stroke.

To assure square edges, hold a block of wood, the faces of which should be perfectly square, firmly against the bottom of the plane and the outer edge of the board.

When driving nails, grip the hammer handle near the end.

In assembling, when it is necessary to drive pieces together, hammer directly on a soft block of wood.

Long nails may be withdrawn without bending or marring the wood by placing a block of wood under the hammer head.

Dents or bruises in wood may be removed by applying several thicknesses of cloth or blotters soaked in water and then applying a hot pressing iron (not too hot) to the blotters or cloth.

Stop boring as soon as the point of the bit comes through the underside of the wood, turn the piece over and finish boring from the other side.

When fastening pieces of wood together with screws, bore holes for the screws with a bit or drill of slightly less diameter than that of the core or root of the thread of the screw. In the case of hardwoods, use a bit with a diameter slightly smaller than that of the plain shank of the screw to bore the hole through the piece through which the screw passes.

Soap placed on the threads of screws makes them turn more easily in the wood.

Large holes in wood may be filled by inserting pieces of wood that match the original piece. Small holes and cracks may be filled with thick paste made by mixing a quantity of fine sawdust from the wood used and ordinary glue.

Green soap or benzine will remove grease spots from wood.

Raising of the grain of the wood when staining may be eliminated by sponging the wood with warm water before the final sanding.

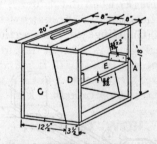

LADDER FOLDED

FOLDING BENCH LADDER

Materials Required. One box, 20 by 18 by 16 inches. Two pieces, 25/32 by 2 by 6 inches, for step cleats (A). Two pieces, 25/32 by 2 by 10½ inches, for step cleats (B). Two hinges.

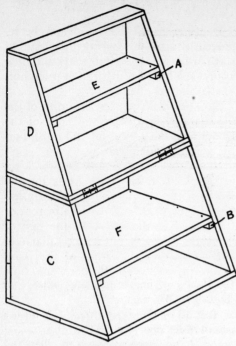

LADDER OPEN

Materials Required. Two pieces 9/16 by 5 by 5¼ inches for ends (A). One piece 9/16 by 5¼ by 18 inches for bottom (B) and (C).

Shape ends (A) as shown. Cut the other piece to form (B) and (C) as shown. Then nail ends (A) to the wide ends of (B) and (C).

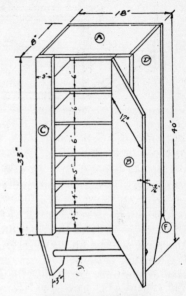

Remove top from box. Cut box at an angle through the ends and sides into two sections (C) and (D), as shown on page 292. If the top of the box is made up of 25/32-inch material, it may be used for steps (E) and (F). Cut these steps to fit in between the ends (E), approximately 5½ inches wide and (F) approximately 10½ inches wide. Secure these intermediary steps to cleats as shown, halfway between the sides of the box. Note cleats (A) are on top of (E) when the ladder is folded. Cut a handhole in the narrow side of section (C). Hinge the two sections together.

LINEN CLOSET

Materials Required. Seven pieces 7/16 by 6⅞ by 16⅞ inches for shelves and top end (A). One piece 9/16 by 12 by 33 inches for door (B). Two pieces 9/16 by 3 by 33 inches (C). Two pieces 9/16 by 6⅞ by 40 inches for sides (D). One piece ¾-inch doweling 18 inches in length for towel rod (E). One piece 9/16 by 18 by 33 inches for back (F). Two butts (hinges). One cupboard catch.

Shape bottom ends of sides (D) as shown and bore ¾-inch holes through them for towel rod (E). Nail sides (D) and back (F) to top end of closet and shelves (A). Nail front strips (C) in place. Hinge door (B) to (C). Attach catch to door.

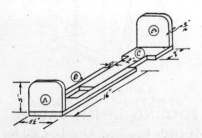

ADJUSTABLE BOOK ENDS

Because this holder can be adjusted, one or a number of volumes may be kept in it.

TOOL CHEST

Materials Required. One box 32 by 12 by 8 inches (A). One piece 11/16 by 12 by 32 inches for lid (B). Two pieces 5/16 by 2 inches by inside length of box (A)

[293]

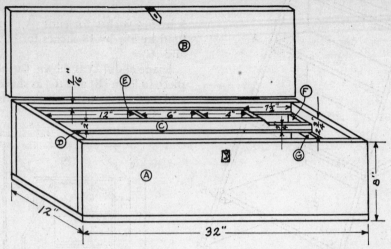

for tray sides (C). One piece 5/16 by 6 inches by inside length of box (A) for tray bottom (D). Four pieces 5/16 by 2 by 5⅜ inches for partitions (E) and end of tray. One piece 5/16 by ¾ by 5⅝ inches for tray end (F). Two pieces 5/16 by 1 inch by inside width of box (A) for cleats (G). Two butts (hinges). One hinge hasp and lock.

Shape tray sides (C) as shown. Nail sides (C), end (F), partitions (E), and bottom (D) together to construct tray. Nail cleats (G) to ends of box (A), as shown. Hinge lid (B) to box.

by 5¼ by 5¾ inches (D). One piece, 5/16 by 4¾ by 5¾ inches (E).

Round off the top of back (A). Bore a small hole near the top as shown. Cut ends (B) to dimensions given, then nail (A) and (D) to these ends. Hinge top (C) to (A) 6 inches from the bottom. Then nail bottom (E) in place.

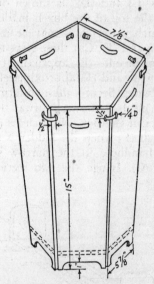

WASTE-PAPER BASKET

Materials Required. Five pieces, 7/16 by 7⅛ by 15 inches, for sides. One piece, 7/16 by 10¼ by 10¼ inches, for bottom.

Taper the sides from a width of 7⅛ inches at one end to 5⅞ inches at the other as illustrated. On the piece for the

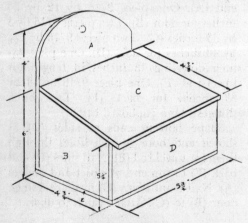

SALT BOX

Materials Required. One piece, 5/16 by 5¾ by 10 inches (A). Two pieces, 5/16 by 4⅛ by 6 inches (B). One piece, 5/16 by 4⅞ by 5¾ inches (C). One piece, 5/16

bottom lay out a circle of 5-inch radius, divide this circle into five equal parts, draw lines connecting these divisions, and then saw along these lines. You will then have the pentagon-shaped bottom. Bore two 1/4-inch holes 1 1/2 inches down from the wide end of each side piece 1/2 inch from the edges. Cut out the hand openings. Nail each of the five sides to one of the sides of the bottom piece 1 1/2 inches from the narrow end. Tie the tops together with buckskin or rawhide. Paint attractively.

should protrude 4 inches. The other two cleats should be nailed in the corners of the back end of the box. Construct the flooring as shown and secure it to the bottom of the box. The holes supply ventilation under the floor. Remove the top from the other box and cut to a triangular shape. Nail the roof boards over this framework, which should fit over the projecting ends of the vertical cleats. The sections may be held together by hooks and screw eyes.

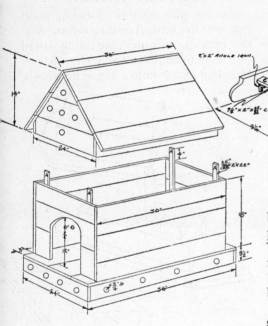

DOG HOUSE

Materials Required. One box, 30 by 24 by18 inches. One box, 30 by 24 by 14 inches. Four pieces, 25/32 by 2 by 22 inches, for cleats (A). Pieces, 25/32 by 36 inches, for roof. Pieces, 25/32 by 24 by 36 inches, for flooring. Two pieces, 25/32 by 5 1/2 by 34 7/16 inches. Two pieces, 25/32 by 5 1/2 by 24 inches.

Remove the top and bottom from the larger box. Cut the entrance out of one end and nail two cleats on each side of this opening as illustrated. The ends

SLED

Materials Required. Two pieces, 25/32 by 3 1/2 by 36 inches, for runners (A). One piece, 9/16 by 9 by 20 inches, for seat (B). Three pieces, 25/32 by 2 by 9 1/2 inches, for cleats (C). One piece broom handle 11 inches long. Four 2-inch angle-iron braces.

Shape runners (A) as illustrated. Cut a slot 1 by 6 inches midway between the ends. Bore a hole near the front end of each runner for the short piece of broom handle. Nail cleats (C) between the runners 5/8 inch below the top edges—one cleat 5 1/2 inches from the rear ends of the runners, one 23 1/2 inches from the rear ends, and a third midway between the other two. To strengthen the joints between the runners and the front and rear cleats screw two angle irons to the underside of each. Then nail seat (B) across cleats (C). Half-oval or flat iron pieces 36 inches long and 3/4 inch wide screwed to the bottom edges of the runners will save them and make the sled slide better.

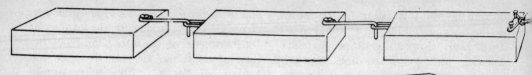

PLANK TRAIN

To make plank train, plane and sand-paper several pieces of wood. Fasten together by putting a large hook on one plank and a staple on the next into which the hook will fit.

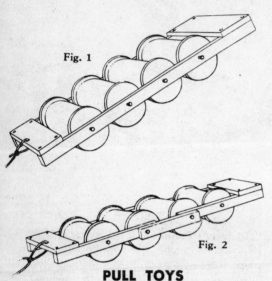

Fig. 1

Fig. 2

PULL TOYS

Use several spools of the same size, the larger the better. Cut two pieces of wood, about 12 by 15 inches long and narrower than the diameter of the spools. Place two crosspieces to fasten the strips together at the back and front as shown in Fig. 1. Place the spools between the strips so that they do not touch. Hammer nails through the strips of wood so that they go into the holes in the spools and form axles on which the spools will turn. Attach a pull string to the crosspiece at one end.

With a little more trouble this toy can be made with joints (Fig. 2) so that it will pull over door sills, rugs, etc. Cut the wooden side strips just long enough to join two spools together. Overlapping strips can then be used to attach the pairs of spools into a train of any desired length.

WOODEN WAGON

Nail or glue together blocks of wood that give the general outline shown. Button moulds, or round moulding sawed into sections about half an inch wide may be nailed loosely onto a wagon for wheels.

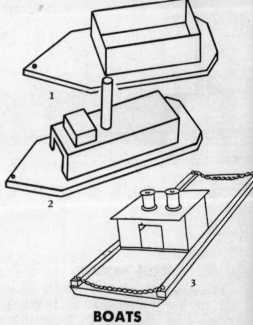

BOATS

Boat 1 may be made by pointing one end of a 1 by 4 by 14-inch board to give it a boat shape. A narrow, open, wooden box, about 3 by 6 inches by 2 inches deep, screwed to the board, makes loading possible. The child may pull his boat if a screweye is screwed into the front end for a string. A ferry boat (2) and a freight barge (3) may be made as suggested above.

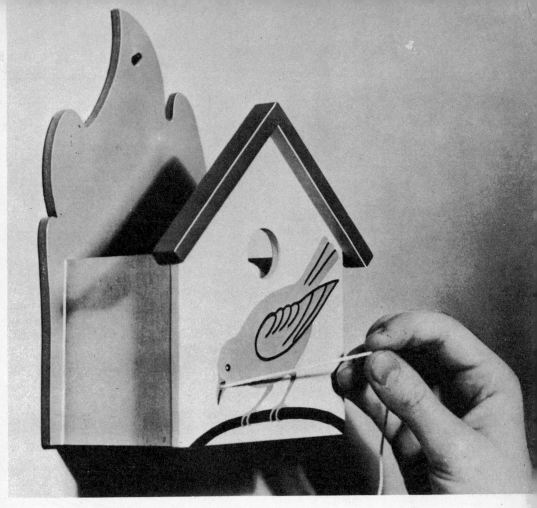

STRING HOLDER

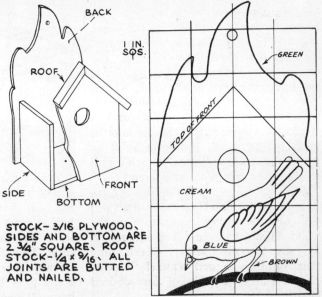

BACK

ROOF

SIDE

BOTTOM

FRONT

1 IN.
SQS.

GREEN

TOP OF FRONT

CREAM

BLUE

BROWN

STOCK- 3/16 PLYWOOD.
SIDES AND BOTTOM ARE
2 3/4" SQUARE. ROOF
STOCK- 1/4 x 9/16. ALL
JOINTS ARE BUTTED
AND NAILED.

[297]

CHILD'S DESK

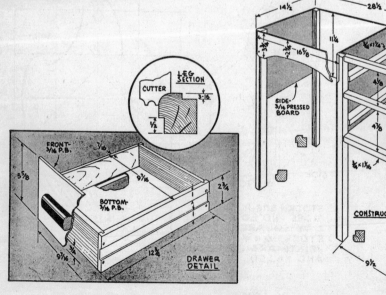

LEG SECTION

CUTTER

DRAWER DETAIL

FRONT- 3/16 P.B.

BOTTOM- 3/16 P.B.

SIDE- 3/16 PRESSED BOARD

BACK- 3/16 P.B.

CONSTRUCTION

LEGS 1 5/16 SQ.

As you become more skilled in working with wood, you will want to add power tools to your equipment. When you have reached this stage, you will enjoy making the projects that follow.

CHILD'S DESK

Here is a child's desk that is both easy and inexpensive to make, yet attractive and practical. Pressed wood is used for the top, sides and back. This should be the hardboard variety, and can be either ⅛ or 3/16 inch thick. The drawing is dimensioned for 3/16-inch stock, and if any other thickness of plywood or pressed board is used, the necessary allowances in the way of the leg rabbets, etc., should be made.

All of the legs are cut with the same circular saw setup, but vary slightly, as can be seen in the drawing. Rabbets extend the full length of the leg stock. The center leg at the rear is a plain square. All of the others have either one or two rabbets and rounds.

Notice that the drawer rails are let into the backs of the front legs. The rabbets at the top of the center and left legs, which take the apron piece, can be cut on the shaper or jointer, fitting the apron later to the curve at the end of each cut.

Assemble the right and center leg with the drawer rails, then add the left leg with the apron. The sides and back can then be nailed or screwed in place to complete the framework. The drawer slides are cut from ¾-by-1¼-inch stock, and are screw-fastened to the pressed board. The top is pressed board or plywood, 15 by 29 inches, rounded over on the top edge all around. Oval head screws can be used for fastenings, or the assembly can be made with finishing nails set flush with the surface.

The drawing shows the drawer construction. Both drawers are the same size. Drawer pulls can be round or keystone shape, and are screw-fastened from the inside of the drawer front.

Finishing. All pressed board used in the construction is finished natural with shellac or varnish, with the exception of the drawer fronts and apron, which are painted medium green or buff. Legs are finished dark green. If used with other painted furniture, the color scheme would be varied to suit.

Chair. A matching chair can be easily made up by following the same general type of construction.

MODERN NIGHT TABLE

Simple in both design and construction, this modern night table makes an attractive and useful project. It can be made up nicely in white pine for a paint or lacquer finish, or constructed in hardwood if a varnish or other bright finish is desired.

As can be seen in the cutaway drawing, the construction is almost "box-like" in its simplicity, being relieved only by the moulded top of the base and the two turned legs. Standard 1-inch stock dressed to ¾ inch is used for the greater portion of the work. Plywood of the same thickness can be used for the base and top to eliminate the glueing job which will probably be necessary if you use stock lumber.

This procedure is only feasible where a paint finish is to be used, since the edge grain of the plywood does not take kindly to varnish.

The drawer is not shown, except in section, but is standard construction with the end and front pieces boxed or rabbeted into the sides. A dado groove all around affords the best manner of fitting the bottom of the drawer. Another job for the dado head is the rabbeting of the rear legs to take the plywood back. This job can be done equally well on the jointer or by routing on the drill press. Either mortise-and-tenon or doweled joints can be used in the assembly of the upper portion of the table, while the base joints are satisfactorily made with cleats screw-fastened into place.

The job of making the long cylindrical shape which comprises the larger portion of the front legs can be simplified and a perfect surface insured by using a small block plane instead of the skew chisel. The plane is held against the turning with the blade at an angle to the revolving stock. The heel of the plane should be supported by the tool rest. This method of working results in a perfectly smooth and even surface, something which cannot always be said of the same operation with the skew.

Finishing. A paint finish is recommended. This does not include the inside of the drawer, which makes up to better advantage in hardwood finished bright.

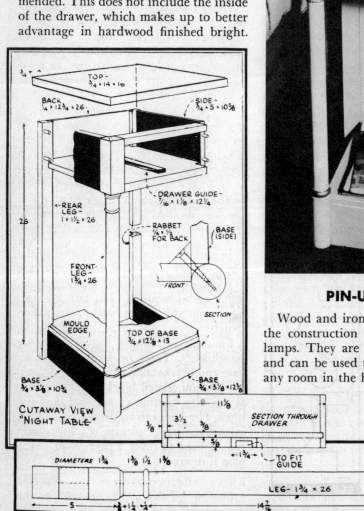

PIN-UP LAMPS

Wood and iron combine effectively in the construction of these useful pin-up lamps. They are quite simple to make, and can be used to advantage in almost any room in the home.

Start by making the base. In overall size, this will measure about 4½ inches wide by 10 inches long. Any of the samples shown can be used, or you can originate some other pleasing shape. A shallow groove to take the metal bracket must be let into the face side of the base. This is best done with a ⅝-inch-thick

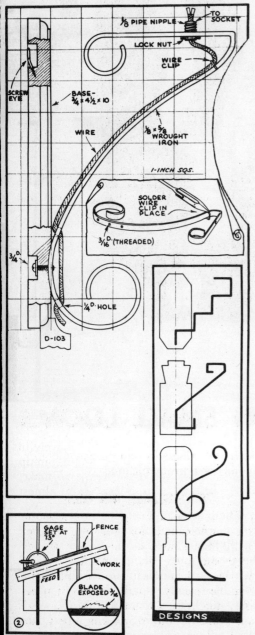

dado head combination, set to cut ⅛ inch deep.

The bracket is made from ⅝-inch-wide wrought iron. This stock is readily bent to shape cold. The various holes required for mounting, wiring, etc., are then drilled.

In order to keep the wiring neatly in place, metal clips are soldered to the bracket, as shown in the drawing, locating these as required. The lighting unit is a standard socket with turn-button switch.

Finishing. Finishing has considerable possibilities. Paint or lacquer on both base and bracket offers the simplest method. Chrome-plated brackets are effective, as are also hammered and polished finishes. The base can be decorated with an inlay banding. A picture or photograph can be used to cover a part or all of the base if desired.

EASY WEAVING ON SMALL LOOMS

Weaving, reduced to fundamentals, is going over and under taut threads known as the "warp" with another thread called the "weft." The pattern is usually made with the weft thread as illustrated later in this chapter. This principle applies to small looms as well as large ones. Naturally, for the beginner, small looms provide the best introduction to weaving. With them you can make many lovely and practical articles for personal use and the home. The particular advantage of the small loom is that you may carry it with you wherever you go, and put idle moments to profitable use.

MATERIALS TO USE

There are many exciting materials on the market used for weaving, but for small looms such as the two described here—the purse loom and the square weaver—it is important to use only those that have elastic quality. Yarn is probably the best. Choose a four-ply wool yarn and, if you are working out a pattern, select a neutral color for the warp or background and a bright contrasting color for the pattern or weft. If you do not string your loom with a thread that will "give," the warp threads become very taut before the weaving is completed.

WEAVING WORDS

In directions for weaving, these terms are often used:

Beater. Flat stick with which each row of weft is "beaten" after it is shot through the warp, to make the work firm and even.

O. Over.

U. Under.

Warp. Lengthwise threads used to string loom.

Weave Plain. To weave under and over each thread until row is completed.

Web. The material woven is sometimes called the web.

Weft. Crosswise threads with which pattern is woven.

With these words in mind, you will easily understand what we have to say about weaving on the pages that follow.

PATTERN WEAVING

In all weaving the loom is first strung with the warp threads and the pattern woven in with weft, or the thread carried on the shuttle.

Weft thread is usually of a contrasting color. However, there is one exception to this rule. Plaid designs are made by stringing warp threads of different colors and changing the color of the weft thread frequently in order to get the plaid effect.

For simple pattern weaving, string the loom with warp threads in one color. Use a contrasting color for the weft. The pattern is made by going under or over the warp threads and skipping several occasionally in order to bring out the pattern. If you weave over and under each thread the result will be a plain weave or darning stitch.

It is a simple problem to block out your own weaving designs. Take a piece of graph paper and block off twice as many squares as you have pegs or nails in your loom or as many squares as there

are warp threads. The design is made by first making all squares involved in the pattern a solid color. Each square represents one thread. The pattern is always put in with the over stitches.

The following graphs and directions for weaving will give the beginner an idea of how to develop an original pattern, and may be used in the projects given in this chapter, as well as others. Try this on the purse loom we will show you how to make:

From right (bottom to top):
Row 1. U3, O1, U3, O1, etc.
Row 2. O, U, O, U, O, U, etc.
Row 3. O3, U1, O3, U1, etc.
Row 4. U3, O1, U3, O1, etc.
Row 5. Same as row 3.
Row 6. Same as row 2.
Row 7. Same as row 1.

(Left) Same design as above, with light background. *(Bottom)* A purse loom.

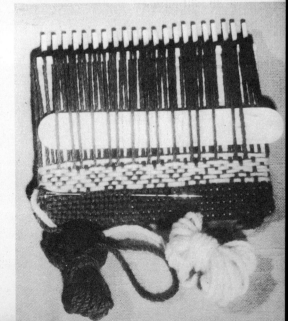

THE PURSE LOOM

You may make many handsome purses in different patterns on this little loom. Here is how to make your loom:

Cut a piece of three-ply wood, the size of purse desired. Add a strip of wood on either side of top of loom, about ¼-inch thick as shown in Fig. 1. This will hold the warp threads away from the loom to facilitate weaving when nearing the top.

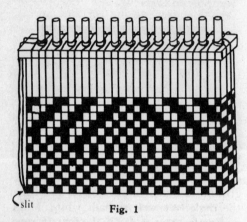

_{slit}   **Fig. 1**

Drill holes about ¼ inch apart across top of loom large enough to receive ⅛-inch pegs. Cut a small slit at two lower corners to hold thread while stringing loom (Fig. 2). Cut ⅛-inch dowels in 1-inch length for pegs. The number of pegs used depends on the size of the purse you wish to make, but it should always be an odd number.

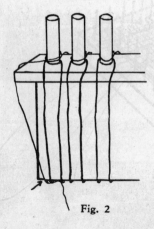

Fig. 2

DIRECTIONS FOR STRINGING LOOM

Fasten yarn in slit in lower left-hand corner of loom, leaving an inch for holding. Carry yarn up narrow end of loom around first peg from left to right, then down same end and fasten in slit.

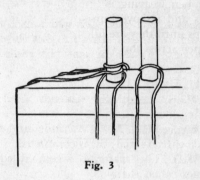

Fig. 3

Next, bring yarn up front of loom around first peg from left to right down front of loom and up back and again bring yarn around first peg, going from left to right. The first peg now has three loops around it (Fig. 3).

Bring yarn down back of loom, then up front and around second peg left to right, down front and up back around second peg left to right, and so on until all pegs have two loops around them (Fig. 2). Be sure warp threads are not crossed on either side.

End stringing, fastening thread on slit at bottom of loom, and then put two extra strands on other end as in the beginning. This means the last peg on right has three loops and the end is fastened in slit. *Do not stretch yarn.*

HOW TO WEAVE PURSES

Thread weft thread (1 yard or 1½ yards in length) in weaving needle and begin at lower right-hand corner. Weave under one thread and over the next all the way across to left of loom. Push down thread with beater. Weave over and under two end threads, on left side of loom, then turn loom over and continue weaving until back where you started.

After weaving two rows, force weft

threads under loom with needle to make bottom of bag. Continue weaving around and around the loom until you have reached the top. Leave all short ends of yarn when ending and starting a new thread on either end of loom . . . weave them in and out of purse, being careful not to interrupt design, and cut close.

When weaving is completed, pull out pegs and remove purse. Weave through loops until they are filled. Line and sew a zipper across top.

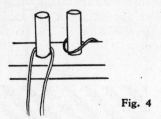

Fig. 4

Note: For tapestry weaving or materials heavier than yarn, the warp threads must be farther apart. String loom by putting only one loop over each peg (Fig. 4). You may use patterns as described earlier.

THE SQUARE WEAVER

The beginner will also find the square weaver easy to make and use. This loom is designed for weaving 4-inch squares which can be sewed together to make

almost any article in which yarn is employed. The loom can be made larger by adding more nails to each side but the weaver will find it much easier to handle a small loom and a 5- or 6-inch needle that will pick up the warp threads in one operation. When the square is completed there will be 15 loops on each side. These are matched with the loops on other squares and sewed together with a darning needle and matching piece of yarn. Sew together on wrong side with overcast stitch (see sewing instructions in the chapter "Fun with Felt"). After all squares are joined, block to shape by covering with damp cloth and pressing lightly with warm iron.

The squares can be woven into different designs as shown later in this chapter, or sometimes it is better to use a plain weave. It is simple to make up your own designs. Take a piece of graph paper and make a square by blocking off 3-inch squares on each side. Make the background or warp threads black and leave the design or weft threads white. Make any design you wish on the first 16 rows and complete the squares by repeating backwards on your pattern.

HOW TO USE PATTERNS

The squares can be used to make almost any article you wish to make from yarn. First make a paper pattern and fit the squares to it. Do not worry if the pat-

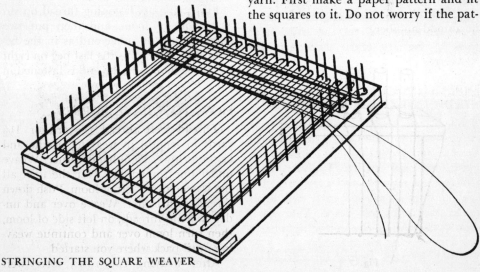

STRINGING THE SQUARE WEAVER

tern calls for a rounded corner such as the top of a mitten. Follow the line of the pattern in the seam by sewing a running stitch, turn the right side out and press flat by using a damp cloth and warm iron. If the corners are too bulky, sew seam on sewing machine and cut away extra lengths. Four-ply hand-knitting worsted is the most satisfactory yarn to use for weaving the squares. Do not attempt to use a cotton thread or material that is not elastic in quality. The warp threads become too taut for weaving before the square is completed.

DIRECTIONS FOR MAKING SQUARE WEAVER

To make the loom, cut 4 pieces of wood ½ by ½ by 5 inches and miter the corners. Use only soft wood such as pine or bass as it is very difficult to drive the nails into hard wood. Glue the 4 pieces together to form a square and reinforce corners with a small nail if necessary. Use ¾-inch headless nails, if they are available, to form top of loom. If not, buy 1-inch small nails and cut off heads with wire clippers.

First drive a nail in each of two corners diagonally across from each other as shown in the illustration. Then add 15 nails ¼ inch apart along the four sides. Draw a guide line in the center of the frame and follow it while adding the nails. This is important in order to weave a perfect square. Drive the nails in at least ¼ inch to make them firm for weaving.

DIRECTIONS FOR STRINGING LOOM

Note that there are nails in two corners of the loom. Place the loom in front of you so that there is a nail in the lower left-hand corner. Tie yarn onto this nail and string loom by carrying yarn back and forth around each nail until nails are completely filled. Your yarn should then be at the upper right-hand corner and ready for weaving.

Wind the yarn around the outside of

the nails *eight* times in order to measure the amount of yarn needed for weaving the square. Thread the long needle and weave over and under each warp thread and bring the needle out just above first nail at top on left. Continue weaving back and forth until each nail is covered. Your square is completed when you bring your needle out beside the nail where you started.

Remove square by pushing it off carefully from the nails and weave the two ends into the edge of the square.

Here are some patterns that will give you good-looking results on the square weaver.

DIAGONAL WEAVE

Row 1. Weave plain—U, O, U, etc.
Row 2. O2, U2, O2, etc; end U1.
Row 3. O2, U2, O2, etc; end U1.
Row 4. O1, U1, O2, U2, O2, etc; end O1.
Row 5. U2, O2, U2, etc; end O1.
Row 6. U1, O1, U2, O2, etc; end U1.
Repeat 3, 4, 5 and 6.
Last row weave plain.

IRISH CHAIN

Row 1. Weave plain O, U, O, etc.
Row 2. U, O3, U, O3, etc; end O2.
Row 3. U, O3, U, O3, etc; end O2.
Row 4. *Repeat* row 3.
Row 5. U2, O, U, O, U, O, U, etc.
Row 6. U, O, U, O3, U, O3, U, O3, etc; end U1.